D1714407

The Story of God Bible Commentary Series Endorsements

"Getting a story is about more than merely enjoying it. It means hearing it, understanding it, and above all, being impacted by it. This commentary series hopes that its readers not only hear and understand the story, but are impacted by it to live in as Christian a way as possible. The editors and contributors set that table very well and open up the biblical story in ways that move us to act with sensitivity and understanding. That makes hearing the story as these authors tell it well worth the time. Well done."

Darrell L. Bock
Dallas Theological Seminary

"The Story of God Bible Commentary series invites readers to probe how the message of the text relates to our situations today. Engagingly readable, it not only explores the biblical text but offers a range of applications and interesting illustrations."

Craig S. Keener
Asbury Theological Seminary

"I love The Story of God Bible Commentary series. It makes the text sing, and helps us hear the story afresh."

John Ortberg
Senior Pastor of Menlo Park Presbyterian Church

"In this promising new series of commentaries, believing biblical scholars bring not only their expertise but their own commitment to Jesus and insights into today's culture to the Scriptures. The result is a commentary series that is anchored in the text but lives and breathes in the world of today's church with its variegated pattern of socioeconomic, ethnic, and national diversity. Pastors, Bible study leaders, and Christians of all types who are looking for a substantive and practical guide through the Scriptures will find these volumes helpful."

Frank Thielman
Beeson Divinity School

"The Story of God Bible Commentary series is unique in its approach to exploring the Bible. Its easy-to-use format and practical guidance brings God's grand story to modern-day life so anyone can understand how it applies today."

Andy Stanley
North Point Ministries

"I'm a storyteller. Through writing and speaking I talk and teach about understanding the Story of God throughout Scripture and about letting God reveal more of His story as I live it out. Thus I am thrilled to have a commentary series based on the Story of God—a commentary that helps me to Listen to the Story, that Explains the Story, and then encourages me to probe how to Live the Story. A perfect tool for helping every follower of Jesus to walk in the story that God is writing for them."

Judy Douglass
Director of Women's Resources, Cru

"The Bible is the story of God and his dealings with humanity from creation to new creation. The Bible is made up more of stories than of any other literary genre. Even the psalms, proverbs, prophecies, letters, and the Apocalypse make complete sense only when set in the context of the grand narrative of the entire Bible. This commentary series breaks new ground by taking all these observations seriously. It asks commentators to listen to the text, to explain the text, and to live the text. Some of the material in these sections overlaps with introduction, detailed textual analysis and application, respectively, but only some. The most riveting and valuable part of the commentaries are the stories that can appear in any of these sections, from any part of the globe and any part of church history, illustrating the text in any of these areas. Ideal for preaching and teaching."

Craig L. Blomberg
Denver Seminary

"Pastors and lay people will welcome this new series, which seeks to make the message of the Scriptures clear and to guide readers in appropriating biblical texts for life today."

Daniel I. Block
Wheaton College and Graduate School

"An extremely valuable and long overdue series that includes comment on the cultural context of the text, careful exegesis, and guidance on reading the whole Bible as a unity that testifies to Christ as our Savior and Lord."

Graeme Goldsworthy
author of *According to Plan*

2 CORINTHIANS

Editorial Board
of
The Story of God Bible Commentary

Old Testament general editor
Tremper Longman III

Old Testament associate editors
George Athas
Mark J. Boda
Myrto Theocharous

New Testament general editor
Scot McKnight

New Testament associate editors
Lynn H. Cohick
Michael F. Bird
Dennis R. Edwards

Zondervan editors

Senior acquisitions editor
Katya Covrett

Senior production editor, Old Testament
Nancy L. Erickson

Senior production editor, New Testament
Christopher A. Beetham

The Story of God
Bible Commentary

2 CORINTHIANS

Judith A. Diehl

Tremper Longman III & Scot McKnight
General Editors

ZONDERVAN
ACADEMIC

ZONDERVAN ACADEMIC

2 Corinthians
Copyright © 2020 by Judith A. Diehl

ISBN 978-0-310-32721-9 (hardcover)

ISBN 978-0-310-59910-4 (ebook)

Requests for information should be addressed to:
Zondervan, *3900 Sparks Dr. SE, Grand Rapids, Michigan 49546*

Cover design: Ron Huizinga
Cover image: iStockphoto®
Interior design: Kait Lamphere

Printed in the United States of America

20 21 22 23 24 25 26 27 28 29 30 /LSC / 15 14 13 12 11 10 9 8 7 6 5 4 3 2 1

To my husband, David, with gratitude for his willing heart,
for his able editing skills and his great patience.
He has truly been my *Paraclete* in the flesh.

Old Testament series

1. Genesis—*Tremper Longman III*
2. Exodus—*Christopher J. H. Wright*
3. Leviticus—*Jerry E. Shepherd*
4. Numbers—*Jay A. Sklar*
5. Deuteronomy—*Myrto Theocharous*
6. Joshua—*Lissa M. Wray Beal*
7. Judges—*Athena E. Gorospe*
8. Ruth/Esther—*Marion Taylor*
9. 1–2 Samuel—*Paul S. Evans*
10. 1–2 Kings—*David T. Lamb*
11. 1–2 Chronicles—*Carol M. Kaminski and Christine Palmer*
12. Ezra/Nehemiah—*Douglas J. Green*
13. Job—*Martin A. Shields*
14. Psalms—*Elizabeth R. Hayes*
15. Proverbs—*Ryan P. O'Dowd*
16. Ecclesiastes/Song of Songs—*George Athas*
17. Isaiah—*Mark J. Boda*
18. Jeremiah/Lamentations—*Andrew G. Shead*
19. Ezekiel—*D. Nathan Phinney*
20. Daniel—*Wendy L. Widder*
21. Minor Prophets I—*Beth M. Stovell*
22. Minor Prophets II—*Beth M. Stovell*

New Testament series

1. Matthew—*Rodney Reeves*
2. Mark—*Timothy G. Gombis*
3. Luke—*Kindalee Pfremmer DeLong*
4. John—*Nicholas Perrin*
5. Acts—*Dean Pinter*
6. Romans—*Michael F. Bird*
7. 1 Corinthians—*Justin K. Hardin*
8. 2 Corinthians—*Judith A. Diehl*
9. Galatians—*Nijay K. Gupta*
10. Ephesians—*Mark D. Roberts*
11. Philippians—*Lynn H. Cohick*
12. Colossians/Philemon—*Todd Wilson*
13. 1, 2 Thessalonians—*John Byron*
14. 1, 2 Timothy, Titus—*Marius Nel*
15. Hebrews—*Radu Gheorghita*
16. James—*Mariam J. Kamell*
17. 1 Peter—*Dennis R. Edwards*
18. 2 Peter, Jude—*C. Rosalee Velloso Ewell*
19. 1, 2, & 3 John—*Constantine R. Campbell*
20. Revelation—*Jonathan A. Moo*
21. Sermon on the Mount—*Scot McKnight*

Contents

Acknowledgments

Special thanks to my editors, Scot McKnight, Michael Bird, and Katya Covrett. My pastoral, research, and teaching backgrounds were not specifically in the area of Pauline studies, but Scot had confidence in me anyway to accomplish this volume. For that I am grateful, as I thoroughly enjoyed reading and writing about "Pastor Paul." It was a project that matched who I am and my experiences, while it educated me and deepened my love of God's Word. Thank you all for your support to improve my manuscript.

Thanks to Dr. Craig Blomberg at Denver Seminary, who observed that I was a "bunny-hopper" in my NT studies. I kept finding new and interesting things to discover, which took me offtrack from my assigned research many times, but I learned so much. I am also grateful for the guidance of Prof. Larry W. Hurtado at the University of Edinburgh, who guided my doctoral studies and helped me to develop as a writer. Thanks, too, to Dr. Linda Belleville, for sharing her love of the Pauline epistles and for giving me confidence. Through the years, as I learned to explore and appreciate scholarship, and knit together my thoughts in writing, I used countless biblical commentaries as well as other resources. It is my sincere hope that this commentary will be just as helpful to current readers—students, pastors, teachers, missionaries, Christian leaders, and readers today who are "servants of Christ" in a challenging world.

Finally, thanks to all those people who supported me with their prayers and their words of encouragement. Family and friends have been very tolerant during this writing process. I could not have done it without you.

The Story of God Bible Commentary Series

The word of God may not change, but culture does. Think of what we have seen in the last twenty years: we now communicate predominantly through the Internet and email; we read our news on iPads and computers; we can talk on the phone to our friends while we are driving, while we are playing golf, while we are taking long walks; and we can get in touch with others from the middle of nowhere. We carry in our hands small devices that connect us to the world and to a myriad of sources of information. Churches have changed; the "Nones" are rising in numbers and volume, and atheists are bold to assert their views in public forums. The days of home Bible studies are waning; there is a marked rise in activist missional groups in churches, and pastors are more and more preaching topical sermons, some of which are not directly connected to the Bible. Divorce rates are not going down, marriages are more stressed, rearing children is more demanding, and civil unions and same-sex marriages are knocking at the door of the church.

Progress can be found in many directions. While church attendance numbers are waning in Europe and North America, churches are growing in the South and the East. More and more women are finding a voice in churches; the plea of the former generation of leaders that Christians be concerned not just with evangelism but with justice is being answered today in new and vigorous ways. Resources for studying the Bible are more available today than ever before, and preachers and pastors are meeting the challenge of speaking a sure word of God into shifting cultures.

Readers of the Bible change too. These cultural shifts, our own personal developments, the progress in intellectual questions, as well as growth in biblical studies and theology and discoveries of new texts and new paradigms for understanding the contexts of the Bible—each of these elements works on an interpreter so that the person who reads the Bible today asks different questions from different angles.

Culture shifts, but the word of God remains. That is why we as editors of The Story of God Bible Commentary series, a commentary based on the New International Version 2011 (NIV 2011), are excited to participate in this new series of commentaries on the Bible. This series is designed to address this generation with the same word of God. We are asking the authors to explain what the Bible says to the sorts of readers who pick up commentaries so they can understand not only what Scripture says but what it means for today. The Bible does not change, but relating it to our culture changes constantly and in differing ways in different contexts.

When we, the New Testament editors, sat down in prayer and discussion to choose authors for this series, we realized we had found fertile ground. Our list of potential authors was staggering in length and quality. We wanted the authors to be exceptional scholars, faithful Christians, committed evangelicals, and theologically diverse, and we wanted this series to represent the changing face of both American and world evangelicalism, with both ethnic and gender diversity. I believe this series has a wider diversity of authors than any commentary series in evangelical history.

The title of this series, emphasizing as it does the "Story" of the Bible, reveals the intent of the series. We want to explain each passage of the Bible in light of the Bible's grand Story. The Bible's grand Story, of course, connects this series to the classic expression *regula fidei*, the "rule of faith," which was the Bible's story coming to fulfillment in Jesus as the Messiah, Lord, and Savior of all. In brief, we see the narrative built around the following biblical themes: creation and fall, covenant and redemption, law and prophets, and especially God's charge to humans as his image-bearers to rule under God. The theme of God as King and God's kingdom guides us to see the importance of Israel's kings as they come to fulfillment in Jesus, Lord and King over all, and the direction of history toward the new heavens and new earth, where God will be all in all. With these guiding themes, each passage is examined from three angles.

Listen to the Story. We believe that if the Bible is God speaking, then the most important posture of the Christian before the Bible is to listen. So our first section cites the text of Scripture and lists a selection of important biblical and sometimes noncanonical parallels; then each author introduces that passage. The introductions to the passages sometimes open up discussion to the theme of the passage, while other times they tie this passage to its context in the specific book. But since the focus of this series is the Story of God in the Bible, the introduction leads the reader into reading this text in light of the Bible's Story.

Explain the Story. The authors follow up listening to the text by explaining each passage in light of the Bible's grand Story. This is not an academic series, so the footnotes are limited to the kinds of texts typical Bible readers and preachers readily will have on hand. Authors are given the freedom to explain the text as they read it, though you should not be surprised to find occasional listings of other options for reading the text. Authors explore biblical backgrounds, historical context, cultural codes, and theological interpretations. Authors engage in word studies and interpret unique phrases and clauses as they attempt to build a sound and living reading of the text in light of the Story of God in the Bible.

Authors will not shy away from problems in the texts. Whether one is examining the meaning of "perfect" in Matthew 5:48, the problems with Christology in the hymn of Philippians 2:6–11, the challenge of understanding Paul in light of the swirling debates about the old, new, and post-new perspectives, the endless debates about eschatology, or the vagaries of atonement theories, the authors will dive in, discuss evidence, and do their best to sort out a reasonable and living reading of those issues for the church today.

Live the Story. Reading the Bible is not just about discovering what it meant back then; the intent of The Story of God Bible Commentary series is to probe how this text might be lived out today as that story continues to march on in the life of the church. At times our authors will tell stories about what this looks like; at other times they may offer some suggestions for living it out; but always you will discover the struggle involved as we seek to live out the Bible's grand Story in our world.

We are not offering suggestions for "application" so much as digging deeper; we are concerned in this section with seeking out how this text, in light of the Story of God in the Bible, compels us to live in our world so that our own story lines up with the Bible's Story.

SCOT McKNIGHT, general editor New Testament
LYNN COHICK, JOEL WILLITTS, AND MICHAEL BIRD, editors

Abbreviations

AB	Anchor Bible
BDAG	Danker, Frederick W., Walter Bauer, William F. Arndt, and F. Wilbur Gingrich. *Greek-English Lexicon of the New Testament and Other Early Christian Literature.* 3rd ed. Chicago: University of Chicago Press, 2000
CBQ	*Catholic Biblical Quarterly*
DLNTD	*Dictionary of the Later New Testament and its Developments.* Edited by R. P. Martin and P. H. Davids. Downers Grove, IL: InterVarsity Press, 1997
DPL	*Dictionary of Paul and his Letters.* Edited by Gerald F. Hawthorne and Ralph P. Martin. Downers Grove, IL: InterVarsity Press, 1993
ICC	International Critical Commentary
IVPNTC	IVP New Testament Commentary
JBL	*Journal of Biblical Literature*
JETS	*Journal of Evangelical Society*
JSNT	*Journal for the Study of the New Testament*
NIDNTT	*New International Dictionary of New Testament Theology.* Edited by Colin Brown. 4 vols. Grand Rapids: Zondervan, 1975–1978
NIGTC	New International Greek Testament Commentary
NAC	New American Commentary
TynBul	*Tyndale Bulletin*
WBC	Word Bible Commentary
WUNT	Wissenschaftliche Untersuchungen zum Neuen Testament

Introduction

It has been said that communication in the twenty-first century has been greatly improved with the advent of technology; we cannot function without our cell phones, tablets, and the Internet. Certainly, our ability to communicate with those who live far away is much faster, more reliable, and less expensive than it was decades ago. However, there are people who insist that there is nothing quite as effective as a face-to-face interchange between people. Thus, for some, technology makes things better; for others, it makes things worse. In a similar fashion, the written communications between the apostle Paul and the church of Corinth lacked the close, intimate nature that can only be achieved with a visit in person. Then, as now, communications can be misinterpreted and misunderstood, or something may have needed further explanation. It appears that Paul persevered in communicating effectively with his distant churches, and for that, we are grateful, because we still have some of those letters. Even as we struggle today to "understand fully" (1:14) the words of Paul, we realize that it helps to have personal contact with one another to resolve issues and mend fences.

Have you ever had to write a very hard letter to someone? The apostle Paul had to write a very troublesome letter to people he loved in the ancient city of Corinth. In truth, he very well may have written more than one hard letter to his brothers and sisters in the church at Corinth. Of the two letters that we have recorded in the New Testament that were sent there, our 2 Corinthians appears to have been the more difficult and problematic letter to compose. It runs the spectrum of human emotions: it is tearful, joyful, gentle and loving, bold and threatening.

Apologia. The "heart" (overall theme, content, and emotions) of 2 Corinthians 1–7 is Paul's *defense* of his apostolic ministry, while chapters 10–13 are the *validation* of his message and his authority in response to the strong opposition that was given to his position as an apostle. Another way of looking at these divisions is to see chapters 1–7 as an explanation of his *conduct* as God's messenger (especially 2:14–7:16), and chapters 10–13 explain his *mission* as a God-appointed apostle to the Gentiles.[1] While his personal reputation as

---

1. Murray J. Harris, *The Second Epistle to the Corinthians*, NIGTC (Grand Rapids: Eerdmans, 2005), 127–28.

God's appointed messenger was at stake in this congregation, Paul's most fervent desire was for the church to mend their ways, flourish, mature, and be "built up" in their Christian faith. Scholars have called the first seven chapters of the letter Paul's *apologia* to the Corinthian readers.[2] That is, we see Paul clearly arguing for the *defense* of his appointed apostolic ministry among them. As he defended his ministry, Paul asked his readers to help him complete an important relief-fund project in chapters 8 and 9. In the last four chapters, Paul was *validating* his calling and his concern for his readers in contrast to opposing rival missionaries who were damaging the health and the future of the Corinthian church.

A Trial and a Courtroom Scene. Another way to visualize this letter is to imagine a courtroom scene. On one side of the room, there are persuasive *"prosecutors"* who accuse Paul of numerous offenses. Their *"opening arguments"* begin in chapter one. Specific offenses brought against Paul are not clearly outlined as we do in our courtrooms today, but we can discern many of their charges from Paul's own responsive words: Paul was charged with being weak, indecisive, and capricious because of his abrupt change of travel plans. Perhaps Paul was unreliable and could not keep his word. He was bold in his letters, but face-to-face, he was a weakling (10:10). Furthermore, grief and sorrow were caused by Paul on an earlier visit to Corinth and in earlier letters. He was a poor speaker and was obviously inferior to other teachers in their midst. Maybe the "prosecutors" raised suspicions about Paul's motives concerning the collection of money from the Corinthians; he could be a fraud, intending to keep the money for himself. In a dramatic sense, Paul was blamed for having neither care nor concern for the congregation at Corinth. These opponents were present in the church, strategically positioned in leadership during Paul's absence, and were teaching and directing the church in a manner that was very different from their founding teacher, Paul.

The trial *"spectators,"* of course, were the people in the church at Corinth, Christian believers, many of whom considered Paul their pastor. Some of them had made up their own minds about Paul even before his "trial" began. Members of this group were primarily Gentile believers; some were being duped by other Greco-Roman teachers who were promoting ideas that were in opposition to Paul's gospel message. In addition, some spectators in the church were Jewish by ethnicity, and it is possible that they were heavily influenced by Jewish Christians who came from outside the church to "correct" or

---

2. Paul B. Duff, "Transformed 'From Glory to Glory': Paul's Appeal to the Experience of His Readers in 2 Corinthians 3:18," *JBL* 127.4 (2008): 761. See also, Victor Paul Furnish, *II Corinthians*, AB (New York: Doubleday, 1984), 35.

"add to" Paul's teachings. Thus, in view of criticism from inside and outside the community, it may have been very natural for the relatively new believers to look intently at Paul and say, "Who is this man, really? He was not one of the original twelve disciples of Jesus. How do we know that he is authentic in his message? Where did he come from, and who can vouch for him?"[3] Suspicions breed suspicions. Further, just by looking at Paul, they may have had doubts about his seemingly poor physical health and appearance. If, indeed, he was a true apostle of Jesus, would God allow him to be in such poor health?

The Case for the Defense. On the other side of the room, then, is Paul, the "*defendant.*" He had no high-priced lawyer defending him against such accusations, only God and his Lord Jesus Christ. Despite their objections to his intentions and his fiscal motives, and from the very onset of the "trial," Paul had supreme confidence in his "defense team," in a certain victory, and in his vindication as one called by God to ministry. His defense begins in earnest in chapter 1 (1:12) and continues until the end of the letter. Paul had to answer questions concerning his travel schedule, hardships, weaknesses, and persecutions that, paradoxically, authenticated his apostleship. The reason Paul had such confidence in his message and his ministry was because he knew that it all came from God; his message was far superior to any message touted by his rival teachers (3:1–6).

In his defense, there were other "*witnesses*" in the courtroom. Sitting beside Paul, or behind him, were his colleagues, other missionaries serving Jesus, ready to "take the stand" in his defense. These men traveled across the region preaching Jesus and supporting established Christian assemblies. They, too, had endured trials in ministry work with Paul (6:1). A few of his colleagues are named in this letter, such as Timothy (1:1), Silas (1:19), and Titus (2:13; 7:6, 14; 8:16–24). We can observe the author's consistent use of plural pronouns ("we," "ours," and "us"), implying that Christian ministry is a team effort. What a relief to know that Paul did not stand alone in his ministry, or in his motives, toward the Corinthians.

The Evidence and Rebuttal. While the charges leveled at him by his adversaries were feeble at best, Paul still needed to respond in his own defense. The *prosecution* presents evidence to the court against the accused. In this letter, the charges against Paul were primarily demeaning, discrediting verbal slander: he was indecisive, a mediocre speaker, timid and weak in his discipline and in his tone. In short, he did *not* have the credentials or the character to hold the apostolic authority that he claimed to possess.

---

3. Duff, "Transformed," 763.

As a *rebuttal* to these accusations, Paul did two things: first, he clarified his genuine "weapons" in the argument. He was, in fact, strong in the Lord, and empowered by God to do his assignment as the apostle to the Gentiles. That is, Paul fought against his enemies with unexpected "weapons," those very unlike the "standards of the world" (10:2–6). Paul was not using weapons of human pride, arrogance, and manipulation. Instead, he dealt firmly with the slanderers in Corinth not with weapons such as swords but with meekness, gentleness (10:1), forgiveness (2:5–8), and concerned love for the people (i.e., 6:11–13). Second, Paul was bold enough to turn the mirror on his accusers and show the "jury" what the *prosecutors* were really like (2:17; 3:6). He presented evidence of his adversaries' "secret and shameful ways" (4:2), and their misleading teachings (11:4). Furthermore, it was evident that his rivals were abusing and exploiting the congregation for their own interests, using oppressive rules and prohibitions (11:16–20). Dripping with irony, Paul admitted that he was "too weak" to behave in the manner of his opponents (11:21). In short, the evidence of the prosecution against Paul had no foundation.

In the first seven chapters Paul was very open about his care and concern for his readers (7:11–13). He honestly spoke of his love and affection for them (6:11–13; 7:2–4). His tone is very positive: he showed confidence in them and was proud of them in their faith (7:4). Paul had great hope for the Corinthians, and he was encouraged by whatever devotion they showed to him and to his colleagues (7:5–7; 12–13). He even confirms his joy over the readers' concern for him in 7:7. This is really "feel good" stuff for the "press gallery"!

Ironically, the suffering and hardships Paul faced were direct evidence of his calling from God and the empowering effects of the Holy Spirit. While the Corinthians were impressed by the power and position of the tyrannical leaders of the Roman Empire, Paul insisted that his power came from God and was exhibited through human weakness. He boasted gladly about his own weaknesses and expressed his meekness and gentleness as direct evidence of his authentic apostleship, because Christ himself was meek and gentle (10:1) and was "crucified in weakness" (13:3–4). In view of all the evidence, and in contrast to Paul, it was certainly the false apostles who were dishonest, self-serving, and not ministering for the benefit of the congregation.

The Verdict. In this case, as with others, the Judge, of course, is God. He proclaims the final *verdict.* As in many courtroom scenes, the verdict may be quite unexpected. The last four chapters of the letter shift in tone and purpose as Paul prepared his readers for a "closed case." The unexpected verdict was that, in truth, the *congregation* was on trial and needed to prove their devotion to Jesus Christ and to his apostle, Paul. And the judgment imposed on his opponents? Through the first chapters of the letter, Paul does not verbally attack or directly condemn his opponents. Yet, in chapter 11 he accused the prosecutors of being false apostles, and servants of Satan who were deceitful, counterfeit messengers. God would judge the deceivers correctly, and Paul had no anxiety about how God would judge him.

The Case against Paul. In the modern American judicial system, a case begins with opening arguments, usually before a jury, evidence and witnesses are presented, and then closing arguments are imparted. The *prosecution* always begins the opening arguments, followed by the *defense.* The *prosecution* also has the last word and gives the final closing statements, after the *defense.* In the case of 2 Corinthians, Paul's opponents, the false apostles or competing teachers who invaded the congregation he had established, began the case with degrading, accusatory charges against Paul and his ministry. Paul had to defend his methods, ministry, and motivations. Chapters 1–9 are his opening arguments in his own defense. True, godly evidence of Paul's life, and the godly witnesses for him (his fellow workers) were presented to the Corinthian readers. The final chapters of the letter, chapters 10–13, are Paul's closing arguments in the case, addressing the misleading notions and erroneous beliefs of his opponents.

Following the American system, the prosecution would still have the final, closing words in the case against Paul. Yet, in this letter, Paul turned the table on his opponents and testified to their deceptions, self-interest, and even abuse of the congregation. Because of their dishonesty, they were not allowed the final word. Knowing the *Jewish* laws as he did, Paul implied that because he was innocent of the false charges, the prosecutors themselves were held responsible for condemning an innocent man:

> If a malicious witness takes the stand to accuse a man of a crime, the two people involved in the dispute must stand in the presence of the LORD before the priests and the judges who are in office at the time. The judges must make a thorough investigation, and if the witness proves to be a liar, giving false testimony against a fellow Israelite, then do to the false witness as that witness intended to do to the other party. You must purge the evil from among you. (Deut. 19:16–19)

The Case Today. Thus, it is our job as modern-day readers to investigate the developments in this courtroom drama as we delve deeply into the known facts and evidence against Paul. This case is still relevant today. Unfortunately, it is not unusual for churchgoing Christians today to oppose, persecute, and condemn pastors and Christian leaders on unwarranted charges, such as how one looks, or dresses, or speaks, or how a leader fails to nurture and show compassion as expected. Leaders are judged on the stands they take on certain (sometimes thorny) social issues, or how a leader fails to promote a specific social cause. For any pastor or leader who has been unjustifiably opposed and condemned by the people he or she loved, this letter is strength and encouragement. For people who have selfishly and indefensibly charged a pastor or leader, this letter is a stern warning. Furthermore, this letter is a "head check" and a "heart check" for Christian leaders to be absolutely certain that they are preaching, teaching, and living the true, authentic gospel of Jesus Christ. It is still against human nature to see suffering and hardship as part of the process of maturing as Christians, but this letter gives us insight into that paradox. For the Christian church today, it is critical that we understand Paul's instructions and objectives, and that we see how the church of Christ fits into God's grand Story of human redemption, reconciliation, and conduct in the world.

Author: The Apostle Paul

The influence and the inspiration of the apostle Paul on the Christian church in his generation *and in ours* cannot be overstated. Quite probably, Paul was the author of our two canonical Corinthian letters. First Corinthians is by far the better known of the two letters, but there are similarities in both letters in vocabulary, literary style, and rhetoric, as well as topics, themes, and his manner of argumentation. While we can recognize that each Pauline letter in the NT addresses some kind of need, uncertainty, or difficulty in a Christian assembly, 2 Corinthians is very obviously an attempt on the part of a concerned pastor to address specific issues that were detrimental to the church in Corinth.

Following proper Greco-Roman epistle customs, Paul introduced himself to his readers in a similar form in the two Corinthian letters (1 Cor 1:1 and 2 Cor 1:1). He was both an "apostle, called by God" and an "apostle of Christ Jesus by the will of God." "An apostle" was a common title he used for himself in other letters (see Romans 1:1; Galatians 1:1) to emphasize that his calling and commission were directly from Father God and the Lord Jesus Christ. In each of the Corinthian letters, Paul named a fellow Christian worker (Sosthenes and Timothy) who served as a devoted witness to Paul's mission and ministry. At the outset of each letter, then, Paul testified to his God-given authority as a messenger of Jesus Christ.

Paul's Conversion

His life before his conversion to Christianity was already influential and outstanding. Born sometime between 10 and 5 BC, much of his life coincided with the life and ministry of Jesus.[4] As the Hebrew Saul, he was a loyal, committed Jew, even to the point of violently persecuting those Jews in his society who recognized Jesus as the Messiah. We have only snapshots of his pre-Christian life story in Acts (9:1–30; 22:2–21; 26:1–32), and by Paul himself in the letters to the Galatians (1:11–24), the Philippians (3:4–7), and to his colleague Timothy (1 Tim 1:12–14). Saul, the man Paul was before he was a Christian, was a highly-educated Jew, a Pharisee, and a Roman citizen, a man of fervor and zeal for God and for his people. Saul's great enthusiasm for the Torah was what drove him to persecute the followers of Christ, whom he regarded as misdirected and disobedient to the one God he knew. Surely this background affected who he became as Paul, the thoughtful, dedicated Christian preacher, teacher, church planter, and missionary.

An amazing encounter with the risen Jesus on the road out of Jerusalem and on the way to Damascus transformed Paul's life. A revelation, as an act of divine grace from God, changed his life forever. Jesus appeared to him in a flash of glory and gave him his assignment for serving the Lord: the devout Pharisee was instructed to convert Gentile people to faith in Jesus.[5] After this life-altering experience and an intense education from Jesus, Paul then preached the gospel of Jesus Christ boldly and fearlessly (Acts 9:27–28). Jesus made him temporarily blind so that eventually Paul would see the truth. In service to his Lord, Paul traveled thousands of miles over many years by land and by sea across the ancient Near East. He abandoned his previous way of life in Judaism (Gal 1:13), and he "died to the law" in the wake of his extraordinary redemption and restoration by Jesus Christ (Gal 2:19).[6] His stories (and his theology) are captured in epistles he wrote to the people he saved and served in ministry. It was not an easy assignment. In 2 Corinthians alone, Paul shared four passages about the trials and hardships he experienced during his years of ministry (1:8–11; 4:8–12; 6:4–10; 11:22–28). He highlighted his suffering to demonstrate his reliance on God, the one who assigned him to his tasks, and who daily empowered him to complete his assignments (1:9; 11:30–31; see Rom 8:28, 35–36).

Paul the Missionary

Paul's personality and background were a perfect fit for the kind of service to which he was called. His fine education as a young man in Tarsus, his roots in

4. Michael F. Bird, *Introducing Paul* (Downers Grove, IL: InterVarsity Press, 2008), 31.

5. James D. G. Dunn, "The Christian Life from the Perspective of Paul's Letter to the Galatians," in *The Apostle Paul and the Christian Life* (Grand Rapids: Baker, 2016), 4.

6. Larry W. Hurtado, "'The Paul Dialogue': Barclay & Wright," June 16, 2016, https://larry hurtado.wordpress.com/?s=the+paul+dialogue.

the Torah, and his keen insight into the plans and purposes of God prepared him for a challenging ministry to the Gentiles. Paul was a deep theological thinker who reflected on what he learned; he was educated in the art of rhetoric and was deliberate about the words he used in his communications. After his conversion, Paul carefully connected the dots between the OT laws and prophecies and the Messiah, Jesus. On the mission field and in the unfamiliar land of Gentiles, he spoke in their language (metaphorically and physically) and understood their foreign culture. He geared his message of the gospel to what his audience knew and accepted as truth, and then disclosed God's truth in a way they could grasp. Yet, his thoughts and insights were profound, and his letters were weighty (10:10). Thus, "Paul is our theological master, our pastoral mentor, our spiritual advisor and our missionary hero."[7]

Extremes seemed to characterize Paul's story: there were prophecies, and miracles performed (Acts 19:6, 11), amazing visions and revelations received (2 Cor 12:1–6), and deep friendships established (Acts 19:8–10; 20:17–38). On the other hand, ministry is difficult; Paul experienced extreme hardships and dangers, physical and mental (see 2 Cor 11:23–28). As he narrated his own life for the people he served, he always gave the glory and the honor to God, taking none for himself. In addition to his service to the churches, Paul practiced his trade as a tentmaker in Gentile cities (Acts 18:1–4) to pay his own way as he traveled and established congregations. However, in Roman society this was *not* a profession with high status, class, or recognition, and it must have seemed very odd to others that Paul did not accept high fees for his teaching and speaking. It was countercultural that someone in his social position was most concerned about other people rather than himself and his own ambitions. As the quintessential pastor and shepherd, Paul was conscientious, compassionate, and giving of himself. Although they were substitutes for Paul's presence, letters served as instructions, exhortations, admonitions, and encouragement to the Christian converts. Unfortunately, readers today cannot hear all of the converts' side of the conversations, so we must gain an understanding of Paul's missionary work strictly from his side of the interactions. We also know that his letters were passed around to other Christian assemblies in different cities and shared extensively ("circular letters"; see 1 Thess 5:27; Col 4:16). Thus, Paul's Corinthian letters were "occasional letters," written for a particular group of new Christians, but he attempted to reveal collective Christian truths that applied to believers beyond the specific historical situations.[8]

---

7. Bird, *Introducing Paul*, 12.
8. Ben Witherington III, *Conflict and Community in Corinth* (Grand Rapids: Eerdmans, 1995), 5–35.

The Roman Empire and the Gentile Mission

With respect to the Gentile mission, it is essential that we remember that Paul's ministry was conducted in the context of the first-century AD Roman Empire. Alexander the Great (356–323 BC) expanded his Greek Empire by military force. He brought together all the Greek city-states (with the exception of Sparta) into the "Corinthian League" (also called the "Hellenic League") to accomplish a military invasion of Persia. When they met at Corinth, it was the first time the states were unified in an effort to increase Alexander's empire. As he conquered the region, the Greek sovereign established Hellenism everywhere—the Greek language, the culture, and the philosophies.

After Alexander, and still two centuries before Paul and Jesus, the Romans relentlessly expanded their control over the area of Greece and Asia Minor by military conquest. The Roman imperial power gained solid control through military supremacy. To take control, the army devastated local towns and villages, and massacred and enslaved people. In 146 BC the Romans defeated the Greek city of Corinth and demolished it. Corinth faded in glory, and it was left in ruins for a century. Then, in 44 BC, Emperor Julius Caesar rebuilt the city of Corinth as a Roman colony. His intention was to establish the city as a destination for potentially rebellious Romans: freed slaves, retired military veterans, and rural outsiders who migrated into Roman cities. As a colonized city, Corinth became a major commerce center; its strategic location as a port city made it a hub of products and of people.[9]

The book of Acts records the missionary travels of Paul across the empire, mainly in Greece (Achaia and Macedonia), Asia Minor, Italy (Rome), Palestine, Judaea, and Galilee. He journeyed to major cities across the region, urban areas located on strategic Roman roads.

Paul traveled south to Corinth after he had established Christian communities in Macedonia, including Philippi, Thessalonica, and perhaps Berea (see Acts 16 and 17). Paul's gospel message shared with the Corinthians was essential Christianity, featuring the crucifixion of Christ (1 Cor 2:1–2) and Jesus's resurrection (1 Cor 15; 2 Cor 5). The third person of the Trinity, the Holy Spirit, was made apparent to the Corinthians with a "demonstration of the Spirit and of power" (1 Cor 2:4–5; 2 Cor 12:12). They received the fundamental tenets of the Christian faith, customs, rituals, and behavior, many of which were very foreign to the first-century Romans and Greeks.[10]

---

9. Richard A. Horsley, "The First and Second Letters to the Corinthians," in *A Postcolonial Commentary on the New Testament Writings*, ed. Fernando F. Segovia and R. S. Sugirtharajah (New York: T&T Clark, 2009), 222–23.

10. Furnish, *II Corinthians*, 22–24.

Backgrounds

Bruce Winter suggests that we think about the historical background of the Corinthian letters in two ways. First, the social, political, religious, and *cultural* background of the Corinthian believers was entirely Roman. Second, and in contrast, the *theological* background of the apostle Paul was Jewish, reflecting the OT, intertestamental Judaism, and the Jesus traditions. Indeed, this was a clash of cultures from the very beginning. It is a very helpful reminder to modern readers, however, that the story and plan of God's redemption was unfolding within this Roman imperial culture. Paul's letters must be read in their original imperial Roman context, and Paul's mission must be understood within these complicated social and historical backgrounds.[11]

Certainly, the dominant culture in Corinth was Roman, even if Greek was considered the common language for commerce and trade, as well as written and spoken rhetoric (oration). Corinth boasted of Roman language (Latin inscriptions), temples, and administration. The modernization of Corinth replaced the ancient Greek structures, such as the Temple of Apollo. It was reconstructed to be an intentional imitation of the temple that the Emperor Augustus built in Rome to the same god. The Roman "Venus of the Forum" was rebuilt to be more impressive than the Greek temple to Aphrodite. Her temple was at the center of the city, as the "Mother of the Roman nation" and a "mother" to the Corinthian colony.[12]

Thus, the Corinthian believers did not become Christians in one day; the first-century Roman society was deeply ingrained in them, and they were rooted in what we might call "cultural conditioning." Often the problems that arose within the congregation were the result of the Corinthians' culture and lifestyle, which determined how they responded to situations within their society that were in opposition to the Christian gospel message. Thus they had many questions about how to respond and live as a community entrenched in the overwhelming Roman influence and authority. The canonical letter we know as 1 Corinthians raises at least six such issues, to the point that they had to ask Paul to help them sort out the answers to such matters. These daily issues included sexual behavior and immorality (i.e., 1 Cor 5:1–5; 6:13–20), marriage, lawsuits, and propriety in worship. In 2 Corinthians, Paul had to address questions of idolatry (6:14–7:1), suffering (1:3–7), and finances (i.e., 8:1–12; 9:6–11). Spiritual gifts, extraordinary visions, and miracles were issues in both letters. The very fact that they wrote to Paul with their queries

---

11. Bruce W. Winter, *After Paul Left Corinth: The Influence of Secular Ethics and Social Change* (Grand Rapids: Eerdmans, 2001), xii–xiii.

12. Winter, *After Paul Left Corinth*, 9–10.

is evidence that some people within their community had concerns about what was happening.[13]

We know that Paul ministered to the people in Corinth for about eighteen months (Acts 18:11), but even that was not enough time to encounter all the possible situations that vexed the Corinthian congregation in that culture. So, what happened after Paul left them? It appears that the congregation was still uncertain not so much about doctrine but about proper behavior. As a group of believers, they were neither assured nor in agreement with one another about acceptable actions and conduct for Christ-followers. Thus, confused and divided, they were trying to engage their prevailing culture while still adapting to the truths of Paul's gospel message.[14]

Scholars have advanced additional theories. It has been proposed that Gnosticism infiltrated the church. Perhaps the concept of "over-realized eschatology" blurred their vision of clear, Pauline truths. However, both suggestions fail to deal with all the problems that arise in the two Corinthian letters. A third suggestion is that Paul failed to teach all that was needed, or that he himself changed his mind about Christian freedoms and convictions after he left Corinth. Winter discounts all these suggestions and contends that it was the external challenges of Roman influence and authority that created internal strife in the church. Three significant changes affected the society and impacted the lives of the Corinthian believers. The first was the location of the Isthmian Games. This event in Corinth was one of three crucial religious and athletic festivals held annually in the empire. Attended by the emperor and his family, local elites competed for the best venue. Civic dinners were staged by the elites, and the entire city of Corinth was invited to attend the festivities. Perhaps this was the setting for Paul's instructions on eating and idolatry (1 Cor 8:9).[15]

The second change was three severe grain shortages during the early years of the church. Such a shortage resulted in poverty and famine for the common person in the region (see 2 Cor 8:1–2). An imperial official superintendent was assigned by the government to distribute the grain supply in local areas, and most often, he was able to manipulate the market for the benefit of those with wealth and power at the expense of the lower-class population.

Third, a "federal" imperial cult was created in about AD 54 as an outward, public display of loyalty to and veneration of the emperor (see more about the imperial cult, below). While the worship of the emperor as divine was legally

---

13. Winter, *After Paul Left Corinth*, 1–2.
14. Winter, *After Paul Left Corinth*, 1–7.
15. Winter, *After Paul Left Corinth*, 5–6.

voluntary (especially in the eastern provinces), it was socially mandatory. This was a change for the Christian congregations in the empire who were looked down upon as "deviant" Jewish sects, or as "atheists" who worshiped an "unseen" god. Many Christians refused, at their own peril, to worship the emperor or any of the local and national gods and goddesses.[16]

Thus, the promised peace in the empire (Pax Romana) in the first century was a fallacious dream of human achievement and human ambition that resulted in greed, envy, self-preservation, and destruction. Christian congregations across the empire attempted to exist in the "kingdom of God" and grow within the power, prestige, and control of an earthly "kingdom." Despite this, the Christian church spread and expanded rapidly in the first and second centuries. The Corinthian letters, as a first-century source, are perhaps the "best composite witness to life in a Roman colony in the East."[17]

Paul's message was clear to some people, but opaque to others. To unbelievers in the Gentile world, Jesus was the picture of weakness and degradation, crucified on a cross as a common criminal. His crucifixion by the Romans was a form of execution reserved for seditious, rebel leaders. Yet, to believers, "Jesus is Lord" (1 Cor 12:3–4) and was the transforming power of God that broke into their world (2 Cor 3:18). The paradox of God is that outward appearances are not reliable, and supreme worth is not what the world supposes it to be. Further, the approval of God through Christ matters far more than human status, recognition, and accolades. In a culture brimming with military might, self-praise, and self-commendation, Paul rejected such signs of acclamation, and centered his success and "boasting" among the Gentiles in the triumphs of God. The epitome of true meekness, Paul "boasted" lavishly in whatever demonstrated his own weaknesses and drew his readers' attention to the power of God.

Jewish Christianity

Under the Roman imperial scheme, thousands of people living in the Palestine region were deported and moved to other parts of the empire. Jewish communities and Jewish Christians settled in the *diaspora*, and those ethnic Jews living in Roman cities were assimilated by varying degrees into the established culture. Some became the so-called "Hellenistic" or "Grecian" Jews (see Acts 6:1). Under Roman rule, two things happened: first, there were numerous "peasant revolts" in the Palestinian region, which gave birth to Jewish resistant

16. Winter, *After Paul Left Corinth*, 28. Also, see Larry Hurtado, *Destroyer of the Gods: Early Christian Distinctives in the Roman World* (Waco, TX: Baylor University Press, 2017).
17. Winter, *After Paul Left Corinth*, 28.

movements (like the Zealots) and popular, seditious (yet false) prophets (Matt 7:15; 24:23–25; 2 Pet 2:1). Second, a high-priestly, wealthy, elite aristocracy formed in Jerusalem, which chose to associate themselves closely with the client kings established by the Roman government (such as King Herod).[18]

Conversely, Michael Bird contends that Jesus's mission was "Israel-centric," that the restoration of the nation of Israel included the salvation of the Gentiles (see, for example, Acts 1:7–8). As a continuation of that vision, and amid Roman domination, Paul upheld the "Israel-centric" mission of Jesus. In the mind of Paul, his mission was to and through Israel, not through Rome; a godly, transformed nation would therefore transform the world—even the Roman world. The Christian church, through Jesus, was to be the unified "people of God" including both Jews and Gentiles: "the new Israel and the renewed humanity. The church was to be charismatic (Spirit-endowed), multi-ethnic (Jew and Gentile), Christocentric, unified ("one body"), part of society, but not a reflection of it."[19]

Paul wrote that the reconciliation of all humanity and the restoration of the people of God were achieved by—*and only by*—the death and resurrection of the Messiah Jesus. What happened to his own people, the Jews, was important to Paul (see Romans 9–11), but his God-given assignment was to extend the grace of God to the Gentiles, to suffer and serve so that all people could become Jesus-followers (see Acts 9:15–16). Combined into one "new temple," or "one body," both believing Jews and Gentiles were indeed called to be the light to the nations (2 Cor 4:6). The unity of Christian believers made the light so much brighter in the dark world of the Roman Empire.

The Grand Story of God

Paul was a man of vision and foresight. In an intellectual sense, Paul was equipped and well-trained in the proper use of Greek rhetoric; in the geographic sense, he saw a big plan, and anticipated a time when he could take the gospel message to Spain (Rom 15:28). In a spiritual sense, Paul could sense an eschatological necessity for delivering the life-saving message of Christ to people who were led astray by the world around them. He could perceive that he was a strategic part of the "Grand Story of God," a cog in the wheel of God's eternal plans and purposes for all of humanity, the Jews and the Gentiles. Paul seemed to realize that his was a unique role in the Christian missionary movement, called and empowered by God (Rom 15:25–27). It was his intention to bring all of his converted believers into full maturity in Christ (see Eph 4:13).

---

18. Horsley, "First and Second Letters to the Corinthians," 224–25.
19. Bird, *Introducing Paul*, 56. Also, see Horsley, "First and Second Letters to the Corinthians," 224.

Paul faced opposition and hardships with grace and perception, never losing sight of the "big picture." His distinctive calling and his mission were worth defending and protecting from the accusations and attacks of opponents, and his congregations were worth the trials and efforts (see 2 Cor 13:10). Finally, as Bird wrote,

> Paul left us neither a travel diary nor a systematic theology textbook to follow. At the end of the day, we have only a "Reader's Digest" account of his life from Luke (in the Acts of the Apostles) and some thirteen pastoral postcards he sent to the churches of his day. He wrote letters for a variety of reasons: to encourage and rebuke congregations, to exhort individuals in their ministry, to defend his authority and ministry and to establish fellowships with Christians he did not know personally.[20]

"New Perspective" on Paul and his New Testament Letters

It is appropriate here to comment briefly on the "new perspective" of Paul and his writings. Readers can learn a great deal more about this "old/new perspective" discussion in related books found in the bibliography. The scholarly discussion about Paul and his theology has been smoldering for about the last forty years and has been reignited in current NT scholarship. Briefly, the "old perspective" on Paul focused on "my standing before God." That is, in the past, we have interpreted the writings of Paul as criticism of human guilt (sin) before a righteous God, and how to resolve that problem.[21] Paul insisted that if a person commits to faith or belief in Jesus Christ as Lord and Savior, then he or she can reap the benefits of God's salvation, redemption, and grace. This perspective raised concern about how Paul viewed the Jewish people (his own people) who rejected Jesus as the Messiah and did not follow Christ as the promised Messiah. Some scholars concluded that Paul was critical of Judaism as a "legalistic work-religion" (deemed a "caricature" of Judaism), where only obedience to the law placed a person in right standing with God.[22] This would be a sharp contrast to Paul's view of Christianity, which was outside of the law and based on faith in Jesus alone.

While the "new perspective" on Paul neither denies nor makes light of personal salvation and grace through belief in Christ, it poses a different central

---

20. Bird, *Introducing Paul*, 12–13.
21. Scot McKnight, "The New Perspective and the Christian Life: The Ecclesial Life," in *The Apostle Paul and the Christian Life*, ed. Scot McKnight (Grand Rapids: Baker, 2016), 136.
22. Patrick Mitchel, "The New Perspective and the Christian Life: Solus Spiritus," in McKnight, *Apostle Paul*, 72.

message of Paul's writings, which is more ecclesial in nature.[23] "The personal redemption theme of the old perspective is not the central concern of Paul here, nor is the Torah-shaped behavior for Jews and somewhat for gentiles the focus. . . . His concern is that the church is a fellowship of *differents*" (that is, a fellowship of different types of people).[24] The Pauline "mystery" as presented in his letters to the churches (Eph 1:9–10) is that Gentiles have the opportunity to become an addition to the people of God not through the law, but through faith in Jesus Christ (e.g., Eph 2:11–22). Therefore, Paul sees the church as one fellowship, a mixed bag of sinners, Jew and Gentile, Greek and Roman, male and female, all redeemed by the same Savior, and filled with the same Spirit (1 Cor 12:8–11).

Enduring Stories

In this letter to the Corinthians, we enter into the life of Paul the apostle through his stories, written down and shared with his readers: he relates his own near-death experience, his own version of the story of Moses and the glory of Sinai, of valuables in clay jars, his own physical hardships, the generosity of the church at Macedonia, of his encounter with his opponents, a narrow escape from Damascus, and even being "caught up to paradise." As readers we thirst for more details from his stories, more information and explanations; however, we don't get them. Unfortunately, the lack of details in his stories tends to raise speculation by modern-day readers about circumstances, dates, motivations, and identities that seem to be irrelevant to Paul's purposes. In addition, while Paul's stories are important to his message and to his audience, he intended them to move the focus off of himself and on to God and to the Lord Jesus (see 2 Cor 11:30–33). He did not carry reams of written commendations (or recommendations) from church to church, publicizing his own abilities and success stories. In fact, he punctuated his own weaknesses in ministry. No doubt it appeared odd to the church that Paul came to them with a unique witness of "weakness and fear" (see 1 Cor 2:1–5).

The "Story of God" is revealed in Paul's stories, and the two are so inseparable that we could say that Paul's story is God's story in a snapshot format. While we are focusing on one picture, one letter sent at one time to one church in one ancient city, the truths found in 2 Corinthians are God-given truths that are still relevant today in Christian churches everywhere. Paul was simply an instrument in the Master's hand to give us messages of truth and fidelity. God's life-giving Holy Spirit does not fade with time or

---

23. McKnight, "New Perspective and the Christian Life," 139.
24. McKnight, "New Perspective and the Christian Life," 139.

circumstances, and the life he gives to all believers is eternal and unrestricted by human time or geography.

Audience: The Corinthian Believers

In addition to what we know about the writer of 2 Corinthians, we can also make some postulations about the audience to whom Paul wrote. Why did Paul find it necessary to write the things he did to the Corinthian believers? Because he loved the church so much, he was using all his rhetorical power and principles to persuade the Roman audience to follow in the ways of Christ that he had taught them. Perhaps his corrective rhetoric in 1 Corinthians was not sufficient, and the prevailing powers of numerous outside influences were injuring the young believers.

Living in the shadow of Rome, Paul's readers had their own backgrounds, religions, ethnicities, social norms, social aspirations, and secular ethics. The established Roman forces controlled and grounded their everyday lives. Since we are aware that Paul planted this church, we can assume that they were converted and trained by Paul in the basics of Christianity, in contrast to their known Roman culture, religion, and politics. The readers were saved and blessed, "sanctified in Christ Jesus" (1 Cor 1:2) and were a part of a larger family of Christian believers "throughout Achaia" (2 Cor 1:1). Initially, they were an "assembly of believers," gathered together in a home or homes for teaching and prayer. For this reason, Paul had a special love for his "spiritual children" in Corinth and was anxious for them to succeed and grow in Christ. In setting the course for their redemption and their maturity, Paul placed great hope in the Corinthians; he anticipated the potential of this small assembly to grow and become an example of the Christian church in the entire region (2 Cor 10:14–16).

In total, the population of Corinth was quite large by first-century standards: perhaps 70,000 to 80,000 inhabitants. The inhabitants were Roman citizens, freedmen and women, veterans, slaves, and immigrants. As a result, the Christian church was an amalgamation of people from all parts of the Roman society, as well as a number of Jewish Christians.[25] On the one hand, the earliest Corinthian Jesus-followers may have included people of high ranking in society, both educationally and socially. These "elites" were people of wealth, position, and power in the city, many of whom may have tended toward arrogance and an overstated view of themselves. On the other hand, the Christian gathering also appealed to the common person living in the

25. Linda L. Belleville, *2 Corinthians*, IVPNTC 8 (Downers Grove, IL: InterVarsity Press, 1996), 14–15.

rural areas around Corinth with a minimal amount of education and material wealth. Perhaps these people gained a sense of value and worth within the Christian faith, something they did not have in their society. Paul recognized that some of the people were of lower classes:

> Not many of you were wise by human standards; not many were influ-ential; not many were of noble birth. But God chose the foolish things of the world to shame the wise; God chose the weak things of the world to shame the strong. God chose the lowly things of this world and the despised things—and the things that are not—to nullify the things that are . . . (1 Cor 1:26–28).

So, for example, there were divisions among the believers when it came to the celebration of the Lord's Supper. Some people of the upper class did not wait to eat supper until the others had arrived. Often the early Christian fellowships held a meal in connection with the partaking of communion (the "agape meal"), not unlike our church potluck suppers. In Corinth, the wealthier, elite people brought more food than the poorer members, and they ate their fill before the others (the "working class") arrived at the gathering. The poorer members were left hungry. As a result of their differences, there were those who defiled the Lord's Supper with their superior attitudes and selfishness (1 Cor 11:17–22). Of course, this was unacceptable to Paul, and it negated the meaning and significance of the memorial supper initiated by Christ. As we could guess, dissention and divisions were apparent within the congregation concerning members' status, position, and "worldliness" (1 Cor 1:10–13; 3:3–5).

Bruce Winters employs the Latin term *Romanitas* to describe the values of the Corinthians. The concept affected most of the known empire in the first century, especially the colonies. It refers to Roman values and social conven-tions. Corinth was populated by people born and raised in the thoroughly Roman culture. The Roman way of life touched every aspect of their lives, from A to Z—from architecture to the god Zeus. When Paul introduced the gospel message of Jesus Christ to the Corinthians, his words were in conflict with the known Roman society, their laws, judicial system, ethics, titles, and religious worship. The depths of this "Romanization" of a formerly Greek city-state cannot be overstated. Yet, the mere fact that the church wrote to Paul asking specific questions about the "new" Christian life was evidence that some people in the church did not perceive some "old" behavior in the culture as appropriate.[26]

---

26. Winter, *After Paul Left Corinth*, 1–2, 10–28.

Second, and perhaps even more influential, was the Roman concept of "*cursus honorum*" which was, briefly, the path to fame and fortune. Very little exceeded the Romans' appetite for personal social status and honor. Not unlike the "Yuppies" of recent memory, the young, affluent Roman men did everything they could to climb the social ladder to success. Often the more successful, prestigious citizens were duly honored with statues or monuments in their cities, and their accomplishments brought honor to the whole city or colony. They gained their status by noble birth, excellent military service, generosity (gifts often given to those of yet higher social strata), and/or superior public speaking abilities. This concept expanded to an "honor and shame" culture within the empire. Notably, the more fame and honor one received, the more one could boast about one's importance. Boasting was not only acceptable, it was assumed, because this status concept became very competitive. One's status was flaunted by appropriate clothing and extravagant public banquets and events. "Honor was a public verdict; it was also intoxicating."[27]

There were other outcomes of this notion of *cursus honorum*. First, the society became highly structured in leadership. Very few elites actually gained the fame and fortune they sought, but in keeping with the human drive for status, local associations, trade groups, clubs, and sub-cultures adopted the concept. That is, "what the upper class does, others imitate."[28] Furthermore, since generosity was a virtue, the upper crust of society accepted the role of benefactors or patrons who financially aided the lower strata of artists, tradesmen, workers, civil servants, and teachers. Patrons developed a network of "friends" (or "clients") and could therefore manipulate power in exchange for exclusive loyalty. Those in the upper strata of the population were powerful enough to secure unjust advantages in the court system in the empire: they could afford to bribe judges, juries, and even witnesses. They could obtain food when the famines made it difficult. In fact, with status came the opportunity to acquire almost anything (materially) that one could desire, even at the expense of the needs of those in the lower classes. With this structure in place, the upper class of people could afford to affect political decisions, control agricultural production and distribution, and sway the decisions of the judicial and banking systems.[29]

Social Status

Thus, in view of these prominent ideologies, social honor and position were important among the residents of Corinth. The nature of one's status was

---

27. Scot McKnight, *Pastor Paul: Nurturing a Culture of Christoformity in the Church* (Grand Rapids: Baker, 2019), 134.

28. McKnight, *Pastor Paul*, 134.

29. Winter, *After Paul Left Corinth*, 188.

apparent in his or her wealth and position in the city and at the temples, and in one's political power. Status is an important motif found in Paul's letters; it is regarded as a liability to one's character. One critical example found in 2 Corinthians is the concept of "boasting." This *cursus honorum* idea begins in 1 Corinthians and moves into 2 Corinthians. Negatively, Paul addressed the issue of the Corinthians being "proud" and "boasting" (1 Cor 5:2, 6), especially as it related to the behavior of an incestuous man in their midst. A concern for status could very well have influenced the way the church regarded this man. Conveniently, the church may have overlooked the blatant, corrupt behavior of this member because he was a person of wealth and status in the community. Paul used this example as a statement on their personal boastful attitude as a whole.[30] Then, in 2 Corinthians, he repeatedly used the idea of "boasting" about himself ironically, subverting their own high regard for something Paul regarded as vain and worthless in the eyes of God.

In reality, honor and status provided many benefits only to those at the top. By rebuking the power and prestige of the Romanized elites, Paul was damaging the ability of those who thought they could control not only society, but also the Christian church. However, he continued to try to convince his readers that status was derived from one's position in Christ, rather than in the Roman hierarchy (1 Cor 1:30; 2 Cor 5:10; 8:9).

The Romans were accustomed to great traveling orators and philosophers who were seeking higher status and recognition for their ideas. Indeed, like many large cities, the moral ethos of Corinth was low: it was "spiritually and intellectually empty," with "crass materialism, ungracious and uncultured" residents.[31] People found their identity in the Roman culture by trying to find their place in the social and economic structure. Immigrants poured into Corinth, seeking a better life in the colony, each with his or her own background, religion, and experiences.

On the religious front, above the city on the hill known as the Acro-Corinth stood "Venus of the Forum" (the former "Temple of Aphrodite" for the Greeks), which was built to revere the popular goddess of love, beauty, and fertility. It is also probable that she was the patron goddess of prostitutes and was highly celebrated with festivals and feasts. Other temples were dedicated to Asklepios (or "Asclepius"), the "god of healing," of physical, mental, and emotional health. Another attraction in the city was the temple to Tyche, "the goddess of good fortune," or fate or luck.[32] Thus, the city was a center for

---

30. Winter, *After Paul Left Corinth*, 53–55.

31. Furnish, *II Corinthians*, 10–13. See also Ralph P. Martin, *2 Corinthians*, WBC 40 (Waco, TX: Word, 1986).

32. Belleville, *2 Corinthians*, 14–15; Furnish, *II Corinthians*, 16.

healing rituals and offering sacrifices to deities for health and prosperity. Paul's imagery of the "body of Christ" would have been very effective with people who were especially concerned about their physical ailments and health. The Egyptian goddess Isis was also popular in Corinth as the "goddess of the sea." The nearby port at Cenchreae was strategic in trade and commerce, and it brought a diverse population from Egypt and beyond to the area of Corinth.[33] Thus, many assorted powers other than the Jewish God shaped the everyday lives of the Corinthians.

Preserved stone inscriptions from the ancient city have revealed acts of civil government and administration, city planning, and even dining instructions. These historical markers also indicate strong divisions in the population that were seen in both politics and economics. The gap continued to widen between the controlling "elites" and the "non-elites," or the laboring and serving strata of people. Evidently, this separation of society spilled over into the Christian community as well.[34] Indeed, there was a dramatic inequality in Roman Corinth. The elite landowners prospered as the city grew and flourished. This prosperity was passed on to the middle class of tradesmen and service people who supported the wealthy. In return, proper social behavior was expected within the hierarchy; appropriate loyalty, reciprocation, and honor was due those in controlling positions. In the end, the rich got richer, and the poor of the region got poorer, often suffering in such circumstances.[35] Clearly, Paul responded negatively to the hierarchy of people in the empire; he objected to accepted norms, political and social issues, and a culture of reciprocity and class inequality.

Imperial Cult

Perhaps most important, Corinth was also a city devoted to the established Roman Emperor. This is a third aspect of the *cursus honorus* culture that raised the sitting emperor to the very highest realms of status, rank, title, and esteem. Corinth had a temple (probably build during the Claudian period, AD 41–54) in veneration to the emperor and his family. The Roman emperor was comparable to the "father" of the entire realm, and he received honorable titles such as "benefactor" "savior," and "son of god." When Paul arrived in Corinth, he perceived the emperor's presence everywhere—coinage, statues, temples, monuments, and inscriptions. Every four years the "Isthmian festival" and

---

33. Furnish, *II Corinthians*, 16.
34. James R. Harrison, "Introduction," in *The First Urban Churches: Roman Corinth*, ed. L. L. Welborn and James R. Harrison (Atlanta: SBL Press, 2016), 1–45. See 1 Cor 1:10–13.
35. L. L. Welborn, "Inequity in Roman Corinth," in Welborn and Harrison, *First Urban Churches*, 47–84.

games were held in Corinth, in honor of the "deified Julius Caesar" and the current reigning emperor.[36] Without a doubt, Paul also responded negatively to this imperial cult in Corinth. As a monotheistic Jew, Paul rebuked idolatry, and he taught the exclusivity of the Christian Trinitarian God: Father, Son, and Holy Spirit. He rebuked any other human being, god, or goddess as "divine," or "lord" or a "son of god." He disdained the adoration of a human leader, and he chastised the people for committing this "idolatry" (1 Cor 10:7, 14; 2 Cor 6:14–18). We can read counter-imperial themes in passages such as 2 Corinthians 4:1–6. It is even suggested that the "god of this age" in 2 Corinthians 4:4 may be a reference by Paul to "the deified Augustus Caesar" instead of to Satan.[37] Human participation in the worship of the emperor and local deities was socially expected and highly encouraged across the empire. The veneration of the emperor was positioned alongside other shrines and temples in Corinth, which dated back to the earlier Greek pantheon.

Today, scholars debate the extent of the emperor cult in the first century, both in geography and in intensity. Apparently, it was a more common practice in the western part of the empire because of its proximity to Rome itself; but strategic cities in the eastern section of the empire (such as Corinth and Ephesus) vied for the attention, prosperity, and recognition of the sitting emperor. To validate this ideology, it has been said that, "We stress that the pervasiveness of Roman imperial theology's emperor cult across the Mediterranean was one of the key features of Paul's world. It was the glue that held the civilized world together. In any city that Paul visited, evidence of emperor worship appears repeatedly in present excavations."[38]

Furthermore, communication with the "spirit-world" was very common and desired in the Greco-Roman culture. Members of the church at Corinth placed great honor and prestige in their misconception of the power of the indwelling Holy Spirit (1 Cor 1:5–7; 2:10–13; 2 Cor 11:3–4). Paul implied that it is the spirit of Satan that controls and influences aspects of the Roman world (2 Cor 2:11). So, the Trinitarian God of the Christians was difficult to understand. With fear and apprehension, if a person turned to salvation in Jesus Christ and decided to follow him (and was therefore "filled with the Holy Spirit"), that person was normally expelled from society altogether: household, family, neighborhood, trade unions, and any civic activities.

---

36. Furnish, *II Corinthians*, 17.

37. Fredrick Long, "'The God of This Age' (2 Cor 4:4) and Paul's Empire-Resisting Gospel at Corinth," in Welborn and Harrison, *First Urban Churches*, 219–61.

38. John Dominic Crossan and Jonathan L. Reed, quoted by Colin Miller in "The Imperial Cult in Pauline Cities of Asia Minor and Greece," *CBQ* 72 (2010): 316.

It took unusual courage, therefore, for a Gentile to commit to the Christian way of life and ritual as stipulated by Paul.[39]

Jews in Roman Corinth

Far less is known about the Jewish population in the empire, yet we know there were Jews in Corinth. At the time of Paul, the Roman government was tolerant of varied religions across the empire, including the practicing Jews. However, the very orthodox Jewish belief system prevented them from entering into many social and cultural practices in a predominantly pagan city. We do know that many Jews and Jewish Christians fled to Corinth after they were expelled from Rome:

> Under Claudius (AD 41–54), many Jews were forced to leave Rome, this time because of an imperial edict which was evidently prompted by strife between the Jewish community as a whole, and those of its members who had become Christians. According to Acts 18:2, this edict caused Aquila and his wife Priscilla to flee Italy to Corinth. In fact, Acts attests to the existence of a sizable Jewish community in Corinth in Paul's day (Acts 18:4–17).[40]

The Jewish immigrants discovered that in the city of Corinth, "no distinction can be made between its 'sacred' and 'secular' institutions."[41] To be part of the colony (or city) was to be a part of the Roman system.

In short, both the literary and archaeological evidence demonstrates the huge diversity of people and of belief systems in Roman Corinth. The mixture of ideologies affected the behavior and the practices of the society and the newly-formed church. Feelings of superiority and inequity characterized the Christian gathering: Jew and Gentile, rich and poor, urban and rural, sophisticated and uneducated, family and state. It is very possible that there were even some disagreeable "unbelievers" (seekers?) in their mixed gathering who frustrated the teaching and nurturing efforts of Paul (see 1 Cor 5:9–11; 14:22; 2 Cor 6:14–18). Idolatry was an especially thorny issue, as some people accepted the divinity and worship of Jesus, but he was not their exclusive Savior. They found it necessary to add something else to salvation, such as another local pagan god, or another ritual, another law or requirement to follow. The dramatic influence of the culture and the responses made by the Christian

---

39. Kathy Ehrensperger, "Between Polis, Oikos, and Ecclesia," in Welborn and Harrison, *First Urban Churches*, 105–32.
40. Furnish, *II Corinthians*, 21.
41. Furnish, *II Corinthians*, 15.

believers, especially after Paul left their community, may help to explain the conduct, dilemmas, and conflicts so apparent in the Corinthian letters.[42]

Culture of Orality

At the time of Paul, his was a predominantly oral culture. Most common people did not read or write, while the highly educated persons were avid advocates of poetry and rhetoric.

> Given recent estimates of literacy in the early Roman period (ca. 10–15% of the general population), many, perhaps most, believers of this time were unable to read at all. Many others likely had limited reading competence [but could not write]. Very few came from the sort of elite circles that [were] linked with high-quality pagan manuscripts. In short, there was a spectrum of reading competence in early Christian circles, with very few believers having the level of reading ability characteristic of the cultured elite.[43]

Yet the Roman culture was highly rhetorical; that is, it was all about "persuasion." Oral persuasive speech was everywhere, in pronouncements, on statues, inscriptions, imperial propaganda, and even oratory contests. Educated men were expected to speak in public forums and debates. Therefore, Paul used preaching as his most persuasive vehicle to appeal to his Greek-speaking target audiences, and he was skilled in rhetoric. Letters and texts were merely a secondary form of communication when Paul could not be present with his converts. It is interesting to note that the phrase the "word of God" in Acts and in Paul's writings always refers to the *oral* proclamation of the gospel message, and not the written text (see 1 Thess 2:13). Yet, letter writing was a significant part of rhetorical higher education. After years of study, one was expected to produce a rhetorical composition using an *epistolary* (or letter) format, following an established structure: an introduction, greeting or opening (prescript), a proposition, an objection, an argument, and an ending, conclusion, or postscript (that is, *exordium, narratio, propositio, probatio, refutatio, peroratio*). Today, the skill of ancient letter writing and literary rhetoric in Paul's letters are highly debated among scholars, but a basic understanding

---

42. Winter, *After Paul Left Corinth*, 28.

43. Larry W. Hurtado, "What Early Christian Manuscripts Can Tell Us about Their Readers," https://wp.me/pYZXr-2cJ. See his complete essay in *The World of Jesus and the Early Church: Identity and Interpretation in Early Communities of Faith*, ed. Craig A. Evans (Peabody, MA: Hendrickson, 2011).

of this art form helps us to avoid reading Paul's letters in the same manner as we read our written texts today.[44]

Thus, the NT documents, including Paul's letters, were written more for a *listening* audience than for literate readers. Only the wealthy elites in the culture could afford to collect written "books." Lectors (those who could read texts) were hired to read documents, and they did so out loud for everyone to hear. The ancient Greek written texts, of course, did not have the separation of words, sentences, or paragraphs, much less chapters and verses. A talented lector read aloud, discerning the text in an appropriate manner. Paul's audiences, therefore, would gather together as a community to *hear* his letters, perhaps collected in codices and passed around among the congregations. The NT letters were not private communications but were written for *groups* of people (with possible exceptions). In fact, these oral communications were sometimes close to a drama, a speech, or a performance that "plays out" the written word in front of an audience.[45]

> Indeed, one of the observations we can make on the basis of earliest Christian manuscripts (as well as references in early Christian writings themselves) is that already in the earliest centuries (and probably earliest decades) Christians were heavily involved in writing, copying, reading, exchanging, and disseminating a great number of texts. In recent decades there has been a good deal of justifiable interest in ancient "orality", the spoken word, and oral "performance" as features of early Christianity in its ancient Roman-era setting. But, without denying for a moment that oral speech was important in that period, I must emphasize the prominent place of texts as a distinguishing feature of earliest Christianity. Indeed, in the Roman religious environment, early Christianity seems to have been unexcelled, and perhaps unique, in the scale of the production, use, and distribution of texts, devoting impressive personnel and financial resources to the activities involved.[46]

With this in mind, the most accurate terminology for Paul's audience in Corinth would be the *hearers* of the gospel message and of his written letters. However, since we are reading the Corinthian correspondences today, I will use the broad term of "*readers*" in this commentary to include both the ancient and the present audiences.

---

44. Ben Witherington III, "'Almost Thou Persuadest Me . . .': The Importance of Greco-Roman Rhetoric for the Understanding of the Text and Context of the NT," *JETS* 58.1 (2015): 63–88.
45. Witherington, "Greco-Roman Rhetoric."
46. Hurtado, "Early Christian Manuscripts," 2.

Being a Church

The assorted band of believers who gathered in Corinth had never been a "church" before and had no ecclesiastical or theological guide to prepare them for the debates and divisions on how to be a Christian. Thus, an attempt to combine the Jewish Christians and the Gentile Christians (in Rome, Galatia, Ephesus, Corinth, and elsewhere) into *one church* was like mixing oil and water. Paul founded, shaped, and nurtured a community of believers who lived in a very pluralistic society that held very different values from the teachings of Christ. There was no common ground, no accepted set of theological "rules" to follow. They met regularly to pray, learn, fellowship, and worship. Such Christian meetings were not closed to "outsiders," yet this assembly of believers was totally unlike the spiritual festivals, local gatherings, and rituals of their "pagan" neighbors. This kind of radical social behavior took some getting used to. Some differences were obvious to the Corinthians, but deeply rooted cultural and religious ideas and experiences surfaced, leading the assembly into chaos and confusion. In effect, the Corinthian Christians were "getting it" in terms of their head knowledge, but they were not fully understanding what it meant to have faith in Christ in terms of their conduct, behavior, and heart devotion to Christ and to his apostle Paul (1:12–14). If the Corinthian church was "puffed up" about their wisdom and excellence, and if they were (even unconsciously) in competition with their neighboring churches to the north (see 8:1–7; 9:2), then it was a ripe situation for confusion on the inside and for outside intruders to lead them away from their initial ministry conversion by Paul.

Moreover, in the Roman Empire, anything labeled an *ekklesia*, or an "assembly of people," could have highly political implications, especially if the participants were not well-known, loyal Roman citizens. The early Christian churches, initially gathering together in private homes aroused "suspicion and the specter of sedition."[47] It was somewhat dangerous for such gatherings to even meet, much less dine together, learn together, sing together, and pray together. The Romans and the Jews all held tightly their own traditions, ethics, beliefs, and "cultural baggage." Suddenly, the "new kid on the block," Christianity, was an attempt to bring all humanity together under the gospel of Jesus Christ. All things considered, this was not fertile ground for compromise, cooperation, unity, and love. No wonder the problem that nagged at Paul from the beginning to the end of his missionary work in Asia Minor was ecumenical diversity and division.

---

47. McKnight, "New Perspective and the Christian Life," 141.

Church Today

The issues, problems, and solutions addressed by Paul in 2 Corinthians are not confined to one church in the first century. His letters remain as relevant for believers today as they were for his original hearers/readers. We must be aware of sinful pride, selfishness, a deceptive and misleading gospel message, wrong ideas about Jesus's identity, greed and the lack of generosity, false indicators of maturity in Christ, and who can or can't be in our "club." Such issues can cause grave divisions in churches today and are not beneficial as a Christian witness in our world. Paul's message concerning the "church," then, should have an even greater effect on our congregations today. The American church has a difficult time blending all the diversity we find in our churches, as evidenced by the separate congregations on Sunday mornings. We have difficulties "having equal concern for each other" and "valuing oneself and others in the Lord" regardless of our diverse doctrines, backgrounds, wealth, ethnicities, and practices.[48] Like the Corinthians, American Christians can take a lot of pride in their labels, their heritage, and their "mature" spirituality. As Paul demanded in his churches, we need to be united in Christ, in our love of the Lord, and in our Christian love for one another.

Purposes

Why did Paul write this letter? What were his purposes in writing yet another letter to this struggling, disobedient church? Why did he have to defend himself to people he loved? Why did he have to justify his calling and ministry? After all he tried to do for his readers, why didn't he just give up? Why did Paul have to suffer for Christ? Why did he stand up to the lies and deception of his enemies? Why was he so committed to a ministry that was rife with obstacles, challenges, and frustrations? We recognize that Paul did not write a letter *for us*, for Christians living centuries after his ministry, but why has his letter become such a valuable treasure even for Christian believers today? By contemplating the *whys* of this letter, we can better understand both Paul's motivations and our current interpretations of the text today. Has anyone in Christian ministry today ever silently asked the critical question, "Why am I doing this?" No doubt, at some point, that very question must have passed through Paul's mind (consider his trials outlined just in this letter: 1:8–9; 4:8–9; 6:4–10; 11:23–29). Finally, why does this letter remain relevant to believers today?

---

48. David A. deSilva, "The Corinthian Correspondence," in *An Introduction to the New Testament: Contexts, Methods and Ministry Formation* (Downers Grove, IL: InterVarsity Press, 2004), 555.

Linda Belleville suggests that Paul's primary purpose in writing was to establish a closer, more trusting relationship between himself and the congregation he founded in Corinth.[49] As a result of their political and economic situation, he was intentionally calling the Corinthians to separate themselves from the reigning culture of the day. Paul distanced himself from his opponents while mimicking their own words and approaches to emphasize who the real "Son of God" is and how the Christian life was to be lived. He emphasized the validity of his own God-given ministry in the first seven chapters of the letter. Paul defended his own character and his calling as a minister of the gospel of Jesus Christ, a gospel *they had already received for themselves.* In these chapters he attempted to outline his credentials and then make requests of his readers. By explaining his own position and concerns, Paul was hoping the church would see the fallacies of his opponents and of their culture in general. This is an important strategy: he had to build their trust in who he was, to verify what he had taught them, and to make requests of them to prove their trust. Then, in chapters 8 and 9, Paul approached his crucial request with encouragement and confidence: that the church would gladly participate in the relief-fund project for the saints in Jerusalem. Finally, in the last four chapters (10–13), his purposes for this letter were expanded.

Why did the Corinthians allow themselves to be under the spell of evil, deceptive leaders? Paul unleashed his frustrations concerning the adversarial rival missionaries (11:13–14; see Introduction). Evidently Paul made a dramatic change in his tone and content because he needed to *make a shift in the purpose* of this writing. His strong admonition to the church was to immediately turn away from the people who were doing damage to the church with their disparaging self-interests and false accusations. He warned the church that another visit was necessary for Paul to straighten things out, and he did not want it to be a painful one.

At the heart of this communication, Paul's greatest interest was in building up the church at Corinth so that it would truly know truth and not fall prey to erroneous lies and imposters (10:8; 13:10). Central to all of Paul's life, calling, and mission was Jesus Christ. Beginning at his conversion, Paul thought deeply about the Christian life and the gospel message he proclaimed. No doubt his theology developed over a period of time as he reacted to specific circumstances within his young churches and as he helped people to understand the manner in which the Christian life is to be lived. So, a very important purpose in writing this letter was to correct the false teachings about Jesus, specifically about his meekness and gentleness (10:1) and his humiliation on

---

49. Belleville, *2 Corinthians*, 22.

the cross, which paradoxically nullify the distortions about Christ and about Paul that were created by his enemies.

Paul's commitment and love for people he had once considered Gentiles and "foreigners" (Eph 2:11–12) never failed. It is truly remarkable. He suffered, traveled, sacrificed, argued, and fought for the benefit of the Corinthians. Ultimately, he believed that the Christian culture could change the world—the world of self-gratification and human ambition—and that a truly Christ-centered vision could bring a unified life to the network of believers across the empire. The overarching purpose of Paul's ministry is expressed with the single name of Jesus; it was his Lord and Savior who motivated the apostle to live, to minister, to correct, to suffer, and to die (4:10–12). This is a pattern for all of us who live in the comfort of acceptable Christianity.

Key Themes

Citing a case for unity of the letter, Belleville notes four key themes that run throughout: "visit-talk," "dealing with opposition," "Christian suffering and divine power," and the "work of the Holy Spirit."[50] First, in this letter we discern Paul's discussion of actual visits to Corinth in the past, his desire to visit them again (an unfortunate change of plans), and preparations for a future visit. We see real and proposed visits by Paul's colleagues, emissaries sent to show his care and concern for the church. Paul was trying to remove what he regarded as obstacles to an enjoyable visit with the church that would bring "mutual spiritual refreshment" (cf. 7:13b; Rom 15:32).[51]

Paul's Defense

Second, dealing with the "opposition" is a primary theme of the entire letter. It is Paul's defense of his calling and his character. When his ministry and mission were called into question, the result was a "painful visit" (2:1), and Paul wanted to avoid another similar encounter. His competency and his message were planted firmly in the hands of God, through Christ, and were never based on personal gain or recognition. If chapters 1–7 are an apologetic, then chapters 8–9 are a progression from his defense to a tangible sign of their trust in him. Chapters 10–13 progress to feature bold rhetoric, irony, and paradox, which revealed the true nature of his adversaries (i.e., 11:13–15). The very essence of the gospel of Christ was under pressure, and Paul was forced to defend himself and his message. His defense increased as the opponents'

---

50. Belleville, *2 Corinthians*, 21–38.
51. Harris, *Second Corinthians*, 45.

accusations and lies increased. Like a disciplining father, he did not want to act severely in the exercise of this apostolic authority, but he would if he had to (13:10).[52]

Pastoral Ministry and Leadership

Ultimately, however, Paul's defense of his own authority and apostleship were not as important to him as the survival, maturity, and edification of the believers in Corinth. Paul was the consummate pastor, educating, encouraging, warning, correcting, loving, and caring for his people as much as he could under the circumstances in the first century. Planting and leading a church, especially from a geographical distance, are not easy tasks. Paul had no simple or rapid forms of communication with the Corinthians—no Internet, jet planes, or Skype. Yet so many issues were on his mind that he had many sleepless nights (11:27). He wanted to help the poor in Jerusalem; he wanted to unite all the Gentile churches in his region with the Jewish believers; he wanted to encourage his colleagues in ministry; he would have liked to see true, Christ-like lives in this church, and the maturing of his people into self-sacrificing, fruit-bearing believers. Paul's very life proved to be a role model of leadership for the Corinthians, especially in his devotion to Christ and in his own suffering and hardships in the face of opposition. He cited his own suffering more than once to emphasize the fact that pastoral ministry cannot be done except by the "competency that comes from God" (1:9; 3:5).

In contrast to the Roman culture, Paul insisted that positions of authority and leadership were not by virtue of money or position or even being born into the right family. Leadership is self-sacrificing (Matt 20:26–28). Leaders like Paul are "slaves," "ministers," "servants," called and gifted by God to do his work with love and humility. As God's true apostle, Paul was self-emptying; he reversed the honor/shame value system so prevalent in Corinth and put human arrogance and power in conflict with that of God.[53] Perhaps Paul did not have an attractive physical appearance; he confessed that he was somehow afflicted and "stumbling of speech." He chose to be a common laborer, a tent-maker (Acts 18:3) who lacked the dignity the Corinthians expected from their leaders (11:7; 12:7). All of this humble presentation was food for the feast of Paul's opponents. They disparaged his speech and his methods; they relished the idea of appealing to the common cultural expectations of the Corinthians and belittling Paul as a weak and ineffective leader.[54]

---

52. Harris, *Second Corinthians*, 45.
53. Harris, *Second Corinthians*, 31.
54. Harris, *Second Corinthians*, 31.

Paul discovered that it was difficult to maintain the simplicity and focus of
the Christian gospel message in the community at Corinth—that Jesus alone
is Lord, and that "salvation is by God's initiative and grace in Jesus." Other
leaders provided other options, and most were probably less self-sacrificing
and more appealing. The early Christians, not unlike us today, put too much
stock in their leaders, raising them to unhealthy or even unrealistic positions,
and believing them without pondering their words. The church was divided
over leadership, with little coherent agreement or criteria for following a leader
(see 1 Cor 1:11–13). Yet, as Peterson writes, "There is nothing glamorous or
inspiring about even the best of leaders: every one, down to the last man or
woman, is saved by grace."[55] Paul knew this very well from experience, and he
attempted to model it and teach it to his congregations.

Christian Suffering

Third, suffering and persecution for the sake of Christ (4:5) is a theme that
still holds true for Christians across the globe today. "Every chapter echoes
this theme."[56] In place of personal acclaim and wealth, Paul reiterated that his
ministry was defined by speaking the genuine truth, which can lead to trials
and hardships (4:1–2, 7–12, 16–18; 6:3–10). That is, Christian suffering and
hardships lead to reliance on God and not on one's own power and abilities
(1:8–11). Hope, through suffering, comes through the "God of all comfort"
(1:3–7). This letter opens with Paul's familiar, precious, proverbial dictation
on the overflowing comfort of God through Christ amid human suffering
(1:3–7). The theme does reappear all the way through the letter, even as Paul
recorded his own trials in 2 Corinthians 4, 6, and 11. He demonstrated tenacity and courage to keep going despite at least one near-death experience, stoning, floggings, beatings and shipwrecks (11:23–29). Through countless hours
of physical tortures as well as the emotional "pressure of my concern for all
the churches" (11:28), Paul's hope was always in Christ.

"Divine Power in Weakness"

Closely related to the theme of Christian suffering is the theme of God's
power expressed through human weakness.[57] As it was for the ancient Corinthians, this seems to be a contradictory statement to people in our day.
How can weakness be strong, even through the power and strength of the
Lord? Because of his suffering and hardships, Paul knew experientially that

55. Eugene Peterson, *Christ Plays in Ten Thousand Places* (Grand Rapids: Eerdmans, 2008), 186.
56. Belleville, *2 Corinthians*, 36.
57. Belleville, *2 Corinthians*, 36.

he preached and ministered by the power of God, not by his own strength (1:8–11; 3:4–6; 4:7–12). It must have been hard for the prideful Corinthians, who apparently excelled in everything (1 Cor 1:5; 2 Cor 8:7), to grasp the antithetical idea that Paul would boast about his own foolishness and weaknesses (i.e., 10:4; 11:1, 30). But, as Paul wrote, the way of the world is to put stock in human, worldly power and position (10:3; 11:18) instead of trusting in the ways of God. In the world, power is achieved by human effort; to rest in this kind of worldly power is to be foolish in Paul's view. Certainly, Paul's opponents were "worldly," preaching a "different spirit" and a "different gospel" (11:4), thus pretending to be stronger than and superior to Paul. Most critical is the fact that the Corinthians were actually believing the erroneous, self-centered "deceitful workers" (11:13), in sharp contrast to the power of God through Christ, which had already been preached to them by Paul (11:3–4).

The Holy Spirit and Unity among the Corinthians

The fourth key theme is the work of the Holy Spirit in Corinth. The Corinthians had experienced the power and the glory of God's Holy Spirit in their midst (1 Cor 1:4–10). However, they had flawed expectations about their lives in Christ (2 Cor 5:17). Garland is correct in saying that the breach between Paul and the Corinthians was not just theological; the conflicts were "rooted in the Corinthian cultural values that clashed with the Christian values he [Paul] wanted them to adopt."[58] As they did in their old, pagan ways, they assumed the presence and power of the Holy Spirit was an aid to bring them personal recognition, wealth, and an exalted position. Instead, the death and resurrection of Jesus completely reversed "worldly values and expectations" (1 Cor 1:17; 2 Cor 4:10–12). That is, Paul attempted to keep bringing them back to the cross of Christ and to the sufferings of Christ crucified.[59] For the church as a body, it was the Holy Spirit that created and sustained the congregation, and it was the Spirit of God that bonded the believers together in unity. For each believer, it was the Holy Spirit that was in the process of *transforming* each person into "Christ-likeness" (3:18), both in the present and in the life that is to come (4:13–14, 17–18; 5:1–5; 6:6–7; 13:14).

In summary, the themes of this letter were developed by Paul to turn around the readers' thinking, to help them to understand fully (1:14) his gospel message, and to build up the church at Corinth. Paul had to defend his message, his actions, his integrity, and his motivations in response to those

---

58. David Garland, *2 Corinthians*, NAC (Nashville: Broadman & Holman, 1999), 30.
59. Garland, *2 Corinthians*, 30.

who demeaned him for their own benefit. Even after personal visits and letters, the Corinthians had failed to grasp the self-effacing, servant ethos of the
gospel message and the remarkable paradox of Christ crucified. Paul found
it necessary to repeat the heart of his gospel message to counter the culture
and rhetoric of *Romanitas* so familiar to this church. Regrettably, Paul had
to discipline his readers (12:20–21; 13:5–7) and try once again to unite the
church in their support of him and of his colleagues in Christ (7:12–16).[60]

Dates and Structure: The Integrity of 2 Corinthians

What is still debated among present scholarship is the structure of 2 Corinthians and the dates that correspond to the composition of this complex letter.
In fact, the unity and integrity of this letter may be the most controversial
part of the study of 2 Corinthians. Because of the obvious differences in tone
and affect between the first seven chapters and the final four chapters, the
timeline of Paul's written communications and visits to Corinth has become
a bit muddled. Dates and times, visits, and communications are not clear to
modern readers living centuries after the facts. On the one hand, the letter
appears to be one unified document. On the other hand, scholars have proposed the "partition" concept, where separate pieces of two or more letters
were combined to create the whole letter as we have today. This composition
issue, and the integrity of the whole letter, has been a problem for decades,
and it still perplexes scholars today.

Partition Theories

For generations, numerous scholars have suggested that chapters 1–9 and
chapters 10–13 were originally separate documents composed and sent by
Paul to the church at Corinth at different times in his ministry. The first and
obvious reason for this separation is the unexpected and dramatic change of
tone at 10:1. The apparent joy, relief, and confidence expressed by Paul in
chapter 7 is replaced with frustration and "scathing remonstrance and biting
irony" in chapters 10–13. Some have even suggested that a number of smaller
letter fragments were pasted together by an editor well after Paul penned the
communications.[61]

One opinion is that chapters 10–13 were written earlier than chapters
1–9, and form part of the "tearful letter" (or "sorrowful" letter) that Paul
referred to in 2:4. According to the "Hausrath hypothesis" of separation,

---

60. Garland, *2 Corinthians*, 32. See *Romanitas* above, and in Winter, *After Paul Left Corinth*, 18, 28.
61. Harris, *Second Corinthians*, 29.

several passages in chaps. 1–9 "contain intentional allusions to previous statements in chs. 10–13." An example of such an allusion is 10:6 and 2:9.[62] The "Semler hypothesis" gained support in the twentieth century, and proposes the same kind of separation, although Semler suggested the first section of the letter ended with chapter 8. Semler figured that chapters 10–13 were written after chapters 1–9 in response to new occurrences in Corinth.[63] Dozens of scholars have followed in the footsteps of Hausrath and Semler, noting distinctions in themes, words, and phrases, as well as omissions between the two sections. In fact, Taylor proposes that our letter is a composite of five separate letters composed by Paul. He proposed that the earliest fragment, 6:14–7:1, is a portion of the letter referred to in 1 Corinthians 5:9. Like a giant crazy quilt, the pieces of letters were stitched together into our canonical 2 Corinthians to reflect the progression of Paul's relationship with the readers, and to show the intensification of the opposition to Paul within the church.[64] It is possible, of course, to manipulate the text and redact the sections such that we can make the letter say almost anything we want. Still, we have *no textual evidence* of partial letters in any manuscripts.

Another issue is concerned with the amount of time involved in getting communications across the empire. We know facts about first century travel that would indicate that it takes a good amount of time not only to write a letter, but also to send it by the hand of a messenger over land and sea. Frankly, there was just not enough time for Paul to complete all that Taylor suggests.

Furnish sees 2 Corinthians as a composite letter, a combination of "two originally independent letters," chapters 10–13 subsequent to the first nine chapters. He believes that the letter in its present form was finalized in the late first century, sometime between AD 96 and 125. Perhaps two of Paul's letters to the Corinthians (*not* our 1 Corinthians letter) were found about that time that were previously "uncirculated because neither was complete, and that they had edited them [into one letter] for use locally and in Rome."[65]

Yet, Belleville points out that "there is no manuscript evidence to support the notion that chs. 10–13 circulated independently of chs. 1–9 at any given point." Paul hints at his upcoming visit to Corinth in 9:4, but the details and explanations of that visit appear in chapters 10–13.[66] She might agree with

---

62. Harris, *Second Corinthians*, 35.

63. Harris, *Second Corinthians*, 34–38. A. Hausrath proposed his theory in 1870; J. S. Semler presented his theory in 1776.

64. N. H. Taylor, "The Composition and Chronology of Second Corinthians," *JSNT* 14.44 (1991): 67–87.

65. Furnish, *II Corinthians*, 40, 41.

66. Belleville, *2 Corinthians*, 32.

Harris that chapters 10–13 cannot stand alone, and they make little sense without the first nine chapters. In his book about early Christian manuscripts, Larry Hurtado lists writings that came to form the NT dated to the second and third centuries AD (or CE). In his findings, our earliest manuscript evidence of the 2 Corinthians letter does not confirm the existence of multiple letters written by Paul. Today, scholars have one complete manuscript of 2 Corinthians, as well as codices dated to the same time period that contain 2 Corinthians among numerous Pauline letters.[67]

In summary, David deSilva contends that "every argument advanced by a supporter of a partition theory has been countered plausibly by a supporter of a more unified view of 2 Corinthians (whether it is taken as a single whole or as two major letter fragments: 2 Cor 1–9 and 2 Cor 10–13)."[68]

So, it seems that the more complicated the theory, the less likely we have perceived the composition accurately. We can misinterpret the context and miss the author's true intent if we separate and/or reshuffle the sections as we would like to understand the text. Yet Harris rightly notes that what *all* the theories have in common is a "demand of some unspecified interval of time [that] elapsed between the writing of chs. 1–9 and chs. 10–13."[69]

In the end, Murray Harris comes down on the side of literary unity; in his opinion, "what remains perfectly feasible is that, though sent as a single letter, 2 Corinthians was composed in stages and not at a single setting."[70] Harris reminds us that it would be incorrect to assume that Paul sat down and wrote or dictated his epistles completely at one sitting. He writes:

Given the unpredictable yet relentless demands and pressures of Paul's pastoral ministry (11:28), it is antecedently probable that each of Paul's letters, apart from Philemon, was written over a considerable period of time, perhaps days or even weeks or months, and was then sent to the addressees when weather permitted travel and a trusted deputy was available to deliver it, and, if necessary, to explain and reinforce its contents, and perhaps to report back to Paul on the church's reaction.[71]

Thus, putting together what we know, we can surmise that while he was ministering in Macedonia, Paul felt an urgency to write a letter to the church

67. Larry Hurtado, *The Earliest Christian Artifacts: Manuscripts and Christian Origins* (Grand Rapids: Eerdmans, 2006), 20–21, 221.
68. deSilva, "Corinthian Correspondence," 577.
69. Harris, *Second Corinthians*, 38.
70. Harris, *Second Corinthians*, 51.
71. Harris, *Second Corinthians*, 50.

in Corinth, as there were several issues he needed to correct. He penned the first nine chapters to defend his own character and his calling as God's authorized apostle, and to correct some of their theology. In addition, he needed to make a number of appeals to the readers and encourage them, especially since he could not be there with them in person. Meanwhile, Titus reported back to Paul that, on the surface, everything in Corinth was going well; Titus had explained Paul's previous ("tearful") letter to the congregation, as well as Paul's altered travel schedule. For Paul, surely it was wonderful to hear good news about dear friends, and it must have been a relief to Paul to know that the church responded so well to Titus's visit. Paul felt free, then, to urge his readers to proceed with the relief-fund collection that was so critical to Paul (chs. 8–9). Pause. For some reason, there was a gap of time before he could finish the letter.[72]

The attack on Paul's authority in Corinth was not entirely new (see 2:17; 3:1; 4:2–6), but at that time the wounds were becoming infected, and Paul realized that he had to put a stop to the "deception" and "distortions" (4:2) of his adversaries. Paul's joy and enthusiasm were dampened by "the rest of the story" of the intensifying influence of his opponents. Thus, Paul wrote chapters 10–13 from the region of Macedonia (perhaps in the city of Philippi) in northern Greece, where he was visiting churches (see 7:5; 8:1; 9:2). He subsequently sent the whole letter to Corinth in the hands of Titus and his colleagues to clarify the situation and put a halt to the "work of Satan" (11:13–15).[73] Upon completion of the letter, Titus returned to Corinth rather quickly with his co-workers and the letter in an attempt to reconcile the relationship between Paul and the church, reestablish Paul's authority, and stop the bloodletting by his adversaries before he made another visit to Corinth to pick up the funds for the Jerusalem project.

Paul still wanted the Corinthians to have his thoughts from his earlier writing (chaps. 1–9), but he needed to tackle the growing false reports, rumors, accusations, and stories. Likely, Paul's greatest appeal and his most important project, the relief fund for the poor in Jerusalem, was being discredited, along with his own character. This would have been crushing news to Paul. More disparaging actions (11:15), charges, doubts, and suspicions had infiltrated the church and made their way back to Paul, who realized the severity of the problem only after chapters 1–9 were written.

The emotions and events of this letter are a bit like being a parent: even the most kind, encouraging, and soft-spoken parent can reach a limit with his

---

72. Harris, *Second Corinthians*, 51.
73. Harris, *Second Corinthians*, 105. See Belleville, *2 Corinthians*, 20.

or her children. Using a particular look or tone of voice lets children know that they are in deep trouble. When pastors, leaders, or parents face grave disappointment and discipline concerning those they love, their moods and their voices can change radically.

Suggested Timeline

Our knowledge of the life and missionary work of Paul, particularly as it relates to the church of Corinth, is frustratingly incomplete. Outside of the two canonical letters that we call 1 Corinthians and 2 Corinthians, Acts is our main source of information internally. Yet we can offer an estimate of time chronology, visits, letters, and important occasions. It is just a *suggested* timeline—other commentators have assigned various dates.

First Visit and First (Lost) Letter

Paul's first visit to Corinth was the planting of the church, perhaps in AD 50 or 51 (1 Cor 2:3; 4:15; Acts 18:1–18). He stayed there for eighteen months (Acts 18:11), and then returned to Asia Minor (to Ephesus, Acts 19). After his departure from Corinth, perhaps in the summer of AD 51, Paul wrote to his Corinthian church.[74] This is the earliest letter of Paul addressed to the Corinthian church, but it is a *lost letter,* known to us from Paul's mention of it in 1 Corinthians 5:9–11. It appears to be a letter written in response to a letter Paul received from the Corinthians. Right from the beginning there appears to have been some misunderstandings between Paul and his church in Corinth, particularly having to do with living the Christian life and immorality in their midst.

As their founder, it was Paul's desire and intent to guide his congregation in spiritual matters. Yet, Paul was a church planter and he did not intend on staying in Corinth forever. He had to move on to other assignments. It was not possible for him to always be with them; hence, he wrote letters to answer their questions, and to adjust their beliefs and behavior. In addition, Apollos visited Corinth and helped the believers with a better understanding of the initial teachings of Paul (Acts 18:27–19:1).

Second Letter

Right away, the young church at Corinth responded to his first letter and sent a letter back with a number of questions for Paul: "Now for the matters you wrote about . . ." (1 Cor 7:1, see 8:1; 12:1; 16:1, 12). To answer their questions, Paul wrote the long letter that is our canonical *1 Corinthians.* It is our

---

74. Furnish, *II Corinthians,* 22.

first extant correspondence, and Paul's second letter to the church. While we think Paul was still in Ephesus at the writing of this letter, the dating of this letter is obscure. Likely, 1 Corinthians may be dated to the fall of 53 or 54.[75] In addition to addressing issues and answering their questions, Paul wrote this letter to warn his people about divisions within the church that cropped up after Apollo's visit.[76] That is, the primary purpose of this letter was to address specific problems and to advise them on their concerns and their conduct. Paul was very concerned about the church for a number of reasons, and he wrote to give them admonitions about specific situations within the congregation and general warnings about living as followers of Christ.

In the summer or early fall of 54, Paul sent his associate Timothy to Macedonia (northern Greece) and Corinth (southern Greece), intending to follow the same itinerary himself at a later date (1 Cor 16:5–9). However, Paul knew that his already-dispatched letter (our 1 Corinthians) would reach Corinth before Timothy did, so one reason he sent this letter was to ask them to receive Timothy warmly (1 Cor 16:10–11; 4:17).[77] In a way, it could be considered a letter of recommendation about his colleague, Timothy.

Perhaps Timothy reached Corinth in the spring of 55, and upon his arrival, he found a church plagued with difficulties and controversies. One of the main reasons Timothy was sent was to see if the Corinthians were collecting funds for the church in Jerusalem, but this was not possible because of all the other problems burdening the church. So, Timothy took his leave and hurried on to Ephesus to give Paul unfortunate reports about Corinth.[78]

Unplanned Second Visit

As a result, Paul found it necessary to make an emergency visit to Corinth in the spring of 55. This was his *second* visit to the city, and it turned out to be a "sorrowful" (or "painful") one (2 Cor 2:1–2). The letter that we call 1 Corinthians had not been well received, and it did not accomplish Paul's intentions. This "unplanned, emergency visit to Corinth had been a disaster." Furthermore, it appears that during this visit, Paul had a "traumatic confrontation of some kind with one of the members of the congregation" (perhaps slander).[79]

Paul made a hasty exit back to Ephesus "hurt, angered, and perplexed."[80] Apparently Paul had had to rebuke "those who sinned earlier" (2 Cor 12:21;

---

75. Furnish, *II Corinthians*, 29.
76. Lars Kierspel, *Charts on the Life, Letters and Theology of Paul* (Grand Rapids: Kregel, 2012), 120.
77. Furnish, *II Corinthians*, 28.
78. Furnish, *II Corinthians*, 43.
79. Harris, *Second Corinthians*, 57. See also Furnish, *II Corinthians*, 54, 55.
80. Harris, *Second Corinthians*, 59.

13:2). It is likely that someone, perhaps an intruder, degraded Paul and humiliated him in the presence of the church. At that time, the other church members were reluctant to stand up for Paul and his teachings.[81] Later, at some point, discipline was imposed on the offender. Unfortunately, this short visit was a blow to Paul and his relationship with the Corinthians, and he had to rethink his future visits and his relationship with the people.

Planned Visits Revised
Originally, Paul's itinerary included a two-part visit to Corinth: one stop in Corinth to straighten things out there, then on to Macedonia, and then a return visit to Corinth (2 Cor 1:15–17). But Paul's "double visit" plan was altered. He thus had to account for his change of plans with his readers. His change of plans was not arbitrary; his actions were the result of great thought, care, and concern for all parties (2 Cor 1:15–2:4).

Third, "Tearful" Letter (2:4; 7:8–12)
Late in the spring of 55, injured by his second visit to Corinth, Paul sent a letter to the church, which has been called the "tearful letter" or the "sorrowful letter" (2 Cor 2:3–4). Again, we do not have this letter, only Paul's reference to it. Paul had to revise his plans so that he would not be going to Corinth first from Ephesus as he had intended. He would go to Macedonia first, then down to Corinth, which would make his visit weeks or even months after what the Corinthians had expected. So, this is a substitute letter for the first part of his two planned visits. Obviously, the change of plans was a disappointment to the church, but it was a disappointment to Paul as well, who was still reeling from his previous painful visit. This letter was a poor replacement for Paul's personal visit, and the apostle must have boldly confronted the Corinthians about their ethical and internal problems. Because it was delivered by Titus, Paul was quite anxious to meet with Titus and hear about his reception by the troubled church and their response to his letter.

And the drama continued. It is possible that while Titus traveled south to Corinth, Paul ended up in prison in Asia Minor (probably Ephesus). From about AD 53–55, Paul encountered crisis after crisis in his ministry. How could Paul minister to his young churches while in prison? Once again, Paul was blocked from personally visiting his people, and he had more changes of plans. Fortunately for readers today, during this time Paul was able to write letters from prison to his congregations in Greece (see Philippians 1:13–14, and Philemon, for example).

---

81. Harris, *Second Corinthians*, 59.

Probably early in the fall of 55, when he finally did meet with Paul in Macedonia, Titus had lots of news for Paul from Corinth. It is possible that this news was mixed—the good news and the bad news. Despite the content of the "tearful letter," the overall reception of Titus was positive. Yes, some members of the congregation were disappointed that Paul again was unable to visit them; the two planned visits became no visit at all, and Paul had sent only a letter with Titus instead.[82] However, Titus's report also had good news; he brought news of repentance by some of the people, as well as their concern and affection for Paul (7:5–16).

Fourth Letter

Paul was released from prison late in the summer of 55 at about the same time that Titus was visiting Corinth. Paul then traveled to Macedonia (perhaps Philippi), and Titus joined him there with the news concerning the church.[83] In spite of the fact that the report from Titus was generally encouraging, Paul must have thought it was necessary to write to the congregation again. He began the letter that is our canonical *2 Corinthians,* chapters 1–9. It was a letter filled with a spectrum of emotions, from pain and affliction to joy and encouragement. It was necessary to defend his own calling and his character, and to make significant admonitions to the congregation. He was concerned about past visits, present situations, and a future visit. In addition, he was very anxious and appealed to the congregation to finish the commitment they had made to financially help the "saints in Jerusalem." Perhaps some amount of time passed; during his physical absence from the church, animosity against him increased. Finally, Paul had to address the problem of missionary rivals who had overstepped their boundaries and had entered the church, promoting dishonesty and slander.

"Third" Visit

Paul repeated his intention to visit the Corinthians for a third time toward the end of his fourth letter (9:4; 12:14; 13:1). Certainly, his purpose for this visit was to rectify painful accusations and ease any remaining tension between the church and him. It was important to Paul to have a face-to-face meeting to resolve any remaining issues in the minds of his readers. More than one gnawing issue had to be resolved before Paul could collect and deliver the relief fund to the Jewish brothers and sisters in Jerusalem. The entire letter culminates with this anticipated third visit; it is the climax to the story Paul

---

82. Furnish, *II Corinthians,* 141, 144.
83. Furnish, *II Corinthians,* 54, 55.

was writing. "A single coordinating purpose in writing this [entire] letter was to prepare for this imminent visit by seeking to remove present or potential obstacles that could prevent the visit from being pleasant" (13:1, 5–7, 10).[84]

We cannot know with certainty the conclusion of the story of the Corinthians, and how their story fits into the big story of God. If Paul's letter to the Romans was written from Corinth after the Corinthian letters, it can give us some clues.[85] That is, if Paul made his third visit to Corinth in the early spring of AD 57, he likely sent a letter to Rome from there. In Romans 15:25–27 Paul writes that the churches in "Macedonia" (i.e., the Philippians) and "Achaia" (i.e., Corinth) "were pleased to make a contribution for the poor among the Lord's people in Jerusalem," implying that Corinth did, indeed, collect the funds Paul had solicited. Assuming this to be the case, Paul may have departed for Jerusalem, with his colleagues and the relief funds, in the summer of AD 57.[86] As he wrote to the Roman church from Corinth, Paul was still recalling the sting of the opponents' darts, urging his readers in Rome to, "watch out for those who cause divisions and put obstacles in your way that are contrary to the teaching you have learned. Keep away from them. For such people are not serving our Lord Christ, but their own appetites. By smooth talk and flattery they deceive the minds of naive people" (Rom 16:17–18).

However, Acts is frustratingly silent about the reception of what appeared to be a rather hefty sum of money from Greece for the believers in Jerusalem. We know that, at first, Paul's reception in Jerusalem was warm (Acts 21:17). Despite this, the Jews in Jerusalem arose in opposition to Paul and had him arrested by the Roman officials (Acts 21:27–36). Nothing else is said in Acts about the funds, the "service to the Lord's people" (2 Cor 8:4), in which Paul had placed so much hope.

Finally, very little is known about the Corinthian church after Paul departed for Jerusalem (with the collection?). At the end of the first century (AD 96 or 97), the church in Rome sent a letter to the Corinthian Christians, which we call *1 Clement*. The Roman church sent a delegation of church leaders to Corinth with this noncanonical letter that called for peace and order in the congregation, in response to a schism in the church. Apparently, the division was caused by "a few rash and self-willed individuals."[87]

The completion, then, of the two canonical letters that Paul wrote to the Corinthians may have taken as many as five to seven years to complete. During that time, we can assume that the Corinthian ministry was a difficult

---

84. Harris, *Second Corinthians*, 44.
85. Furnish, *II Corinthians*, 55.
86. Furnish, *II Corinthians*, 55.
87. Furnish, *II Corinthians*, 55–56.

one for Paul, at best. But Paul never gave up on this congregation. No doubt this is a reality for Christian church planters today: it takes time. To be sure, converting new believers (in a very foreign culture) and growing them into mature believers is not an overnight task. Paul was an absentee pastor for much of that time, ministering in other cities from Asia to Macedonia.[88] More than any other Pauline letter, in this letter we see his physical and spiritual struggles, as well as trouble within and trouble from outside, encountered with great godly confidence, humility, and faith.

Paul's Opponents

One of the most intriguing questions confronting scholars today is the identity and intents of Paul's opponents as perceived in 2 Corinthians. Paul's opponents are usually expressed in the plural, except perhaps in 2:5 when we see that a particular person caused a serious offense, probably slander, against Paul. This offense was so damaging that Paul felt it necessary to write the "tearful" or "sorrowful" letter (2:4) to the congregation to seek punishment for the offender. Yet, we do not know the number of persons who were challenging Paul's message, authority, and competence. Scholars cannot agree on exactly how many opponents were actually regular attenders of the Corinthian church and/or how many interlopers infected the church from the outside. Furnish speculates that there may have been only two or three people who created havoc in the church, but they held a high view of themselves and were apparently successful in "setting themselves up in Corinth as his competitors."[89] Regardless of their numbers or their precise intentions, the effect they had on the assembly affects the way we interpret Paul's arguments throughout the letter.

Paul's opponents on the missionary field are referred to by different designations in different letters, as evident if we compare 2 Corinthians and the letter to the Galatians: "false teachers," "rival apostles," "interlopers from Palestine," "agitators," "fools."[90] This can be confusing. One reason why it is so difficult for us to identify the opponents in Corinth is that there may have been more than one group of these dissenters. In fact, we should *not* assume that Paul's opponents in Corinth were exactly the same as the opponents in other settings. Many conflicting issues among the churches were the same, rooted in misleading theology and/or selfish motives, but many were unique to a location and to local circumstances. On four missionary journeys,

---

88. Belleville, *2 Corinthians*, 22.
89. Furnish, *II Corinthians*, 49.
90. Harris, *Second Corinthians*, 71–73.

over thousands of miles, Acts relates that Paul encountered major opposition in many places: in Lystra (14:19–20), in Philippi (16:22–24, 37), in Ephesus (19:23–41), and in Jerusalem (22:24–29; 23:12–24; 25:3). It is certainly possible that Paul faced rival missionaries or challenging adversaries in every location where he planted or visited a church. He therefore found it necessary to adjust his defense and counterattacks against various rivals in each situation he encountered and in each letter he penned.

Tracking Paul's opponents through 1 Corinthians into 2 Corinthians may give us an insight into the identity of his rivals in Achaia. In 1 Corinthians, other "apostles" do not appear to be adversaries, but were a part of Paul's struggles, hardships, and efforts. Paul used irony to help Corinthians recognize the "foolishness" of their own self-exaltation and spiritual immaturity in comparison to the "apostles," a group of evangelists serving God across the Roman Empire (1 Cor 3:18; 4:8). Ironically, Paul called the "apostles" "fools for Christ," "weak, brutally treated, persecuted and slandered"; the ministers of God were serving God in different places in different ways, but they were considered the scum of the earth by the popular world (1 Cor 9–13). And yet, these ironic designations are exactly what we see in 2 Corinthians as the real description of the accusations thrown at Paul by his opponents. Moreover, he told the Corinthians that he had to fight "wild beasts" in Ephesus, no doubt a reference to human enemies in that city who placed Paul in grave danger (1 Cor 15:30, 32). He concluded that in his church-planting ministry, from Ephesus across to Macedonia and into Corinth, he was fully aware that "there are *many* who oppose me" (1 Cor 16:8–9, my emphasis). As modern readers, then, we have some idea what the agitators *did*, but we still do not know exactly who they *were*. While the background information in 1 Corinthians gives us an insight into the afflictions and trials Paul recorded in 2 Corinthians (1:8–10; 4:7–12; 6:4–10; 11:12–15, 19–20), it does not clearly reveal the identity of his human rivals in Corinth.[91]

Gentile Opposition

Since we have already established that the Roman Empire in general, and the Corinthian church specifically, was made up of an amalgamation of diverse people, social groups, and cultures, it seems very plausible that *more than one type* of oppositional group was present and active in Corinth; at least *two* groups may have been in conflict with Paul and his message, disparaging his character and his competence.

---

91. Kierspel, *Charts on the Life, Letters and Theology of Paul*, 63–64.

First, it is altogether possible that there were influential, wealthy, powerful Roman attendees of the house-church who clustered together to create a clique of superiority and status within the congregation. McKnight calls this a "personality cult," when some members followed one particular leader or ideology (see 1 Cor 1:10–13; 3:3–11), even selecting their leader depending upon his status, not his message. Paul did not fit in with their style of boasting, proper clothing and appearance, smooth speech, and "worldliness" (1 Cor 1:27; 3:1, 19). What mattered to these formerly pagan Gentiles was not holiness, godly wisdom, and the righteousness of God, but social status, worldly wisdom, and selfish honor. Paul had to demonstrate that the ambitions of these rival leaders were not compatible with their devotion to Christ.[92]

First-Century Sophists

To get a better idea of his Roman challengers, we must consider a movement among the Gentiles in the Roman Empire. Winter suggests that the intellectual sophists were quite possibly high candidates for oppositional leaders, since they were a significant force in the world of the Greeks and Romans. This faction of philosophy was another great change in the first century Roman social culture. The First Sophistic movement began in Athens in the second half of the fifth century BC, and there was a renaissance of the movement in the first century AD. The term "sophist" is derived from the Greek words for wisdom (*sophia*) and for a person who is wise (*sophos*). The sophists were "wise men," or professional teachers who traveled about, educating young, elite Greek men. A student was called a "disciple" of the instructor, and the latter would charge a large fee for the training. Often, they would establish expensive schools to educate the next generation of wealthy, high-class youth in the challenging world of excellence and virtue.[93] Furthermore, there was stiff competition between the sophists, for money and for students. Recommendations about a teacher for prospective students (and parents) from former and continuing students were crucial. Students revered their instructor and were quite loyal to a teacher and to his philosophies.

Originally, the early sophists recognized a distinction between the unchanging reality of nature and that which was contrived by human thought and speech (and was therefore changeable). But by the first century AD, there was an emphasis on the power of speech (*logos*), rational thought, and rhetoric that could change the human mind. Reality was shaped by persuasive speech, knowledge, wisdom, and opinion. Great respect was shown to those who could

---

92. McKnight, *Pastor Paul*, 136.
93. Winter, *After Paul Left Corinth*, 32–33.

influence other human intellectuals in political gatherings through the art of rhetorical persuasion. The intellectuals engaged in verbal battles of words and logic.[94] Paul, for example, held his own at a Council meeting in Athens where he spoke the Christian gospel message (a "new teaching," Acts 17:16–34). The Greek philosophers argued with him (v. 18), but some men and women were convinced by his spoken rhetoric (v. 34). Just after this elevated event in Athens, Paul left and went to Corinth for his initial visit (Acts 18).

Later, what we see in the Corinthians letters—a desire for wisdom, knowledge, persuasion, bold self-aggrandizement, recommendations, and the assumption of payment to the teacher—all fit the ethos of the sophists. In contrast, Paul, the "newcomer," was not like any of the teachers with which they were familiar, and his gospel of Jesus Christ went against all that the highly respected teachers were promoting. Paul, however, declared that his wisdom was unlike the worldly, self-serving wisdom of these teachers (i.e., 2 Cor 10:2–6).

Jewish Opposition

The second group of adversaries may have been Jewish by ethnicity. It is possible that Jewish missionaries ("teachers") arrived in Corinth from the Palestine region to add to or to directly oppose the teachings of Paul.[95] There were a number of different groups of Christian missionaries traveling in the Gentile world; some may have had their own ideas and theology that were not identical to those of Paul. It is not unreasonable to surmise that both groups of opponents (Roman and Jewish) were present in the church at separate times, or even at the same time. The first Christian believers were primarily converted Jews who considered Jesus as God in their devotional life, worship, and behavior. This was erroneous and even dangerous to the devout Jews (like Saul) who adhered to the worship of only one Yahweh God. To include Jesus as the divine Son of God with God in their devotion and practice was a grave offense and punishable by the kinds of actions we see perpetrated on Paul in 2 Corinthians 1:8–9 and 11:22–28.[96] "In terms of the religious scruples of the Jewish tradition, the most striking innovation in earliest Christianity is the treatment of the glorified Jesus as an object of cultic devotion in ways and terms that seem otherwise reserved for the God of Israel."[97]

---

94. Winter, *After Paul Left Corinth*, 36–40.

95. Donald Guthrie, *New Testament Introduction* (Downers Grove, IL: InterVarsity Press, 1970), 422–23.

96. Larry W. Hurtado, *How on Earth Did Jesus Become a God?* (Grand Rapids: Eerdmans, 2005), 178.

97. Hurtado, *How on Earth*, 197.

His opponents in Galatia were Jews (Gal 1:6–7; 2:15–16), for example, but may not have been the same group who were active in Corinth. If such opponents were, indeed, Jewish Christians from Jerusalem or Antioch (or a similar locale), they were "doing missions" across the Roman Empire, not unlike Paul himself. Some group of Jewish "interlopers" may have "invaded" Paul's territory after he established the church at Corinth and disgraced him to the congregation *in his absence.* Paul noted that his persecutors were Jewish Christian *believers,* saved and redeemed through Christ, just as Paul. Paul recognized them as "Hebrews, Israelites, Abraham's descendants [and] servants of Christ" (see 2 Cor 11:22–23). For this reason, it becomes difficult for us to fully understand why fellow Jewish believers were attempting to convince the church at Corinth that Paul was unfit in his character and his message was untrustworthy. Sadly, it may have been this group of Jewish missionaries who overstepped their limits and invaded Paul's territory of ministry, thinking they were better than Paul and boasting of their ministry successes in the field (10:12–18). They demeaned his character and abilities, invaded his mission territory, took credit for his efforts, promoted themselves, and disparaged his apostolic authority and his credentials.[98]

Paul implied that they were ethnic Jews who had a sense of superiority over the Gentile Christians because of their heritage in their forefather, Abraham (11:21–22). It is also likely that they were attempting to impose Jewish concepts, practices, and observances (3:7–18) as requirements on the Gentile believers in Corinth. In other words, as false teachers, they taught that the only way a Gentile could be accepted by God as one of his people was to follow the established Jewish belief system and then *add* belief in Jesus Christ as the Messiah. Perhaps his opponents believed in the life and death of Jesus, but not in the resurrection of Jesus (see 1 Cor 15).[99] Such teachings were refuted by Paul, and he consistently proclaimed that Jews and Gentiles were united in Christ and equal (1 Cor 12:13; Gal 3:28–29; Eph 2:11–18; Col 3:11).

So, among the dissenters in the region, there may have been both Jewish Christians hanging on to their former laws and Greek sophists and/or Roman elites who looked for acknowledgment for their positions, their excellence in reason, and their practice of rhetoric. In any event, while Paul does not mention any of his rivals by name, certainly the congregation knew who he was writing about. Perhaps, in keeping with the ancient rhetorical style of not even granting one's enemies the status of being named as a person, Paul clearly identified neither his Roman nor his Jewish enemies.[100] More important than

---

98. Belleville, 2 *Corinthians,* 33.
99. Guthrie, *New Testament Introduction,* 423.
100. Furnish, *II Corinthians,* 49.

who they were was *what* they were trying to do in Corinth. The key to the conflict was doctrinal differences with Paul; the opposing preachers were advocating a different "Jesus, a different spirit, and a different gospel" (2 Cor 11:4). That is, they were proclaiming deceptive doctrine and theology, and in doing so, they also claimed superiority over Paul and his message (11:5–6). "These so-called apostles are 'false' in Paul's opinion because their intent is not to preach the gospel and upbuild the congregation, but to inflate their own ego. Financial gain and the desire for dominance are their motivations."[101]

Paul's commitment and calling were to bring the Gentiles in as full citizens in the kingdom of God; any other view of Christianity was inadequate. Christ was to be the center of the Gentiles' devotional life and their ethical behavior, regardless of their social and religious backgrounds. Indeed, the Gentile believers in Corinth and throughout the Roman Empire were people of God, redeemed and bought with a price, just like their Jewish Christian brothers and sisters. Syncretism of Jewish laws and traditions *in addition* to Jesus-devotion was, in Paul's mind, completely unacceptable. It was not unlike the combination of the worship of the God Yahweh and the worship of various pagan gods and goddesses in the Gentile culture.[102] That is, all Christians, Jew and Gentile alike, are molded together into the righteous people of God by the gracious work of Jesus Christ (5:20–21). The words of Paul in his letters to the Jewish *and* Gentile believers were intended to benefit them and help them on their Christian journey, to "build them up" (13:10) in the faith. "His proclamation of full enfranchisement of Gentile Christians into the elect people of God without requiring them to make a full conversion to Jewish observance of the Torah (including, for males, circumcision) certainly brought opposition from some other Christian Jews (see Gal 5:11–12)."[103]

His criticism of such teachers (as ethnic Jews like himself) became even more bitter than his disapproval of his Gentile opponents (see 2 Cor 11:3–6, 13–15). He considered them "false apostles, deceitful workers" (11:13) who rejected not only Paul's message of salvation in Christ alone, outside of the Jewish laws, but also his attempt to promote the unity and meshing of two very diverse cultures (Jews and Gentiles). The Jewish Christians may have found it quite disagreeable to jump on Paul's bandwagon and welcome Gentile believers into their midst with open arms and open minds. As a result of their self-exaltation, these opponents were injuring and dividing the church only to benefit themselves. He perceived these adversaries were misleading his

---

101. Belleville, *2 Corinthians*, 35.
102. Hurtado, *How on Earth*, 174–75.
103. Hurtado, *How on Earth*, 174.

beloved Corinthian church, misusing the word of God, taking advantage of the believers, and preying on the new Christians. Paul denounced those who were "enslaving" the people, probably with strict rules and requirements, and "taking advantage" of them and their lack of knowledge of the Jewish laws. The rivals even used physical violence to push them into submission (see 11:20). Paul was most critical of their fraudulent, unscrupulous, cunning deceit (4:2; 11:3).[104] So, he found it necessary to contend with them fiercely in this letter: "he vigorously lambasts them (11:13, 15), yet he takes their charges seriously and seeks to show that they are groundless."[105] His direct designation of the imposters as "servants of Satan" (11:15) implies that he knew the *real* source of their malicious words and actions.

"Our Ministry Will Not Be Discredited" (6:3)

The opposition, whatever their previous connections or their present intentions, was determined to dispute Paul's apostolic authority, mission, and message in Corinth, and to demean his character in a church he founded. They accused Paul of intentionally frightening the people with his potent written communications while actually being weak and ineffective in person. He lacked the education and rhetorical style of the sophists, and he carried no letter of commendation that might authenticate the apostleship he claimed. His "new" gospel message was unclear and "veiled." Furthermore, he refused to accept any financial remuneration from the congregation for his ministry services, which was viewed as an insult to the Roman church and a demonstration of Paul's lack of love for them (11:11; 12:15).[106] That is, his Jewish opponents wanted visual "signs" to prove Paul's authority (12:1–7), and the Romans wanted special "wisdom" to prove Paul's knowledge and status (11:5–6, 13:3).

Paradoxically, Paul's primary argument for his case against both opponents was the cross of Jesus Christ (13:4).[107] His main concerns were to expose these rivals, to defend his own apostolic ministry, and to build up a struggling congregation (13:10). Paul had a completely different picture of what it meant to be a follower of Jesus. At the center of Paul's life, message, pastoral care, and concern was the Lordship of Jesus Christ. Some Roman Christians thought they were above Paul and his message because of their sense of value, honor, and status. His fellow Jewish Christians were still committed to their own religious heritage, augmented by faith in Jesus as their Messiah. His Jewish rivals had no intention of allowing full unity within the pagan culture, and they may have

104. Harris, *Second Corinthians*, 72.
105. Harris, *Second Corinthians*, 72.
106. Harris, *Second Corinthians*, 69–70. See also Belleville, *2 Corinthians*, 35.
107. McKnight, *Pastor Paul*, 138.

worked diligently to keep the new believers separate. This was poles apart from Paul's message to be a community united in Christ. No one wanted to alter their own culture and traditions just to accommodate the other believers on the congregation. N. T. Wright captures the "new" mind of Paul and his mission:

> What he does say over and over again, is that the church, this symbolic community, must be *united* on the one hand, and *holy* on the other. The unity across traditional boundary lines—Jew/Greek, slave/free, male/female—is well known. Church unity looms much larger for him even than justification. . . . We can grasp Paul's constant emphasis on unity, without going soft on Paul's insistence on "faith alone" as the marker of justification. . . . He sees the church itself as the powerful sign to the watching world, and for that matter to the watching principalities and powers, that a new way of being human has been launched upon the world.[108]

Certainly, this was more than just a slight disagreement between missionaries about methods or styles of ministry. From this letter, we can discern that Paul felt that the complete truth and the significance of the gospel of Jesus Christ were at stake. This letter was more than just an attempt to bolster Paul's reputation among his churches. In the shadow of this conflict in Corinth, the existence of the entire community of believers was in peril; to completely discredit Paul and his message in Corinth could severely damage the Jesus movement across the Roman Empire.

Response to Opponents: Subversion

Linda Belleville suggests that 2 Corinthians is "one of the most personal and pastorally challenging of Paul's letters."[109] Emotionally, it cuts us to the core to imagine his own fellow believers, leaders in the community of Christ, could be so vindictive toward Paul. How did he do it? How did Paul handle his difficult tasks and his brutal opponents with godly confidence and compassion, and with demonstrated love for humanity? Numerous and diverse, the accusations throughout the letter touched the core of who Paul was as a person and as a leader, his ministry motivations, his gifts, his intentions, his integrity, and even his personal appearance. Anyone experiencing this kind of attack would certainly run and hide from the unjust, vicious verbal beatings. One could even consider Paul's maltreatment as a "verbal crucifixion."[110]

---

108. N. T. Wright, *The Paul Debate* (Waco, TX: Baylor University Press, 2015), 183–84.
109. Belleville, *2 Corinthians*, 41.
110. McKnight, *Pastor Paul*, 139.

Yet, Paul responded to his enemies and to an unjust worldly system with the literary weapon of subversion. Subversion is the act of challenging and changing an established system (usually political) by working from within it, often in subtle ways, so as not to raise the ire of the current system. Paul fought against his enemies with unexpected "weapons," those very unlike the "standards of this world" (10:2–5). He refused to use the weapons of human pride, arrogance, and manipulation. Like Jesus, Paul did not openly defend himself as a person. Instead, he dealt firmly with the slanderers in Corinth not with swords, but with meekness, gentleness (10:1), forgiveness (2:5–8), and a concerned, deep love for the people (i.e., 6:11–13). The epitome of true "meekness," Paul "boasted" lavishly about things that demonstrated his own weaknesses and what called his readers' attention to the power of God. His rebuttals were clear but concealed. He subverted their boasting and accusations with his intentional self-deprecation. Paul's humility was an unexpected response to his accusers and their selfish claims. His use of irony and paradox in this letter is clear evidence that Paul was doing something rhetorically that was understood by his readers without putting them or himself at risk. He refused to play the game of his adversaries, and so Paul addressed his opponents' accusations (his "weakness"), their expressions ("riches"), and their own definitions (of power) with "potent irony that unmasked" his rivals. That is, using clever rhetorical language, Paul attempted to subvert his readers away from the Roman power and systems to a "kingdom" ruled by Christ.[111]

Paul was faithfully committed to the integrity of his ministry and his message. Indeed, he was a minister of a new work of God in the world (the "new covenant"). Despite constant opposition and numerous trials and hardships, Paul knew the comfort and the presence of God every step along the journey. As an ambassador for Christ (5:20), his job was to reconcile the Jews and the Gentiles into one people of God, reprimanding his opponents' felonious theology and self-interest. He met discouragement, tests, and adversity, but Paul never gave up living and proclaiming the true word of God. "When the gift of grace becomes the reigning idea in church relations (including leadership), a subversive power is unleashed."[112]

Dealing with Opposition Today

Even today, Christian ministry is very challenging. Paul is a role model for us as we confront modern-day opposition and struggles in ministry: on the missionary field, in the pastorate, in chaplaincy, and in Christian counseling.

---

111. McKnight, *Pastor Paul*, 138.
112. McKnight, *Pastor Paul*, 138.

Society assaults parents, teachers, and Christ-followers attempting to live Christian lives at home and on the job. Not unlike Paul's experiences, many Christian leaders and biblical truths are denounced by our society. Those people who question motives and falsely accuse Christians usually have significant issues in their lives outside of what they call "religion." Opponents criticize Christians as "uneducated," or "intolerant" or "too judgmental," often with little basis for their hostility.

Unfortunately, the attitudes, speech, and behavior of some self-proclaimed believers do verify the oppositional claims. In contrast, like Paul, we must focus on "pure devotion" to Christ, teaching, preaching, and living only for "Jesus Christ and him crucified" (1 Cor 2:2). Intentionally, then, Christian leaders must become aware of what "worldliness" is breeding in our churches "and subvert it to nothing less than the cross of Christ."[113] We must be the "letters of recommendation" for the Christian faith, "known and read by everyone" (2 Cor 3:2–3). Like Paul, Christians must take our callings seriously, know we are accountable for our actions and our words, and trust in God, who is ever-present with us, whose Holy Spirit empowers us, and whose "love compels us" (5:14) to serve Christ every day. We might be amazed at what God can do in a culture of humility and grace and the leading of the Spirit in place of jealousy, greed, personal acclaim, pride, and ambition.

Outline: The Letter of 2 Corinthians

I. Introduction (1:1–11)
   - A. Salutation and Personal Greeting (1:1–2)
   - B. Comfort, Affliction, and Praise (1:3–7)
   - C. Deliverance from Affliction in Asia (1:8–11)

II. Paul's Account of His Conduct and His Commission in Corinth (1:12–2:13)
   - A. Assurance of Motives (1:12–14)
   - B. Explanation of Canceled Visit (1:15–24)
   - C. The Painful Visit (2:1)
   - D. A Tearful Letter (2:2–4)
   - E. Offense and Joy (2:5–11)
   - F. Anxiety in Macedonia (2:12–13)

III. Paul's *Apologia*: Nature of True Apostolic Ministry Described (2:14–7:16)
   - A. Superiority of Paul's Ministry (2:14–4:6)

---

113. McKnight, *Pastor Paul*, 148.

Resources for Teaching or Preaching

Blomberg, Craig L. *Neither Poverty nor Riches*. Grand Rapids: Eerdmans, 1999.

Fee, Gordon D. *Paul, the Spirit, and the People of God*. Peabody, MA: Hendrickson, 1996.

Hafemann, Scott J. *Suffering and Ministry in the Spirit: Paul's Defense of His Ministry in 2 Corinthians 2:14–33*. Grand Rapids: Eerdmans, 1990.

Köstenberger, Andreas J. and David A. Croteau. "'Will a Man Rob God?' (Malachi 3:8): A Study of Tithing in the Old and New Testaments." *Bulletin of Biblical Research*, 16.1 (2006): 53–77.

Peterson, Eugene. *Christ Plays in Ten Thousand Places*. Grand Rapids: Eerdmans, 2008.

———. *The Contemplative Pastor*. Carol Stream, IL: Word, 1989.

Plantinga Jr., Cornelius. *Not the Way It's Supposed to Be: A Breviary of Sin*. Grand Rapids: Eerdmans, 1995.

Stott, John. *The Radical Disciple*. Downers Grove, IL: InterVarsity Press, 2010.

Wright, N. T. *Surprised by Hope*. New York: HarperOne, 2008.

Yancey, Philip. *Where Is God When It Hurts?* New York: Zondervan, 1990.

CHAPTER 1

2 Corinthians 1:1–11

 ## LISTEN to the Story

¹Paul, an apostle of Christ Jesus by the will of God, and Timothy our brother, to the church of God in Corinth, together with all his holy people throughout Achaia: ²Grace and peace to you from God our Father and the Lord Jesus Christ.

³Praise be to the God and Father of our Lord Jesus Christ, the Father of compassion and the God of all comfort, ⁴who comforts us in all our troubles, so that we can comfort those in any trouble with the comfort we ourselves receive from God. ⁵For just as we share abundantly in the sufferings of Christ, so also our comfort abounds through Christ. ⁶If we are distressed, it is for your comfort and salvation; if we are comforted, it is for your comfort, which produces in you patient endurance of the same sufferings we suffer. ⁷And our hope for you is firm, because we know that just as you share in our sufferings, so also you share in our comfort.

⁸We do not want you to be uninformed, brothers and sisters, about the troubles we experienced in the province of Asia. We were under great pressure, far beyond our ability to endure, so that we despaired of life itself. ⁹Indeed, we felt we had received the sentence of death. But this happened that we might not rely on ourselves but on God, who raises the dead. ¹⁰He has delivered us from such a deadly peril, and he will deliver us again. On him we have set our hope that he will continue to deliver us, ¹¹as you help us by your prayers. Then many will give thanks on our behalf for the gracious favor granted us in answer to the prayers of many.

Listening to the Text in the Story: Psalm 23:4; 71:21; 119:50, 52, 76, 82; Lamentations 3:19–25; 1 Corinthians 16:10–11, 13.

"Comfort ye, O comfort my people," says your God.
—*Isaiah 40:1 NASB*

"Praying with Eyes Open"
Blessed are those who mourn
Flash floods of tears, torrents of them,
   Erode cruel canyons, exposing
   Long forgotten strata of life
   Laid down in the peaceful decades:
   A badlands beauty. The same sun
   That decorates each day with colors
   From arroyos and mesas, also shows
   Every old scar and cut of lament.
   Weeping washes the wounds clean
   And leaves them to heal, which always
   Takes an age or two. No pain
   Is ugly in the past tense. Under
   The Mercy every hurt is a fossil
   Link in the great chain of becoming.
   Pick and shovel prayers often
   Turn them up in the valleys of death.
         —Eugene Peterson[1]

Have you ever received a bad letter? Perhaps you were jilted by an ex-spouse in the form of a letter. Maybe you received a letter of termination by mail from a former employer, or were turned down for a desired position, and you wanted to tear it into pieces. Somehow bad news in the form of a letter is even worse than a verbal offense. On the other hand, perhaps you have had to write a merciless letter when you really did not want to. It was your duty to fire an employee or to reject a manuscript; it was imperative to quit a job or to end a relationship. Certainly, it can be very difficult to put into words the emotions and the hard decisions that erupt on paper. Either way, hard letters are painful to read and to write.

During World War II, many American soldiers were sent overseas for duty, assigned to a post across the ocean for months or even years. As time passed, the wives and girlfriends of the GIs who remained back home changed their minds, moved in a new direction, and found someone new. She could not wait for the old boyfriend to return and found someone who was much closer to her in every way. So began the "Dear John" letters, sent from the girls left behind to the soldiers sent abroad. The exact origin of that phrase is lost to history, but the infamous letter was a painful reminder that relationships, especially

---

1. Eugene Peterson, *The Contemplative Pastor* (Carol Stream, IL: Word, 1989), 75.

long-distance ones, are so fragile. Perhaps the love of his life was gone; perhaps this marriage was to end in divorce. Not only did he have to endure fatigue, combat, and dangerous situations, but then the soldier was informed that no one was supporting him with her love anymore. Instead of affectionate words of longing and love, the "Dear John" letter was torture for the recipient.

In much the same way, Paul discovered that it was difficult to write hard letters to the very people he loved and to whom he ministered. Regrettably, the letter we know as 2 Corinthians gives us only hints about a previous "tearful letter" (2:3–4) he was compelled to write, as well as a "painful visit" by Paul to the congregation (2:1). From the start, this letter is emotionally charged as Paul pours out his feelings, opening his letter with troubles and distress, sufferings and endurance. It may be quite the opposite of a "Dear John" letter, but Paul was just as emotional in this epistle.

Everyone experiences human pain and trials, often even to the point of depression and despair. Then, we see miserable human conditions across the globe, much worse than our own, and we must repent of our whining and self-centeredness. In comparison to the plight of other Christians who are persecuted for their faith, or victims of powerful weather storms, corrupt governments, hunger, oppression, diseases, and neglect, I know that I have it rather easy. By nature, it seems that human beings question the presence of pain and suffering in our lives; we avoid it at all costs. We question the care and love of God. Why is there so much suffering in the world? Why do we have to suffer? As we listen to this text, we must hear the voice of Paul loud and clear saying that maybe we need a different view of suffering, trials, and troubles. We need to be reminded of the significance of trials and weakness, as well as the source of great comfort, salvation, endurance, and hope.

EXPLAIN the Story

The opening section of Paul's letter, 1:1–11, sets the tone and establishes the themes that will follow in this complicated letter. The congregation at Corinth was calling his apostolic authority into question, so Paul needed to set the record straight about his mission, his message, and his own character. Oddly, it was the suffering that Paul experienced that validated his divine calling. This is peculiar even for today's readers, who are surprised that Paul's authority and qualifications for ministry are validated through his suffering! Even so, Paul's opponents no doubt used the sufferings against Paul, assuming that one correctly called by God would not suffer so many "perils" in ministry. As Garland writes,

How does he prove that he does not make his own decisions according to the self-centered wisdom of this world, but that he always has their best interests at heart? How does he defend his sufficiency as Christ's apostle when he appears to be so weak and afflicted? How does he change their attitudes toward his afflictions and suffering as an apostle?[2]

While God called Paul to a ministry that included suffering, God also sustained Paul and ultimately delivered him from key trials. The power of God is perceived in the comfort of God. In fact, Paul learned to rely on God through his perils, knowing that the God who resurrected Jesus Christ would surely uphold Paul and his ministry colleagues in doing what God had called them to do. Thus, through his accounts of danger and troubles, the church can see Paul's faithfulness in the face of adversity and can be encouraged by Paul's unfailing gratitude toward a merciful, powerful God. The people in Corinth were privileging their own opinions and the accusations of other people over Paul and his authority.

Salutation and Personal Greeting (1:1–2)

Similar to the greeting Paul wrote to the church in his previous canonical letter (1 Cor 1:1–3), Paul begins this letter with a description of himself, recognition of who the readers are, and a brief blessing. Certainly, it was not unusual for Paul to open a letter with a reference to his apostleship (i.e., Rom 1:1; Eph 1:1; Col 1:1), but this is especially vital as a reminder to the readers in this letter. His whole identity, of course, was based on the "will of God" (2 Cor 1:1). Under the direction of God, and not by his own accord, Paul was "an apostle of Jesus Christ." Paul made a special point of referring to himself as an "apostle," which is, literally, "one sent forth." This is a special commissioning, by Christ himself, and is the very basic issue in conflict between Paul and the Corinthians. Was Paul really qualified and authorized to be an "apostle"? Obviously, from the second word of the letter (in Greek), Paul was confident that he was "sent forth" from God, and he was about to prove this to his Corinthian audience.

As readers today, we can see that the first seven chapters of this letter are a description and a defense of his apostolic ministry: called, commanded, and confirmed by God through Christ. As we move through this dense letter, he begins by describing himself and his transparency before the readers. Then, we can observe Paul's consistent, unswerving defense of his ministry in the face of human opposition and disagreement: he perceived no distinction between himself and "the Twelve" disciples found in the Gospels (i.e., John 6:67, 70),

---

2. Garland, *2 Corinthians*, 29.

and he demonstrated that he fulfilled all the requirements to be an apostle (i.e., 2 Cor 12:12).

However, the unusual (even ironic) tactic used by Paul to bring to light his unique identity and his apostolic defense was his *humility*. The unusual characteristic about this letter is that Paul does not "blow his own horn" or chastise the church in order to endorse and promote himself, even when he was rebuked and criticized by others. Rather, he stood in the shadow of the cross of Christ. He affirmed God's power and authority, as demonstrated through the life and ministry of a fallible, weak, and only too human Paul.

A witness to Paul's commission and his authority, his brother in Christ, Timothy, is mentioned as a fellow worker and co-missionary with Paul (1:1; see Acts 18:5; 1 Th 1:1; 2 Th 1:1; Phil 1:1). Timothy was from Lystra, a city in the area of Galatia, through which Paul had traveled on his first missionary journey (see Acts 14:8–21; 16:1–5). As a young man, Timothy traveled across the ancient Near East and Greece with Paul, planting churches and taking the gospel message to people throughout the Mediterranean region. His name here may imply that Timothy was a co-sender of the letter with Paul; in any event, we can assume that Timothy was an envoy from Paul to many of the churches in the area: Philippi (Phil 2:19), Thessalonica (1 Thess 3:2), and in Macedonia (Acts 19:22). As such an important part of Paul's ministry, we suspect that Timothy also shared in Paul's trials, sufferings, and opposition. No doubt the congregation in Corinth knew Timothy well, as he was sent by Paul earlier to settle some problematic issues in Corinth (Acts 18:5; 1 Cor 4:17; 16:10–11).[3] In addition, in this letter Paul considered Timothy a "brother" in the ministry, implying an equality of position, something beyond a master and a student relationship. Paul may have used this word intentionally to enhance Timothy's influence in the church; that is, an association with Paul lent more credibility in the eyes of the readers.[4] All of this is evidence that Paul never failed to show his love for his fellow missionaries and always encouraged the congregations to warmly accept his co-workers when they were sent to visit (1 Cor 4:17; 2 Cor 7:6–7).

Further, the people receiving this letter are converted Christians, or "saints," "those who have been set apart" as "God's people" (1:1; see Rom 1:7; 1 Cor 1:2). The "church of God" was the house church, or a community of believers in Corinth, where primarily Gentile (Greek and Roman) Christians met together. This community was started by Paul on his second missionary journey, perhaps around AD 50–51. At that point in time, the Roman Empire

---

3. Bruce Barton et al., *Life Application Bible Commentary: 1 and 2 Corinthians*, ed. Grant Osborne (Carol Stream, IL: Tyndale, 1999), 262–63.

4. Furnish, *II Corinthians*, 104–5.

was ruled by the Emperor Claudius. In contrast to Emperor Caligula before him, Claudius declined the idea of statues and temples built in his honor, rejecting compulsory emperor worship throughout the empire. Instead, it was the local Jews who were hostile to Paul and to his message. Acts relates that in Thessalonica, the "jealous Jews" accused Paul of "defying Caesar's [Claudius] decrees saying that there was another king, one called Jesus" (Acts 17:5, 7). So, when Paul went to Corinth, he met considerable Jewish opposition, and he decided to preach only to the Gentiles (Acts 18:1, 5–6). The Jews in Corinth "made a united attack on Paul and brought him into court." Paul was accused of advocating a religion not recognized by Roman law, as Judaism was (Acts 18:13). The formal case was said before Gallio, the Roman governor of the region, who rejected the case of the Jews (Acts 18:14–17). Although Claudius had held a rather tolerant view of the Jews in Corinth, unrest in any portion of the empire was unacceptable. The emperor expelled all Jews from the city of Rome in AD 49 "on account of Chrestus"[5] (see Acts 18:2). This "edict of expulsion" caused Christian Jews like Priscilla and Aquila to flee to places like Corinth where they met Paul.[6] Thus, Paul was able to quietly continue his ministry and gain a significant following among Jewish and Gentile believers in Corinth. He had the opportunity to stay in Corinth for about eighteen months, safely securing the new believers in their Christian faith.[7]

The phrase "in Achaia" (2 Cor 1:1) indicates that Corinth was in the southern peninsula of Greece, not in the northern Macedonian area. This congregation is introduced to modern readers in our first canonical letter to the Corinthians, so a fuller understanding of the people in the Corinthian church can be gained by reading this letter. It is worth noting that, in general, Achaia was an area of poverty, while the urban area of Corinth was quite wealthy. Thus, there was an economic disparity in the region that could not be ignored by the church.[8] They were in Corinth, yet they are together with all the believers, rich and poor, Greek and Jew, over a larger geographical area (1:1). That is, the church had to see itself as one part of a very large, unified whole. They were the "holy ones," the "chosen ones," "set apart for holiness" with all the other believers throughout the region. Harris notes that this "church of God" is part of "that worldwide and yet heavenly community which is the church of God as it finds real and representative expression in the local congregation of believers at Corinth."[9]

5. Suetonius, *Claudius* 25.4.
6. Kierspel, *Charts on the Life, Letters and Theology of Paul*, 15, 19.
7. Barton et al., *1 and 2 Corinthians*, 263.
8. Garland, *2 Corinthians*, 50.
9. Harris, *Second Corinthians*, 133, 135.

Recognizing who they were in Christ, Paul then cited a very typical blessing/greeting to his friends in Corinth: "Grace and peace to you from God our Father and the Lord Jesus Christ" (1:2). This is a greeting that Paul used repeatedly in his letters to the churches; we see it in the first chapter of Galatians, in Ephesians, Philippians, and in Colossians (but without reference to Christ, oddly). In his first letter to the Thessalonians, Paul greeted them with only "Grace and peace," but the second letter has the complete greeting with references to "God our Father and the Lord Jesus Christ." The important aspect of this greeting is that "grace" is Paul's adaptation of a common Greek salutation, and "peace" is a form of a Hebrew greeting. The readers needed to understand that this was neither the kind of Pax Romana peace promised by the Roman emperors, nor was it the kind of grace conferred on someone in an inferior position. Paul uses this phrase often to cleverly include both the Jewish and the Gentile believers in the church.

Typically, Paul used "God the Father" and "the Lord Jesus Christ" in tandem, linking them together to emphasize that both God and Christ bless the believers with grace and peace. Jesus's life, death, and resurrection is the ultimate expression of God's grace to humanity ("God's unsought and unmerited favor in Christ"), and the Hebrew expression *shalom* ("fully rounded well-being") connotes the wholeness and fullness that, for Paul, is completed only in following Christ.[10] Believers, therefore, are blessed with both grace and peace through the Father and the Son. Together with the third person of the Trinity, the Spirit, believers are sanctified and sustained.

On a literary note, we can notice Paul's use of numerous first-person plurals ("we," "us," "our"); these appear throughout 2 Corinthians 1–7. Some scholars consider these words to simply be the use of the editorial plural (or generic plural), which is a literary expression that does not necessarily indicate that other people were with Paul. However, these plural words could also imply that Paul was not alone in his ministry.[11] He may have intended to emphasize to his readers that he was not a lone apostle but was aided by a wider circle of co-workers and co-missionaries. Timothy has already been mentioned, and Silas and Timothy are mentioned as fellow workers in 1:19. It appears that Titus ministered closely with Paul (2:13; 7:6, 13–16; 8:16–23). Are we to assume that Paul was not alone when he experienced his "near-death experience" as related in 1:8–11? It would be very unusual for one man to travel extensively alone across the Roman Empire. Still, we should understand that Paul is clearly writing about himself in this letter, explaining his own calling and ministry, and

10. Harris, *Second Corinthians*, 135.
11. Harris, *Second Corinthians*, 140.

even taking personal blame for misunderstandings (i.e., 7:8–9). Certainly, he is the primary object of the debates and discussions in this letter. It is his ministry, his message, and his personal character that are on the line in Corinth.

Comfort, Affliction, and Praise (1:3–7)

Verses 1:3–7 are very much like a prayer of praise; it has been considered to be a "Jewish blessing, heavily influenced by the Jewish liturgical tradition."[12] In Greek, verses 3–4 are one sentence, a tightly composed blessing or praise to God and Christ. Paul did not bring just good wishes to his readers; he brought a sacred blessing from one who was uniquely qualified to do so. What is distinctive about this prayer, however, is the combination of two antithetical themes of God's comfort and human affliction in one blessing. Human affliction is contrasted with divine comfort. Thus, the missionaries are afflicted for the readers' comfort, yet comfort is always supplied by God for endurance through affliction.

In 1:3, three names are given for God in Paul's exclamation of praise: he is the "Father of the Lord Jesus Christ," the "Father of compassion," and the "God of all comfort." This is perhaps Trinitarian in effect, revealing the nature of Father God, his Son Jesus Christ, and the "Paraclete," the Advocate (John 14:26; 16:7). The word "compassion" is actually written in the plural in the Greek language, so we can interpret it as "compassions" or "mercies," indicating a wide range of divine empathy. As the "Father," God is tender, gentle, and gracious toward his "children"; his "great love" and "compassions never fail" (see Lam 3:19–25). Used ten times in five verses, the word *paraklēsis* means literally a "calling alongside" or "consolation." It is related to the word used for the Holy Spirit (as in John 14:16), and it is worth noting that the complete "triune God" pictured here in Paul's blessing is the source of "all comfort" (2 Cor 1:3). Furthermore, in the book of Isaiah, we see that "comfort" is an action, referring to tangible intervention, usually performed by Yahweh (Isa 40:1). It is not just a kind thought; comfort is concrete support through an affliction. Paul uses it as a "consolatory strengthening in the face of adversity that affords spiritual refreshment."[13] In the OT, the people of God were very aware of God's comfort through their hardships, and they realized that "suffering was a time of judgment and cleansing" of the nation.[14]

Further, Paul's concept of affliction is exemplified by the "sufferings of Christ" (2 Cor 1:5). The early Christian believers understood that the death

---

12. Furnish, *II Corinthians*, 116.
13. Harris, *Second Corinthians*, 143.
14. Furnish, *II Corinthians*, 118.

and suffering of Jesus on the cross were necessary to complete the redemption of humanity. That is, the "passion" or the "suffering" of Christ (Acts 1:3) that is found in the Gospels is the foundation of Paul's words in 1:5. The believing Christian is a participant in that "suffering of Christ," yet Paul emphasized the fact that the responding *comfort* of Christ "overflows" into the believer. The sufferings of Christ abound or overflow into each of our lives because Jesus suffered and died for each one of us. So then, the comfort of Christ should overflow from us to others, and we can comfort others in their affliction. Believers are unified in the sufferings of Christ, and they are then unified in his remarkable comfort (2 Cor 1:7).

All human beings encounter "troubles" or "oppression, tribulations, afflictions" in this life—no exceptions (1:4). The reason is that we are then able to comfort other people, just as God comforts us. It is interesting that God comforts us in all our sufferings, as we are going through them. God may not choose to eliminate our afflictions, but his comfort is enough to get us through the troubles. Since Paul had experienced both affliction and comfort in his ministry, he tells the readers that he did so for their benefit (1:6). As God encourages people in their trials, so Christians should help one another with encouragement and prayer: suffering and encouragement go hand in hand (1:7). By helping each other, when the afflictions do pass, the church will emerge more faithful, stronger, and better equipped to encourage others in need of comfort. This time will come, Paul assured them, after "patient endurance" (1:6). The believers should not despair, but be encouraged, just as Paul remained firm in his hope that God will continue to deliver them (and him) from all their troubles. In summary, the purpose of suffering is to prepare believers to be comforted by God and to comfort other people in the same way. Comfort (encouragement) leads to endurance, and endurance leads to hope. Paul had a great deal more to say about his own trials and suffering as we progress through this letter.

This passage may be difficult for some believers to hear: we must share in the sufferings of Christ as well as the comfort and salvation of Christ. It is almost a paradox for Paul to wish his readers grace and peace (1:2), and then immediately tell them they will have great troubles and suffering (1:4). Perhaps some believers had in mind that once one is "saved" and commits to faith in Christ, suffering and trials would end. Paul reminded them that is simply not the case. People tend to think that religion is supposed to lift them up, not drag them down with suffering. Yet, Jesus even warned his followers that, "I have told you these things so that in me you may have peace. In this world you will have trouble. But take heart! I have overcome the world!" (John 16:33). While certainly believers will suffer, the Christian is not alone in his or her hardships, and suffering builds endurance. The church's very existence is to suffer together and comfort one another. Ask any marathon runner if he or she has ever experienced any suffering in running over 26 miles at one time; but of course, each twisted ankle, each pulled muscle, each pain, each difficulty builds determination and endurance—and a hope that one day the runner will win the race! Also, most marathon runners do not succeed in achieving the prize without assistance from many patient people.

Logically speaking, it is a bit difficult to see how the suffering of one man, like Paul, can be an agent of "comfort and salvation" of many people (2 Cor 1:6). Christ, of course, is our quintessential example of this (1:5). Laura Alary suggests that there are "numerous similarities between Paul and the [OT] prophets—both of whom suffer, proclaim, teach, exhort, reconcile and console." Certainly, this may be an illustration of how the "suffering of one can benefit the many."[15] It is also true that the sufferings of one, shared with others, can bring encouragement and comfort to many other people. Someone who has been through cancer treatments can minister to other cancer patients in a way that I could not, since I have never experienced such affliction. The troubles and suffering of one person in the church, or in a school, or in a neighborhood, can strengthen and unify the entire community with the common goal of love and support for one another. Ironically, as "partners" in Christ's death and suffering, all believers are "partners" in Christ's comfort that leads to endurance (see 4:10–11).[16]

In these verses, we see that Paul wanted to secure the compassion and understanding of his readers and gain their support for him as a person before he addressed their damaged relationship. He wanted to explain and defend himself before he attended to the controversial issues that plagued the church on the inside, and those rivals from the outside who were degrading and discrediting him. As a matter of fact, Paul was so certain of this hope of comfort (1:10) from God, and from the prayers of others (1:11), that he shared with his readers the crushing hardships that he faced in the province of Asia and the hope that followed.

Deliverance from Affliction in Asia (1:8–11)

Immediately following Paul's comforting thoughts of vv. 3–7, he related a story about his own deliverance from adversity and the comfort of God in times of suffering. Using a typical Jewish formula for worship, Paul praised God for his blessings (1:3–7), and then called attention to blessings in which

---

15. Laura Dawn Alary, "Good Grief: Paul as Sufferer and Consoler in 2 Corinthians 1:3–7. A Comparative Investigation," ProQuest Dissertations and Theses 2003, http://ezproxy.net.ucf.edu/login?url=http://search.proquest.com/docview/305263639.

16. Furnish, II Corinthians, 120.

he himself had participated (1:10–11). Paul's hardship in Asia was so over-whelming and devastating that he "felt the sentence of death" (1:9); only God could intervene and spare his life (1:10).

Regrettably, we do not have many details about the nature of this deadly experience or its exact location. In the first century, "Asia" referred to the large Roman province that lay to the east of the Aegean Sea. Paul had ministered all across this region from Antioch to Troas. It is possible that his readers had heard something about his deadly experience, but they had no idea of the severity of the situation; it was "beyond what a person could bear."[17] This hardship had two results, which Paul wanted his readers to understand. First, Paul tells this story to support and summarize the blessing that precedes the story. His personal suffering led to comfort from God and reliance on God. This reliance on the Father is a key theme in this section because God's grace and comfort are sufficient for believers, even in a time of affliction. There is no room in this story for pity or condolences from the Corinthian church. Paul had learned an important, valuable lesson. After this deadly ordeal, Paul gave up on self-reliance in ministry and learned to put his hope and trust in God for his physical and spiritual health. It is one thing to talk theology about the comfort of God, and quite another thing to experience it. That is, Paul suffered just like the Corinthians suffered—like all of us suffer—and this helps us to identify more closely with Paul in his ministry struggles. Later in the letter, Paul recorded this divine promise that was evident in his own life from the very beginning: "My grace is sufficient for you, for *my* power is made perfect in [your] weakness" (12:9, my emphasis).

Second, it appears that the Corinthians were faithful in their prayers of intercession for Paul, and he was grateful for their concern (1:11). Paul knew that God graciously answers the prayers of his people, and that he could not do his ministry effectively without their prayerful support. Paul shared his horrific experience in Asia with the church so that they could see that he, too, had suffered mightily, and that his delivery was from God. The church became a part of the partnership of Paul's sufferings and his hope (1:10). The prayers, the dangerous experience, and their concern for him deepened the pastor-congregation relationship.

Paul's opponents in Corinth must have accused the apostle of being weak and ineffective; this is seen especially in chapters 10–13 (see 10:1, 10). In this brief opening section, Paul began his rebuke against such accusations and introduced the concept that, ironically, God's power is evidenced through his human weakness. Human hardships and afflictions are the ideal opportunity

---

17. Harris, *Second Corinthians*, 155.

to see the power of God at work. In the end, at the point of despair, we may finally rely on God (1:9–11, see also 12:9–10).

The opening of this letter to the Corinthians is different in many ways from his other letters. Paul set the tone of his communication at the outset with blessings, encouragement, and a personal story of suffering and comfort. Unlike the letter to the Philippians, for example, Paul did not offer thanksgiving for the Corinthians in his opening greeting; unlike Galatians, his tone was not remedial. With mixed emotions, Paul necessarily began his letter with encouragement and praise. Ultimately, he knew that his reputation was at stake in Corinth; but more than that, his relationship with a church that he loved needed restoring. That is what this letter must do.

LIVE the Story

How many times over the last centuries, in difficult, painful situations, have Christians read and re-read 2 Corinthians 1:3–7 for their own comfort and encouragement? At a time of tears, I remember a friend calling me on the phone and reading this passage of Scripture to me aloud. And it was a comfort! While 1:3–7 is a familiar and precious passage, we usually neglect to read the following passage (1:8–11), where Paul narrated his own real-life example of suffering. He was transparent and bears his soul about an excruciating, near-death experience. Keeping things in perspective, we can see that Paul's words in 1:3–7 are not just heavenly platitudes that he invented. Paul spoke from experience; he did suffer greatly, and yet he was still able to see his afflictions in the proper light. This is not an easy task.

I remember trying to explain to my children that whatever pain they were going through "was for their own good." Difficult to explain and even more difficult to swallow, those words can ring true. Paul's answer to the purpose of suffering is that we are to comfort others as God has comforted us. Some Christians mislead others into believing that the Christian life paves the way to an easy life; truly, our entire society is predisposed to avoid suffering. Yet, following Christ (who suffered greatly for us) does not exempt us from common (and constant) tension, problems, worry, conflicts, and stress. Physical difficulties such as jobs, family, health, and finances can result in emotional strain and anxiety. We can get so lost in an attempt to intellectually figure out the "why" of suffering, that we neglect to recognize the "who" of the one who ultimately brings much-needed comfort (1:3). It is the Spirit of God within us who comforts us, encourages us, and admonishes us to share that care, compassion, and love with others who are hurting.

The "Beauty of Pain"

One of my favorite books by author Philip Yancey is *Where is God When it Hurts?* In this memorable work on human suffering, Yancey asks crucial questions:

Why is there such a thing as pain?
Is pain a message from God?
How can we cope with pain?
How does faith help?

Humans suffer pain physically, mentally, emotionally, psychologically, and even spiritually—sometimes all at the same time! We do everything within our power to avoid pain, from using a bandage on a scratched knee to powerful, addictive medical painkillers. Yancey demonstrates that pain has a purpose. In fact, it has many purposes, and should not be regarded only as an attack on the human person. Yancey begins his discussion with the science of physical pain. He says that "the mechanism of pain in the human body operates much like a warning system. . . . Pain sensors loudly alert my body to danger and force me to concentrate on the problem area."[18] He is convinced that pain "gets a bad press" because we always see the "problem of pain" and attempt to offer weak and empty reasons for it. In fact, we need to see pain in "an entirely different light." To repeat an amazing paradox, pain has a purpose, and it is for our protection. The "marvels of the pain network" inside and on the human body are astounding.[19] An understanding of the network reveals that pain is not a divinely inspired mistake; it "reveals a marvelous design that serves our bodies well."[20] Further, the visible, physical pain we all know so well serves as a vivid metaphor for unseen, mental, psychological, and spiritual pain as well.

As a real-life illustration of the pain network, Yancey introduces his readers to Dr. Paul Brand, a medical doctor who was head of a team at a leprosarium (a hospital for the treatment of leprosy) in Carville, Louisiana. The same disease we read about in the Bible, leprosy is a disease that affects the nervous system; it is the oldest recorded disease, and is still dreaded today. Affected patients have a defective pain system, and the disease numbs the person's extremities.[21] Brand was awarded a large financial grant to design an artificial pain system especially created for leprosy (and diabetes) patients "who are in danger of losing fingers, toes and even entire limbs simply because their

---

18. Philip Yancey, *Where Is God When It Hurts?* (Grand Rapids: Zondervan, 1990), 12.
19. Yancey, *Where Is God When It Hurts?*, 13.
20. Yancey, *Where Is God When It Hurts?*, 17.
21. Yancey, *Where Is God When It Hurts?*, 23–25.

warning system of pain had been silenced."[22] Their research among the afflicted in America and in India made Dr. Brand and his colleagues acutely aware that leprosy patients were "living in great danger because of their painlessness."[23] Ultimately, the entire project was abandoned, because the God-made nervous system in the human body was far too complex for even the most sophisticated human technology to replicate.

Certainly, pain is unpleasant; it can be miserable and crippling. Yet, Brand's scientific investigations proved to be evidence that pain saves us from destruction. First, if we had no warning sign of a physical problem, the issue could destroy us. Simply put, if I cut myself deeply and felt no pain, I could bleed to death. Medical doctors and researchers have developed intricate tests for signs of cancer in the human body because various forms of cancer can be a "silent killer," as they can be without symptoms and without pain. Without hesitation, Dr. Brand declares, "Thank God for inventing pain! I don't think he could have done a better job. It is beautiful."[24]

The second purpose of pain is to remind us of our humanity, our frailty, and our dependence. There are those people who are convinced that the "sole purpose of life is to be comfortable [and] suffering vastly complicates that lifestyle."[25] Likewise, some religious belief systems attempt to deny all pain, and followers endeavor to rise above it. Granted, the human condition in this world is out of whack and we live in a fallen state. The megaphone of pain can produce two opposite reactions: the human pain and suffering of this world can turn people against God for allowing such wretchedness, or it can drive a person toward God for comfort. For the Christian, it is the latter choice. We recognize the reality of the dual nature of this great-but-fallen world, and accept the veracity not only of the present condition of this world, but also of our own human nature (which Paul calls "the flesh").[26] Moreover, if a person cannot feel any physical pain, that person also cannot feel any positive senses of touch, like a hug.

In faith, pain brings us to our knees to consider the greater issues of life and death and the meaning of both. Pain is caused by our own sin and by the fallen nature of the world around us. God permits suffering because it screams to us about our own need for restoration and redemption.[27] Paul recognized this when he wrote,

---

22. Yancey, *Where Is God When It Hurts?*, 18.
23. Yancey, *Where Is God When It Hurts?*, 25.
24. Yancey, *Where Is God When It Hurts?*, 18.
25. Yancey, *Where Is God When It Hurts?*, 60.
26. Yancey, *Where Is God When It Hurts?*, 61.
27. Yancey, *Where Is God When It Hurts?*, 61.

We know that the whole creation has been groaning as in the pains of childbirth right up to the present time. Not only so, but we ourselves, who have the firstfruits of the Spirit, groan inwardly as we wait eagerly for our adoption to sonship, the redemption of our bodies. For in this hope we were saved. But hope that is seen is no hope at all. Who hopes for what they already have? But if we hope for what we do not yet have, we wait for it patiently. (Rom 8:22–25)

Make It Count!

When we suffer, we can make a request to the Father of all compassion to please make this experience *count*. Let it count toward making me a better person. That means asking "What do I need to learn from this trial?" and "Who can I help because I had to go through this?" I realized that my friend who is a cancer survivor has a unique perspective and a valuable ministry to other cancer patients that I will never have. Another friend is blind, so she listens to the Scripture and locks every word in her memory, which is difficult for me as a visual learner. I depend on my ability to read a passage instead of memorizing it. Finally, we can say, "Please Lord, teach me what I need to learn from this trial because I do not want to go through it again!"

Compassion in Community

In the life of the church, trials, suffering, and hardships give believers the opportunity to comfort one another, which leads to unity and love among them. The gifts of grace and peace are never to be hoarded, they should flow out of grateful hearts to others. I don't think human beings were ever intended to go through pain and suffering alone; the community is the strength and support to help one another in hard times. Even when we ourselves are suffering, we may be called to minister to another person who is in even deeper despair. The writer Henri Nouwen, who knew suffering and pain, wrote,

> To follow Christ means to relate to each other with the mind of Christ; that is, to relate to each other as Christ did to us—in servanthood and humility. Compassion, then, can never be separated from community. Compassion always reveals itself in community, in a new way of being together. Fellowship with Christ is fellowship with our brothers and sisters. This is most powerfully expressed by Paul when he calls the Christian community the body of Christ. . . . It is in the Christian community that we can be open and receptive to the suffering of the world and offer it a compassionate response. For where people come together in Christ's name, he is present as the compassionate Lord (see Matt. 18:20).

Jesus Christ himself is and remains the most radical manifestation of God's compassion.[28]

Moreover, human suffering shifts the control of life from us to God. Through the perils of life, when all else fails, we learn to lean on God (1:9–10). Within the Christian community, we may attempt to help one another, but very often there is little we can do for someone *except to pray*. Paul recognized the help he received from the church in the form of the "prayers of many" (1:11). What is irritating is the flippant comment from someone who pats you on the back and says, "Wow, too bad. I'll pray for you . . ." Insincerity and artificiality from fellow Christians can hurt more than the hardship itself. Pray and love with empathy and sincerity. Fully aware of life, of suffering and hardships, and with humility, sincerity, and compassion, we must learn to gladly pray for one another with hope focused on the "God of all comfort."

"Power of God Comes through Suffering"

Paul's power, authority, and effectiveness were questioned by those who were attempting to discredit him and his ministry. How like Paul to reverse what was expected and to tell a story of his human weakness! No doubt Paul was bothered by his own reputation in Corinth, but his real concern was about the forces that were dividing and misleading the community of believers. Where did their loyalty lie: with self-serving, human power and authority, or with God's power that, paradoxically, comes through human (Paul's) weaknesses? Unfortunately, human power cannot totally alleviate human suffering in this world, regardless of what some might imagine. More often, human power *produces* suffering, such as inhumane governments and radical terrorists. It has been said that "absolute power corrupts absolutely." In the Roman Empire, where Paul preached, the imperial authorities were perfect examples of the corruption of power. The Corinthians knew this; they were used to following imperial power and authority under the threat of treason or even death. Yet, we see that Paul was secure enough in the power and the love of God not to depend on his own situations and abilities. The congregation could not understand the paradoxes that were apparent in Paul's life: the goodness of suffering and power in weakness. By giving up our own comfort, as Paul did, we can act in love toward others. By suffering well, we love well.

---

28. Henri J. M. Nouwen, *The Only Necessary Thing: Living a Prayerful Life*, ed. Wendy Wilson Greer (New York: Crossroad, 1999), 129.

2 Corinthians 1:12–2:13

LISTEN to the Story

¹²Now this is our boast: Our conscience testifies that we have conducted ourselves in the world, and especially in our relations with you, with integrity and godly sincerity. We have done so, relying not on worldly wisdom but on God's grace. ¹³For we do not write you anything you cannot read or understand. And I hope that, ¹⁴as you have understood us in part, you will come to understand fully that you can boast of us just as we will boast of you in the day of the Lord Jesus.

¹⁵Because I was confident of this, I wanted to visit you first so that you might benefit twice. ¹⁶I wanted to visit you on my way to Macedonia and to come back to you from Macedonia, and then to have you send me on my way to Judea. ¹⁷Was I fickle when I intended to do this? Or do I make my plans in a worldly manner so that in the same breath I say both "Yes, yes" and "No, no"?

¹⁸But as surely as God is faithful, our message to you is not "Yes" and "No." ¹⁹For the Son of God, Jesus Christ, who was preached among you by us—by me and Silas and Timothy—was not "Yes" and "No," but in him it has always been "Yes." ²⁰For no matter how many promises God has made, they are "Yes" in Christ. And so through him the "Amen" is spoken by us to the glory of God. ²¹Now it is God who makes both us and you stand firm in Christ. He anointed us, ²²set his seal of ownership on us, and put his Spirit in our hearts as a deposit, guaranteeing what is to come.

²³I call God as my witness—and I stake my life on it—that it was in order to spare you that I did not return to Corinth. ²⁴Not that we lord it over your faith, but we work with you for your joy, because it is by faith you stand firm.

²·¹So I made up my mind that I would not make another painful visit to you. ²For if I grieve you, who is left to make me glad but you whom I have grieved? ³I wrote as I did, so that when I came I would not be distressed

by those who should have made me rejoice. I had confidence in all of you, that you would all share my joy. [4]For I wrote you out of great distress and anguish of heart and with many tears, not to grieve you but to let you know the depth of my love for you.

[5]If anyone has caused grief, he has not so much grieved me as he has grieved all of you to some extent—not to put it too severely. [6]The punishment inflicted on him by the majority is sufficient. [7]Now instead, you ought to forgive and comfort him, so that he will not be overwhelmed by excessive sorrow. [8]I urge you, therefore, to reaffirm your love for him. [9]Another reason I wrote you was to see if you would stand the test and be obedient in everything. [10]Anyone you forgive, I also forgive. And what I have forgiven—if there was anything to forgive—I have forgiven in the sight of Christ for your sake, [11]in order that Satan might not outwit us. For we are not unaware of his schemes.

[12]Now when I went to Troas to preach the gospel of Christ and found that the Lord had opened a door for me, [13]I still had no peace of mind, because I did not find my brother Titus there. So I said goodbye to them and went on to Macedonia.

Listening to the Text in the Story: Psalm 34:2; 44:8; Matthew 6:12, 14; 18:15–20; Luke 11:4; Romans 16:20; Colossians 3:13; Revelation 12:9–12.

Father, walk with me in my pilgrimage as a pastor
To mountain peaks that I may see Your purposes clearly,
Lush pastures that I may be nourished by Your truth,
Valleys of discouragement that I may be supported by Your strength.
May Your gentleness make me great. Amen.
                    H. B. London and N. B. Wiseman[1]

If you have ever done so, you know that travel in a foreign country can be a little tricky. While weeks (or even months) of planning can go into a travel itinerary, plans are often subject to significant changes in an instant: a train is missed or a plane is delayed; a sudden change of weather foils the outdoor plans; sickness or injury in a foreign place can upset the whole apple-cart.

---

1. H. B. London and Neil B. Wiseman, *The Heart of a Great Pastor* (Ventura, CA: Regal, 1994), 175.

One key element of travel is flexibility, or travelers can lose tempers, money, and valuable relationships!

When I was a teenager, I had the opportunity to study the French language in France one summer. I quickly learned how much I did not know, and how American I was! I had made some typical tourist purchases, and I wanted to send them back to the States by post. I went to a store similar to our hardware stores to get brown wrapping paper to cover the box I was mailing. I tried to ask for a roll of brown paper, and the poor clerk tried even harder to understand my fractured French. He took me to down an aisle of the store and showed me a roll of aluminum foil. It was a roll, so he got part of the picture, but he did not understand me completely (my fault, not his). Likewise, Paul realized that the Corinthians misunderstood many aspects of his ministry and his relationship with them.

As indicated in the introduction to this commentary, this letter to the believers in Corinth that we call "2 Corinthians" is not really the second letter Paul sent to the church. In fact, the passage under study can be confusing because of multiple letters and multiple visits by Paul to Corinth, such that the modern-day reader can be puzzled. In this section of the letter, we hear Paul beginning to defend his message, his ministry, and his own conduct. Yet he begins his defense in a very unclear manner because we as readers are only privileged to part of the story.

Paul wrote this letter to the church in Corinth from Macedonia. Apparently, some folks in the Corinthian congregation were upset with Paul because they did not fully understand him or his motives. He changed his travel plans, and they took it as an offense that he changed his mind about visiting them. Again, Paul had been experiencing great persecution in Asia Minor, and we must remember that travel was difficult in Paul's day. Travel plans could change quickly, and one did not just jump on the next plane to make up for lost time. What we hear behind the text is disappointment on the part of the congregation because his plans did not materialize as they expected. In addition, because they did not understand his motives, his readers had speculations and doubts about his intentions and commitment to them. Perhaps someone promised you something that was very important to you. You looked forward with anticipation and then, suddenly, they reneged on that promise; yes, it can hurt.

Why would Paul do that? Was Paul really the wise apostle they thought they knew? Why were there opponents within the congregation who slandered him and used his (perceived) weaknesses to vilify Paul and his ministry? Why had he written such a bold and confrontational letter to them? Could the church be reconciled to him? And what is all this "boasting" about anyway?

EXPLAIN the Story

Assurance of Motives (1:12–14)

After a very emotional introduction to this letter, with an admission concerning his own personal trials and hardships (1:8–11), Paul began the actual body of the letter in 1:12. It was important to defend his own trustworthiness and character before he proceeded with any further matters. Because the Corinthians had complaints about Paul, he had to reassure his readers so that they "will come to understand fully" (1:14) both the mission and the heart of Paul. (The introductory section of this commentary includes a timeline of Paul's communications with the Corinthians and attempts to clarify Paul's letters and travel plans for readers today.)

This passage begins with the word "Now . . ." (1:12), clearly introducing a new theme following the introductory section of the letter. This new theme involves Paul's own personal character, which is the foundation of his relationship with the Corinthians. In his actions, behavior, and motives, Paul had been nothing toward his readers but righteous and totally sincere.

The theme of "boasting" is inaugurated in vv. 12–14, as Paul declared that the readers can "boast" of him and his integrity, and he can "boast" of them. To "boast" is usually a pejorative word to modern-day readers, so we are anxious about the use of this word. It is interesting to note that Paul used it more in his letters than any other NT writer.[2] Actually, Paul used some form of this word more often in the Corinthians letters than elsewhere (38 of 55 instances), and most of these occur in 2 Corinthians (10 times in chapters 1–9 alone). Further, Paul repeated the concept of "boasting" 18 times in the final section of his letter, chapters 10–13, so we will encounter this word again as Paul continued to defend his ministry in Corinth.[3]

Normally our first reaction to "boasting" is revulsion; in our culture, we cringe when people constantly brag and boast about their positions, power, or prestige (or even their grandkids!). Yet the idea of "boasting" is used by Paul in a manner different from what we imagine today. That is, to "boast" is closely related to "have confidence in" something or someone.[4] Interestingly, Paul's "boasting" can be understood in a positive sense (1:12), but the "boasting" of his opponents is seen in a negative light (11:21). Throughout this letter we sense a play on words that Paul is using to compare and contrast his true confidence in God with that of his adversaries.

---

2. Furnish, *II Corinthians,* 126.
3. Furnish, *II Corinthians,* 127.
4. Furnish, *II Corinthians,* 126.

On the one hand, in the Bible we often get a glimpse of the idea of "boasting" that is most appropriate, even encouraging and beautiful. In the Old Testament we read:

> In God we make our boast all day long,
>   and we will praise your name forever. (Ps 44:8)

And Paul wrote:

> May I never boast except in the cross of our Lord Jesus Christ, through which the world has been crucified to me, and I to the world. (Gal 6:14)

> For it is by grace you have been saved, through faith—and this is not from yourselves, it is the gift of God—not by works, so that no one can boast. (Eph 2:8–9)

The believers in Corinth were living proof that salvation did not depend on human effort. So when someone was saved, Paul said, "Let him who boasts [of their salvation] boast in the Lord!" (1 Cor 1:31); he then repeats this exclamation in 2 Corinthians 10:17. Paul boasts about the Thessalonians' perseverance and faith (2 Thess 1:4), and Paul himself "boasts in the cross" (Gal. 6:14). Our English word "pride" in 7:4 is the same word used for the affirming "boasting" done by Paul in 7:14. We "boast" about those good and positive things for which we are grateful and "proud" (like grandchildren!).

On the other hand, there is certainly the negative kind of boasting in the Scriptures: it is used in the epistle of James (3:14; 4:16) where it is declared evil (4:16), as well as in Ephesians 2:9, 1 John 2:16, Jude 16, and even in 1 Corinthians 3:21; 5:6. Boasting about oneself and one's own accomplishments is always placed in a negative position. No one can boast about saving the spiritual life of another person; only God can do that through Jesus Christ. Moreover, Furnish suggests that in this particular passage, boasting carries the idea of a "verdict of blamelessness to be pronounced at the Parousia when the Lord Jesus will come to judge (see 1 Thess 2:19)."[5] If so, in this case Paul is referring to a "boasting" that is an *eschatological* confidence. He is confident in the future of his readers, and proud of the fact that his ministry has made his readers ready for "the day of the Lord Jesus" (2 Cor 1:14). Yet, it appears that Paul is also boasting about their acceptance of his message of

---

5. Furnish, *II Corinthians*, 126.

Jesus Christ as Lord and Savior in the present. His readers showed confidence in his proclamation as they believed his gospel message, and he can "boast" in their salvation and posture before God.

What concerned him the most was their "full understanding" (1:14) of Paul and of his ministry. A primary purpose of this letter, Paul desired that his readers would fully receive his written explanations concerning his message, his motives, and his conduct. The Corinthians had first-hand knowledge of Paul, as he had spent 18 months with them (Acts 18:11). They were not to give in to the "worldly wisdom" that surrounded them in their culture. Outside rivals were touting false accusations and another kind of wisdom that had shaken the readers' confidence in him. Thus, it was Paul's hope that, in the end, no matter what his opponents said against them, Paul and his colleagues would be a "boast" for the congregation, just as the congregation was a "boast" for Paul and his fellow workers in ministry (2 Cor 1:14). In view of the slander aimed against Paul, he was setting up the defense of his ministry to the Corinthians that began with the strength and integrity of his own character (1:12).

Explanation of Canceled Visit (1:15–24)

His integrity was challenged by those who took offense at Paul's change of travel plans. Not surprisingly, there was a perfectly logical rationale for the recent unexpected change in his plans. Paul realized it was necessary to explain his behavior as an expression of his "holiness" and "sincerity" of intentions, and not a result of someone else's "worldly wisdom" (1:12, 17). In fact, his opponents in Corinth may have accused him of creating a convoluted scheme to trick the church, collect the financial aid for Jerusalem, and get out town quickly! In their "worldly wisdom," they may have speculated an ulterior motive devised by Paul since he would not take fees for his ministry (1:17; cf. 2:17; 7:2; 8:20–21;11:7–11;12:13–18). The readers did not fully understand Paul's motives and were falling prey to the deceptive words of his adversaries. Paul had to straighten things out.

Thus, the *original plan* was for Paul to make *two* short visits to Corinth (in the south of Greece), one before and one after his visit to Macedonia (in the north of Greece). The original plan was "so that you [the Corinthians] might benefit twice" (1:15–16). This was a careful plan to leave Ephesus, visit Corinth, then head north to Macedonia. He would return the same way for a second short visit at Corinth, specifically to pick up their funds for the collection for the believers in Jerusalem. Such a plan was for the Corinthians' benefit, and Paul fully intended to keep it as much as he was able. Because "God is faithful," so Paul's statements were honest and faithful (1:18).

The Faithfulness of God

In the middle of the justification of Paul's travel plans, we find a short paragraph on the faithfulness of God (1:18–23). As readers, we must back up for a moment and follow Paul's line of thinking from 1:12 to discover two points he is making in his apostolic defense. First, Paul assures his readers that the gospel message that he and his colleagues "preached among you" was not ambiguous, and it was from God (1:18); it is true and authentic in its content. In fact, Paul emphatically stated that Jesus is "*the* Son of God"; that his unique relationship with the Father as well as his unique status as the Son were not only key to Paul's message, but also supported its authenticity (1:19). This may have been a subtle rebuttal to the Gentiles who considered the Roman Emperor as a "son of god." Paul used this full title for Jesus only four times in his letters, indicating that it was not a favorite or frequent title for Jesus (see 2 Cor 1:19; Rom 1:4; Gal 2:20; and Eph 4:13). The use of the definite article "*the*" implies that, for Paul, Jesus's divine sonship was an unambiguous certainty and foundational to his theology and to his proclamations.

> The designation "son of god" was not common in Greco-Roman paganism, and seems to have been used as a title only by Roman Emperors. . . .
> Paul views Jesus' divine sonship as unique, and does not accord Jesus membership in a class of other figures who may be regarded as sons of God such as we encounter in the Jewish or pagan sources.[6]

Paul was very clear with his readers concerning the veracity of his gospel message, so they could rest assured that his message and the promises of God were certain (2 Cor 1:20). The Corinthians had experienced God's power in their lives and the complete affirmation of God's promises through Jesus Christ. It was God who called Paul and his associates to proclaim this message, not a human whim or curiosity. Thus, Paul did not conduct himself in the ways of the world: he did not make decisions lightly, speak vaguely, or live haphazardly (1:12–17).

Second, it is the presence of the Spirit among the Corinthians that is evidence of their faith and a guarantee of their future inheritance (1:21–22). We know that the Corinthians could get this wrong; much of 1 Corinthians was written against a misunderstanding of how the Spirit works in believers.[7] Here Paul reminds them that God "anointed us" (that is, all of us, v. 21). Then he used a vivid metaphor, assuring his readers that God "set his seal

---

6. Hurtado, "Son of God," *DPL* 901, 903.
7. Furnish, *II Corinthians*, 150.

of ownership". on all of them; his Holy Spirit was a deposit given to them, "guaranteeing what is to come" (1:22; Eph 1:13–14). If they are truly "sealed by the Spirit," then they know that Paul's message is true. The Spirit affirms God's absolute faithfulness, and because God is faithful, Paul was faithful to deliver the clear, true word of God (1 Cor 1:8–9).

The Painful Visit (2:1)

Therefore, Paul's *actual plan* had to unfold in an unusual (and painful) way. He made one quick "emergency" visit to Corinth from Ephesus after he received a negative report from Timothy about the congregation. This quick visit was probably unplanned, but Timothy's report made it plain that Paul needed to get to Corinth. All the circumstances for this change of plans are uncertain, but it appears that when Paul left Corinth after his first church-planting visit there, the people had serious questions about Paul's author-ity, intentions, and actions. There must have been allegations about Paul's character and motivations, no doubt provoked by his rival missionaries who wanted the people to believe that Paul was self-serving, a weak messenger, and quite unreliable. What actually happened at this emergency meeting (2:1) is not totally clear, but it is possible that during this visit someone viciously slandered Paul and the church did not stand up for him. Paul forgives this personal attack in 2:5–11, saying that the offender hurt the whole church, not just Paul. Whatever was said or done drove Paul away from Corinth in a hurry, and with a heavy heart.[8]

A Tearful Letter (2:2–4)

On the heels of this painful visit, Paul wrote a (scathing?) letter to the Cor-inthians. This communication no longer exists, so we cannot be certain of what it said, but we know that it was an emotional nightmare for Paul. He could not bear to return to Corinth in person, so he wrote to them out of grief (1:23; 2:2–3). This so-called "tearful letter" (also called the "sorrowful letter," 2:4) is *not* our 1 Corinthians, but it is a letter lost to us today. It was written after 1 Corinthians and after the painful visit Paul just mentioned. This "tearful" or "severe" letter is very likely a primary reason for the writing of 2 Corinthians, as Paul needed to explain his motivations behind why it was written (2:3, 4; see 7:8–10) and redeem his relationship with his readers. In this letter, Paul addressed his readers with boldness and confronted them for their moral failures.[9] That is, in verse 2:9 he explains the reason for this letter

8. Furnish, *II Corinthians*, 159.
9. Garland, *2 Corinthians*, 135.

was "to see if you would stand the test and be obedient in everything." If the readers were truly "saved" and had truly repented of their sins, their moral and ethical behavior even in a very pagan culture would be demonstrated in their Christ-like lives and practices. He had real confidence in them and found joy in their faith (2:3). Yet, it is this "tearful letter" that is a key matter of dispute between Paul and the Corinthians, and a catalyst that nearly ruined their pastor-congregation relationship.[10]

Furthermore, this corrective (disciplinary) letter was sent in place of the first of the two visits to Corinth that Paul had promised (1:15). The "tearful letter" was not well received. It was a disappointment to some members of the congregation; the letter was a sore substitute for the promised visit.[11] In his absence, the relationship between the founder and the congregation had deteriorated rather quickly. Paul knew that the larger issue of his credibility as an apostle was becoming more significant. Their doubt was deepening, and his personal accountability was draining. Had he failed them? Was he too harsh? What happened next?

Thankfully, we see the rest of the story in chapter 7. Paul was able to rejoice at the effects of this "tearful letter": he knew the letter had caused them "godly sorrow," but "only for a little while" (7:8). And, by the grace of God, this "tearful," dreadful letter brought about the Corinthians' "repentance that leads to salvation" (7:10). Finally, and not to be missed, Paul emphasized that the emotional "tearful letter" was a pledge of "the depth of my love for you" (2:4) and was meant for the good of the Corinthians (2:9; 7:8–9). As a parent sends an emotional, pleading, correctional letter to a son or daughter out of love and concern, Paul wrote to people he truly loved and cared about; the letter caused as much pain for Paul to write as it did for the recipients to read it.

Offense and Joy (2:5–11)

Paul was called by God to a ministry that was first and foremost the proclamation of the gospel of Jesus Christ to unbelieving Gentiles. One of the fruits of this ministry was a church of believers in Corinth. Yet the Roman Gentiles had never seen a church before, and they had no idea what that meant. They had listened to many voices and speakers, and had heard other messages, but Paul and his message were different. He was different because he really loved them (2:4) and did not speak out of self-interest. Although they experienced the same empowering Holy Spirit in their lives, they were very diverse in their membership and had a variety of opinions. They were still divided over

---

10. Garland, *2 Corinthians*, 134.
11. Furnish, *II Corinthians*, 141, 144.

a number of issues (see 1 Cor 1:10–17). In response to their doubts and confusion, Paul began here in chapter 2, and moved through chapter 7, to explain to his readers just exactly what his ministry required and how it was distinctive from any other messages that they may have encountered. In view of the unfortunate events that took place in the church during the "painful visit," verses 2:5–11 are about forgiveness in ministry and the intentions of Satan. Then, verses 2:12–13 explain why Paul was writing to them from the northern area of Macedonia.

The effects of Paul's "painful" visit to Corinth (2 Cor 2:1) were not as he had hoped. The majority of the congregation may have accepted the corrective actions, but there must have been at least a portion of the church that disapproved of Paul. At some point in time, someone (an individual) had been the cause of Paul's grief (2:5). Very likely, this person spoke against Paul in some way or accused him of something, sharply denigrating his ministry and his character. Paul was challenged both personally and publically, yet he said "I have forgiven—if there was anything to forgive . . ." (2:10).

While we know neither exactly what was said about Paul nor the motivation behind the intentions of the offender, this incident has repercussions throughout this letter. No doubt the offense hurt Paul more than he lets on. If we surmise that Paul's opponents in Corinth were verbally disparaging him in the congregation, we can label such an offense what it really is—human sin. It may have been that the rival missionaries and "false apostles" (11:13) were envious of Paul and his position, and so labored to discredit, demean, and demolish Paul. These adversaries did not want to take over Paul's ministry as much as they wanted to promote their own authority and their own selfish interests. They were not working to provide encouragement and benefit for the congregation, but for themselves. Thus, the activities of his enemies were the result of raging envy, resentment, anger, and pride. "Envy, like the pride that spawns it, is inevitably comparative. Envy is resentment of someone else's good, plus the itch to despoil her of it." Envious people enjoy hurting others and rejoice in their misfortunes.[12] Perhaps these people were worried that Paul had an unfair advantage over them in Corinth because he was so well known that he did not need any recommendations from other people (3:1–3). Perhaps they were jealous of his ministry successes and easily found weaknesses and appearances that could be used against Paul.

Certainly, it was a personal injury between Paul and the one who caused the offense, but Paul was aware that this one incident touched the whole

---

12. Cornelius Plantinga Jr., *Not the Way It's Supposed to Be: A Breviary of Sin* (Grand Rapids: Eerdmans, 1995), 167–69.

congregation (2:5). Sin has a way of doing that—it does not affect the perpetrator only, but all the people around the sinner. It divides people and disrupts
unity within a church. Paul warned the believers against blatant sins within
the congregation that can destroy a church (see Rom 13:11–14). Furthermore,
from chapter 2 we can jump to chapter 12 of this letter, where Paul increased
his warnings against the destructive "wrong-doers" who polluted the church
at Corinth. In chapter 12, Paul was concerned that when he visited the
Corinthians for a third time, he would be "grieved," that he would find no
repentance, and see a continuation of the same sins that were the root of the
problems in 2:5: "For I am afraid that when I come I may not find you as I
want you to be, and you may not find me as you want me to be. I fear that
there may be discord, jealousy, fits of rage, selfish ambition, slander, gossip,
arrogance and disorder" (12:20; see further comments on this passage).

Forgiveness in the Church

Nevertheless, it appears that the church (or at least an obedient majority) had
confronted the one sinner in 2:5 and disciplined the individual in some way.
Paul indicated that the church's punishment was sufficient (2:6). Like the sin
committed against Paul and the entire church, forgiveness, comfort, and love
for the offender must be granted for the sake of the entire church (2:7–10).

One of the most demanding and the most healing elements of Christian
ministry is forgiveness. Necessary and often difficult, ministers must forgive
terrible words, intentions, attitudes, and behaviors of the very people whom
they try to serve. Paul stood up for this person, which may have been exactly
what the congregation did *not* do for Paul during the "painful visit." The
offense by this person toward Paul and the lack of support for their founder
by the other church members was the cause of the "tearful letter" (2:4).

In forgiving the sins of this individual, Paul set an example for the whole
church that forgiveness can be the agent of reconciliation, a topic we will see
in chapter 5. This person is not the same "immoral brother" that we see in
1 Corinthians 5:1; in that case, the immoral behavior was not a slanderous
insult against Paul personally as it was in 2 Corinthians 2:5–11. It is interesting, however, to see that in both cases the entire congregation is affected
by one person's malfunction. In both cases Paul reflects on the role of Satan
in human sinful nature (1 Cor 5:5; 2 Cor 2:11). Paul does not spend a lot of
time discussing Satan in his letters, but we can see in 1 Corinthians 5:11 how
immoral behavior is one example of the subtle but tenacious designs of Satan
that are hostile to churches and to God's ministry. Although to call oneself a
Christian and continue to live an intentionally sinful life is reprehensible and
gives a false testimony about Christ, the lack of forgiveness in a congregation

can be like an evil cancer that spreads and rots the bonds of love, trust, and confidence. Here, Paul warns the church to be on their guard because "we are not unaware of his schemes!" (2 Cor 2:11). "Paul could well be thinking of how Satan can take advantage of an unforgiving, overly legalistic attitude to sow division and dissension in the church."[13]

Thus, Paul forgave the offender "in the sight of Christ for your sake" (2:10). For the sake of the whole church, he called upon Christ as his witness to the forgiveness of this one who hurt him. We might say that Paul's act of forgiveness is a test case, or a case in point for the entire congregation. The test was, as Christ-followers, were they being obedient in everything that Paul had taught them, in behavior, in attitudes, and in actions (2:9)? Since he had to write the "tearful letter," it is likely that they were not living the kind of moral and ethical lives Paul expected. Moreover, to reject Paul's warnings and criticisms was to reject Christ. "Sin is disruption of created harmony and then resistance to divine restoration of that harmony. Above all, sin disrupts and resists the vital human relation to God, and it does all this disrupting and resisting in a number of intertwined ways."[14] How the church responded to Paul's admonitions was proof of their true character.

While the Corinthians held strong interest in using their spiritual gifts and the power of the Holy Spirit (as seen in 1 Corinthians), they were also susceptible to other sinister spiritual invasions. That is, Paul must have seen clear evidence of demonic attack on the church and within the congregation (2:11). One man among them was a part of an immoral sexual union (1 Cor 5:1–5; 6:12–20). Other believers were participating in idolatrous temple rituals and feasts with their pagan neighbors (1 Cor 10:18–22). Hence, Paul had to send words of warning to them in this letter. In the first half of 2 Corinthians Paul recognized the work of Satan in the false verbal accusations and slanderous injuries about Paul's apostolic mission and ministry. In 11:13–15 we discover that the "false apostles" in the church were "masquerading as servants of righteousness," but in reality, were part of the deceptive "schemes" of Satan.[15]

In addition, the punishment for the sin of the wrongdoer must be appropriate to the offense; excessive punishment could "overwhelm" the sinner with "excessive sorrow" (2:5–8). The purpose of church discipline, Paul reminded them, was to urge repentance and promote reconciliation. Indeed, this situation was a perfect opportunity for Satan to fill the offender with resentment and hostility instead of repentance and humility, thereby further injuring the

---

13. Belleville, 2 *Corinthians*, 76.

14. Plantinga, *Not the Way It's Supposed to Be*, 5.

15. See comments on 11:13–15 for more details concerning Paul's views on Satan and his "masquerading" imagery.

entire congregation. How does a church cope with Satan's "schemes"? We are blessed to have Paul's famous imagery of the "armor of God" given to every believer to use against satanic forces; this is found in Ephesians 6:11–17, and it applies to individuals as well as to entire congregations.[16]

Testing, Testing

Paul explained that he wrote the "tearful letter" (2:4) for the purpose of "seeing if you [the Corinthians] would stand the test" and be "obedient" (2:9). The idea of testing is repeated in 13:5 where Paul challenges the people to examine their own hearts. Yet, this kind of testing is not the same as an academic exam with which we are familiar today. In this case, Paul was trying to discern the worth or quality of his readers; literally, he was writing "that I might know your quality." Scientists perform this kind of examination to determine if a product (like a dam or a pharmaceutical drug) maintains the highest possible quality to insure consumer trust. It was the actions of the believers that indicted the true authenticity of their faith. The specific test in 2:9 was related more to their obedience to the gospel teachings of Paul and to their rejection of sin in their midst, and less to doing anything wrong (13:6–7). Thus, the groundwork of Paul's ministry to the Gentiles rested in his readers' obedience to the Christian message proclaimed by Paul (2:9; Rom 6:16–18). The "test" or the "quality" of their obedience was demonstrated in the sincerity of their love for fellow-believers and their commitment to Christ (2 Cor 8:8).[17]

Later when Paul reiterates the concept of testing, he is less tactful in his instructions. Paul warned that he was ready to "punish every act of disobedience" among the Corinthians until "your obedience is complete" (10:5–6). He asked the Corinthians to prove that their faith in Christ was genuine (13:5). That is, he was hoping that on his next visit to Corinth, he would find that the readers had cleaned up their act. They would fail the test if they were not properly living their faith in Christ, but were listening instead to the "false apostles" (his opponents, see details in chapter 13).

Anxiety in Macedonia (2:12–13)

Pressing on with this ministry, what Paul experienced in Troas is not unusual for people in Christian leadership (2:12–13). The story of a visit to Macedonia begins in 1 Corinthians 16:5 with Paul's promised visit to this area in northern Greece. But at this point, he was feeling pulled in two opposite

---

16. Barton et al., *1 and 2 Corinthians*, 293–94.
17. Furnish, *II Corinthians*, 157.

directions, literally. While he was given an excellent opportunity to minister to those in Troas, he was still anxious and apprehensive about the Corinthian church. Should he go to Troas on the Asian coast, or should he return to Corinth in southern Greece? Thus, in these two verses, Paul was attempting to explain his dilemma and decision, and why he was ultimately writing this letter to them (2 Corinthians) from Macedonia. He was in a battle for his call to ministry and his conduct, and he felt the pressure of overcoming the hindrances of Satan (2:11). Second, often it is difficult to minister in one situation when one's heart and mind are consumed by anxiety about another situation. Conflicts at Corinth, the "painful visit" and the "tearful letter," Paul's rival opponents, slander, rumors, doubts, and fears were all contributing to his uneasiness and "no peace of mind" in Troas (2:13). The conflicts disturbed Paul so much that he was unable to be an effective evangelist in Troas. As Garland writes, "church strife never speeds up the gospel's advance."[18]

"My Brother Titus"

In these verses, we see the first mention of Paul's co-worker, Titus, who was a Gentile Christian and a very important asset to Paul's ministry (Gal 2:1–5). He was a "true son" to Paul, perhaps converted by Paul to Christianity (Tit 1:4), and a valuable "partner and fellow worker" on the missionary field (2 Cor 8:23). From what we read in this letter, we can see that Titus was a key player in the reconciliation of Paul and the Corinthians, and in collecting the funds for the "saints" in Jerusalem (see 2:13; 7:6, 13–14; 8:6, 16–21; 12:18). Apparently, Titus was a problem solver: he was assigned to appoint elders in the newly founded churches and deal with difficult dissenters, "idle talkers and deceivers" in the communities (Titus 1:1–14). Not an easy job. Titus was sent by Paul to Corinth where he did encounter problems including, but not limited to, the very same false teachers that were disparaging Paul and questioning his apostleship.

Titus was probably the bearer of Paul's "tearful letter" to the church. He relayed a message of correction and (in their view) of broken promises concerning Paul's visits to Corinth. So, Paul was anxious to hear from Titus about how he got along within the deteriorating Corinthian situation (2 Cor 2:13). When he discovered that Titus was unable to connect with Paul in Troas, Paul's anxiety only increased. No doubt he was concerned and worried about Titus's travel safety, how he was received in Corinth, and how the church reacted to Titus's visit. We know that eventually Paul and Titus did join one another, and it was a blessing to Paul. God's plans did take precedence over those of Satan, and Titus had a glowing report for Paul about the Corinthians.

---

18. Garland, *2 Corinthians*, 133.

For the rest of the story, we need to jump over to chapter 7 of this letter, where we see parallel themes repeated. The narrative continues in 7:5–16 when Paul finally connected with Titus and received his desired good report. The emotional trauma ("grief and sorrow") of chapter 2 is seen as redemptive, "godly sorrow" in 7:8–10. The divine comfort in chapter 1 is reiterated in 7:6–7. To their credit, the sorrow and grief in the church (2:5) was transformed into "happiness" for Paul (7:7, 9) and an "encouragement" (7:13). That is, both Paul and his readers experienced the deliverance and salvation of God through the suffering, grief, sorrow, and hardships of human life. Despite his trials and disappointments, Paul punctuated the key principle expressed in 1:9—that God's grace is always sufficient, and that human weakness is God's opportunity to display his power. "Thanks be to God," Paul exclaimed, despite his difficulties, and then Paul demonstrated how Christians are led in triumph by God in Christ (2:14–17).

LIVE the Story

How many of us have experienced a change of plans that causes a run-in with a relative or upsets business colleagues? Have you ever written an email to avoid a conflict with someone face-to-face? Human communication is easy to misinterpret and misunderstand, especially back in a time when it depended on slow, written transmission. Even short emails today lack the intonation and emotions that aid in understanding. The church misunderstood Paul's motives and his message (1:14), yet Paul was hopeful that he could rectify the situation so they could all live together as brothers and sisters in Christ.

With regard to co-workers in ministry, Paul loved Titus like a son or a brother in Christ; he was very concerned about his fellow worker. This is a paradigm that can be shared with all Christian ministries. Following Paul's example, we must work together as a team on ministry staffs, caring for each other without malice or competition. In fact, we must take responsibility for the safety and welfare of all those people who are in our "family of God," that is, the church. Awareness is a key: Who is missing from regular worship or other church gatherings? Who haven't you seen for a while? What action can you take to let them know you are concerned?[19] Leaders can be very protective of "their" ministries, sometimes at the expense of the ministry of other people on staff. As an example, once a lead pastor told the women of his church that they could neither promote nor attend a regional women's ministry retreat that was to take place in their city.

---

19. Barton et al., *1 and 2 Corinthians*, 298.

Unfortunately, the church calendar got confused, and the all-church revival was planned for the same weekend as the women's retreat, which was already scheduled by the state organization. The lead pastor said that the all-church event took precedence over the women-only event. Misunderstandings and calendar conflicts can and do happen. Yet our attitude should be one of cooperation: How can we work together to resolve these issues? How can I support you in your ministry? It is all important in the big kingdom picture.

Forgiveness

One offender (2:5) damaged Paul's relationship with the entire church; one bad apple spoiled the whole bunch. Today, the denigrating, back-stabbing, slanderous rumors concerning a pastor (often begun by only one person) can infiltrate the church and will ruin the pastor-congregation relationship. While the offense affected the entire church, Paul then instructed the entire church to forgive the one who initiated the hurt (2:7). How could Paul do this? Is he just ignoring the sin, the injury, the lies? What is a pastor to do?

The first reality we all must face is that human beings are sinful creatures. Even those who have confessed Jesus Christ as their Savior fall back into old selfish habits. The nicest people in the world can thoughtlessly criticize and pass judgment on others in a way that injures multiple relationships. The author of 1 John is speaking truth when he wrote, "If we claim to be without sin, we deceive ourselves and the truth is not in us. If we confess our sins, he is faithful and just and will forgive us our sins and purify us from all unrighteousness. If we claim we have not sinned, we make him out to be a liar and his word is not in us" (1 John 1:8–10). This author casts no blame; this is not a judgment on or condemnation of humanity. It is simply a diagnosis, an insightful view into the nature of human beings. Must we say, "oh well, that's just the way I am" and ignore the veracity of our transgressions? If not, how are we released from the bondage of this sinful condition?

God is in charge of the spiritual laundry. It is he who "cleanses" us and deletes our sins (1 John 1:7). Eugene Peterson says that if we are pretentious enough to deny our sinfulness or marginalize our sins, then the result may be perfectionism. That is, if I try hard enough, and use the right methods, programs, and procedures, I can project a veneer of being without failure—I can achieve excellence. This can easily happen in the trials of ministry; perfectionists can become workaholics living under the constant strain of their own goals and achievements.

By ignoring the ubiquity of sin they persist in the illusion that if they accomplish just one more mission, master just one more act of devotion, successfully avoid contamination with just one more sloppily living Christian, get one more program up and running, they will emerge head and shoulders above all others.[20]

The perfectionist ends up without the forgiveness of God and without the love of other people.

Thus, Peterson says, "the only sane (and biblical) approach to sin is through the expiation/forgiveness, the sacrificial and operative center of which is Jesus Christ—forgiveness moved by love."[21] Only God is the beginning and the end of the kind of love that forgives human failings.

Recognition of personal sin does affect the entire church, as Peterson writes further: "A life of love in the community is secured by a life of forgiveness by God. That which we cannot do for ourselves through education or government or business is done for us by God in Christ. This is the foundation, the only foundation, on which a community of love can be formed."[22]

Satan's Schemes

In the introduction to *The Screwtape Letters*, C. S. Lewis wrote, "There are two equal and opposite errors into which our race can fall about the devils. One is to disbelieve in their existence. The other is to believe, and to feel an excessive and unhealthy interest in them."[23]

In agreement, Paul does not write excessively about devils in his letters, yet we can surmise that he was well aware of the spiritual battle that rages against believers in general and against anyone in the service of the Lord in particular. The battle continues to this day. It is Satan's desire to divide and destroy the Christian church, the family of God, and the family unit of human beings. He would love to sidetrack, discourage, or effectively negate all Christian ministry. We ignore Paul's warning in this letter (2 Cor 2:11) at our own peril. Satan can successfully steal our encouragement, our confidence, and our joy (7:4). His tools include doubt, injury, unforgiveness, and disappointment. We cannot let him win. The great Reformer Martin Luther said, "The best way to drive out the devil, if he will not yield to texts of Scripture, is to jeer and flout him, for he cannot bear scorn."[24]

In view of Satan's schemes, perhaps church discipline is the most difficult

---

20. Peterson, *Christ Plays in Ten Thousand Places*, 320.
21. Peterson, *Christ Plays in Ten Thousand Places*, 321.
22. Peterson, *Christ Plays in Ten Thousand Places*, 319–20.
23. C. S. Lewis, "The Screwtape Letters," in *The Complete C. S. Lewis Signature Classics* (New York: HarperSan Francisco, 2002), 183.
24. Lewis, "Screwtape Letters," 181.

part of ministry. Even as redeemed creatures, humans can and do sin; we can be disobedient and intentionally injure one another. Discipline, then, is necessary and in the best interest of the entire church and all of Christendom. It can help keep the church "pure" (7:1) and "obedient" (2:9), but its purpose is not to humiliate and destroy the person. Kind and thoughtful discipline should bring wrongdoers to repentance, restoration, and reconciliation. Jesus talked about church discipline in Matthew 18:15–20, where he initiated what we might call "corporate confrontation": take one or two witnesses when confronting the person to be disciplined, and if he or she refuses to listen, tell it to the church.

I am personally aware of people who have been excommunicated from the church, injured, and dishonored, because of abortions, divorces, and embezzlement. Often sinful people are injured, hurting people. They are determined to never return to a church that cannot forgive, redeem, and restore. Satan tries to harm the church by tempting leaders to use discipline in an unforgiving, unloving way. C. S. Lewis writes, "Readers are advised to remember that the devil is a liar," and he is to be scorned for his deceptions.[25] It is the job of the church to unmask his lies. Then, we must lovingly, respectfully, and carefully allow God to show us how to redeem and heal. Personal anger, greed, power, and position must never be expelled under the "guise of church discipline."[26]

The war in heaven, the fight of good versus evil, was started before anyone can remember. At the birth of Jesus, Savior and Redeemer, God came to earth to take back all of humanity from the malicious grasp of the forces of evil. Sin, iniquity, immorality, and wickedness are conquered ("whitewashed"), and Jesus Christ, the sacrificial Lamb, is triumphant:

> And the dragon stood before the woman who was about to give birth, so that he might devour her child the moment it was born. . . . Then war broke out in heaven (Rev 12:4b, 7).

> This birth's a signal for war. Lovers fight,
> Friends fall out. Merry toasts from flagons
> Of punch are swallowed in the maw of dragons.
> Will mother and baby survive this devil night?
> I've done my share of fighting in the traffic
> Kitchen quarrels, playground fisticuffs;
> Every cherub choir has its share of toughs,

---

25. Lewis, "Screwtape Letters," 183.
26. Barton et al., *1 and 2 Corinthians*, 295.

And then one day I learned the fight was cosmic.
Truce: I lay down arms; my arms filled up
With gifts: wild and tame, real and stuffed
Lions. Lambs play; oxen low,
The infant fathers festive force. One crow
Croaks defiance into the shalom whiteness,
Empty, satanic bluster against the brightness.[27]

---

27. Peterson, *Contemplative Pastor*, 171.

LISTEN to the Story

¹⁴ But thanks be to God, who always leads us as captives in Christ's triumphal procession and uses us to spread the aroma of the knowledge of him everywhere. ¹⁵ For we are to God the pleasing aroma of Christ among those who are being saved and those who are perishing. ¹⁶ To the one we are an aroma that brings death; to the other, an aroma that brings life. And who is equal to such a task? ¹⁷ Unlike so many, we do not peddle the word of God for profit. On the contrary, in Christ we speak before God with sincerity, as those sent from God.

³:¹ Are we beginning to commend ourselves again? Or do we need, like some people, letters of recommendation to you or from you? ² You yourselves are our letter, written on our hearts, known and read by everyone. ³ You show that you are a letter from Christ, the result of our ministry, written not with ink but with the Spirit of the living God, not on tablets of stone but on tablets of human hearts.

⁴ Such confidence we have through Christ before God. ⁵ Not that we are competent in ourselves to claim anything for ourselves, but our competence comes from God. ⁶ He has made us competent as ministers of a new covenant—not of the letter but of the Spirit; for the letter kills, but the Spirit gives life.

Listening to the Text in the Story: **Triumphal Procession**, 1 Thessalonians 4:15–18; **Fragrance**, Genesis 8:20–21; Exodus 29:18, 25, 41; 30:22–38; Leviticus 1:9, 13, 17; Ezekiel 20:40–41; Ephesians 5:2; **Tablets of Stone**, Exodus 24:12; 31:18; 32:15–16; 34:1–14; Ezekiel 11:18–20; 36:26–27; Jeremiah 31:31–34; Proverbs 2:1–5; 3:5–6; Psalm 1; 111:10; **Letters**, Romans 16:1–16; Philippians 2:19–29; **Worship**, Exodus 29:18, 25, 41; 30:22–38; Leviticus 1:9, 13, 17; Ezekiel 37:14; **New Covenant**, Jeremiah 31:31; Ezekiel 11:19–20; 36:26; Isaiah 42:8–9; 48:6; 65:17; 66:22.

In this passage, we can *smell* the story! In the summer of 2015, there was an oddity in the Denver Botanic Gardens greenhouse. On display was the rare "corpse plant," a giant (4–5 feet tall) plant that decides to bloom only once about every ten years. When it does finally open, the one huge blossom has a rank odor that reminds one of burning flesh—hence, the appropriate nickname. Unfortunately, the rare blossom is observed from behind a window because the smell is so bad. Fortunately, the blossom lasts only about 48 hours, so it is barely tolerated by interested professional and amateur botanists. In the same way, soldiers tell us that the "smell of death," or burning flesh on the battlefield never quite leaves their nostrils; the smell is so repugnant, it is unforgettable. Pleasant fragrances and aromas, as well as horrific smells, augment human understanding and jog human memory. Paul masterfully uses olfactory images to heighten the readers' appreciation for the demands of Christian ministry.

After a word of praise to the Father, Paul employs three distinct metaphors in only four verses (2:14–17). Just three brief Greek sentences are translated into three verses in English in most of our Bibles. Yet, this short passage is rich and deep, teeming with Paul's triumphant faith in Jesus Christ. These three verses open a dense passage that demonstrates Paul's confidence and competence in his own Christian ministry that takes his readers to the beginning of chapter four. Here in chapter two, Paul uses the familiar imagery of a triumphal procession, then he uses aroma imagery as unmistakable as the stinky plant at the botanic gardens. Third, Paul uses the picture of a peddler or a merchant who sells his wares for a living. How is it possible that these three images are related to each other? More specifically, how are verses 14 through 16 related to verse 17? What do these verses teach us about Paul's triumphal faith? We will look at these images separately and then try to connect them to fully understand what Paul is saying in this dense passage.

If 2:14–17 provides pictures of the nature of the Christian gospel and the responsibilities of those who are called to proclaim it, then 3:1 anticipates the allegation from his readers that Paul may be boasting about his own strength and evidence of his abilities. He reminded his readers that he and his companions did not need proof of their authenticity, as other false teachers may have supplied. There was no need for such letters about him and the legitimacy of his ministry because there was already plenty of proof within the church—the Corinthian believers themselves.

In 2:16, we hear Paul asking a key question, "Who is equal to such a task?" In truth, are any of us truly qualified and proficient to proclaim the gospel of Jesus Christ in such a manner that is pleasing to God? It is a demanding task for human beings to teach, preach, and transmit the word of God correctly.

Paul gave his short answer in 2:17b in sharp contrast to the false teachers who opposed him: "*we* speak before God with sincerity, as those sent from God." Then, in 3:4–6, he expanded his answer more fully. While the apostle may not have felt confident in his own human strength and knowledge, Paul's great confidence and his competence were from God, and were nothing that he earned or produced by himself. Paul had no capacity even to evaluate the results of his own ministry (3:5) because the results are left up to God. He completely rejected any credit for himself and acknowledged that all the activities of ministry are credited to God. Finally, Paul states that he has confidence and competence in ministry because he and his colleagues are "ministers of a new covenant" (3:6). It is the first time he mentions the "new covenant" in this letter, and Paul will expand on this concept in the remainder of the third chapter and into chapter 4. He is reminding his readers that God is doing a "new thing" with the gospel of Jesus Christ, and Paul is a part of it. Finally, he wraps up this short section with the repetition of two memorable antitheses of "death and life" (3:6; see 2:16) and "the letter and the Spirit," (3:3, 6).

EXPLAIN the Story

Triumphal Faith (2:14–17)

Paul had no peace of mind in Troas (2:13), even though he was assured of two things: he was called by God to ministry in Corinth, and he was faithful to that call. So, in 2:14–17, Paul reveals the characteristics of Christian ministry, in Paul's day and in ours. Paul goes on to develop these aspects of Christian ministry more fully in chapters 3–7 so his readers would get a fuller picture (a fuller understanding, 1:14) of what his ministry was all about.

Abruptly, Paul shifted to a scene of thanksgiving and victory: "But thanks be to God who always leads us . . . in Christ's triumphal procession . . . " (2:14). One of the most common themes we see throughout Paul's epistles is thanksgiving. His words of gratitude pop up periodically in his writing because Paul can be overwhelmed with his thoughts about God's mercy and grace toward Paul himself and toward God's redeemed people.[1]

Following the outburst of praise, Paul made reference to a "triumphal procession" (2:14). Perhaps the imagery is that of the Roman emperor victoriously parading into a city, leading the conquered enemy. A festive celebration, the imperial procession would include the military victor (the emperor himself or high-ranking military leader), the victorious soldiers in regal dress,

---

1. See Rom 1:8; 1 Cor 1:4–6; Eph 1:16; Phil 1:3–6; and Col 1:3–4.

and the enslaved captives taken from the city or region. The common people lined the streets to watch, cheering and applauding the conquerors, and jeering the defeated.[2] Banners were waved, and often the air was filled with the sweet smells of burning spices to greet the emperor. An alternative suggestion could be a religious procession of people, singing and dancing, going toward a temple of pagan gods or goddesses. In fact, the verb "leading in triumph" is from a related noun that was a "hymn sung to the god Dionysus (or Bacchus) during festal processions."[3] The Gentiles in the Roman Empire would be reminded of the firmly established traditions of burning incense as a sacrificial act to the pagan gods in their local temples. It was important to honor the deity or the emperor with incense, so the air would be filled with a great deal of noise and aromas in a celebratory fashion. Either way, the sights and smells of a triumphal procession would be very familiar to the Corinthian people.

In verses 14–16, Paul created a vivid, sensory rift: there are those people who have received the gospel message and those who have not. Through Christian believers, God spreads the fragrance of the knowledge of Christ across the world (v. 15). That is, believers who know Christ are a sweet "aroma" to God! Yet, those who reject the gospel are perishing without the knowledge of Christ, and to them, those who proclaim the message are the smell of death (2:16). Despite trials, he pictured himself and his ministry colleagues as victorious partners with God in the battle of the gospel of Christ. To be sure, the true ministers of the gospel were "the aroma of Christ to God" (2:15 NRSV), in contrast to so many others who proclaimed the wrong gospel (2:17). Thus, we see the dual character of the "fragrance" of the gospel message. On the one hand, those who preach and teach the knowledge of Christ and the true gospel are an appealing "aroma" to God (2:15), and the remarkable victory of Christ is the sweet "fragrance" of life in those who are "being saved" (2:16). On the other hand, to those who proclaim a false gospel that is not able to save people, the true ministers of God (like Paul) are the "smell of death." Like the imperial procession, there are those who are "saved" and victorious in the battle, and those people who are "perishing," still enslaved in chains of sins and ignorance.

Another plausible option for Paul's reference to "fragrance" in 2:15–16 is connected to the burnt offerings and holy sacrifices that were offered to and accepted by the Lord. In the OT, we see that the sacrificial offerings that

2. Paul Brooks Duff, "Metaphor, Motif and Meaning: The Rhetorical Strategy behind the Image 'Led in Triumph' in 2 Corinthians 2:14," *CBQ* 53.1 (1991): 79–92.
3. Harris, *Second Corinthians*, 243.

pleased the Lord exhibited the faithful worship of him by his people as the One True God. The offerings made to the Lord by fire or the "pleasing aroma" of burnt offerings delighted God, in a figurative sense, and were symbolic of his delight when his people faithfully worshiped him (see Exod 29:18, 25, 41; Lev 1:9, 13, 17). Burnt offerings were offered to the Lord every morning and evening in the temple in ancient Israel. Like hamburgers being barbequed outdoors in my neighborhood, the smell of these sacrifices reminded the people of something good and expressed their constant devotion to God. In contrast, the odor of sacrifices offered to false idols is repugnant to the Lord and demonstrates the disobedience and rebellion of his people (1 Sam 15:22–23; Ezek 20:39–44; Pss 51:16–17; 106:28, 36–39).

In addition, special fragrances were holy reminders for the people of their God, Yahweh. In the days of Moses, perfumes and fine spices were made into holy anointing oil ("a fragrant blend") for the Tent of Meeting, to consecrate the ark, the accessories, and the altar, as well as the priests themselves. As directed by God, fragrant spices and a blend of incense were made for the Tent of Meeting, the place where God met with Moses. Thus, it became a sacred formula and very "holy to the Lord" (Exod 30:22–38). In the same way, Paul uses the image of the "fragrant offering" for Jesus himself; the sacrifice of Jesus for his people is the supreme "fragrant offering" and the superlative offering acceptable to God (Eph 5:2).

Paul cleverly tied the two images together: the "triumphal" victorious gospel message and the sweet "fragrance" of Christ for those who believe it. Yet, the image of a "peddler" in verse 17 seems awkward and out of place. Literally, Paul wrote that "we are not like the many peddling or huckstering the word of God."[4] How is a "peddler" attached to a "victory" scene? Again, a picture from the first century will help us to understand the connection. The word used by Paul here is unique in the NT and can have both a neutral meaning (a "retailer, merchant") or a pejorative meaning. In a negative sense, this person was the middle man between the product wholesaler and the retail customer. This middle man could adjust prices or manipulate goods to his own advantage and financial profit.[5] His reputation was generally not a good one, since it was assumed he would be deceitful and may have had mercenary intents. He would sell the spices and fragrances to people for their festive processions and pagan worship. Indeed, crooked peddlers often claimed to sell a drug or an elixir as a therapeutic medicine to aid in healing physical ailments. Some medicinal products (spices, perfumes) were even said to give life to the

4. Furnish, *II Corinthians*, 191.
5. Harris, *Second Corinthians*, 253.

patient (for a tidy sum). This was quite a contrast to the sweet fragrance of Christ that really did give life to the believer.[6]

Employing these images, Paul declared that he was not a fraud, and his motives were not selfish greed. Instead, his message was rooted in Christ, and his ministry was not one of deception or worldly wisdom (1:17). Paul spoke and acted by the grace of God with sincerity, as one who represented God in his proclamations (2:17). He denied being motivated by material or financial gain, deception, or recognition. He confessed that there was a dual effect to his ministry; he recognized that it could be received and accepted, or it could be denied and rejected.[7] Further, Paul's use of the antithetical imagery ("life and death") in this section of his letter is to remind the readers of the two antithetical kinds of knowledge. That is, the Corinthians can pursue the worldly knowledge that Paul reveals in his first letter to the Corinthians (1 Corinthians 1:18–31), or they can accept and embrace the wisdom of God (1 Cor 3:18–23) that was a central point of Paul's ministry. The truth of Paul's message is that Jesus came to overcome death and give eternal life to believers (see John 6:61–64; 10:28; 11:25–26; 17:2; 1 Cor 15:20–26; 2 Cor 2:16; 3:6; 4:10; 5:4). They must choose one or the other—life or death.

This was the nature of Paul's gospel message. It is not the one who merely delivers the message who does the splitting between belief and unbelief. As God's representative, Paul could do nothing but proclaim the truth that he had been given and let the chips fall where they may. He proclaimed this essential message as one sent from God, and then the people who heard the message had the duty to accept or reject the knowledge of Christ. In 2:17, Paul answered his own question posed in 2:16.

Indeed, these verses are our first insight into the false teachers who had infiltrated the Corinthian church, attacking Paul's apostolic authority, his personal integrity, and his intentions. There may have been accusations that his gospel was obscure or misleading, but Paul could defend himself and his ministry by arguing that he and his colleagues preached the true life-giving gospel of Jesus Christ with complete sincerity and were not seeking to profit from their work. His adversaries, on the other hand, were seeking a financial harvest from the Corinthians, and they were certain they were quite able to carry out the demands of a gospel messenger under their own capabilities (2:16).

A key passage in the development of Paul's depiction of his opponents is 2:14–17, showing one aspect of their lack of integrity that the readers must

---

6. Tzvi Novick, "Peddling Scents: Merchandise and Meaning in 2 Corinthians 2:14–17," *JBL* 130.3 (2011): 543–49.

7. Novick, "Peddling Scents," 548.

not forget as Paul continued on with this defense (see 4:5; 5:12). The three images in 2:14–17 illustrate to the readers the outpouring of God's grace in the triumphal faith of the believers and the adequacy of that grace to give a fragrant life to each one who believes. No matter how threatening life (and ministry!) can become, it is God's grace through Jesus Christ that is victorious.

Ministry Credentials (3:1–3)

Students often ask their professors to write a recommendation for them to attend a college, a graduate school, or for a career position. Bosses may write recommendations for employees who leave a company for another opportunity. In our culture, as in Paul's society, it would be very unusual for a person to apply for a job or to take a post without a résumé or a *curriculum vitae* in hand. The first century Roman Empire was a mobile society, so there was a need for introductory letters or letters of personal achievements and references that a person carried as verification of one's position. For an itinerant speaker, teacher, or orator, it was mandatory to carry such a letter as one traveled from town to town to verify one's authority and credibility.[8] As in our day, there was always a suspicion that a teacher/speaker could be an imposter who would likely claim to have new and better ideas or all the right answers. Knowing how important they are, Paul had actually written required recommendations for his friends and fellow workers, such as Timothy and those who had worked very hard as listed in Romans 16:1–16.

Yet, after explaining his gospel message, his commissioning by God, his purpose, and his intentions in 2:14–17, Paul asked his readers if they still needed more proof that he was legitimate. Apparently, the readers had fears that Paul was unable or unwilling to produce these kinds of acceptable credentials about himself ("letters of recommendation," 3:1). But Paul had founded the Corinthian church, and as a missionary in a new area of work, he had no established congregation to send him with a letter of recommendation.[9] The self-seeking "peddlers" in 2:17 may have carried falsified letters of recommendation that they were willing to flash before the Corinthians as "authentic" proof of their position. Paul recognized that the words he spoke or wrote could be twisted and misunderstood in an antagonistic manner by his challengers who said that they were the legitimate teachers of apostolic truth. It is possible that the false teachers may have presented the community with false or forged letters, again demonstrating their boastful, unethical, and self-serving methods. However, because Paul did not carry around such letters

---

8. Belleville, *2 Corinthians*, 87.
9. Furnish, *II Corinthians*, 193.

about himself on his missionary journeys, this was an easy point of attack by his opponents attempting to discredit him and his message. In fact, the phrase "to you or from you" in 3:1 implies that these false teachers were open to receiving recommendations for themselves and taking credit for the efforts of others.[10] Paul writes that he does not need such confirmation because he was doing a new thing in Corinth, planting a new church, which was his own work. Thus, the work that he had already accomplished in the lives of the Corinthians was enough evidence of his competency and his trustworthiness (3:2–3).

Regardless of their motives, Paul neither condemns nor accuses his opponents outright, but points to the readers themselves as a credible substantiation of his successful missionary efforts. The presence of the Holy Spirit (1 Cor 1:5–7; 2:4–5) and the transformed lives of the Corinthian Christians were the result of the efforts of Paul and his companions, and that was simply enough credibility. Not only were they changed as a result of Paul's message, but the change was evident to "everyone" (2 Cor 3:2). This implies that the impact of Paul's work in Corinth was plain for all to see and was pervasive in the region, in spite of what his opponents said. Simply stated, Paul saw his role as a true apostle as one of servanthood—not to serve his own interests, but those of Christ. This basic theme is foundational to chapters 2–5.

Paul then employs a clever play on words in 3:3. Reflecting on the acceptable, written, physical letter of recommendation, he refers to a "letter from Christ," or a spiritual confirmation, that is seen in the transformation of the Corinthians themselves. This spiritual transformation is not visible on paper (or parchment) like a letter, but is written on "human hearts" (3:3). Words written in ink on parchment or papyrus (common in biblical times) may fade with time, and stone tablets can be broken. It is important to note here that Paul is thinking about the ancient tablets of stone that were the laws given to Moses as part of the old covenant (Exod 34:1–14). The sharp contrast between the "letter" (of the law) and the "Spirit" (in the human heart) that Paul uses here reflects the influence of the OT prophets Jeremiah (31:31–34) and Ezekiel (36:26), who spoke of a new, "everlasting" covenant that is "written on their hearts." The contrasting images of the old and the new covenants continue in Paul's arguments in 3:7–11. The Corinthians must remember that no words written by human hands on destructible materials can survive as long as the words of "the Spirit of the living God" and the eternal life that he gives (3:3).

The "Spirit of the living God" in 3:3 is identical to the "Holy Spirit," "the Spirit of God," "his Spirit" and "the Spirit of Christ" (see the discussion of 2 Cor 1:22), titles employed by Paul that all refer to the Third Person of the

---

10. Belleville, *2 Corinthians*, 88.

Trinity. Gordon Fee has done a great deal of research concerning the Holy Spirit in the letters of Paul, and Fee insists that while Paul's primary focus in his Corinthian letters is the work of Jesus Christ, he refers to the "Spirit" by various titles 140 times throughout his writings. In other words, there is an emphasis found in Paul's writings on the Spirit of God that is often overlooked by Christian readers today. Numerous texts indicate to us that Paul knew the indwelling Spirit of God, whose presence was not only in the individual believer, but also in the midst of his people. That is, "God's Spirit means the presence of God himself and that by putting 'my Spirit in you . . . you will live'" (Ezek 37:14).[11] "When Paul attributes to the Spirit the "writing" of the letter from Christ, this is in full accord with his conviction that his gospel has been able to take root in places like Corinth because of the powerful working of the Spirit (e.g., 2 Cor 1:22; 1 Cor 2:4; Gal 3:2–5; 1 Thess 1:5–6)."[12]

Because the "Spirit of the living God" had taken up residence in and among the Corinthian believers, in ways so evident that there was no need for any other recommendations, the gospel and ministry of Paul were surely the apostolic truth and needed no more confirmation (see 1 Cor 1:7; 2:4).

Confidence and Competence in Ministry from God (3:4–6)

Paul's confidence level at this point in chapter 3 is through the roof. He knew where his confidence originated and credited his successful ministry to God through Christ (2 Cor 3:4). He reported to his readers that he and his companions in ministry were empowered by God, so their confidence and their competence rested securely not in themselves, but in divine authority, strength, and abilities. The achievements listed on their résumés were confirmed not by written documents or references, but by the internal, spiritual faith of the Corinthian believers and their transformed lives.

In 3:6, Paul reiterated the earlier theme of "life and death" (2:15–16) and introduced the new topic of a "new covenant." Most important, he insisted that "the Spirit" created the competence of the "new covenant" ministers. This was a reminder for the Corinthians of Jesus's words at the Lord's Supper: "this cup is the new covenant in my blood" (Luke 22:20; 1 Cor 11:25). The "new covenant," then, is spiritual; the Spirit brings to life the ministry of Paul and his colleagues. Through the "new covenant," God demonstrates his gift of salvation to his people; it is life-giving, and is the fulfillment of the promised everlasting covenant as verbalized by the OT prophets:

---

11. Gordon D. Fee, *Paul, the Spirit, and the People of God* (Peabody MA: Hendrickson, 1996), 16–17.

12. Furnish, *II Corinthians*, 195.

I will give them an undivided heart and put a new spirit in them; I will remove from them their heart of stone and give them a heart of flesh. Then they will follow my decrees and be careful to keep my laws. They will be my people, and I will be their God. (Ezek 11:19–20)

I will give you a new heart and put a new spirit in you; I will remove from you your heart of stone and give you a heart of flesh. And I will put my Spirit in you and move you to follow my decrees and be careful to keep my laws. (Ezek 36:26–27).

Paul was certain that something remarkably new was taking place in Corinth "through Christ before God" (2 Cor 3:4). Their whole world was changing. Recalling the old laws written on tablets of stone that were given to the Israelites at Sinai, Paul declared that the old laws were unable to save humanity and brought about death. In the same way, the writer of the NT book of Hebrews quotes the prophet Jeremiah (31:31–34) and adds that the new covenant will replace the "obsolete and aging" old covenant (Heb 8:13). The author of Hebrews also indicates that after the work of Jesus Christ, to return to the old system of Judaism would be to return to that which is ineffective. In the same way, if the ones opposing Paul in Corinth were Jewish-Christian missionaries who demanded that Gentiles who converted to Christianity adhere first to Jewish law, it would explain why they were so challenging to Paul, who disagreed with those demands. It would also explain why the Corinthian believers were confused and misled (since Paul was a Jew).

N. T. Wright explains that by using the OT concept of "covenant," Paul was teaching the Corinthian believers "to think Christianly about God, about God's people, and God's future." By doing so, they could create and maintain their Christian community "energized in unity and holiness."[13] That is, God was doing a "new thing" in the world, just as he had promised (Jer 31:31; Ezek 36:26; Isa 42:8–9; 48:6; 65:17; 66:22), through the life, death, and resurrection of Jesus, and through the "consequent gift of the Spirit." The indwelling Holy Spirit (2 Cor 3:3) confirms within each believer and within the church that the new covenant is remarkably different from the old. Wright says that for Paul, there was a new concept of "one God, one people of God [Jews and Gentiles], one future for God's world," united by one Spirit (1 Cor 8:6; 12:3–7).[14] This brand-new thing that God was doing in the world through the Messiah (the new covenant) is an important concept for Paul, because it

---

13. Wright, *Paul Debate*, 10.
14. Wright, *Paul Debate*, 13.

unites Christians into "one body" and significantly brings the Gentiles into the people of God with the believing Jews. We will see it again in the familiar verse in 2 Corinthians 5:17: "Therefore, if anyone is in Christ, the new creation has come: The old has gone, the new is here!" Paul can hardly contain his excitement! Thus, Paul's argument concerning a new life, the new covenant, and the remarkable change going on in the lives of his readers will continue on into the next section of his letter. He must explain to them the significance of the distinctions between the old covenant and the new covenant in 3:7–11.

 LIVE the Story

I abhor Brussels sprouts. It's not so much the taste of them as it is the smell of them as they are cooking. Now, my husband likes Brussels sprouts. He likes the smell; he comes into the kitchen and takes in the full aroma of the boiling sprouts. We are an example of people who perceive aromas in two completely different ways. In the same way, in 2:14–17, the gospel of Jesus Christ can be received by people in two very different ways. We cannot force people to love and accept Jesus as the Messiah. So, by using three vivid metaphors, Paul discloses the "big picture" of Christian ministry: a victorious faith, and the true, divisive nature of this message and ministry, especially in comparison to the counterfeit ministry of his opponents.

Knowledge of Christ

Paul clearly states the responsibility of a minister of the gospel: such a person is to be God's vehicle for spreading the good news of Jesus Christ. It is first through the preaching and teaching of the knowledge of Christ that the world is exposed to the good news. In other words, God, through us, spreads his message everywhere (2:14). This is a lofty assignment; we must be willing to carry the word of God to wherever God sends us, and to proclaim the gospel message to one person or to one thousand, wherever we may be. Second, Paul illustrates the nature of his ministry. Effectively, his ministry is pleasing to God, a "sweet-smelling aroma" of Christ (2:15a). Third, he shows the effect of his ministry on his audience (v. 15b). In truth, the gospel message splits humanity into two separate parts: those who are in the process of being saved because of their knowledge of Christ, and those who are in the process of perishing because they reject the gospel message proclaimed by Paul and his companions.

These aspects of Christian ministry seen in these verses are serious considerations for Christian leaders today. As God's instrument, the minister is to impart the knowledge of Christ (2:14), which is the essential message that should be on the lips of every minister in every church, "everywhere," from the suburban churches in America to the native huts in Africa. In this passage, it is the knowledge of God, with and through Christ that is the number-one aspect of the Christian gospel message. This may seem obvious to some readers today, but in reality, many people who speak from a pulpit, or minister in the church in other ways, neglect to consider the foundational message that they are asked to proclaim. In our culture, it is too easy for a pastor or a counselor to become caught up in the most recent current ideas, or in human psychological and sociological methods, and neglect biblical theology altogether. It may be easier to preach on "relevant" topics like marriage or morals, and use a couple of passages from the Bible as support for the pastor's personal opinions, but "easier" is not always better. Generally, ministers are people who want to help other people, and in spite of their altruistic motives, they can forget where their wisdom and help originates—in the knowledge of Christ (2 Cor 3:14; Prov 2, 3; Ps 1; Ps 111:10).

Without question, there are a multitude of excellent preachers and pastors serving selflessly in our churches today. We have all been greatly influenced by these talented, dedicated, loving ministers; perhaps you can specifically name a person or persons who have ministered to you, given you much and affected your spiritual life. Moreover, it is worth repeating that serving the Lord in any capacity can be a difficult and thankless job. Unfortunately, in the face of countless difficulties, ministers today can get distracted from their central task of preaching and teaching the word of God by any number of diversions: our own credentials and degrees, a successful, lucrative ministry, or our own charismatic talents can change our focus from God to ourselves. Conversely, ministry can be discouraging because of inadequate supplies and budgets, long hours of counseling, and contentious people. It can all be quite overwhelming to Christian leaders, and it becomes a challenge to "stand firm" (2 Cor 1:24) not only in our faith but also in our calling.

Paul warns us in this passage about losing our focus on Jesus; it is knowledge of Christ, not worldly knowledge, that should be the center of all ministry. Paul knew of false teachers in ministry, and today we are aware of certain people who may be deceptive, dishonest, or distort the word of God. A well-known television pastor preaches "feel good" sermons every week so the people will leave his church happy. He quotes the Proverbs occasionally, perhaps just to add a bit of wisdom to his own words. Other evangelists minister for human praise, for applause, and for financial gain. Vulnerable people send in money because they want to believe impressive human promises that God will bless them and prosper them "a hundred-fold" if they support a particular ministry.

Yet, if Christ is always the central message, then everything we say or do should be a sincere reflection of him.

In addition, in today's competitive market, we tend to push pastors to market themselves and their churches.[15] Pastors are now being videotaped weekly to be on television and on social media sites. They may appear on YouTube, and they may pontificate on social networks in an effort to promote their own church and ministries. "Successful" Christian leaders are urged to publish books and write blogs. These spotlights are not unhealthy for the Christian church in our culture, unless the leaders are claiming glory for themselves and not for the Christ they serve. Clearly, a pastor who endlessly boasts of the size and growth of his or her megachurch, or of the financial wealth of the organization, or of an extraordinary number of souls saved, as a result of his or her ideal sermons would be shunned as a braggart. Where is the balance? How does one obtain the competence and the confidence needed to be a minister of the gospel without being boastful and prideful? Paul is acutely aware of the pitfalls of ministry, and he relates that his "confidence" in ministry is only "through Christ before God" (3:4).

A young minister shared a story with me of taking the message of Jesus Christ to the wasteland of Kenya in the twenty-first century. Southern Kenya is lush, prosperous, and populated, an area that was privileged to receive the gospel message years ago. However, the northern part of Kenya is a desert, with inadequate dirt roads and remote villages. It can be dangerous, and no one really wants to go there. But a local Christian preacher had a vision from God to take the gospel message to the people of northern Kenya. Rejecting warnings from local people and even from longtime missionary workers, a small group of Christian messengers bravely made their way to give the people the knowledge of Jesus Christ for the first time. That is the point of ministry—to go where we are sent from God and to declare the clear message of Jesus Christ. God protected those messengers because they were doing what he asked them to do in Kenya. Now the Christian believers in northern Kenya (while small in number) are God's "letter of recommendation" concerning those missionaries, and a "letter of Christ," just like in 2 Corinthians (3:2–3).

Not everyone is asked to go across the globe to proclaim the gospel. Each one of us is asked to be the "fragrance" of Christ wherever we are, and in whatever position we are placed. There are hundreds of Bible-based organizations in which Christians can participate today, locally and internationally. Yet, spreading the "sweet fragrance of Christ" does not have to be a huge, organized mission across the world. A special card to someone on his or her

---

15. Belleville, *2 Corinthians*, 86.

birthday is a sweet aroma. Opening the door for someone, helping an elderly neighbor, carrying a package, shoveling snow from a driveway, a smile on a bad day, or a word of encouragement all produce a "pleasing aroma" in a needy world. On that note, let it be said that the "social gospel" of today is a good thing, and Christians need to be more involved in making our world a better place. But Paul reminds us that first and foremost, the purpose of ministry is the proclamation of the gospel of Jesus Christ. It is our job to address the eternal, spiritual needs of people everywhere, as well as temporal and physical needs.

Divisive Message

Furthermore, Paul reminds us in these verses that the responsibility of the reception of the gospel message is on the recipients, not the messenger. That is, when the gospel is preached or taught with truth, clarity, vigilance, and under the inspiration of the Holy Spirit, it is up to the ones receiving the word of God to make their own decisions. Paul gives human beings only two options: to receive the gospel and believe, or to reject the message ("those who are being saved" and "those who are perishing," 2:15). Those who hear the true gospel and accept it will have "an aroma that brings life"; those who reject the gospel will experience "an aroma that brings death" (2:16). In today's culture, just two options may seem intolerant, restrictive, and limiting, but Jesus himself said:

> For wide is the gate and broad is the road that leads to destruction, and many enter through it. But small is the gate and narrow the road that leads to life, and only a few find it. (Matt 7:13–14)

> Jesus answered, "I am the way and the truth and the life. No one comes to the Father except through me. If you really know me, you will know my Father as well. . . ." (John 14:6–7)

In the latter passage, note the definite article "*the*." Jesus declares himself as "the way," not "a way"; he is "the truth," not one of many, optional truths; he is "the life," not one of many alternative lifestyles to enjoy. There are only two responses to the hearing the Christian gospel, which is an idea that is not well received by present-day cultures that promote tolerance of a plethora of views, opinions, and expressions. Paul writes that if anything outside of the knowledge of Jesus Christ is preached, it is not the gospel.[16]

---

16. Belleville, *2 Corinthians*, 83.

Therefore, we must be very conscious of the primacy of Christ and the content of our messages. It may be true that sometimes the audiences in our culture are partially to blame because they respond positively to misleading ministry practices. Heavily swayed by modern-day false teachers, people send their money to self-seeking preachers in the hopes that their sensational healings and promises are real. In addition, churchgoers demand more entertainment and excitement than true worship in our churches.[17] Huge megachurches can attract famous Hollywood speakers and musicians. They can provide full musical and dramatic productions, including live animals for Christmas and Easter productions. Entertainment may attract visitors, but does it really enhance the true gospel of Jesus Christ? Does it detract from the true message? Paul wants to discourage any kind of ministry that is not Christ-centered.

On the one hand, as members of a Christian congregation and participants in a church family, we are called to fairly evaluate the effectiveness and the significance of a church and its leadership. These kinds of comments are common, although they are thoughtless and not beneficial:

"He is a great speaker, so his church is growing like crazy."
"Her church is very 'socially minded,' and they put their faith into action."
"My church is bigger and better because we have more programs in which to participate."
"I don't go to church anymore because all they do is ask for money."

In contrast, Christians should evaluate a church according to whether or not Jesus is the main focus. Is the knowledge of Christ taught and preached? Is worship focused on him, and are people finding salvation by his grace and by the sincerity (or truth) of proclamation?

Competent Ministers

On the other hand, certainly many Christian pastors have struggled with feelings of inadequacy and incompetence at some point in their ministries; it would be inhuman not to have such feelings. We cannot overlook Paul's comment in 2 Cor 2:16, "And who is equal to such a task?" because it is such an important question for both pastors and congregations to consider. Paul answers this hard question honestly in 3:4–6. Ministry is so very demanding, whether it is in a pulpit or in a jungle (is there a difference?), that sometimes we wonder why anyone accepts the charge at all. Often it is a thankless,

17. Belleville, *2 Corinthians*, 86.

24/7 job, sometimes with inadequate pay and few benefits. Ministers hold the hands of people from birth to death and through innumerable crises in between, sometimes not even knowing for certain if they are making any kind of difference in human lives.

Christian communities can place pressure on pastors and Christian leaders that is unforgiving and unrelenting. It is often assumed that leaders are without sin (especially sexual sins); they have perfect families (especially teenagers); they drive modest cars that never pollute the air; they have (spotless) homes that are less than ostentatious on the outside, but can hold forty parishioners for a potluck dinner on the inside. They are expected to be exactly what someone needs at exactly the time he or she needs it: grief counselor, career counselor, prophet, teacher, advisor, marriage and family therapist, cook, janitor, nurse, a shoulder to cry on, and at least a relatively good golfer. Paul wants to discourage this kind of thinking while still encouraging his fellow workers to place their confidence in God, who gives them their sense of competence. Christian leaders are called to "boast in the Lord" (1 Cor 1:31; 2 Cor 10:17), and to establish firmly their confidence and competency in "Christ before God" (3:4).

A very wise minister in the Church of Scotland recalled his first scary years as a brand-new parish pastor:

> I soon realised that newly ordained ministers, and their spouses, are like newly hatched chicks. They need love and support . . . I also learned how mistaken I was in imagining I would be like the Lone Ranger, riding around single-handed, righting wrongs, responding to cries for help, leaving silver bullets behind to let people know I had been on the job. It was so very different.

And significantly, one of his elders said to him: "We know God called you to minister to us. Now we realise that we are also called to minister to you!"[18]

Over the last few decades, the job of the pastor (or, more often, the pastors) of a church has expanded and the nature of ministry has broadened. Someone once said that pastors are lucky because they only worked on Sunday mornings. If that was ever the case, certainly those days are gone! The world is very complicated, and so is ministry. As an example, my uncle was a Methodist minister in Mississippi during the days of the civil rights movement. In those days, there was a "white" Methodist conference and a "colored" Methodist conference in the same geographic area. A small delegation of pastors decided it was time to

---

18. James Simpson, "Ministering to Ministers," *Life and Work: The Magazine of the Church of Scotland* (October 2016): 58.

combine their tasks and the talents, and to unify the two conferences into one. The congregation in my uncle's ("white") church was not at all happy with his attempt to integrate the two conferences. There were threats to him and to his family, and his own people attacked his house, his position, and his motives. They tried hard to have him removed from the church. No one in seminary taught my uncle how to take charge in such a situation or prepared him for that aspect of ministry. Fighting for civil rights was not part of the initial job description. But he was equal to the task, even to the point of putting his family in danger. The integration of the churches was successful. Today, we could say "Why would Christians, followers of Christ, treat their pastor in this manner?"

Thus, in this section of his letter Paul articulates critical, timeless truths about Christian ministry. Perhaps not as obvious as we think, Christian ministry should first and always be Christ-centered. Second, Paul indicates that human beings have only two options as a result of hearing the gospel of Jesus Christ: when the true gospel is preached, people will either receive the gospel message or they will reject it. This is a rather sobering thought to realize that Paul tells his readers that the only two options are life and death (2:16). There appears to be no middle ground. Third, because Christians are given the Spirit at conversion, we are Spirit-filled believers; do we act like that? God's very presence is *always* with us. Fee summarizes:

> Life in the Spirit also includes every other imaginable dimension of the believer's present end-time existence, including being empowered by the Spirit to abound in hope, to live in joy, to pray without ceasing, to exercise self-control, to experience a robust conscience, to have insight into God's will and purposes, and to endure in every kind of present hardship and suffering. To be a believer means nothing less than being filled with and thus to live in and by the Spirit.[19]

Fourth, Christian leaders should serve as people sent from God, and it is from God that leaders gain a sense of confidence and competency, not from their audience or from their own talents, gifts, and efforts. For Paul, competency and confidence in ministry rest in the truth of the knowledge of Christ. He is only the human "container" of the message, but the triumphal victory of his Lord urges him on to continue to spread the message everywhere, in spite of (or as a result of) trials and opposition. This kind of confidence in God and in one's own calling leads Christian leaders into a deeper understanding of what we are called to do and why we are called to do it.

---

19. Fee, *Paul, the Spirit, and the People of God*, 184.

CHAPTER 4

2 Corinthians 3:7–18

 LISTEN to the Story

⁷Now if the ministry that brought death, which was engraved in letters on stone, came with glory, so that the Israelites could not look steadily at the face of Moses because of its glory, transitory though it was, ⁸will not the ministry of the Spirit be even more glorious? ⁹If the ministry that brought condemnation was glorious, how much more glorious is the ministry that brings righteousness! ¹⁰For what was glorious has no glory now in comparison with the surpassing glory. ¹¹And if what was transitory came with glory, how much greater is the glory of that which lasts!

¹²Therefore, since we have such a hope, we are very bold. ¹³We are not like Moses, who would put a veil over his face to prevent the Israelites from seeing the end of what was passing away. ¹⁴But their minds were made dull, for to this day the same veil remains when the old covenant is read. It has not been removed, because only in Christ is it taken away. ¹⁵Even to this day when Moses is read, a veil covers their hearts. ¹⁶But whenever anyone turns to the Lord, the veil is taken away. ¹⁷Now the Lord is the Spirit, and where the Spirit of the Lord is, there is freedom. ¹⁸And we all, who with unveiled faces contemplate the Lord's glory, are being transformed into his image with ever-increasing glory, which comes from the Lord, who is the Spirit.

Listening to the Text in the Story: Exodus 34:29–35; Jeremiah 32:38–40; Isaiah 55:3; Ezekiel 11:19; 36:26; Psalm 118:5; 119:32, 45; Isaiah 61:1–8; Luke 4:17–19; John 8:32; Galatians 5:1; Romans 12:2; 6:18.

> "The days are coming," declares the LORD,
>   "when I will make a new covenant
> with the people of Israel
>   and with the people of Judah.
> It will not be like the covenant

> I made with their ancestors
> when I took them by the hand
>   to lead them out of Egypt,
> because they broke my covenant,
>   though I was a husband to them. . . .
> I will put my law in their minds
>   and write it on their hearts.
> I will be their God,
>   and they will be my people."
>   —*Jeremiah 31:31–32, 33*

I had a cell phone for about two years before I got a new one for Christmas. At first, it was rather daunting to be shown all the functions my new phone could accomplish. My old phone was so simple, and I liked it. I was just happy to function under the old system that I was used to. It was not a bad phone, really, it was just old. Technology advances so quickly that it could easily pass me by. I had no idea that the newer phones could increase my productivity, my communications, and my fun!

In much the same way, the Jewish people lived for centuries under the old covenant, the old rules and regulations that had been given by God to help mold the nation into his people. Remembering that Paul himself had been an educated, orthodox Jew who had lived under the Mosaic law for a long time, this section of the letter to the Corinthian believers is rather surprising. Even today, biblical scholars have studied and debated these verses in the attempt to try to discern what the apostle was really saying to his audience.

First, it is important to listen to this section of text in a broader context: the wider context of this passage is Paul's defense of his own integrity and Christian ministry in spite of external opposition (1:12–7:16). Paul confirmed for his readers both the extent of, and the nature of, his divinely-appointed calling in 2:14–3:6. He pointed out that his competence and confidence is from God, and not of himself. Then, in 3:7–18 he moved into an illustration of the superiority of his ministry over every other message, and the superiority of the true apostle who is appointed by God to proclaim the new covenant. It is likely that Paul's opponents in Corinth (see Introduction) were preaching a gospel message that contradicted Paul's proclamations. These rival missionaries insisted on holding on very tightly to the rituals and traditions of the old covenant. Ancient ill feelings rooted in Judaism and feelings of superiority over the Gentiles were not easily forgotten even by those who received Jesus as the promised Messiah. After all, Jesus came first to the Jewish people (e.g., Matt 15:21–28). Thus, some contended that anyone (especially Gentiles) who was to be considered a part of God's people must adhere to Torah first. Yet, for Paul, it was the Spirit of God alone that identifies the people of God under the new covenant.[1]

Second, it is critical for modern readers to realize that Paul is using his interpretation of an OT narrative to make the point of his argument. His interpretation of the events of Exodus in this passage may be a variation of our scholarly interpretations of this passage today. Clearly Paul knits together the ancient Hebrew text, known Jewish traditions, and perhaps even non-biblical material, which was an acceptable method of interpretation in his day.[2] After his encounter with the risen Jesus, and with eyes of faith, Paul was seeing the Exodus events not as obsolete, but as fulfilled in the new covenant brought about by the Spirit (2 Cor 3:6).

Third, and perhaps most important, we cannot ignore the main theme of verses 3:7–18, which is "glory." This word, with the adjective "glorious," appears ten times in 3:7–11, and twice in verse 3:18 alone. Why the emphasis on glory? Why does Paul use this OT narrative in his own defense, especially with a primarily Gentile audience in Corinth? Is he attempting to glorify himself or his own ministry? What is the point of this appraisal of the OT covenant, and how is this related to Paul's attempt to establish a basis for his bold outspokenness among the Corinthians (see 3:12)?[3] At first glance, it is difficult to tie together all the threads of this complicated passage: covenant, glory, Moses, ministry, boldness, the veil, the Spirit, freedom, and transformation.

EXPLAIN the Story

Superior New Covenant Ministry (3:7–11)

After bringing up the topic of the new covenant in 3:6, Paul employs an OT narrative to illustrate why God is doing a "new thing" among his people, and Paul is a part of it. Paul relates to his readers the events of Exodus 34:28–35 in an attempt to illustrate the superiority of the ministry of the new covenant in Jesus Christ over the old covenant of the law (2 Cor 3:6). His argument revolves around the gracious revelations of God to humanity, pictured by the "veiling" (or "hiding") and "unveiling" (the "revelation") of Moses.[4]

---

1. Fee, *Paul, the Spirit, and the People of God*, 100.
2. Linda L. Belleville, *Reflections of Glory: Paul's Polemic Use of the Moses-Doxa Tradition in 2 Corinthians 3:12–18* (Sheffield: Sheffield Academic, 1991), 17.
3. Garland, *2 Corinthians*, 168.
4. Belleville, *Reflections of Glory*, 15.

In Exodus 32, the Lord God gave to Moses the "two tablets of the Testimony" (better known to us as the Ten Commandments). It was understood that in ancient days, each party of a covenant agreement had a copy of said agreement. Thereafter, both copies of the tablets (God's and Israel's) were preserved in the Israelite ark of the covenant (Exod 25:21). At that time, this was a new thing that God was doing; he gave the letter of the law to his people to establish a covenant relationship (Exod 24:12; 31:18; 32:15–16). God graciously took his people out of Egypt and into the land of promise, where he confirmed a covenant with them. Moses told the people all of the words and laws of the Lord, and the people promised to obey and do everything the Lord had said (Exod 24:3, 7). Nevertheless, when Moses descended from the mountain with the tablets of stone, he saw the Israelites had fallen into grave disobedience, having made a golden calf (an idol) and worshiped before it. The Lord threatened to destroy the "stiff-necked" people (32:9–10) and disown them for breaking his covenant with him. Moses, too, burned with anger at the people and he "threw the tablets out of his hands, breaking them to pieces at the foot of the mountain" (32:19). When his anger subsided, Moses considered making atonement before the Lord for the sin of his people (32:30, 33, 34). His intercession was successful, and God made Moses the mediator between the people and God.

The story continues in Exodus 33, where the Lord God confirms Moses's leadership to the Israelite people, and says he is pleased with Moses (33:17). Then, Moses asks God directly, "Now show me your glory" (33:18). In hindsight, the Israelites had seen the glory of the Lord in the two stone tablets that were the gracious, glorious revelation of God himself through his laws and his covenant with the people. "Written on stone tablets" (2 Cor 3:3) was a common way to express the glorious revelation given to Moses on the mountain. The covenant established morals, ethics, and modes of behavior for living together as a unique nation of God's people. It outlined the meaning and function of worship of the one, true God, and secured the presence of God with his people in the tabernacle (and later, in the temple). This covenant with Israel was formalized and sanctified by the sacrificed blood of animals, as we see in the sacrificial system in the OT, where the various sins of the people were "covered" by the blood (Exod 24:8).

Thus, in Exodus 34 the nation of Israel gets a "mulligan," a "do-over," or a second chance to keep the covenantal law. God forgave the idolatry, the wickedness and sin of the people, and renewed his promise to confer on them their "inheritance" (34:9). Once again, the people pledged to obey the words of the covenant. God reiterated the covenantal laws (made earlier in chapters 19–24) and granted to the people two new stone tablets (34:28). When Moses received the new tablets and descended once again from the mountaintop to the people, the tradition of the glory and the veil began. God's glory was revealed in the giving of his law to his people and was reflected in the face of Moses. When Moses returned to the people, he was unaware that "his face was radiant because he had spoken with the Lord" (34:29). Moses therefore "put a veil over his face" (34:33) when he spoke with the people, hiding or concealing his radiance. The climax of these events is when Moses, the one who had asked to see God's glory (33:18), actually reflected that very same divine glory to the nation.

This powerful Exodus narrative did four important things: it established Moses as their leader, mediator, and representative before God; it demonstrated God's loving forgiveness toward his people without ignoring their disobedience and rebellion (Exod 34:6); it provided a new revelation of God, who chose to define and secure his relationship with his people; and finally, it renewed the gracious gift of the Mosaic covenant and chiseled the letter of the law into the minds of the people.

Unfortunately, despite all the revealed glory and radiance of the law given by God to his people, Paul narrates that the light from Moses's face faded in time, as did the Israelite's resolve to obey and worship God (2 Cor 3:7–11). The "veil" becomes a metaphor for Israel's disobedience and unbelief. Paul uses a "lesser to greater" type of argument in these verses to say that the glory of the Holy Spirit, given by God to Christian believers, is even more glorious than the old law. We must see that the law of the old covenant was not declared wicked or evil; elsewhere Paul describes it as "holy, righteous, good, and spiritual" (Rom 7:12, 14). The law was good, given by a gracious God, but it exposed their sins. The people who broke the law brought condemnation upon themselves because of their own disobedience and rebellion. The covenant written on stone tablets, as glorious as it was at the time, could neither eradicate that evil nor remove the penalty of death. If a condemnation ministry is "glorious," then how much more glorious is Paul's contrasting ministry of Jesus Christ "that brings righteousness" (2 Cor 3:9)?

The weakness of the covenant of law, according to Paul, was that it did not include the empowering Holy Spirit. A written code of laws required obedience, and disobedience brought death (3:7). In contrast, the ministry of the Spirit that brings righteousness (3:9) is a surpassing glory that gives life (3:10). The new covenant presented by Paul in his ministry endures forever and does not fade with time. It is the new revelation of God, "unveiled," and is much more glorious than the old covenant (3:11). "It is through the Spirit that we behold—and are transformed into—the glory of the Lord. The promised new covenant has replaced the old, and the gift of the Spirit proves it."[5] Nevertheless, Paul notes, the Jews who rejected the Messiah and the ministry of the new covenant were (and are) still "veiled," unknowing and living in the dark, because "only in Christ is it taken away" (3:14–16).

Many years after the Mosaic covenant was established, the Hebrew prophets foretold of a time when the writing of the law would be not on stone or papyrus, but on "tablets of human hearts" (3:3). Both Jeremiah (31:31–34; 32:39–40) and Ezekiel (11:19; 36:26) spoke of the laws that would be written not with ink, but "with the Spirit of the living God" (3:3).

The passage from Jeremiah (31:31–34) clearly gives the reason that a new covenant was necessary: the people of God broke their old covenant with him. The new covenant surpasses the old because the Spirit of God transforms human hearts on the inside so that people can know God and can be obedient to his commands. The stone law broke into pieces; it could not save the people from the captivity of their own sin and defiance. The promised Spirit, as part of the glorious new covenant, produces the righteousness the former covenant failed to produce. Paul understands that for Jew and Gentile alike, the Spirit is the replacement of the Torah and a fulfillment of the Torah's requirements.[6] The concepts of the new covenant and the gift of the life-giving Spirit to all believers (Jew and Gentile) are so glorious and so groundbreaking that they become the foundation of Paul's confidence in his ministry to the Corinthians (3:4). God has once again graciously broken into human life with the new covenant that was made official by the sacrificed blood of Jesus Christ (Luke 22:20; Rom 3:25; 5:9; Col 1:20). "As Moses' face had once radiated the splendor of the old covenant, the splendor of the new covenant is now to be seen in Christ (v. 6)."[7]

In Paul's mind, there was a very good reason to use this Israelite narrative to teach his primarily Gentile audience about him and his new covenant ministry. N. T. Wright explains that Paul has already instructed the Corinthian believers that "we have the mind of Christ" (1 Cor 2:16). Therefore, he is trying to get the Corinthians to think in a whole new way, to think "Christianly."[8] The followers of Christ must become mature in their thinking (1 Cor 14:20) and be transformed by the renewing of their minds (Rom 12:2). Because of the death and resurrection of Jesus, because of what he did for all believers, both Jews and Gentiles are, incredibly, new creatures (see 2 Cor 5:16–17). If Paul's aim was to establish a community of unified, holy people of God, it was through new thinking and the transformed lives

---

5. Fee, *Paul, the Spirit, and the People of God*, 100.
6. Fee, *Paul, the Spirit, and the People of God*, 101.
7. Furnish, *II Corinthians*, 248.
8. Wright, *Paul Debate*, 1.

of Christ-followers. Wright says that through the "extraordinary act of new creation in and through Jesus and his death and resurrection, Paul believed it was the start of a new world."[9]

Furthermore, the ministry of the Spirit (3:7) is not a supplement or an addendum to the ministry of the law. The splendor of the old covenant "faded away" (3:7, 11, 13–14) and has thus been removed and replaced with a permanent covenant and a permanent Spirit. The glory of the new covenant is far greater than the old covenant: it is more enduring, and it brings life and righteousness instead of death and condemnation. By way of summary, then, a chart may be helpful to compare the old covenant of the law and the new covenant of the Spirit of Christ:

	"Old"	"New"
1.	Letters of recommendation (3:1)	You are our letter (3:2)
2.	Writing in ink, on stone (3:3)	Spirit of the living God (3:3)
3.	Competence of human agents (3.5)	Competence from God (3:5)
4.	External letter (3:6)	Internal Spirit of God (3:3, 6)
5.	Letter kills, leads to death (3:6, 7)	Spirit gives life (3:6)
6.	Glory of law to Moses (3:7)	Surpassing glorious ministry (3:10)
7.	Law brings condemnation (3:9)	Spirit brings righteousness (3:9)
8.	Transitory (3:11)	Lasts forever (3:11)

Superior New Covenant Minister (3:12–18)

"Therefore," Paul continues in 3:12, in an effort to connect his thoughts in 3:6–11 to the following thoughts in 3:12–18. As a result of understanding the superiority of the new covenant over the old covenant, Paul goes on to show how, as a minister of the new covenant, he is superior to the patriarch Moses. It was, of course, Moses who brought the old covenant, written on stones, to the people of Israel. However, Paul and his ministry colleagues brought the good news of the new covenant to the Gentiles as well as the Jews. Both Moses and Paul served as intermediaries between God and his people. Unity is achieved through reconciliation, as the Israelites were unified and reconciled

---

9. Wright, *Paul Debate*, 6.

to God through the Mosaic Law. Under the new covenant, it was Paul's ministry of reconciliation that unifies God's people (see 5:11–21).

Using a type of Jewish logic, perhaps even a traditional "midrashic" interpretation, Paul demonstrates to his readers how he is a superior minister.[10] Paul emphasizes his own boldness in contrast to Moses's timidity and reserve (3:12–13). That is, a major difference between the ministry of Moses and that of Paul has to do with human fear. When Moses returned from the mountaintop to the people of Israel, they were afraid to look at Moses. The anger of the Lord "burned" against the people (Exod 32:10) in their rebellion and disobedience. Like a child who knows very well that he or she is in trouble with the parents, the nation recoiled in fear and was disciplined by God with a plague (Exod 32:35). The radiant glory of God on Moses's face had to be covered because the people were afraid, knowing that their disobedience "brought death" (2 Cor 3:7).[11] In an act of timidity, Moses hid the glory of God, knowing he could not undo their sins or remove their guilt; thus, all he could do was to beg God for atonement.[12]

In contrast, Paul revealed the glory of God, clearly visible as the Spirit present in his own life and ministry, and which removed human fear. Paul's ministry of the Spirit was a message of hope (3:12) that allowed people (even sinful people) to "encounter the glory of God without being destroyed."[13] That is, Paul was the superior minister because of the presence of the indwelling Spirit directing all of his life and ministry. It is the "Spirit of Christ" (which is identical to the "Holy Spirit" and the "Spirit of God") that brings life and hope to all those who had once been living under a ministry that brought condemnation (3:7). Thus, Paul was not looking for personal accolades, nor was he promoting himself; Paul was the superior minister because he ministered in the Spirit, reflecting God's glory (3:18).

> The glory of God has been imaged for us in the one true human who bears the divine image, Christ himself; and by beholding his "face" we see the glory of the eternal God (3:18; 4:4, 6) . . . Christ has put a human face on the Spirit as well. Not only has the coming of Christ changed everything for Paul, so too has the coming of the Spirit.[14]

Minister of Hope

Although there are various kinds of hope mentioned in Paul's letters (3:12), there is one essential feature that is consistent in such references: humanity

---

10. Furnish, *II Corinthians*, 230, 232, 244.
11. Garland, *2 Corinthians*, 171.
12. Furnish, *II Corinthians*, 232.
13. Garland, *2 Corinthians*, 175.
14. Fee, *Paul, the Spirit, and the People of God*, 25.

has new expectations because the coming of the promised Christ created a new situation for both Jews and Gentiles. In his ministry, Paul announced that the new hope that people have in Christ includes position, power, and promise: salvation (1 Thess 5:8), righteousness (Gal 5:5), resurrection in an incorruptible body (1 Cor 15:52ff; Acts 23:6; 24:15), eternal life (Tit 1:2; 3:7), being transformed into the image of Christ (2 Cor 3:18, and see 1 John 3:2–3), seeing the glory of God (Rom 5:2), knowing the reality of his calling (Eph 1:18; 4:4), faith and love (Col 1:5), reconciliation through the gospel (1:22), and glory itself (1:27). In addition, Paul's Greek word for "hope" is a word that has an "objective quality of certainty."[15] In other words, as a minister of the new covenant, Paul announced good things to come, things worth waiting for, that will inevitably come to pass. His ministry was full of unconditional hope because of all the promised glory yet unseen (3:18).

Ministry of "Boldness"

Because Paul had this great hope, he could deliver the gospel message "very boldly" (3:12). Here, Paul used a word that conveys not just a general sense of bravery, but also implies a specific boldness of speech, even despite strong opposition (see also 1 Thess 2:2; Phlm 8). Paul insisted that he had the right to speak freely while he made every attempt to also speak openly and clearly.[16] Two things may be happening here. First, the veil was used by Moses as a cautionary cover, so that the people could not see the fading of his radiance, so he may have felt a restriction of his speech with the Israelites. But Paul and his fellow ministers ("we," 2 Cor 3:12) were "not like Moses"; as true Christian ministers, they were filled with the Spirit of God. Indeed, something new happened that made the new ministers very courageous in their speech and presentation of the gospel message.

Second, Paul was attempting to justify his apostolic ministry over Moses in response to his opponents in Corinth who may have been accusing him of not keeping his promises or following through with what he had said (1:15–2:2). An unexpected result of their allegations against Paul was to encourage him to speak all the more boldly in proclaiming his message. Thus, Paul and his colleagues were up-front, open, and courageous in their proclamations. These superior ministers of the new covenant were able to be daring in speech and action because they were bringing a new hope to the audience.

Still, the Corinthians might ask, why do some of the Jews reject the "more glorious" gospel message that Paul was so enthusiastically teaching? This is a

---

15. E. Hoffmann, "Hope," *NIDNTT* 2:242.
16. Belleville, 2 *Corinthians*, 102.

critical question in response to Paul's argument concerning the superiority of the new covenant and of his own new covenant ministry. From 3:12 to 4:6, Paul describes why some fellow Jews rejected the gospel message, even in view of this hope and glory. Paul explained that their "minds were made dull" (3:14) and "a veil covers their hearts" (3:15). Both their minds and their hearts prevented the Jews from seeing precisely what Paul had seen: the glory of the Lord (3:18). Thus, with dull minds and hardened hearts, they could not perceive the glory of God through their own intellect (their minds or the law), or through their own spiritual awareness (their hearts). How could anyone see the glory of God behind a veil that was intended to hide the radiance? Paul addressed this "hardening" at length in his letter to the Romans, chapters 9–11 (see especially 9:18). Again, an unexpected result of the hardening of the hearts of the Jews was the acceptance of the Gentiles into the community of God's people (Rom 11:11–16).

"But," Paul says in contrast, the people who believed his message and placed their faith in Jesus as the Messiah are unveiled (2 Cor 3:16). Those who believe in the Lord Jesus have uncovered ("unveiled") faces that "reflect the Lord's glory." As a new minister, with a new message, Paul shared a new revelation of God to both Jews and Gentiles. Those who refused his message and rejected this revelation in Christ could not perceive the glory shown to Paul. While the old covenant was exclusively given to the Israelites, the glorious new covenant is inclusive for all humanity (Gal 3:26–29).

Ministry of Freedom

In the OT, the concept of "freedom" (2 Cor 3:17) was inextricably linked to the redemption of the nation of Israel by God himself. It was God who set the people free by his saving acts, such as their exodus from the land of Egypt. Freedom was never taken lightly, and it was only by God's grace that it was experienced. It was both political and theological in nature; both national and individual freedoms and liberty were always a gift from God. The nation was never independent from God, and Israel was only free when they were bound in obedience to God.[17] With this background in mind, Paul uses the word "freedom" (and its derivatives) more than any other NT writer.

However, the term is not used in reference to political freedom or to individual liberty to do as one pleases. The verb ("to set free") is uniquely used for the consequences of the work of Jesus on the cross (John 8:32; Gal 5:1; Rom 6:18). Further, Paul goes beyond the OT concepts in that he sees freedom as a release from the powers and forces that restrain the human being: sin

---

17. For example, see Pss 118:5; 119:32, 45; Isa 61:1–3; Luke 4:17–19.

(Rom 6:18–22; 8:2–3), Satan (Eph 6:12), death (Rom 6:20–23; 8:21), and even the law itself (Rom 7:3–6; 8:3; Gal 2:4; 4:21–31; 5:1–13). Paul reminds the Corinthians, "Am I not free? Am I not an apostle? Have I not seen Jesus our Lord? Are you not the result of my work in the Lord?" (1 Cor 9:1). So the readers know that Paul is in a unique position, called by God, with a unique ministry to speak freely and boldly about the new covenant. What Paul calls the "old self" (Rom 6:6; Col 3:9), is the person before he or she is "in Christ"; and the "old self" is in the process of being released (or "freed") from the old covenant of condemnation and death (2 Cor 3:12–18). Positively, Paul says that freedom is a state of being "where the Spirit of the Lord is" (3:17); the believer is a "new creation" (5:17), set free to speak and minister boldly in the Spirit.[18]

Verse 3:17 should be understood as the end of a sentence that started in 3:6. We read that "the Spirit gives life . . . ," so then, "where the Spirit of the Lord is, there is freedom." That is, it is only by "turning to the Lord" (3:16) that people can find "freedom in Christ." True freedom exists only in relationship with the Holy Spirit. What the law demanded has been rescinded and replaced by the "Spirit of the living God," in the form of the freeing, life-giving grace of the new covenant. Those who are Christ-followers enjoy a new freedom *from* the law of condemnation and *toward* a new relationship with God.

The Spirit of the Lord

Paul's discussion of the "the Spirit" begins in this letter in 1:22, where it is Christ who has "put his Spirit in our hearts," in contrast to the veiled hearts of unbelieving Jews (3:15). The Spirit was the primary sign of belonging to Christ (1:22; cf. 11:4). It is the gift of the Spirit, neither earned nor demanded, that is given to those who believe at the beginning of one's Christian life (Gal 3:2–5, 14; 1 Cor 6:11). The Spirit initiates the process of salvation in one's life and carries it through to completion. It is a sign of ownership; the believer becomes a possession of Christ (1 Cor 6:19). Thus, all Christian believers are baptized "by one Spirit, into one body," so individuals become members of the one people of God (1 Cor 12:13).

In addition, the Spirit is the divine power that enables believers to live out their lives in Christ. Where the Israelites did not have the power to fully and completely follow God's law, it is the Spirit that distinguishes a Christian believer from an old-covenant Jew and makes it possible to live in the new covenant (2 Cor 3:6–8). While there may be continuing tensions between what Paul calls "the flesh" and the Spirit in this life, there is hope (3:12) for believers in a total triumph by the Spirit. We might say that the gift of the

---

18. J. Blunck, "Freedom," *NIDNTT* 1:716–18.

Spirit in individuals as well as in the corporate body of Christ is a "down-payment and the guarantee" that God will complete the work done by Christ and through the Spirit.[19] The glory of God, far superior to the glory of the given law, will be fully revealed in the complete transformation of believers (3:18). "As with Moses, and now by the Spirit, we are unveiled as we enter the sanctuary to behold the glory of the Lord. The Spirit of the Presence has now removed the veil . . . so we can behold the glory of the Lord himself in the face of God's Son."[20]

Further, Paul had certainly encountered the Holy Spirit in his own life, and he witnessed to that fact. No doubt Paul experienced the fulfillment of the Old Testament prophesies that promised a time when the law would be written on the heart and not tablets of stone (3:3, 7). He was excited to see and feel a time when all people could know God for themselves and could pray and worship God intimately without a human mediator of tradition.[21] In this sense, Paul's message was superior to every other message, and Paul was superior to every other messenger. God graciously gives his people his Spirit who indwells, empowers, and frees people to live a life pleasing to God, and to accomplish his purposes. Moreover, the Corinthians had also experienced, to a great extent, the work of the Holy Spirit in their own lives (1 Cor 1:4–9). They should have recognized that the bold proclamations by Paul were indeed from the Holy Spirit because they had encountered such power. It is the presence of the Spirit in the lives of the believers that most clearly defines the old from the new. In fact Dunn writes:

> Of the NT writers, Paul most deserves the title, "the theologian of the Spirit," for he gives a more rounded and more integrated teaching on the Spirit than we find in any other literature of that time, or indeed for several centuries before and after. . . . The Spirit constitutes that immediacy of personal relationship with God which Moses had fitfully enjoyed (2 Cor 3:13–18) and which Jeremiah had only foreseen from afar (2 Cor 3:3, referring to Jer 31:33).[22]

Transformed from Glory to Glory

The crown of Paul's complicated discussion is verse 3:18. Paul confirmed what he has just written, completed his thoughts, and created a basis for what is to follow in 4:1–6. In just this one verse, Paul declares that:

---

19. J. D. G. Dunn, "Spirit, Holy Spirit" *NIDNTT* 3:701.
20. Fee, *Paul, the Spirit, and the People of God*, 21.
21. Dunn, "Spirit," 702.
22. Dunn, "Spirit," 700.

1. *All* believers are involved, not just Moses and the Israelite nation.
2. Outwardly and boldly, unveiled believers *reflect* the glory of Christ, who is himself the glory of God.
3. They are being *transformed* into Christ's likeness "with ever-increasing glory."
4. This gift of glory to believers, from God, is evidenced by the indwelling *Holy Spirit.*

The first part of this verse says literally, "And all of us, with unveiled faces, seeing the glory of the Lord as though reflected in a mirror . . ." (NRSV). This implies that when anyone who believes in Jesus looks into the mirror and sees his or her own reflection, what that person sees is the "same image" as the Lord Jesus himself. That is remarkable! Paul is expanding his thoughts about the boldness of those who are in Christ. Only Moses was privileged enough to witness the glory of the Lord at Sinai; now, the new covenant allows *all* believers to see the divine glory. The idea of a mirror reflection in verse 3:18 involves a "visible representation (or reflection) of some reality."[23] Certainly the mirror image of something may be indirect and imperfect, but it can also be an accurate, "unhidden" representation of true reality. But, how can this be? Can flawed, sinful human beings reflect the glory of God?

Believers are being "transformed" by the Spirit of God into that very image of Jesus, so that Christians can then reflect that image to the world (3:18). In Paul's thinking, the "transformation" (or, the "*metamorphosis*") of the believer is a major change of the "inward person," not the "outward" person, which is "wasting away" (4:16). Yet, the "whole person" is a "new creation" (5:17) demonstrating the inward transformation through outward Christian actions and behavior. It is also interesting to note that in this verse Paul omits words such as "dimly" or "blurring" concerning the reflection (see 1 Cor 13:12); believers are a clear reflection of the divine glory.[24] In contrast to Moses, and without hesitation, every believer can bravely, outwardly show the glory of God that has transformed his or her life by the redemption of Christ Jesus (3:14).

The powerful theme of glory is prevalent throughout the NT, and it is a major theme in this section of Paul's letter. The Greek word (or a derivation of it) that Paul uses is found in every verse from 3:7 to 11 and culminates in 3:18. It is the word *doxa,* from which we derive the English word "doxology." Foundationally, this word is from the Hebrew word *kabod,* which implies

---

23. Harris, *Second Corinthians,* 314.
24. Harris, *Second Corinthians,* 315.

God's majesty, splendor, honor, and worthiness. In the OT, *kabod* was used to refer to God's self-revelation. The presence of God among his people, manifested as his glory, took the form of divine events and actions in salvation history. This included events such as the exodus, as well as in the tabernacle and temple, where it was said that God's glory "resides."[25] Paul was using these Jewish concepts in this passage. He explains that it is the glory of God, his self-revelation to his people, that shined on the face of Moses (Exod 34:30; 2 Cor 3:7, 13, 18); yet, the reflection of that divine glory faded from the human face with time. After the life, death, and resurrection of Jesus, it was replaced by a greater glory.

The greater glory, of course, is Jesus himself. In the NT, the concept of glory is expanded by the recognition of the power of God operating in the world and within his people. Further, and just as important, is the concept that human beings can share in the glory of God, or will share in it at some point in the future. On the one hand, all of the values attributed to God's glory—revelation of himself, his power, and exaltation—have been fulfilled in Christ, in the work that he accomplished for the salvation of humanity (Heb 1:3; John 17:1, 24; 2 Cor 4:4, 6). On the other hand, Paul knows that because of Christ, the eschatological hope that is the glory of God will be accomplished in completely transformed humanity. Through grace, believers share in Christ's suffering; yet, at some point in the future, believers will also share fully in his glory (Rom 8:17). In 3:18, Paul explains that those who believe in Christ, who is "the radiance of God's glory" (Heb. 1:3), will one day be totally transformed and will completely "reflect the Lord's glory" (2 Cor 3:18). Expanding upon another Jewish concept, Paul summarizes the Christian hope as "the hope of glory" (3:12; Col 1:27; Eph 1:17–19).[26] Perhaps the greatest gift of God to the Christian is to be with Jesus and to see fully, completely, and unveiled, his eternal glory and splendor (see John 17:22–23). As we cannot separate the sun and the brilliant light that proceeds from it, in the same way, the Son and the Father cannot be separated. As Jesus reflects the glory of the Father, believers reflect the glory of the Father and the Son through the Holy Spirit (2 Cor 3:17–18). While complete transformation of all persons may be yet in the future, Paul tells his readers that they are Spirit-filled believers who can and must reflect the glory of God in a world that desperately needs its light.

Further, Paul says that *all* believers are being transformed into the image of the risen Christ "with ever-increasing glory"; literally, believers "are being changed from glory to glory." This is an unusual phrase, and scholars have

25. S. Aalen, "Glory," *NIDNTT* 2:45–46.
26. Aalen, "Glory," 47.

debated how to accurately translate it. Suffice it to say that most often Christians have understood this phrase to mean that believers are "glorified" at the time of their initial conversion to Christianity, and then there is a more intense glorification sometime in the future. Yet, this interpretation diverges dramatically from Paul's immediate argument concerning Moses and the old and new covenants. It also has little to do with Paul's main focus, which is the defense of his person and his ministry. An alternative view suggests that the believer's "transformation" is the consequence of the glory of one ministry succumbing to the superior glory of another ministry. In 3:17–18, it is the Spirit of God who frees the believers from the condemnation of the old covenant, and Christians are being "changed into" the image of Christ as a result of the filling of the Spirit of God. It is the Spirit that allows (and helps) Paul to speak openly and boldly to the Corinthians (3:12), and the Spirit grants the readers the ability to receive Paul's message unhampered. Thus, one expression of glory in the ministry of Moses is compared to another, greater expression of God's glory in the ministry of Paul ("from one glory to another glory"). The transformation is from death to life, from Moses's ministry to Paul's superior ministry.[27]

Again, a chart may be helpful to see how the work of the Spirit of God that began in 3:6 has significantly changed the lives of believers through the minister Paul, who works in that Spirit and under his direction:

"Old" minister of law	"New" minister of the Spirit
Moses veiled with caution (3:13)	Paul's boldness of speech (3:12)
Dulled minds, hardened hearts (3:14, 15)	Ministry of Spirit (3:17)
Obstructed faith of unbelievers (3:14, 15)	Freedom for those who believe (3:14,16)
Awareness of sin, death (3:13)	Transformation into his likeness (3:18)
Only Moses reflected glory (3:13)	All believers reflect divine glory (3:18)

In the end, Paul wanted his readers to have the correct perception of him, of his ministry, and of his message. He contrasts the old legal system and its leader to the new spiritual message and its minister, who was commissioned

27. Paul B. Duff, "Transformed 'From Glory to Glory': Paul's Appeal to the Experience of His Readers in 2 Corinthians 3:18," *JBL* 127.4 (2008): 775–76.

to illustrate the ongoing process of God's revelation to his people. Because the Corinthians had an obscured perception of Paul and his purposes (1:12–13), he wanted to make sure that his message was understood and received properly. In addition, Paul wanted the Corinthians to remember their own position in Christ, and to have a correct perception of not only their own transformation process, but also of the evidence of the Holy Spirit moving among them (1 Cor 1:5–9). Truly, it was the apparent presence of the "Spirit of life" in the lives of the Corinthian believers that separated Paul's ministry from any other competing messages.

LIVE the Story

Paul Duff summarizes this section for us by writing,

> So, all believers can clearly see God's power in the resurrection of the executed Christ. We believers can see this in ourselves because we are being transformed into the same image, the image of the resurrected Christ. Like Christ, we are being transformed from the ministry of death to the ministry of life ("from glory to glory") because Moses' glorious ministry brought condemnation and the sentence of death upon us (Gentiles). But Paul's ministry of the Spirit and righteousness brings reconciliation with God which is tantamount to life. All of this has come about because the Lord God who raised Christ is also the Spirit who is present in our own ministries.[28]

"Ministry of Condemnation and Ministry of the Spirit and Life"

However, Gordon Fee writes that "with no intent to be judgmental, I observe that in much of its subsequent history, the church has lived somewhat below the picture of the life of the Spirit just outlined."[29] Indeed, in the Christian church, we still have both "ministry of condemnation" and a "ministry of Spirit," which brings life. Historically, from the medieval times to the present, the Christian church has had stringent rules and regulations that were put in place by people, not so much to transform people, but to mold the individual into an acceptable pattern of behavior. Nevertheless, Jesus Christ did not leave us a set of external rules to follow, but with his very own internal Spirit to change us from within. The primary distinction between the two ministries

---

28. Duff, "Transformed," 774 (my emphasis). The very same Spirit that empowered Paul's ministry is in our own ministries today.

29. Fee, *Paul, the Spirit, and the People of God*, 184.

is, indeed, the presence of the Spirit of God. At the time of Moses and the early Israelite nation, the Spirit of God filled one person only temporarily, for a specific speech, action, or behavior. Certainly, Moses experienced the Spirit of God upon reception of the stone tablets, but the common person did not have such an experience. Only later did God set his law "on tablets of human hearts" (3:3) for all people, and today, Christian believers are promised the presence of his Spirit on a permanent basis (3:11).

Yet, perhaps unknowingly, the Christian church today can restrict the Spirit of God. It can be condemning, unwelcoming, and judgmental. The church tends to judge people, especially those outside of its doors, even more harshly than society judges them. At one point in time, some Christians erroneously believed that the HIV/AIDS epidemic was God's righteous judgment on sinful people. Such self-righteous Christians demonstrated a lack of love and compassion for ailing human beings. Often the church can hold on too tightly to the old way of doing things, assuming it is the only right way of doing things. We become very set in our ways, and there is a sense of security in doing the familiar and relying on old rules and regulations.

A friend of mine was invited to her friend's daughter's wedding. The ceremony included a full mass celebration, where attendees of the wedding were invited to partake of the communion elements. When my friend stood up to get in line to take communion, her friend looked at her and stopped her in her tracks with a horrified look on her face. My friend, of course, was a Protestant and was not allowed to participate in the Holy Eucharist ritual. As a committed believer, it was hard for my friend to understand why she was banned from a ceremony that was so significant to her. It may be wrong, but that was the rule.

"Ministry of Death"

One of the most stunning examples of a modern-day "ministry of death" is seen in the formation of religious cults, where leaders are autonomous dictators and members become so brainwashed that they follow strictly enforced rules and regulations out of fear and deliberate ignorance. A prime example is the Reverend James ("Jim") Warren Jones, who was the despotic leader of the Peoples Temple, originally formed as a church in the 1950s in Indiana. Eventually, Jim Jones moved his loyal and captivated multiethnic community to Guyana. Here he established a community named for himself as Jonestown; it was to be a "socialistic paradise" and a "sanctuary" away from American media inquiry. He is best known as the organizer of the mass murder-suicide event on November 18, 1978, in Jonestown, when 909 members (including 304 children) "voluntarily" committed suicide (Jones called it "Translation") by ingesting cyanide poison in a grape-flavored drink. Jones himself died of a gunshot wound to the head, arguably self-inflicted, as he sat in a deck chair.

But that is not all. Earlier the same day, a delegation of people visited Jonestown on a fact-finding trip because of allegations of an abuse of human rights within the compound. This delegation included American Congressman Leo Ryan, concerned relatives of some of the inhabitants, NBC broadcasting crew employees, and other journalists. Jones appeared to be cooperative and hosted a reception for the delegation at the compound. When one of the Peoples Temple members attacked Congressman Ryan with a knife, the delegation decided to depart in a hurry. When they left, they took 15 of the Peoples Temple members with them who had expressed a desire to leave, and Jones did not stop them. At the airfield, two small planes were waiting to take off from Guyana. Jones's armed guard, the "Red Brigade," arrived suddenly and opened fire on the delegation. Congressman Ryan and four other people, including a reporter, a photographer, and a cameraman, were killed. Seven people, including several defecting members of the Peoples Temple, survived the carnage. In total, the events in Jonestown comprised the greatest single loss of American civilian lives in a deliberate act until the events of September 11, 2001.[30]

It is possible to go backward from 1978 to unravel the chilling tale of Jim Jones as a person and to search for answers about how and why such atrocities could take place. Since these events, numerous books have been written and documentary films have been made, based on eye-witness reports, photographs, and interviews with Jim Jones's family. The FBI has reviewed reels of tapes made by Jones and his followers. We know that for decades, Jim Jones was an "integrator," appealing to Americans to "love one another," regardless of race, creed, economics, or ethnicity. He preached sermons on tolerance, the virtues of the social gospel, social responsibility, and equality. He attracted quite a following and gained the public support of prominent politicians in California and on the national level. Yet, underneath his humanitarian spirit was a darkened soul who outwardly confessed his allegiance to communism and Marxism. His desire to create social change and make the world a better place masked his own personal demons: his demands for personal loyalty and obedience, his lack of love as a child, and his degradation of the Bible and

30. Documentary films include "Jonestown: Paradise Lost," an interview with Stephan Jones (son) on Discovery Networks (2007); "Jonestown: Mystery of a Massacre" (1998); "CNN Presents: Escape from Jonestown" (2008); "Witness to Jonestown" (2013); and "Jonestown: the Life and Death of Peoples Temple" (2006) on PBS.org. See also, "The Jonestown Death Tape," transcript No. Q42, Federal Bureau of Investigation, Department of Justice, Washington, DC; RYMUR 89-4286-2303, pp. 11–42. A copy of this transcript can be viewed at the website of the department of religious studies of San Diego State University (https://jonestown.sdsu.edu/?page_id=29081).

Christianity. As a leader, Jones grew in self-aggrandizement. He boldly stated that he was an atheist, yet he saw himself as God. He was "the reincarnation" of Mahatma Gandhi, "Father Divine" (George Baker), Jesus, Gautama Buddha, and Vladimir Lenin, all rolled into one. Further, he told his flock, "I'll be your father for those that don't have a father . . . I'll be your savior . . . If you see me as your God, I'll be your God . . . There's only one hope of glory; that's within you. Nobody's gonna come out of the sky; there's no heaven up there. We have to make heaven down here."[31] Unfortunately, the personal tragedies of the life of Jim Jones spread like a cancer to other vulnerable human beings and led to one of the worst tragedies in American history.

Certainly not all modern ministries are so intensely evil, but sometimes messages can condemn people to a less-than-fulfilling life by maintaining unnecessarily extremely legalistic positions. For a time in America, black people were not allowed to go inside of a "white" church, or a "white" hospital, or a "white" restaurant, and they could not sit at the front of a city bus. There was a time when the Christian church in America told people what to wear, what to sing, what to read, what to eat (fish on Friday) and what to drink (no alcohol), what games not to play (poker), and even what activities were considered very "unchristian" (like a homecoming dance). As a young teenager, my son was told that he could only read the King James Version of the Bible, as all other versions were "not allowed." He was told that "everything that came out of Egypt was evil," and he was too young to understand this false teaching. The youth leaders in his church actually wanted to take away his NIV Bible. If all of this sounds absurd to us today, recall that it is not unlike the 613 laws, rules, and traditions that the Jews were compelled to follow in the first century AD.[32] Do such rules, regulations, and human-instigated traditions raise people to their best? Do they bring an end to the human propensity toward greed, corruption, sexual sins, power, and selfish interests of some so-called religious people?

In summation, Jesus *is* life (John 1:4; 14:6), and if Jesus came to bring the "fullness" of life (John 10:10), then any message that contradicts who he is, why he came, and why he died and was raised again to life is a "ministry of death." One of the deepest and most significant messages of Jesus was that he came to bring light and life to those living in darkness. This is the hope of his followers, that *all* believers have eternal life (John 3:15, 36). Messages and laws created for increased human power, manipulation, and self-interest will die, and "whoever wants to save their life will lose it, but whoever loses their life for me will find it" (Matt 10:38, 39; 16:25).

---

31. "Jonestown: The Life and Death of Peoples Temple," (2006) American Experience, PBS.org.
32. Belleville, *2 Corinthians*, 95.

"Ministry of the Spirit"

The "ministry of the Spirit" in the new covenant is even more glorious than the older ministry of condemnation (3:9). The Spirit of God and of Jesus Christ, written on human hearts, can make unjust, human-made laws powerless and ineffective. There are legalistic rules about not allowing women to fully function in church leadership, but no one can convince me that I should be prevented from ministry in the church simply because of my gender. I know that it is God who gives gifts of the Spirit for the edification of the body:

> There are different kinds of gifts, but the same Spirit distributes them. There are different kinds of service, but the same Lord. There are different kinds of working, but in all of them and in everyone it is the same God at work.
>
> All these are the work of one and the same Spirit, and he distributes them to each one, *just as he determines.* (1 Cor 12:4–6, 11, my emphasis)

It is the Spirit that directs "the manifestation of the Spirit for the common good" (1 Cor 12:7 NASB). Any institutional traditions, rules, or regulations that condemn and destroy human life or that deny or limit the Spirit of God in the lives of all believers should be abolished. It is the job of the Spirit of God to transform human lives, not the power and control of other people (3:18).

Of course, we live in a world of laws, rules, and regulations, even more so today than the Israelites did in ancient times. Like the Jews of Paul's day, people today can understand the role of the law to be a necessary boundary, to control human behavior and actions to align the individual with the community in a political sense, and to align the person with God in a theological sense. There is a perceived dichotomy between law and freedom that is very much a part of our society today. Although laws may appear to limit or hamper our freedoms, laws are required as a standard of stability and order to preserve freedoms in a society. Hence, freedom and law must go hand-in-hand to complement each other. Without laws in a society, there would be anarchy. "The constant danger is rejection of the law in the name of a misconceived freedom which is purely arbitrary, because it is willing to grant itself more freedom than it is willing to grant to others."[33]

On the other hand, laws are not designed to transform the individual from the inside out (3:18). The human transformation declared by Paul implies a complete change of mind-set from the pattern of the world. In the end,

---

33. Blunck, "Freedom," 715.

Paul says, this transformation is "more glorious" than outward compliance to human-made laws. What does it look like in today's world?

"Transformation"

Pastor Francis Chan presented a sermon which was recently uploaded onto YouTube.[34] In the video, perhaps unknowingly, Chan made a distinction between two ministries in our society today that are similar to the ministries Paul discussed in 2 Corinthians 3:7–18. Chan elaborates on the "ministries of condemnation" that should be eliminated from the church today and the "ministries of life" that the Christian church should be promoting and expanding. The basis of Chan's sermon is a passage in Colossians. In Colossians, Paul not only addressed "freedom from human rules" (Col 2:16–3:8) but also defined and upheld the idea of the transformation of Christian believers, visible in one's "new self." Like his words to the Corinthians, Paul wrote to the Colossians:

> Do not lie to each other, since you have taken off your old self with its practices and have put on the new self, which is being renewed in knowledge in the image of its Creator. Here there is no Greek or Jew, circumcised or uncircumcised, barbarian, Scythian, slave or free. But Christ is all, and is in all.
>
> Therefore, as God's chosen people, holy and dearly loved, clothe yourselves with compassion, kindness, humility, gentleness and patience. Bear with each other and forgive one another if any of you has a grievance against someone. Forgive as the Lord forgave you. And over all these virtues put on love, which binds them all together in perfect unity (Col 3:9–14).

In contrast to condemnation and judgment, surely this is the essence of the "ministry of life": that every Christian believer is worthy and is "holy and dearly loved" by God, which is the force behind our desire to be totally transformed by him into the image of his Son.

Second, Chan spoke about a ministry of "blending in with the world" in contrast to a distinctly Christ-centered ministry (that is, "Christ is all, and is in all," Col 3:11). The Christian church today may be guilty of slowly becoming so much like the world around it that eventually it could be indistinguishable from it. We can be a consumer-driven church, appealing to the human desire for bigger and better entertainment, for human convenience, and falling into the trap of shameless competition.[35] The appeal to draw in great numbers of

---

34. All references from Francis Chan's sermon, "A New Attitude Toward People," https://www.youtube.com/watch?v=35nokZ_Z9t0.

35. Belleville, *2 Corinthians*, 86.

people overshadows the emphasis on transforming the people in it. We must live differently from the world; the Christian's life should be different on the outside because of our changes on the inside. Paul says our lives should be characterized by "compassion, kindness, humility, gentleness and patience" (Col 3:12) in a world that promotes self-interest, competition, wealth, success, and power. God does not want his people to be conformed to the patterns of the world, but to be transformed by his own Spirit.

Third, Chan observes that the church has placed too much importance on individual salvation and has neglected the call to serve with others in community. For generations in the American church, evangelism was individualistic. In the past, evangelistic efforts focused on salvation of the person so that he or she can go to heaven after death. This is a shallow emphasis that played on human fear. People are not "saved" or converted to Christianity only for their own peace and comfort in view of their future physical death; we are all "saved" to be an important part of the family of God in the present and to serve in a whole community of Christians, "all baptized by one Spirit so as to form one body" (1 Cor 12:12–13). The focus of the act of conversion has incorrectly been an end product instead of a fresh beginning.

In our self-centered world, some people insist that they do not need the institutional church to worship God or to maintain a good connection to him. They assume that they can read the Bible and pray to God "just as well on a mountaintop, alone, as in an old building with a bunch of people I do not know." And yet, this view of one's salvation is incomplete as well. Paul makes it very clear that we are saved *from* something (sin and condemnation), *to* something (to service and to glory!). Each individual believer is an integral part of the "body of Christ" (the church), where there is a role and purpose for each of us as planned by God (1 Cor 12:18–20).

On one side of the coin, we find that a person's identity may be based on the group to which one belongs: Are you a Baptist, a Presbyterian, a Roman Catholic, a "liberal" or a "conservative"? Such titles can create divisions, judgments, condemnation, and discord. In fact, and quite simply, we are all the "chosen people, holy and dearly loved" by God (Col 3:12), regardless of any other descriptions that tend to separate us. On the other side of the coin, some people search endlessly for their identity; they seek the "perfect" group to which they can belong. These folks constantly move about from church to church, never finding a community that suits all their needs: the pastor is boring, the people are unfriendly, the parking lot is crowded. Instead of worrying about how we are being served, we should worry more about how we can serve others.

It is the "ministry of the Spirit" that develops "holy" people, not a "ministry of condemnation" that is merely judgment based on individual preferences, needs, behavior, and human-made rules. Perhaps we would be changed people if we truly understood how much God really loves each one of us in spite of our own shortcomings. As his beloved children, the people of God are a family, with all of our dysfunctions, and we should love one another as the Father loves us. Paul reminds us that all believers are privileged to have "life" and "hope" and "freedom" in Christ (2 Cor 3:6, 12, 17), and the Spirit transforms and unites all of us so that we can reflect the "glory of God" to the world (3:18).

"Glorious Ministry"

The people of Israel were afraid to approach Moses and his radiant face. Are we the same? What are we afraid of? Are we afraid of what other people will say about us if we reveal our faith? It is the Spirit of God who sets people free to speak publicly, openly, frankly, boldly, and with empathy and understanding. Who will make known the Lord's glory in this world if not his own children (believers)?

Francis Chan relates that God wanted an entire nation to call his own, and he chose the nation of Israel. He wanted a community of people to reveal his glory to the world around them. Individually and corporately, they were to be distinctive, a "holy and loved" people, fearlessly set apart to reflect God's splendor. They were to be a blessing to other nations and yet remain distinct from them. This was a difficult, if not impossible, task for them to accomplish, because they were not indwelt by God's Holy Spirit on a permanent basis. But we are. As believers in Christ, we can speak boldly about our glorious faith because we are loved, and we are empowered by God's Spirit. We are released from the bonds of sin and death, to be used of God to reflect his glory all around us in a world that needs that light and hope (3:12).

Success in our society is often determined by one's own competency and our own ability to complete a given task. Success is signaled by material wealth, consumerism, and positions of power. Paul had none of those things, yet he considered himself a successful minister. It is difficult to fully grasp Paul's unique calling, his unique suffering and opposition in the first century. But his words in this section of the letter are very potent for all Christians today, especially for those who have heard the call to be ministers of the gospel of Jesus Christ. Paul's "new" ministry surpassed all ministries before him because it was a ministry for all people, for all time, regardless of their ethnicity, their gender, or their past. This is not because Paul is so remarkable, but because of the overwhelming power of God and the Holy Spirit. We can begin to identify with Paul and his ministry tasks as we begin to grasp the idea that the power of transformation (and boldness) is from God, and not from ourselves.

"Good News to Unbelievers"

Given that the tremendous power of God is what empowers human beings to minister in the name of Jesus, every believer is called to live in and through God's Spirit, reflecting the glory of God to everyone around us. For example, one segment of our population that has not embraced the glorious new covenant message is the Jews today, living all over the world. Linda Belleville refers to this as "corporate darkness," as the nation's "inability to discern the truths of salvation history because of a condition of spiritual blindness."[36] In spite of this national veil that remains even to this day (3:14), there is still great hope, and still the possibility of individual personal response to the new covenant (see Rom 9:1–11:36). In the Exodus narrative, Moses turned to Yahweh the Lord; the Lord to whom a person must now turn is the Spirit of Christ (2 Cor 3:17–18).[37]

Another one of the most unchurched groups of people in America today are young people from ages 18 to 35. People in this generation have been raised with captivating technology, from the Internet to phones and tablets, and their lives revolve around such devices. Further, many of these young people have little experience with the terrors of war across the globe. Some have been condemned by the institutional church for their behavior, or their appearance, or their nontraditional views of sexuality and marriage; some have never been told about the unconditional love and grace of Jesus Christ. It takes a special, bold filling of the Holy Spirit in young believers to share the new covenant with other people in their own age group.

Finally, although it is painful, it must be said that there are radical extremists in today's world whose message is one of death. Certainly not all Muslims are radical, extreme terrorists, but those who willfully bring about their own deaths and the deaths of hundreds of innocent people in the name of religion are woefully misguided. The world has shared in the grief, the cruel, groaning pain of determined death and destruction by extreme terrorists. Whether it is in New York, London, California, Belgium, Africa, or the Middle East, terrorism is a vivid reminder of a misleading, ill-conceived ministry of death and condemnation that is exactly the opposite of the God's "Spirit of life."

God's Spirit (2 Cor 3:17–18)

"The Lord is the Spirit";

He is God in my heart, in my arms, and in my voice.

The very blood within me, the very breath I breathe is his Spirit (2 Cor 3:6).

---

36. Belleville, *2 Corinthians*, 107.
37. Belleville, *2 Corinthians*, 109.

He never leaves me or betrays me.

Invisible, I see him clearly, hear him sharply and pursue his voice.

"Where the Lord is, there is freedom";

He breaks the chains of my tiny little prison of *self.*

He soothes my pains and dries my tears.

He comforts me so that I can comfort others (2 Cor 1:3–4).

Free to feel and to do the truth.

"We have unveiled faces";

He makes me see things as they really are; lies are exposed.

He helps his Word come alive in me and answers my doubts.

He strips me naked and still loves me.

"We all reflect the Lord's glory";

The unfathomable glory of the living Christ is an echo in me.

A mirror image of Christ is being seen in me.

"We are being transformed into his likeness, from glory to glory."

Even so, in this poor life:

His Spirit pervades and transforms and reshapes,

Molding me as clay into the vessel he has in mind,

Enriching every aspect of my existence.

"Glory comes from the Lord, who is the Spirit."

Shekinah glory of the Father guides and leads;

The sacrificial glory of the Son chooses, appoints;

The Spirit who is the Father, proceeds from the Father,

To the Son (John 16:14).

The Spirit who is the Son proceeds from the Son

To me.

The Son gave his very own glory to the ones he loves (John 17:22):

Teaching, revealing, sustaining, forgiving,

Nurturing, giving joy, and loving his own.

The glorious, incomprehensible plans and purposes of God,

realized through his own Spirit,

through me, through all believers,

united as one, in his Spirit.

Three-in-One. Inseparable. Omniscient. Omni-present.

"Don't you believe that I am in the Father,

and that the Father is in me?"

"On that day, you will realize that I am in my Father,

and you are in me, and I am in you." (John 14:10, 20)

AMEN.

by J. Diehl, 2018

CHAPTER 5

2 Corinthians 4:1–6

 ## LISTEN to the Story

> ⁴:¹Therefore, since through God's mercy we have this ministry, we do not lose heart. ²Rather, we have renounced secret and shameful ways; we do not use deception, nor do we distort the word of God. On the contrary, by setting forth the truth plainly we commend ourselves to everyone's conscience in the sight of God. ³And even if our gospel is veiled, it is veiled to those who are perishing. ⁴The god of this age has blinded the minds of unbelievers, so that they cannot see the light of the gospel that displays the glory of Christ, who is the image of God. ⁵For what we preach is not ourselves, but Jesus Christ as Lord, and ourselves as your servants for Jesus' sake. ⁶For God, who said, "Let light shine out of darkness," made his light shine in our hearts to give us the light of the knowledge of God's glory displayed in the face of Christ.

Listening to the Text in the Story: Genesis 1:2–4; Isaiah 9:1–2; 48:3–5, 17–19; John 3:16–21; Hebrews 1:3; Acts 9:1–19; 26:4–18; 1 Thessalonians 2:12; Romans 9:1–5; 10:1–4; Philippians 3:4–6.

"For my eyes have seen your salvation,
    which you have prepared in the sight of all nations,
a light for revelation to the Gentiles
    and the glory of your people Israel."
           —*Luke 2:30–32*

Christian ministry is a difficult undertaking, at best. Paul is not guilty of sugarcoating his call to ministry; he reveals to his readers the obstacles that he faced in doing what God had called him to do. A pastor once admitted, "Ministry is easy; it is the people who are difficult." Most people have no idea that it can be a thankless, 24/7 job. Perhaps the most painful aspects of ministry are the rebukes, reprimands, and verbal weapons against ministers from their own people, despite their hard work and compassion. Because it is so difficult, one might ask, "Why would anyone go into Christian ministry at all?" If one's call to ministry is real, then serious consideration must be given for anyone thinking about church leadership, the mission field, chaplaincy work, or a related endeavor. Christian work is not for the faint of heart, or for the person sitting on the fence about a deep commitment to God and to Christ. Knowing full well that it will not be an easy task, what is it that God is calling us to do? What is so bothersome to us that it pricks our minds constantly so that we cannot let it go?

The opening six verses of chapter 4 are inextricably tied to what comes before it; in addition, the remainder of chapter 4 is tied to the beginning section of chapter 5. Following his remarks concerning the old covenant ministry and its minister, Moses, and the new covenant ministry and his own calling as a new covenant minister in 3:7–18, Paul persists in an attempt to defend his ministry to his readers in 4:1–6. Specifically, both 3:12–18 and 4:1–6 are part of a larger portion of this letter, explaining the competence and courage (3:5, 12) of Paul's ministry that supersedes that of Moses. Furthermore, chapter 4 is an emotional and poignant chapter that explains why the apostle continues to be encouraged as a minister, despite his own weaknesses and the burdens of the job. In his life and in his ministry, Paul experienced suffering—great suffering. No doubt many people today can identify with the struggles and disappointments of ministry, to put it lightly. Paul says he has been there, done that, and has come out on the other side with faith, hope, and glory.

Chapter 3 climaxes in verse 18, with Paul declaring that in Christ, *all* believers are being transformed into the image of the Son of God. Then in 4:1, Paul contends that "we have *this* ministry," which he has already identified as a new ministry of the Spirit (3:18) and of life (3:6), a ministry of righteousness (3:9), and a ministry that is eternal (3:11). Indeed, what a glorious ministry it is, fulfilling that which the ministry of the law and of Moses just could not do.

In his subtle, humble manner, Paul shares with his readers what has been an arduous task for him. He pours out his own story, opens his heart, and recalls his own experiences for their benefit (4:15). The vulnerability of Paul is often missed in his letters, especially when he is attempting to authenticate his position as the apostle to the Gentiles. Also, we can see that Paul is not alone in his ministerial tasks and difficulties; the use of the pronouns "we" and "our" throughout this portion of the letter implies that there are fellow ministers united with him in his personal drive to deliver the gospel message to the Corinthians. Paul boldly (3:12) points out to the readers that the unveiled new covenant far surpasses the glory of the old (Mosaic) covenant, and it is the transforming power for all people who believe in Jesus Christ. In contrast to their ministry of the Spirit, the false, insincere teachers at Corinth have the readers "bewitched" (see Gal 3:1), and their distorted message leaves the world in darkness (2 Cor 4:2, 4).

> Paul's ministry (of the new covenant, of the Spirit, of righteousness) has a splendor that is not only unending but present with a transforming power in the lives of all (not just some) who, through its agency, have turned to the Lord. This is why Paul and his associates do not shrink back, but act with boldness in their dealings with others.[1]

Thus, chapter 4 opens with Paul's validation of his new-covenant ministry calling and his behavior as it relates to that of his opponents who spoke against him (vv.1–6). Paul's steadfast faith in Jesus, through pain and suffering, has led to his unique, personal testimony about Christ. His focus is only on Jesus, and not on what he could achieve to personally benefit from ministering in Jesus's name. In contrast to his adversaries, Paul can give good reason for his own integrity and his motives concerning the gospel message.

In the following section (4:7–15), Paul returned to the notions of power, trials, suffering, and persecution (see 1:3–11). He makes sure his readers know that his afflictions are "for Jesus' sake" (4:5), and not just general human troubles. His trials were not only a part of his ministry, but also actually authenticated it. The persecution that Paul experienced as a result of his message actually separated him from the disputing false apostles (11:13) who opposed him. Paul had plenty of memorable, dramatic ministry experiences to share with his readers that helped them to identify with him on their common spiritual journey in Christ. Finally (4:16–5:10), Paul pondered the eventual outcome, the eternal hope and the glory that awaits those who serve Jesus faithfully, despite human weaknesses and suffering. He demonstrated that he was able to face the obstacles in his life of ministry because through his trials and afflictions he assured his readers that "we do not lose heart" (the opening and closing phrase in both 4:1 and 4:16).

EXPLAIN the Story

Paul's Ministry Defended (4:1–2)
Paul established the content, the conduct, and the challenges of the ministry to which he had been called in these six verses. Chapter 4 opens with a

---

1. Furnish, *II Corinthians*, 245.

connective word, "therefore," reminding the reader of what has been said in 3:6–18. That is, the glory of God has been and is still being revealed in the gospel message as proclaimed by his competent ministers called by God to deliver the message of the new covenant (3:6, 18). The "therefore" reminds the readers of the hope of 3:7–11 that is theirs and confirms the present transformation as a reality in their lives (3:18).[2] Harris notes that the theme of glory (see 3:18) can be seen in first six verses of chapter 4. Literarily, these verses fall into three couplets:

vv. 1–2 The glory of ministry prompts honesty and truth.
vv. 3–4 The glory of the gospel is hidden ("veiled") from unbelievers by Satan.
vv. 5–6 The glory of God is known through the gospel message of Jesus Christ.[3]

Despite personal trials and opposition, Paul said of himself and his companions in ministry, "we will not lose heart" (4:1, 16). In both verses, Paul used a Greek verb that describes someone who is so fatigued that he or she has fallen into corrupt conduct, or the neglect of duties, or has completely lost the courage to finish the task at hand. It is used in this chapter as it is in Ephesians 3:13.[4] Even so, Paul told his readers that nothing, not deception, opposition, or weariness, will halt his ministry or change his effectiveness as a servant of God. Paul also defended his ministry because, through God's mercy (2 Cor 4:1), the Spirit enabled Paul to preach an unveiled gospel message and serve his readers.[5]

In 4:2, Paul began to address not only the accusations pitched at him, but he also strongly hinted at the character and motives of his opponents. In this verse, he pointed out the faults that are practiced by his rivals.[6] Apparently the false teachers in Corinth were ministering through secret and shameful ways; they were guilty of deception, as well as distorting the word of God. In view of these faults, Paul assured his readers that he had totally renounced and rejected their behavior. In fact, he may have been defending himself against some erroneous charges made against him by his adversaries, who had displayed "worldly wisdom" (1:12).

The carefully chosen words "secret and shameful" (4:2) work in tandem to

---

2. Furnish, *II Corinthians*, 245.
3. Harris, *Second Corinthians*, 321.
4. Harris, *Second Corinthians*, 323.
5. Garland, *2 Corinthians*, 205.
6. Garland, *2 Corinthians*, 205.

describe his opponents' behavior. This phrase can mean "the hidden things of shame," or "conduct concealed by shame," where the innermost thoughts of a person are exposed through his or her behavior.[7] Any way we look at it, Paul was definitely warning his readers that the underhanded tactics of the false teachers were despicable and shameful. Another pair of words, "deception" and "to distort" (4:2) further explain the clandestine conduct ways of his adversaries. The word "deception" or "craftiness" or "cunningness" paints a vivid picture because the meaning of this word is derived from "to bait for fish," or "to ensnare."[8] Paul uses this word again in 2 Corinthians 11:3, where he says the serpent's *cunningness* deceives Eve. The intentional deception and distortion of God's word in 4:2 takes the reader back to Paul's defense in 2:17, where he points out that he does not peddle the word of God for profit. Far be it from Paul to ever twist or tamper with the Scriptures (perhaps specifically the Jewish law) for the Gentile Corinthians. He is separating himself from his unethical, dishonest opponents, from their deeds of deception, and their distortion of God's true message.

Then, in the last part of v. 2, Paul tells his readers what he *does* do, in contrast to what he does *not* do. Furnish considers this "the positive side of apostolic boldness."[9] That is, Paul makes it a habit of speaking the truth plainly, of "commending ourselves to everyone's conscience," and his message is only veiled to those who overtly reject it. His truthful bold speech (3:12) stands out against the deception and misuse of God's word by his opponents. In doing so, he is protecting his own behavior and integrity. To differentiate his motives and his conduct from the others, Paul contends that his ministry sets forth the truth plainly (4:2). Paul adamantly explains that he has declared the truth in every circumstance, with full disclosure, and with no hidden secrets. Obviously, the truth and integrity of Paul's message was a primary concern on his mind. Here, he appealed to the conscience of everyone who had heard him proclaim the message of Christ. They could tell that his message and his methods of evangelism and service were always void of any cleverness, trickery, or misrepresentation (see 1 Cor 2:1–5), and the truth needs no certification from someone else.[10] Paul's message, as well as his very own life, was clear, open, and unveiled to those who received it (2 Cor 3:1–18). As forcefully as he denied the cunning errors of his opponents, Paul attempted to be straightforward and honest with the Corinthians in all his ways.

7. Belleville, *2 Corinthians*, 114.
8. Harris, *Second Corinthians*, 325.
9. Furnish, *II Corinthians*, 246.
10. Garland, *2 Corinthians*, 205.

The "Unveiled" Gospel (4:3–6)

Moreover, Paul continued in verse 3 by using a conditional phrase ("*if* our gospel is veiled . . .") to punctuate the fact that the Christian gospel he proclaimed was not veiled to those who received it. The veiled imagery recalls Paul's argument in 3:13–16, where he insisted that if "anyone turns to the Lord, the veil is taken away" (3:16). His rebuttal here says that if the gospel is hidden in language, it is the unbelievers who cannot grasp it. For those in Christ, the gospel message is knowledge of the truth that removes the veil, while the openness of his gospel message did not penetrate the veiled hearts of other people. Paul highlights the spiritual condition of those who are blinded to his gospel message. The veil was not removed from every human heart, so we can see that the "blinded minds" of 4:4 match the "dull minds" of 3:14. Further, the glory that was so prevalent in 3:7–18 reappears in 4:4 and 6, where it is the gospel of the glory of Christ and the glory of God in the face of Christ, placing the focus directly on Christ and thus on Paul's truthful message.[11]

Paul suddenly shifted to a new metaphor in 4:4 to explain that his message was obscure to unbelievers who cannot see the light, while it was clear to those who already know the glory of Christ. An additional reason for the hiddenness is due to the "god of this world" (4:4 NASB), or Satan, who has blinded unbelievers to the truth. That is, it is Satan who is responsible for their unbelief, and not the gospel message itself.[12]

"Light" in the New Testament can have several meanings. By way of explanation, Paul weaves together and overlaps the image of light with the concept of glory. It is difficult to untangle his imagery in these verses, because both "light" and "glory" are words that have deep and varied implications. First, in 4:4, Paul used the image of light as the gospel message itself ("light of the gospel"). This message shines a light on truth and reveals the glory of Christ to those who receive it. The glorious message of Jesus's true identity and what he did for humanity on the cross stands in contrast to the darkness and blindness of sin and unbelief. Second, in verse 6, Paul brings to his readers the remembrance of the words of God at the creation ("let light shine out of the darkness," see Gen 1:2–4), as well as the words of the prophet Isaiah in 9:1–2.

This image of light is often used in the NT with respect to the "new creation" or the new birth (see 2 Cor 5:17 and John 3:16–21). Here, in 2 Cor 4:6, Paul said that the "light" is "knowledge of God's glory displayed in the face of Christ," which is identical to the concept of the gospel of the glory of Christ in

---

11. Garland, *2 Corinthians*, 202.
12. Furnish, *II Corinthians*, 247.

4:4.[13] Those who *know* Jesus Christ as Lord *know* the unveiling of his splendor in their lives. "Light" is knowledge of the gospel message, which exhibits the glory of Christ Jesus and makes itself known through transformed believers who are "the new creation" (5:17; cf. 3:18)—all thanks to the revelation of God the Father through Christ.

Paul formed an interesting visual and theological parallel in these two verses:

4:4 the light of the gospel	the glory of Christ	who is the image of God;
4:6 the light of the knowledge	of God's glory	in the face of Christ.

The juxtaposition of God and Christ tells the readers that Christ perfectly and reliably displays God's glory to the world. Christ is the "radiance of God's glory and the exact representation of his being, sustaining all things by his powerful word" (Hebrews 1:3). Certainly this knowledge of the true identity and glory of Christ is the treasure so precious to believers, and to which Paul refers in the next verse (2 Cor 4:7).

Paul spoke from experience. "Light" is not an ethereal concept to Paul. He was literally transformed by the "light of Jesus." Paul had suffered from the same blindness as his fellow Jews that had darkened the vision of some in Israel.[14] He was uniquely qualified to preach the light of the gospel because he was also blinded to the truth, and then he was actually physically blinded. This is the conversion story of Saul of Tarsus, who became the apostle Paul following an incredible encounter with Jesus on the road to Damascus (see Acts 9:1–19 and 26:4–18):

About noon . . . I saw a light from heaven, brighter than the sun, blazing around me and my companions. (Acts 26:13)

Saul got up from the ground, but when he opened his eyes he could see nothing. So they led him by the hand into Damascus. For three days he was blind, and did not eat or drink anything. (Acts 9:8–9)

Jesus spoke to him, saying, "I will rescue you from your own people and from the Gentiles. I am sending you to them [the Gentiles] to open their eyes and turn them from darkness to light, and from the power of Satan to God, so that they may receive forgiveness of sins and a place among those who are sanctified by faith in me" (Acts 26:17–18).

---

13. Furnish, *II Corinthians*, 250.
14. Garland, *2 Corinthians*, 208.

Often we say that "a light bulb goes on" in someone's mind when that person finally "gets" something; that is, a moment of knowledge or understanding is pictured as a light that comes on in one's mind or heart. For Paul, his moment of realization concerning Jesus came when he encountered the risen Jesus. His 180-degree transformation from Saul the Persecutor to Paul the Proclaimer came about when he realized that only God can be raised from the dead. Likewise, for all of humanity, it is through the life, death, and resurrection of Jesus that redeemed people are transformed and encounter God's glory (2 Cor 3:18).

This striking experience of light and darkness, vision and blindness, was not a minor event in Paul's life. His encounter with the risen Jesus was at the very heart of his ministry to the Gentiles, and the foundation upon which he was qualified to be an apostle (4:5). Jesus displayed his Father God to humanity; he is the image of what humanity was originally created to be. In the same way, believers should reflect the glory of Christ to the darkened world. If we think about Paul's conversion story in Acts 26:17–18, we can see a vivid similarity to what Paul tells his readers in 2 Cor 4:2–6. He insisted that it was the transformed Paul who ministered to the Gentiles. He was eminently qualified to be an apostle, and to show the light of the gospel message, because he was an eye-witness to the "glory of God in the face of Christ" (4:6).

As a result of his experiences, "the god of this age" does not scare Paul in the least, because he knows that the unseen evil power of the unbelieving world is no match for the glory of Christ's gospel. The "god of this age" is a unique phrase, as it occurs only here in the NT. It refers to Satan and the dominion that he has over those who reject God and his agent, Jesus Christ (see 2:10–11). Here, Satan represents lawlessness, darkness, unbelief, moral depravity, and the worship of idols (see 6:16, especially apparent in polytheistic Corinth). Paul is fully aware of Satan as his personal adversary and Satan's attempts to impede Paul's mission and his unique calling to ministry. We can notice, too, that in Paul's view, the power and influence of Satan are limited to "this age." Perhaps his readers knew that Satan was defeated at the cross of Christ (Col 2:15), but they were still aware of his influence in the world, particularly in defiance of God's truth.[15]

Thus, Paul and his companions did not preach "ourselves" (2 Cor 4:5), under their own power and position, or by their own talents and education; on the contrary, they are only the messengers of the gospel of Jesus Christ.

---

15. Garland, *2 Corinthians*, 209. Other Pauline references to Satan appear in Rom 16:20; 1 Cor 5:5; 2 Cor 11:14, 12:7; and 1 Tim 1:20. A recent book of interest on this subject is Derek R. Brown, *The God of This Age: Satan in the Churches and Letters of the Apostle Paul*, WUNT 2/409 (Tübingen: Mohr Siebeck, 2015).

These ministers are described as humble servants of the Corinthians, and everything that they did was "for Jesus' sake" (v. 5). The true gospel message in 4:6 is what Paul conveyed to the Corinthians:

> The light that dispels darkness in the human heart is found in *the face of Jesus* . . . The *face* is the image that we present in public. Christ's *face*, then, is what he presented during his earthly ministry . . . The connection is a relatively simple one: to know Christ is to know God; to not know Christ is to not know God.[16]

Paul's Gospel to the Gentiles and the Jews

Scholars continue to debate the role of Paul and his ministry to the Gentiles, especially with respect to the nation of Israel. What did Paul think about his call to take the new covenant to the Gentiles, and did his heart ache for his own people, the Jews? To fully answer this question, it would be necessary to explore all of Paul's writings, including Romans 9–11. The Gentiles, in Corinth for example, may have questioned why his own people (the Jews) rejected Jesus as the Messiah. If God chose the Jews as his people, why did they execute the One sent by God for the redemption of the nation? What will happen to the Jews who do not accept Jesus as the Messiah? It is obvious from his writings that Paul struggled tremendously with these kinds of questions. Yet, as we know now, he was God's chosen apostle to the Jews *and* the Gentiles, making it even more likely that his opponents in Corinth were from both camps. Second Corinthians 3:12–4:6 reveals Paul's dilemma and imparts important insights into Paul's heart and mind about unbelieving Jews.[17]

Paul already noted that the unbelieving Jews had dull minds and veiled hearts (3:14, 15). Here, he commented that they stubbornly refused to accept the light of the gospel that they had been given (4:4; see Isa 48:3–5). Further, he recognized the role of "the god of this age" in blinding the minds of unbelievers (4:4). This seems to say that the unbelievers of whom he spoke had been given the knowledge and the truth of the gospel, but they had intentionally chosen to reject the message for any number of reasons.

Consequently, Paul did require an affirmative stand toward Jesus as the promised Messiah and Redeemer (see Isa 48:17–19), and that failure to recognize Jesus as such was disobedience to God. Paul's concern about his fellow Jews was two-fold. First, he was hurt and saddened by their refusal to

---

16. Belleville, *2 Corinthians*, 119 (her emphasis).

17. For more information, see Michael Bird, *An Anomalous Jew: Paul Among the Jews, Gentiles and Romans* (Grand Rapids: Eerdmans), 2016.

follow Jesus. Second, it appears that even those who spoke words of acceptance of Jesus as the Messiah and became part of the first-century Christian movement criticized Paul's methods and did not approve of his efforts to expand his ministry to the Gentiles, who had once been Israel's sworn enemies.

 LIVE the Story

Christian Ministry and the Call for Truth
These six verses are ripe with important challenges about proclaiming the Christian message with integrity and about sharing the Christian message in a world of darkness today. His readers may have well understood Paul's imagery of the veiled and unveiled gospel message and, in the same way, we must see the veils that hide the gospel message from people in our own time and in our culture. What is the point of proclaiming the gospel of Christ to other people? Is converting people to Christianity a process to be achieved and recorded, like the number of passes completed by a football quarterback? These verses should make us think deeply about our own commitments to the gospel, about unbelievers, about the role of the church in evangelism, as well as how and why we share the timeless truths of the gospel "for Jesus' sake" (4:5). That is, if we truly "know the light of the gospel," we should have a burning desire to share it with others. How do we, as the Christian church, "set forth the truth plainly" (4:2) about Jesus Christ?

Recently, a Scottish minister summarized the church's role quite accurately as he wrote, "At best, parish ministry is characterised by generosity of spirit combined with an evangelical sense of outreach and a prophetic passion for justice—especially for the outsider."[18]

The "Lost"
In view of Paul's OT imagery of the unveiling of the gospel, who are the "lost" or the "unbelievers" (4:4) in our world today? If Paul was deeply concerned about his fellow Jews who rejected Jesus as the Messiah, who are we concerned about today? Like that of Paul, what role do we have in the lives of unbelievers in our own generation?

These six verses show us an interchange between the role of the human messenger of the gospel and the supernatural work of God (and the Spirit). For us, these two roles are held in an uncomfortable tension. If salvation and

18. Ron Ferguson, "In Praise of Parish Ministry," *Life and Work: The Magazine of the Church of Scotland* (February 2016): 15.

conversion are all God's initiation and work, why should we do anything? Evangelism and education become unnecessary. Or, if the conversion of people to the Christian faith is completed entirely by human effort, why do we need God? The latter position can result in human pride or human fear—pride that our success is determined by how many "souls we have saved," and fear because, in reality, we must confess that we know that we are not fully capable of converting unbelievers on our own. Thus, both human effort and divine direction are necessary; we must trust in the divine sovereignty of God while embracing our responsibility of sharing his word (4:2) and his glory in our hurting world.

"Knowledge" of God

Certainly, Paul implied that "knowledge" of God is possible only through God's self-revelation, first through the law (3:7–15), and then through his Son, Jesus Christ (3:16; 4:4–6). That is, the "knowledge of God's glory" appears to us now in the "face of Christ." What we "know" about God is only that which he has chosen to reveal to us. Through divine revelatory acts, words, promises, and commands of God in the Old Testament, and then through the life, death, and resurrection of Jesus, we "know" what we know about God. Ultimately, God revealed himself through a person—his Son. Therefore, Paul implies, one cannot "know" God without explicitly knowing Jesus: "The decisive new revelation of God is presented in the NT as constituted in Jesus, in light of whom all God's previous revelations find their ultimate purpose in anticipating, prepared for, and now giving way to Jesus."[19]

Yet, all is not revealed. There are still things we have yet to learn through the Spirit of God, and things that have not been revealed to us by the Father. Human beings who speculate about the "end-times" or guess about the timing of things yet to come can be misleading, and their tactics can be pointless. Indeed, N. T. Wright confirms that,

All language about the future, as any economist or politician will tell you, is simply a set of signposts pointing into a fog. We see through glass darkly says St. Paul as he peers toward what lies ahead. But that doesn't mean that it's anybody's guess or that every opinion is as good as every other one. And—supposing someone came forward out of the fog to meet us? That, of course, is the central thought often ignored in Christian belief.[20]

19. Larry W. Hurtado, *God in New Testament Theology* (Nashville: Abingdon, 2010), 46.
20. N.T. Wright, *Surprised by Hope* (New York: HarperOne, 2008), xiii–xiv.

Again, we must focus on what we do know about Christ, and not on what we do not know about God's ultimate plans on the future.

Like Paul, we are called to spread the gospel of Jesus Christ to unbelievers (4:6). If every Christ-follower was, at some point in his or her life, an unbeliever, then we certainly can grasp the concern and importance of Paul's words in 2 Corinthians 4:3–6. We can feel Paul's apprehension about his own people, his friends, and his family members who did not follow Jesus. We may remember when the lightbulb went on, and we experienced the "light of the knowledge of the glory of God in the face of Christ" (4:6) and the pure joy of knowing Jesus, but often we forget to be that light among "those who are perishing." Instead, it seems easier to stay inside our comfortable cocoon of faithful believers, while we quickly (and often thoughtlessly) judge those on the "outside." While we know that we must bring the light of the gospel to a world of darkness, more often than not, we feel insecure about our message, and we are anxious about approaching people of other faiths—those very much unlike us.

Paul would tell us, "do not lose heart" (4:1, 4:16), build relationships, "set forth the truth plainly" (4:2), and pray. Open the doors of the church and walk out of them; do not just hope that people might come in. Pray for the Spirit of God to move against the blindness, the hardened hearts, and against the grip of the "god of this age" (4:4). We must remember Paul's words in Colossians, that we are "holy and beloved" and that we are to be Christ's witnesses with "compassion, kindness, humility, gentleness and patience . . . forgive as the Lord forgave you . . . and over all these virtues put on love, which binds them all together in perfect unity" (Col 3:12–14).

Preaching Jesus

Many fine books have been written on pastoral church ministry, and they can be beneficial to those involved in church leadership. From them, we can see that the profession of a church minister has changed and developed over the centuries from the time of the Reformation until today. Roles have changed, duties have changed, and even titles have changed. At one time, the pastor of a church was always respectfully called "Reverend" or "Brother." We now have "lead pastor," "senior pastor" (only those over the age of 55?), "associate pastors," "executive pastors," as well as "directors" or "coordinators" of specific ministries. The hierarchy is complicated; it can also be competitive and damaging. So, certainly some things do change over time. But from Paul's description of Christian ministry in this letter, we see that some things should not change in Christian ministry. First, a person's calling clearly should be from God, and from no one else:

On the contrary, in Christ we speak before God with sincerity, like [people] sent from God (2:17). . . . Not that we are competent in ourselves to claim anything for ourselves, but *our competence comes from God*. He has made us competent as ministers of a new covenant—not of the letter but of the Spirit; for the letter kills, but the Spirit gives life (3:5, 6). . . . *For what we preach is not ourselves*, but Jesus Christ as Lord, and ourselves as your *servants for Jesus' sake* (4:5, my emphasis).

In fact, there is nothing in this letter as to specific requirements of age, gender, or education to be called by God into ministry. What Paul does require of true ministers is to "renounce secret and shameful ways," to be honest, to protect God's word from distortion (4:2), to speak the truth plainly (4:2), and not to focus on oneself, but to "preach Jesus Christ as Lord" (4:5). Moreover, Christian ministry is *servanthood*, graciously carried out "for Jesus' sake." The underlying requirement for ministry, then, for us as for Paul, is a humble commitment to work with God to accomplish his purposes.

Second, Paul's letters reveal his pastor's heart as he demonstrated his care, concern, and devotion toward "his people," the members of the various Christian communities. Paul was a teacher, an evangelist, and a church planter, but most of all, he was a pastor/shepherd. He had no theology degree, although he had a fine education (Phil 3:4–6) and knew the Old Testament Scriptures well. He never used the title "pastor" for himself; yet, in Ephesians 4:11 he notes that the position of a "pastor" is one of the gifts that Christ has given to his church, with teachers, prophets and apostles. That is, "pastoring" is not an office that one achieves; it is a gift given to the church for the edification of the church (Eph 4:12–13). In Acts 20:28 Paul warned the Ephesian leaders to "keep watch over yourselves and all the flock of which the Holy Spirit has made you overseers. Be shepherds of the church of God, which he bought with his blood."

As a result of God's calling, Paul was committed to maintaining a relationship with the people of God, preparing them for service, unifying them through knowledge, transforming them, helping them mature into the full knowledge of Christ, and being a humble "shepherd" to them, guiding and protecting them as his own "flock." Ultimately, all that is done in ministry must be done under the guidance of the Holy Spirit to honor God and demonstrate his "glory displayed in the face of Christ" (4:6).

Years ago, I worked as a director of women's ministries in a large, suburban church. As such, I devoted many hours to the various activities within that ministry, from a weekly Bible study to fund-raising projects for a home for unwed mothers and their babies. Because of the expanding ministry and the growing time commitment, I asked to be considered a paid, part-time staff member. Yet I was told by my lead pastor that I could get paid as a staff member only if I could prove that my work directly put more bodies in the pews and hence more money in the collection plates. He wanted me to increase the financial giving to the church by the amount of my salary, which was "evidence" that I could run a fruitful ministry. The emphasis by the staff leadership was that we were working for the organization, and not for Jesus. I did not realize until much later that the value given to ministry in that community was not the glorification of Christ. We must recognize that volunteers, paid staff members, lead pastors, janitors, evangelists, or auto-mechanics—everyone contributes to the proclamation of "the glory of Christ" in his or her own way. Each believer who serves the community honestly and truthfully because they are called by God to do so must be valued as a co-worker with all the others, both paid staff and unpaid volunteers.

On the other hand, in our culture today the demands of ministry can be overwhelming for staff and leaders. In the past, a preacher was someone who "married and buried" parishioners; but today's minister is "on duty" day and night, as a therapist, an administrator, a financial analyst, and a plumber who can fix toilets on Saturday nights. The demand for new and expanding ministries to meet the needs of a varied congregation within a limited (often very limited) budget is taxing. A small church in our area does not have the funds for a secretary, so the one who preaches on Sunday morning creates the order of worship, picks the songs and the Scriptures, types, duplicates, and folds the bulletin all by herself. She creates the monthly newsletter, makes hospital visits, takes all the phone calls, and secures maintenance for the church's physical plant. It is no wonder that some overworked and underpaid professional pastors can get "burned out," or resort to unhealthy websites on the Internet, and/or face the temptation of relational sins with others inside and outside their community. Everyone is needed to help the body of Christ function properly; we can all support those in leadership positions in the church with our gifts, our services, our support, our time, and our prayers.

In a book written years ago, in 1981, Murray Thompson wrote that within the "ordered ministry" of his denomination, there are "clergy" and other "full-time servants of the church." The duties of the professional staff are, "oversight, pertaining to the ministries and structures of the church; pastoral, pertaining to life in and service to the fellowship; and service, pertaining to service in and to the world."[21] While this is a fairly traditional understanding of ministry in

---

21. Murray Stewart Thompson, *Grace and Forgiveness in Ministry* (Nashville: Abingdon, 1981), 15.

most Protestant churches, Thompson goes on to remind us that all ministry "starts with God . . . and Jesus Christ." He adds:

> The call to ministry may well be experienced by anyone inside the church or outside it, for there are many whose objectives coincide with the good news of God's saving actions, and God seems to bless their efforts. . . . Jesus' call to all people is "Follow me." Yet within that inclusive call there are specific or personal calls to particular tasks or responsibilities. Without denigrating the worthiness of unconscious acts of service, Christian ministry is to be understood as a conscious response to the call of God.[22]

Thus, professional ministers in paid positions to serve a community must delegate, promote, train, encourage, and edify those in "unpaid" positions, or those in "lay-ministry" positions inside and outside of the church. A fully involved community brings life and warmth to a church. Very talented, qualified people whose calling from God is very real should be emboldened to serve God as they are so called—the school crosswalk attendant, the intensive care nurse, the counselor, and the elderly lady who crochets blankets for infants in Zaire. A person does not need to have a theological degree to serve God in his kingdom. For the Christian, there are no fences between the Lord's work and "secular" work. Thompson says, "hence the excitement and the vitality experienced by members of the laity when they first realize that what they may be doing at home or at work is a ministry in the same sense as that of the clergy."[23] Paul instructs the Colossians that, "Whatever you do, work at it with all your heart, as working for the Lord, not for human masters, since you know that you will receive an inheritance from the Lord as a reward. It is the Lord Christ you are serving" (3:23–24). We cannot forget that, first and foremost, we are all called to glorify Jesus. "The Bible also makes it clear that all of life is important to God. In fact, how you and I act on the job reveals more about our commitment to Christ than how we act on Sunday."[24]

Finally, those committed to Christian ministry must naturally combat injustice and the influence of the "god of this world" in every way possible. The light of the gospel must take the form of human compassion toward both our fellow believers and the unbeliever alike. In an unjust world, Christians must make a difference, in big and small ways. To put it mildly, Christian ministry is extremely difficult in a darkened world that is filled with selfishness,

---

22. Thompson, *Grace and Forgiveness in Ministry*, 16.
23. Thompson, *Grace and Forgiveness in Ministry*, 16.
24. Douglas Connelly, *Wisdom from a Pastor's Heart* (San Francisco: Jossey-Bass, 2001), 133.

greed, a lack of human justice, unfairness, and immorality. It is noteworthy that the perpetrator of a crime who is shot by police is rushed to a hospital where he or she is cared for like any other patient. In the same way, we must attempt to heal the hopeless, care for the careless, and be patient with the rebellious. In the power of the Holy Spirit, we can extend a helping hand to those in need in a broken world, whoever they are, and leave the judgment to God.

Persecution in the Fight for Justice

My uncle, the Rev. James S. Conner, was a Methodist minister in the state of Mississippi during the 1960s when the civil rights movement in America hit a peak of tension. He was a participant in what has been called the "Born of Conviction" statement, which was printed in 1963. Conner was one of twenty-eight white Methodist ministers, frustrated with the lack of words and actions by their authoritative leaders in the conference, who issued a document in support of radical changes in race relations within the Methodist denomination. The historical backdrop for the writing of this monumental document is remembered with grief and disbelief. The stories of heroism are both painful and inspirational. There were deep, ingrained feelings in *favor* of segregated churches and conferences, schools and public transportation. There were also deeper feelings *against* white supremacy, human injustice, and the need for social change, especially within the Christian church. We remember the words, ministry, struggle, and the courageous life of Rev. Martin Luther King Jr., who lived and spoke in extreme contrast to members of the Ku Klux Klan. The KKK members were "respectable, intelligent, highly regarded" members of their churches and their communities, but we are painfully aware of their public and private acts across the South: murders, lynchings, church burnings, cross burnings, and "secret" acts against innocent black people.

At that time, the focus of racial tension became a "theological concern" in Mississippi, and the church was at the center of the debate about racial equality. What was the proper relationship between the church and the world? The perceived central purpose of Methodism was to "win souls to Christ" and not to become involved in political and social reform. It became very important for the clergy to "support the segregated white supremacist system in Mississippi."[25] My uncle and his ministry colleagues refused to do so. Pain, rejection, and acts of dismissal faced those clergy who refused to act in accordance with the rules of segregation. These men put their lives (and the lives

---

25. Joseph T. Reiff, *Born of Conviction: White Methodists and Mississippi's Closed Society* (New York: Oxford University Press, 2016), xvii.

of their families) on the line to promote justice and equality for God's people, regardless of race or color.

To be reconciled with God involves being reconciled with one another, and it begins with reconciliation with brothers and sisters within the body of Christ. Wright concludes:

> This is the foundation, I believe, for the work of hope in the day-to-day life of the church . . . Part of the task of the church must be to take up that sense of injustice, to bring it to speech to help people both articulate it and, when they are ready to do so, to turn it into prayer . . . And of course, evangelism will flourish best if the church is giving itself to works of justice (putting things to rights in the community) and works of beauty (highlighting the glory of creation and the glory yet to be revealed).
>
> There is a new world, and it has already begun, and it works by healing and forgiveness and new starts and fresh energy . . . This is the good news—of justice, beauty, and above all, Jesus—that the church is called upon to live and to speak, to bring into reality, in each place and each generation. What might the life of the church look like if it was shaped, in turn, by this hope-shaped mission?[26]

Thus, Paul defended his own ministry, and that of every committed Christian worker, especially those committed to a life of humble service. A friend of the author Henri Nouwen described this beloved, devoted pastor and his ministry, which is a model for all of us:

> His sermon was like his life—he rolled up his sleeves and threw himself right into the heart of the matter. He didn't have any simple, clichéd answers. Instead, he paid tribute to the anguish we all felt and pointed to it as the place where our hearts must live to be reborn and where our shared humanity is discovered. It was a message of pain and loss but also one of hope and rebirth.[27]

26. Wright, *Surprised by Hope*, 230–32.
27. Andrew Kennedy, "A New Way to Live," in *Befriending Life: Encounters with Henri Nouwen*, ed. Beth Porter, Susan Brown, Peter Coulter (New York: Doubleday, 2001), 41.

CHAPTER 6

2 Corinthians 4:7–5:10

 ## LISTEN to the Story

[7]But we have this treasure in jars of clay to show that this all-surpassing power is from God and not from us. [8]We are hard pressed on every side, but not crushed; perplexed, but not in despair; [9]persecuted, but not abandoned; struck down, but not destroyed. [10]We always carry around in our body the death of Jesus, so that the life of Jesus may also be revealed in our body. [11]For we who are alive are always being given over to death for Jesus' sake, so that his life may also be revealed in our mortal body. [12]So then, death is at work in us, but life is at work in you.

[13]It is written: "I believed; therefore I have spoken." Since we have that same spirit of faith, we also believe and therefore speak, [14]because we know that the one who raised the Lord Jesus from the dead will also raise us with Jesus and present us with you to himself. [15]All this is for your benefit, so that the grace that is reaching more and more people may cause thanksgiving to overflow to the glory of God.

[16]Therefore we do not lose heart. Though outwardly we are wasting away, yet inwardly we are being renewed day by day. [17]For our light and momentary troubles are achieving for us an eternal glory that far outweighs them all. [18]So we fix our eyes not on what is seen, but on what is unseen, since what is seen is temporary, but what is unseen is eternal.

[5:1]For we know that if the earthly tent we live in is destroyed, we have a building from God, an eternal house in heaven, not built by human hands. [2]Meanwhile we groan, longing to be clothed instead with our heavenly dwelling, [3]because when we are clothed, we will not be found naked. [4]For while we are in this tent, we groan and are burdened, because we do not wish to be unclothed but to be clothed instead with our heavenly dwelling, so that what is mortal may be swallowed up by life. [5]Now the one who has fashioned us for this very purpose is God, who has given us the Spirit as a deposit, guaranteeing what is to come.

[6]Therefore we are always confident and know that as long as we are at

home in the body we are away from the Lord. [7]For we live by faith, not by sight. [8]We are confident, I say, and would prefer to be away from the body and at home with the Lord. [9]So we make it our goal to please him, whether we are at home in the body or away from it. [10]For we must all appear before the judgment seat of Christ, so that each of us may receive what is due us for the things done while in the body, whether good or bad.

Listening to the Text in the Story: Job 10:9; Psalm 2:9; Isaiah 9:1–2; 22:24; 29:16; 41:25; 45:9; 52:11; 64:8; 66:20; Jeremiah 18:1–12; Psalm 30:4–5; Wisdom of Solomon 15:7–17; Sirach 27:5; 33:13; 38:29–30; Matthew 5:10–12, 14, 16.

> God never makes you suffer unnecessarily.
> He intends for your suffering to heal and purify you.
> The hand of God hurts you as little as it can.
> Do not waste your suffering.
> Let suffering accomplish what God wants it to in your life.
> Never get so hard that you suffer for no reason and for no purpose.
> —*Fénelon*[1]

Children can ask the most interesting questions. In their innocence and inexperience, children search for simple answers to some of life's most demanding questions. We ponder some questions even into adulthood because the answers are not simple. What happens when we die? Why do we have to experience trials and suffering in this life? These are perhaps two of the most vexing questions posed by Christian believers and unbelievers alike! In truth, both believers and unbelievers often react to the hardships of life in the same ways. The British are famous for their expression, "keep calm and carry on," even if you are up a stream without a paddle.

The Corinthian believers, like some Christian believers today, had a hard time accepting the fact that Spirit-filled Christians experience tough times. In truth, as we listen to this letter, it is difficult to understand how Paul could have such confidence and hope in his ministry in spite of adversity. Typical of all human beings, the Corinthians were "burdened" and "groaning" in this life; they were longing for a better life, a "heavenly dwelling," or an eternity with

---

1. Francois de Salignac de La Mothe Fenelon, *The Seeking Heart* (Jacksonville, FL: SeedSowers, 1942), 30–32.

God (2 Cor 5:2). Certainly, Paul had such thoughts himself. He needed to remind them that if they lost sight of the eternal promises of God and the hope they received from their position in Christ, then they could miss the earthly purposes to which they had been called in this life. While these days and years are short, temporary, and strife-filled, the Christian must remain focused on and confident in the permanent promises of God through the work of Christ. That is, by "living by faith and not by sight," and by pleasing God (5:7, 9), there is no insecurity or apprehension about what is to come in the future.

Further, Paul's church needed to recognize the incredible power of God. Paul's message is a paradox—that God's power is revealed in the suffering of those he has called into ministry. Now, that's odd. What person today would apply for a pastorate position or a counseling position by enumerating his or her frailties, weaknesses, distresses, and ill-treatment by another community of believers? But this is exactly what Paul was doing from 4:7 to 5:10. Paul attempted to answer seemingly unanswerable questions by saying that it is the power of God (4:7) and the life of Jesus (4:10) that gave him strength and endurance in ministry. Even more unbelievable is the fact that it is this very suffering that authenticated Paul's calling as a true minister of the gospel.

The opening phrase of encouragement in 4:1 is repeated in 4:16 ("we do not lose heart"); thus, it is used as a thematic marker for the entire chapter. The intervening paragraphs from 4:1 to 4:15 explain why the apostle continues to be encouraged despite his own weaknesses and the burdens of ministry. We hear the familiar verses that end chapter four (vv. 16–18) that summarize and conclude Paul's argument concerning his ministry that began all the way back in 3:4. The opening six verses of chapter four are Paul's validation of his ministry calling and his behavior as it relates to that of his opponents. Then, Paul shows that suffering and persecution "for Jesus' sake" was a part of his ministry and actually authenticated it. Finally, Paul thinks about eternity and the glory that awaits those who serve Jesus faithfully. Paul was able to face the obstacles in his life of ministry because he was fully aware of the eternal perspective granted to the Christian believer (4:16–18). On the one hand, he claims that the "death of Jesus" is revealed in the believer's "mortal body" and, on the other hand, that Jesus's resurrected life is at work in us, even as we are "wasting away" physically (4:10–12, 16). Then, Paul claimed in chapter 5 that the life and death of a believer reveals the way in which he or she lived (5:9–10). His use of such paradoxical metaphors can be confusing, and we will look at them more closely.

Most modern translations begin chapter 5 with the word "Now," moving the reader forward from 4:18b ("but what is unseen is eternal") to another realization: that believers have the assurance of resurrection after physical death (see also, 4:14). The first ten verses of chapter 5 are a tightly constructed paragraph, where Paul creates a poetic vision of the eternal future of believers. This picture diverges greatly from the earthly life that we experience in the here and now. Paul lifts our spirits from the despair of 4:7–15 to the eternal glory given to each believer in 5:1–10. In these verses, we are presented with sharp contrasts: "life in the midst of suffering, and glory through and after suffering."[2] Eternity continues to be in Paul's mind as he encourages his church to live their earthly lives in Christ, because they have a guarantee of what is to come (5:5). Like some of us, perhaps Paul was struggling with the very idea of his own death. He stared into the face of death in Asia (1:8–11), and he grappled with his own humanity and mortality. Thus, we read Paul making a case for confidence in a God who has guaranteed that his followers will know an eternal state of glory after death. What started out as discouragement in 4:7–12 ends up as encouragement in 5:6–8. Paul expects the Corinthians to respond to his contrasts and metaphors by living a real life in Christ, which is a positive reaction to the promise of an eternity with the Lord (5:9). Living in hope and with confidence leads to reconciliation with God and with one another; in the second half of chapter 5, Paul demonstrates how that can happen.

EXPLAIN the Story

Power of God in Suffering (4:7–15)

Typical of Paul, the apostle suddenly switches metaphors from the "light" (in 4:6) to "jars of clay" in 4:7. With little warning, verse 7 begins with a "but," so we need to read what comes immediately before it for a fuller understanding of the verses that follow. Paul draws a contrast between the glory of God (v. 6) and the frailty of human beings (v. 7). The imagery of the "treasure in jars of clay" is familiar to modern Christian believers; songs have been written and poetry has been read about this passage. Nevertheless, what, exactly, is the treasure that we have, and why does Paul use the lowly, unassuming clay jar?

The treasure is the gospel message of redemption and reconciliation through Jesus Christ. It is a singular noun, indicating that the "treasure" is one particular thing that is of great value and worth. The precious, glorious gospel exists in contrast to the "knowledge" or the "wisdom of the world" that the Corinthians thought was so important before they came to believe in

---

2. Harris, *Second Corinthians*, 365.

Christ (see 1 Cor 1:18–25). Paul's use of this word, "treasure," reminds us of a parable taught by Jesus. Jesus is using figurative language with his audience to explain what the "kingdom of heaven is like" (see Matt. 13:24, 31, 44, 45, 47). Specifically, in Matthew 13:44–46, Jesus says that the "kingdom of heaven" (remember that Matthew's audience was primarily Jewish, so these are his words for the "kingdom of God") is a treasure so incredibly valuable that a person should be willing to give up everything in order to get it:

> The kingdom of heaven is like treasure hidden in a field. When a man found it, he hid it again, then in his joy went and sold all he had and bought the field. Again, the kingdom of heaven is like a merchant looking for fine pearls. When he found one of great value, he went away and sold everything he had and bought it.

Two words stand out in this small parable: "hidden" and "joy." Jesus's primary message was that he was inaugurating the "kingdom of God" with his life, death, and resurrection. His message, therefore, was "good news" to his hearers, filled with the joy of redemption. Yet the message was "hidden" from those who rejected Jesus and his words. In the same way, the "treasure" of Jesus's gospel message was "hidden" from those who opposed Paul; they would not know the joy of the wonderful, valuable message Paul came to deliver (2 Cor 4:3–4).

Earthenware Vessels

"Treasure" and the "jars of clay" (4:7) were familiar images in the Greco-Roman, Corinthian culture; in addition, these pictures were familiar to the readers of the OT. In the first century AD, items of great value were often kept in clay jars simply because such jars were so unobtrusive and inconspicuous; they attracted no attention by their outward appearance. It was not unusual for people to wrap a valuable treasure in a piece of old cloth and bury it in a secret place, since there were no banks or safety deposit boxes in those days.[3] "Clay jars," or "earthenware vessels" were not just common; they were *very* common. Hundreds of years after they were deemed useless, countless shards, pieces, and whole items of pottery have been discovered in archeological digs all over the Middle East. Since clay is easy to find and inexpensive to use, clay pottery has been used by various civilizations from the earliest times.[4] Even the broken shards of clay pottery were put to use as "scrap paper" to

---

3. David Wenham, *The Parables of Jesus* (Downers Grove, IL: InterVarsity Press, 1989), 205.
4. Belleville, *2 Corinthians*, 119.

make lists and notes; such everyday usage tells us a great deal about how the ancient people lived. Certain cultural aspects of each unique civilization can be suggested by the manner in which people created and decorated ordinary pottery. Even so, while the clay vessels were useful, common, and affordable, they also proved to be fragile and easy to break.[5]

The historical-cultural background of these Middle Eastern clay vessels allows us to see why Paul drew this kind of a picture for his readers. In the Greco-Roman culture, the physical body was frequently described as a "container" or "vessel" for "the mind or soul" of the person. Such a vessel "wears out, grows old, dies, and is dissolved," thus appearing inferior like an earthenware pot.[6] It is remarkable that God chose to put the treasure of his gospel message in the hearts of fallible, cracked, chipped, and fragile human beings. God entrusted the most valuable message of all time to common, ordinary, rather unexceptional men and women. Likewise, it is hard to believe that we find bands of gold and silver and gemstones in the most common, ugly, gray rocks.

No doubt Paul could easily recall the "clay vessel" imagery that is prolific among the Jewish writings in both the OT and in noncanonical literature. The picture of frail humanity in the hands of the proficient Potter is familiar to readers, both ancient and modern. The prophet Jeremiah learned many lessons at the potter's house, centuries before the time of Jesus:

> So I went down to the potter's house, and I saw him working at the wheel. But the pot he was shaping from the clay was marred in his hands; so the potter formed it into another pot, shaping it as seemed best to him. Then the word of the LORD came to me. He said, "Can I not do with you, Israel, as this potter does?" declares the LORD. "Like clay in the hand of the potter, so are you in my hand, Israel." (Jer 18:3–6)

The Hebrew word for "potter" can also translated as "maker." It is used this way in Jeremiah 10:16, "for he is the Maker of all things," certainly in reference to God. The Lord's message to Jeremiah through this brief parable is that God is sovereign; God grants promises and threats to his people based on their actions and behavior.

The "potter" imagery is also found in Isaiah's prophetic record, and it is Isaiah who fashions an unexpected ending to this story of the potter and the pottery. In Isaiah 66, the concluding chapter of this lengthy prophetic story

---

5. Belleville, *2 Corinthians*, 120.
6. Furnish, *II Corinthians*, 253–54.

about redemption and purpose, the Lord promises to "gather the people of all nations and languages [that is, Jews and Gentiles], and they will come and see my glory" (Isa 66:18). For those who choose to love God and "consecrate and purify themselves" (v. 17), God will "set a sign among them" (v. 19) and

> they will proclaim my *glory* among the nations. And they will bring all your people, from all the nations, to my holy mountain in Jerusalem as an offering to the LORD. . . . They will bring them, as the Israelites bring their grain offerings, to the temple of the LORD in *ceremonially clean vessels.*" (66:19–20, my emphases)

Accordingly, Isaiah is instructing the faithful believers to do their job. They are to go out, spread the good news, and "bring them" ("all your brothers," including Gentiles) to faith and into God's covenant. Believers are to help bring the promised redemption into the world by proclaiming the glory of the one and only God. Those faithful people who love God and minister in his name (as "clean vessels") will be his instruments in bringing together people from across the globe. This sounds like a picture of the future Christian church, and apostolic leaders such as Paul were called to proclaim the gospel to "all the nations." However unlikely it may seem, God chose to clean up his broken shards of clay and use them to spread the good news of his love and redemption. The prophet's vision of "the last days" will come true through apostles and servants like Paul (Isaiah 2:2–5).

Further reflecting on lessons from Israel's history, Paul asked the believers in Rome, "[d]oes not the potter have the right to make out of the same lump of clay some pottery for special purposes and some for common use?" (Rom 9:21). Using the same imagery, Paul made a distinction between two kinds of clay vessels to illustrate two kinds of people. First, there are those who reject God and become "dishonorable," or "objects (vessels) of his wrath—prepared for destruction." In contrast, there are those who are "honorable" or "objects (vessels) of his mercy, whom he prepared in advance for glory":

> What if God, although choosing to show his wrath and make his power known, bore with great patience the objects of his wrath—prepared for destruction? What if he did this to make the riches of his glory known to the objects of his mercy, whom he prepared in advance for glory—even us, whom he also called, not only from the Jews but also from the Gentiles? (Rom 9:22–24)

With respect to the "potter" imagery, Cranfield suggests that Paul is emphasizing that the Potter (God) has "authority over the clay" (his people):

> The potter—as the potter—must, in order to fulfill the rational purposes of his craft, be free to make, from the same mass of clay, some vessels for noble, and some for menial, uses. The conclusion to be drawn is that God must be acknowledged to be free—as God, as the One who has ultimate authority—to appoint men to various functions in the on-going course of salvation-history for the sake of the fulfillment of his over-all purpose.[7]

In other words, God has the sovereign freedom to choose to fill human beings with his love and power and glory, based on their actions, behavior, and acceptance of Jesus Christ. He has the right and the desire to mold, form, and transform men and women in the way that he sees best. The Corinthian believers who embraced the treasure of the gospel message and loved God are transformed into "objects of his mercy," "clean" and "honorable vessels," who are filled with his glory. Believers are transformed from ignoble "clay pots" to become noble, "clean vessels," useful for spreading the gospel message around the world. Paul refers to humanity as "earthenware vessels," made by the sovereign Potter, who has chosen to fill the menial vessels in Corinth with his glorious, saving gospel.

Still, why would a powerful, sovereign God do this for frail, dishonorable humanity? Paul goes on to say that God wants to demonstrate *his* power, in contrast to the power of human beings (2 Cor 4:7). Paul recognizes the total insufficiency of human instruments, but he also acknowledges God's total sufficiency to achieve his purposes through his servants. Belleville says it well: "God uses what is fragile and yet serviceable so that there might be no mistaking the origin of the gospel minister's power."[8] "This treasure," or the gospel message of "ever-increasing glory" (3:18), is not just human written or spoken words; the power that lies behind the human words is the extraordinary, "all-surpassing" (4:7) power of God—the very same power that raised Jesus from the dead (4:14). Therefore, in the Potter's hand, and under his transforming, "kiln" power, even mud can be fashioned into a vessel worthy of being filled with God's glory.

Paul is very aware of the irony: it is unusual, and remarkable, that a committed Jew, a persecutor of Christians in Jerusalem, would be chosen as the instrument by which the gospel message of Jesus Christ would be conveyed

7. C. E. B. Cranfield, *Romans*, 2 vols., ICC (Edinburgh: T&T Clark, 1979), 2:492.
8. Belleville, *2 Corinthians*, 120.

to the Gentiles! Surely it would have been more logical for God to choose an educated, committed Roman Gentile, like the God-fearing centurion in Acts 10, to minister to "his own kind" in the Gentile world. But God does not always act within human logic. Paul thus fulfills the prophecy of Isaiah by ministering to the Gentile nations, presenting the believing Corinthians to God as his "letters of recommendation (3:1). He continues to demonstrate why he knows that God has called him to ministry and commissioned him to be God's chosen servant.

Trials and Suffering

Furthermore, while we can identify with and appreciate the "jars of clay" imagery that emerged from the OT writings, in the present passage, how do we connect the imagery in 4:7 to the trials and sufferings listed in verses 8–9? Paul admits that, in their human fallibility and insufficiency, it was not easy for him and his fellow missionaries to carry the gospel into Gentile territory. However, their trials confirm to the reader that Paul was able to accomplish what God asked him to do. Paul uses a familiar literary strategy called "catalogue of hardships" in 4:8–9 to demonstrate his hardships and afflictions.[9] This literary strategy is repeated again in this letter (see 6:4–10; 11:23–28; 12:10) and in other Pauline letters (Rom 8:35–39; 1 Cor 4:9–13; Phil 4:11–12). Here, Paul tells his readers that as a minister of the gospel, he has been, ". . . hard pressed on every side, but not crushed; perplexed but not in despair; persecuted but not abandoned; struck down but not destroyed" (2 Cor 4:8–9).

This list is composed of four balanced antitheses, all written grammatically as participles. The first word of each pair of words states a human weakness, while the second word (following the "but not . . .") illustrates divine power (from v. 7).[10] In each case, the second element is more extreme or more forceful than the first. The words in this list are worth investigating because, painfully, those who have been called to be servants of God may too closely identify with many of these challenges in real life. They need to be observed carefully in pairs:

"Hard pressed" (v. 8) is "to cause something to be constricted or narrow; to crowd; to cause to be troubled, oppressed, afflicted"; it is derived from a word that often refers to oppression, affliction, or some kind of distress from outside circumstances.[11] Picture the image of a wrestler, crushed by an opponent in

---

9. Belleville, *2 Corinthians*, 121; Harris, *Second Corinthians*, 341.
10. Harris, *Second Corinthians*, 342.
11. BDAG 457.

a headlock. Paul used the noun with the same root in 2 Corinthians 1:8, translated as "affliction" (NRSV). Yet, Paul never felt himself being "crushed" or restrained. Even in crushing circumstances, Paul found that he always had an escape.[12] Paul got to the end of his rope, tied a knot, and held on. Somehow, he maintained his positive spirit despite circumstances (see, e.g., 2 Cor 11:30–33).

"Perplexed" (2 Cor 4:8) is "perplexity or anxiety" from a verb that denotes "to be in a confused state of mind, to be at a loss, to be in doubt, uncertainty." This word can even imply an "inward debate, bewildered but never at one's wits' end."[13] Even so, Paul was not "in despair"; again, he employs a word that was first used in 1:8 ("we *despaired* even of life"). He has used an interesting pair of words to describe his state of mind; if the first word is "to be at a loss, uncertain," then the second word implies an advanced state of completely having no hope. While the second word is more intense than the first, it is rather difficult to accurately express this pair in English. Helpful scholars have tried to articulate their differences for us. Harris points out that Paul is using a play on words here, and says this is "to be at a total loss, but not lost."[14] Hughes suggests "confused but not confounded."[15] Furnish says he is "despairing but not utterly desperate."[16] Thus, the prime example from Paul's own life and ministry is seen in 2 Corinthians 1:8–10.

The word "persecuted" (v. 9) is used to express harassment, "especially because of one's beliefs." It can imply aggravation "to the point of death," which is in keeping with Paul's words in 1:8–9."[17] This word appears in 1 Corinthians 4:12, where Paul wrote that "when we are persecuted, we endure it." The other word in this pair is "abandoned" or "forsaken" (2 Cor 4:9); it is a compound word derived from a root word that implies "to leave something behind," especially a place or a person."[18] It is like leaving behind one's childhood birthplace with a final glance, never to return home again. This word appears in the Greek OT in reference to the promises of God, who pledged, "[I] will never leave you nor forsake you. Do not be afraid; do not be discouraged" (see Deut 31:6–8). In spite of such a promise, no doubt Paul felt abandoned by his fellow workers at certain points in his ministry. Demas, for example, "loved the world" and left Paul to travel on to Thessalonica. Crescens fled to Galatia,

---

12. Harris, *Second Corinthians*, 343.
13. BDAG 119.
14. Harris, *Second Corinthians*, 343.
15. Harris, *Second Corinthians*, 138n. 7.
16. Furnish, *II Corinthians*, 254.
17. BDAG 254.
18. BDAG 520.

and Titus went on to Dalmatia. They deserted Paul on the missionary field, and only Luke remained with him (see 2 Tim 4:10–11).

The last two words (2 Cor 4:9) both have a broad range of meaning, making it difficult to limit each term to one particular kind of difficulty. "Struck down" or "cast down" means "to strike with sufficient force so as to knock down, or throw down." In the passive form, it implies the blow of someone else on the victim.[19] While Paul may have been knocked down, he was not permanently destroyed. Then, he used the word "perishing" (v. 9), which implies "to cause or experience destruction, to perish, to ruin."[20] He used the word "struck down" nowhere else in his letters, but he does use the verb "to perish, to ruin" elsewhere. Paul used this word in 1 Corinthians 1:18 ("those who are *perishing*") in much the same way he used it in this letter in 2:15 and 4:3. During his life and ministry, Paul may have been "knocked to the ground, but [he was] not permanently 'grounded.'"[21] Such an experience is seen in the city of Lystra, where Paul was stoned by Jews, dragged outside the city, and left for dead (Acts 14:19–20).

In summary, the trials and suffering on this list were not theoretical for Paul; as we see in 2 Corinthians 1:8–9, "pressures" and trials are a very real, memorable part of Paul's ministry. Physically, mentally, and spiritually, Paul was challenged at every turn of the ministry road. Note his use of the word "always" in 4:10 and 11. Certainly, the very real intervention of God in these trials is a key principle of this letter. His lists of hardships were not written to raise Paul's reputation, induce the readers' empathy, or to show his self-sufficiency. They demonstrate Paul's transparency with his readers, his commitment to his divine calling, and the total dependence of a frail human being on God's power. Ironically, "if I must boast, I will boast of the things that show my weakness" (11:30), so that divine power is experienced in the midst of frail human trials and weakness.

More Antitheses

The conclusion to his list is Paul's recognition of what it meant to share in Christ's suffering through his own trials and afflictions (4:10). Again, his use of antithesis ("death and life") in verses 10–12 is very striking. That is, mortal, perishing humanity carries around (4:10) the immortal life of the resurrected Jesus. Paul traveled many miles as a missionary carrying around his physical belongings as well as his mental burdens and emotional scars. Yet he always

---

19. BDAG 514; Furnish, *II Corinthians*, 255.
20. BDAG 116.
21. Harris, *Second Corinthians*, 344.

carried with him the presence and the power of the resurrected Jesus. Paul and his fellow workers toiled very hard in their frail, mortal bodies so that the readers would know the treasure of eternal life in Jesus.

In v. 13, Paul quotes from Psalm 116:10, emphasizing the fact that faith in Jesus leads to testimony about him. This is the "same spirit," the same driving force that pushes Paul to minister among the Corinthians. Paul says that he can't help it; he has to preach the gospel. There is an extraordinary drive that God puts within the hearts of people that nudges, pokes, and prods them into ministry. This drive can be ignored and denied for just so long, until one day, a person gives in to God and says, "I have to do this." So, Paul continued his testimony among the Corinthians for their benefit, attempting to reach more and more people with the story of Jesus. In doing so, he realized that imperfect humanity can reveal the life of Jesus to the unbelieving world. Ultimately, all of Paul's Christian service, and the goal for every believer, is to glorify God (4:15).

Christian Hope and Glory (4:16–5:10)

There are future aspects of the "big" plans of God that are still opaque to all of us. As walking into a dark tunnel, the experience of human death is very difficult to understand, even to those who have read and re-read the scriptural passages on this subject. Every time a pastor prepares a funeral service or holds the hand of a dying person, the doubts and questions return: Where is this person going? What do you say to a grieving family that just lost a four-year-old child? How do you comfort the parents of a shooting victim, or the spouse of a soldier killed on the other side of the world? In the New Testament numerous passages give us just a glimpse of eternal life, of death, resurrection, and the return of Christ at his Second Coming. This section of 2 Corinthians is one of those passages, and it helps to give us an insight into the misty fog of life after death. It is a small window through which we can see hints of what Paul believed about life, death, and resurrection.

The last three verses of chapter 4 (vv. 16–18) serve as a bridge between the previous verses, 4:10–15, and the following section in 5:1–10. That is, verses 4:16–18 are a conclusion to 4:7–15 where Paul wrote of his trials and his life "given over to death" so as to reveal Christ through his earthly life (4:11). These verses also become an introduction to Paul's eschatological discussion in chapter 5 of life and death, of temporary and permanent, of now and later.

N. T. Wright writes that 4:16–18 follows Paul's "long and passionate description" of his own Gentile ministry. He likened his ministry to "treasure in jars of clay" (4:7) to demonstrate that his words and actions were produced by God's power, not his own. With this in mind, Paul then expressed the Christian's future hope, because human suffering and hardships make no sense without that kind of hope (4:16–5:10). In chapter 5, then, Paul used the imagery of a "new house, a new dwelling and a new body" that is waiting for believers "within God's sphere" ("heavenly places"). God is ready to "put it on" (the new body) over the existing earthly body so that even in physical death, the believer is "swallowed up" by life. All of this, of course, is accomplished by the Spirit of God.[22]

This complicated section of the letter needs to be "unpacked" (that is a clothing image!), and we will do so gradually. We begin by looking at these verses literally. In doing so, we can see Paul's propensity to use antithetical statements, in 2 Corinthians in general, and in chapters 4 and 5 in particular. Paul is a master at using stark contrasts to describe the Christian life, the experience of death, and the unique hope of Christian believers. Perhaps a chart will help us see his antitheses:[23]

"death" (4:10a)	vs.	"life" (4:10b)
"death" (4:11a)	vs.	"life" (4:11b)
"death" (4:12a)	vs.	"life" (4:12b)
"outwardly" (4:16a)	vs.	"inwardly" (4:16b)
"momentary troubles" (4:17a)	vs.	"eternal glory" (4:17b)
"seen"(4:18a)	vs.	"unseen" (4:18)
"temporary" (4:18c)		"eternal" (4:18d)

While Paul and his fellow ministers were experiencing the ongoing process of "wasting away" in their human bodies, he knew that they were being "inwardly renewed" by the Spirit of God (3:18; 5:5) to give them strength for ministry (4:16). Perhaps this is true of all of us; the brevity of life on earth becomes more and more evident as the years go by. Even so, Paul repeats the thematic phrase that is an encouragement to us, "we do not lose heart" (4:1, 16), to punctuate their commitment and tenacity in ministry despite physical adversity (4:8–9).

The phrase "outward . . . yet inward" (v. 16) is a concept not foreign to the Greek readers who were familiar with the dualism of Greek philosophy.

---

22. Wright, *Surprised by Hope*, 152–53.
23. Harris, *Second Corinthians*, 344.

They would have understood the "outer nature," or physical body and the "inner nature," or the soul or spirit that dwelt within a person. It was not difficult for the readers to see the contrasts between the visible and invisible, the temporary and the eternal (see Col. 1:16). It is the "inside" of a person that really counts (see Rom 7:22; Eph 3:16; 1 Pet 3:4). However, Paul does not promote this dualism concept as much as he borrows these paradoxical statements to demonstrate his own life and calling and the realities that face every human being. That is, physical strength is fleeting, but spiritual stamina is eternal (see Jesus's parable in Luke 12:16–23).[24] The "outward" person is the part of the human being that is apparent—the physical body, mental strength, and endurance. The "inward" person less apparent; it is the strength of a person emotionally and spiritually. Like a well-trained athlete, the outward signs of strength and vitality are evident through physical performance and mental attitude. Yet, the inward training of emotions and spirit can make or break a champion. We can see this in the physically disabled athletes who may not have the physical or intellectual strength of other athletes, but their inward spirits are strong and relentless.

In fact, Paul observes, every human being is wasting away as our physical bodies age and our mental capacities are reduced. In spite of this apparent and inevitable process, Paul contends that, in Christ, believers are spiritually renewed daily so that inwardly we can maintain a strong, vital spiritual life for eternity. As an example, my father lived to be almost a hundred years old, and I watched his body and his mind fail him, especially in the latter years. He became weaker and weaker almost daily (2 Cor 4:16); at noon, he could not remember what he had for breakfast. He shuffled his feet and could hardly walk down the hall to the dining room, so the mind and the body were crashing. Yet, at the sight of his family, his eyes would sparkle, and he would smile; he couldn't remember our names, but he was so glad to see us! He hugged the caregivers and thanked them for what they did. He could recite Scripture from memory and remembered World War II as if it were yesterday. While death may not be scary to a Christian, the process of dying is. The fragile, imperfect body does not give up easily; we continue to live in pain and suffering now, but Paul was saying that "a Christian in the present life is a mere shadow of his or her future self." In fact, the glorious new body will come![25]

A common expression in our culture, the phrase "day by day" in 4:16, was unique in the first century. Various English translations imply that it is

---

24. Belleville, *2 Corinthians*, 126.
25. Wright, *Surprised by Hope*, 154.

something that happens every day. The progressive growing nature of spiritual strength through Christ counteracts the daily process of physical and/or mental deterioration of the human being. It is interesting to note the intentional use of the plural pronoun "we" in verses 16–18. That is, while we are all wasting away physically in this life, Paul appears to be making a comment about his own ministry and that of his co-workers, who are being spiritually, "inwardly renewed" *for ministry.* As evidence of his apostolic calling, Paul was not defeated by the trials of life (4:9). For those people who are actively serving the Lord in ministry, like Paul and his colleagues, it should be an encouragement that God is with them on a consistent, daily basis, as they are "being renewed day by day," to fulfill the tasks to which they have been called. The work done for the Lord in this life is not "in vain" but has eternal effects (1 Cor 15:58).

Paul learned that through his own trials and sufferings, and through the exhaustion of his own limited, human abilities "for Jesus' sake," his spiritual toughness increased. This is an incongruity that is hard for people of any age to understand. Since, by nature, we resist our own physical sufferings (diseases, disabilities), it is hard to imagine that these difficulties can actually lead to one's own spiritual strength, growth, and maturity. While our personal sufferings seem far larger than what Paul describes as "light and momentary troubles" (4:17), we are almost offended by Paul's lack of compassion for our problems, our anxieties, and our misfortunes.

Yet, Paul continues to explain that our present troubles pale in perspective. Verse 17 is somewhat awkward in Greek; Harris goes for a literal reading: "For this momentary and light affliction of ours is producing for us to an utterly incomparable degree an eternal load of glory."[26] The NRSV translation untangles this verse as, "for this slight momentary affliction is preparing us for an eternal weight of glory beyond all measure. . . ." The weight and height and depth and size of the eternal, future glory that awaits Christians is difficult to explain; it is "beyond all measure." To emphasize what he is saying, Paul again matched pairs of antithetical ideas in just one verse: "momentary" and "eternal," "light" and "weighted," "affliction" and "glory."

God's Gift of Glory

The final promised "eternal glory" is worth more consideration. In the Hebrew, the word *kabod* can mean either "weight" or "glory," which may be the language behind Paul's phrase "weight of glory" (4:17). The antithetical list in this verse gives us a hint that the "weight of glory" is something that

---

26. Harris, *Second Corinthians,* 361.

is "eternal." Yet, the "glory" in this passage is not only some kind of future reward for believers; it is also something that the manageable and temporal troubles are achieving in us right now. "Glory" is the *presence and power of God* manifested in the lives of humanity in a sensory form. All of God's glory has never been revealed, but parts of it can be seen in the OT stories of redemption: God's power in the parting of the sea, in the Passover, in the *Shekinah* fire and cloud. Certainly, the glory of God was vividly and clearly revealed in the incarnation and resurrection of his Son on earth (see John 17:1–4). Oddly enough, God chooses to put his own glory (power and presence) into his people to accomplish the tasks for which he has prepared them.[27]

Belleville writes that, "affliction does not give way to glory; affliction produces glory."[28] The "life of Jesus" that is at work in a believer (2 Cor 4:10–12) is the "tremendous, eternal glory" that is given to his followers (and not earned), and is "undiminished and unaffected by time."[29] Even though there may be present afflictions that seem heavy and burdensome, nothing outweighs the eternal blessings (now and in the future) that are given to those who faithfully persevere. While it may be difficult for readers today to fully comprehend such eternal glory, certainly it may be an important reason why Paul and his fellow ministers did not lose heart.

Verse 18 adds yet another metaphorical layer to explain Paul's understanding of the many paradoxes of the life of all Christians, and especially those who serve as ministers of Christ. The "visible" are the painful events, situations, and conditions that all Christians experience in our present lives. We tend to focus on them because they are the most visible. It is difficult to "fix our eyes" on the "unseen," which is glorious, eternal, and yet beyond our physical grasp. To "fix our eyes" means to "focus our full attention on," or "to watch out for" something (4:18); that is, if we pay too much attention to the negative, present troubles, we can certainly "lose heart" (4:1, 16).[30]

In his own defense, Paul demonstrated how he was uniquely qualified to be a minister of God, to serve the Corinthian believers, and to assure them that their troubles "for Jesus' sake" in this life lead to endurance and eternal compensation. Paul insisted that it is because of his own sufferings that he was divinely qualified to teach the Corinthian believers and exert his apostolic authority. His opponents, the false teachers, did not experience what Paul had endured and therefore were not as qualified to carry the gospel message (10:7–11, 18; 11:5–6, 22–29). His life, with all his physical, mental, and emotional trials,

27. Aalen, "Glory," 40–48.
28. Belleville, *2 Corinthians*, 128.
29. Harris, *Second Corinthians*, 362.
30. Furnish, *II Corinthians*, 263.

was visibly contrasted to the self-serving opponents whose concerns were for their own ease, power, and position in this present life. It is valuable to note that this passage *does not address all human suffering and all personal trials in general.* Paul is addressing the trials of godly ministry and the difficulties humans face "for Jesus' sake." Seen in perspective of "eternal glory" (v. 17), the temporal ordeals of ministry, the rejection, denigration, misunderstandings, and disparagement of serving God that one may experience on this earth shrink in comparison. These contrasting ideas show that whatever suffering he endured while serving Christ was insignificant in an eternal perspective. The familiar verses, 16–18, summarize and conclude Paul's argument concerning his own ministry that began all the way back in 3:1. While these verses were not intended to be used as a quick answer for the complex question of human suffering in the world, they can be a comfort and an encouragement to all Christians, not just to called ministers.

Thus, in chapter 4, we see how Paul uses his personal experiences to advance his gospel message (vv. 1–9), to demonstrate his determination in delivering this message (vv. 10–12), to illustrate his foundational theology behind the message (v. 13–14), and to reveal his steadfast commitment to his ministry (vv. 1, 16–18). After his personal stories and illustrations (4:1–9), he makes use of the "death and life" imagery from 4:10–17, binding the life, death, and resurrection of Jesus Christ to the ministry of which Paul was a part (see 4:14–15 in particular). The resurrection of Jesus and the life and work of Paul are intertwined for the spiritual benefit of the readers and for the spread of the gospel. This leads the reader into 4:16–18 and into 5:1–10, where Paul presented his reasons for having confidence in the face of death. His discussion moves from present suffering to future glory.

Promised Resurrected Life of Believers

Paul's reasoning in 5:1–10 follows closely on the heels of his arguments in 4:7–18. Again, he shifted to new metaphorical pictures and used new imagery with stark antitheses in 5:1–10 in an attempt to explain the inexplicable—that is, the promised resurrected life of believers. Like most Greeks, the Corinthians had a difficult time grasping the ideas of death and the resurrected body. Because Jesus was physically resurrected—an idea that was quite absurd to the Greek thinkers—believers will have a resurrected body in the same mode. When will that happen, and what does that look like?

Murray Harris understands 2 Corinthians 5:1–10 to be Paul's expression of his developed "eschatological thought" (*eschatology* indicating "the end things"): Paul's personal beliefs concerning the Second Coming of Christ (his *parousia*), the time when the human being receives his or her "spiritual body," and the location and state of deceased Christians.[31] These topics were critical and confusing not only to the Corinthians, most Christians today cannot fully articulate or grasp the details of these issues. In this section of the letter, Paul moved from his personal suffering and trials (4:7–18) to the climactic hope of eternity with Christ and the dramatic resurrection of the saints (5:1–10).

Harris considers two other Pauline passages that can help us to decipher Paul's eschatological speech in 5:1–10: 1 Thessalonians 4 and 1 Corinthians 15. First, in 1 Thessalonians 4:15, 17 (arguably written before the Corinthian letters) Paul used the word *parousia* with a meaning that may not be the same as some people interpret it today. It has taken on the familiar meaning of the "coming" of the Lord; but it actually means "presence." In the minds of the original readers, then, a *parousia* was the presence of a supernatural, powerful being who will appear, particularly with saving, healing power. Further, and so familiar in the Roman Empire, the appearance of such a person signaled a "*royal* presence." Just like a king or an emperor who rode into a subjugated city or province, at his Second Coming, Jesus will arrive bodily, and the whole world will be aware of his sudden, transforming presence. As the true Emperor, Jesus will appear one day and rule the world, and all the other human kings (like Caesar) will bow at his feet (see Phil 2:6–11).[32]

When will this take place (which is a gnawing question for modern readers)? Perhaps Paul imagined himself to be alive until the Second Coming (1 Thess 4:15, 17, "we who are still alive . . . until the coming of the Lord"). This is more than an assuring phrase for his readers, but it does not guarantee the time or the place of the Second Coming. In this section of 1 Thessalonians, Paul is giving directions as to how to live on this earth until that time comes, whenever it is (see 1 Thess 4:1). Yet, Paul's phrase surely implies that at the future *parousia* of Christ, some human beings will be alive and will be united with the returning Christ without experiencing a physical death.[33]

Second, in 1 Corinthians 15:12–58, Paul attempted to assure his readers in Corinth that Christ was physically resurrected, and that a new, resurrected body is promised to Christian believers after passing from this earth. Thus, "we will all be changed." This is the ultimate Christian hope: that believers will, indeed, be totally new creations in Christ (2 Cor 5:17), completed and perfected by God so as to live eternally with him.

Moreover, it is the Holy Spirit who transforms and maintains the new resurrection life received at one's "rebirth," when the believer is united with

---

31. Murray J. Harris, "2 Corinthians 5:1–10: Watershed in Paul's Eschatology?," *TynBul* 22 (1971): 33.

32. Wright, *Surprised by Hope*, 128–29.

33. Harris, "2 Corinthians 5:1–10: Watershed in Paul's Eschatology?," 36.

Christ (2 Cor 3:18). The Spirit is the guarantee and the means by which God will transform humanity in the future resurrection as well ("what is to come," 2 Cor 1:22; 5:5). This process of change (or conversion) is begun in the earthly life, and is a renewal of the mind (Rom 12:2), or "made new in the attitude" of the mind (Eph 4:23), or strength "in your inner being" (Eph 3:16), or the renewal of the inner person by the Spirit (2 Cor 4:16).[34]

Paul consistently taught his converts the Jewish concept that a human soul and a human body are one entity. This is a contrast to the Greek philosophy of the duality of the soul and the body; for the Greek, death was desired because it was a release of the human soul from the "intrinsically evil" body.[35] The ancient Greeks decided that the physical body is malevolent and meaningless, while the soul or spirit of the human being is of much greater importance. Paul had to change their thinking, to convince his readers that the "perishable," temporary human body is "sown" like a seed at death, only to be "raised in glory," "imperishable," permanent, and splendid (1 Cor 15:42–44). That is, the remarkable resurrection body of Christ is the paradigm and the promise for the (future) resurrection of believers (1 Cor 15:51; Phil 3:21).[36]

Not unlike the Greeks, people today think that an eternal, resurrected life after physical death is unlikely if not absurd, and it is difficult to "show" them what is yet "unseen" by anyone except those who choose to be connected to the resurrected Christ (2 Cor 4:18). In fact, for Paul the "present time" and the "time to come" are not successive periods of time, one after another. These times actually overlap, concurrently existing together, leading to an "already but not yet" tension in earthly human life. The eternal, spiritual life of a believer begins at his or her "rebirth" (at the point in time he or she places trust in Christ, see Rom 10:9), and is gradually (or rapidly) changed by the Spirit, culminating in the future completion and resurrection of all believers (Gal 6:8). Certainly "Christians still live in 'the present evil age' (Gal 1:4), and there is a Then which is different from the Now." The tie that binds the present and the future is the work of the Holy Spirit in human lives.[37]

Earthly Tents

It is Paul's use of antithetical metaphors that link this passage together: "earthly tent/eternal house or dwelling," "clothed/naked," "at home in the body/away from the Lord," and "away from the body/at home with the Lord."

---

34. Murray J. Harris, *Raised Immortal: Resurrection and Immortality in the New Testament* (Grand Rapids: Eerdmans, 1983), 145–46.

35. Barton et al., *1 and 2 Corinthians*, 337.

36. Harris, *Raised Immortal*, 147.

37. Harris, *Raised Immortal*, 148–49.

In 2 Cor 5:1–4 he described the resurrected body that will (someday) be given to believers. If the "earthly tent" in 5:1 is the present frail human body, then the solid structure, the "building from God," is our resurrected, eternal, permanent body ("house"). The former, flimsy, temporary "tent," is the physical, "seen" aspect of our lives; it will be "destroyed" by physical death. Then, God grants us an eternal, resurrection body that remains unseen now (5:1). As we grow older and our physical "tents" are ravaged by time, disease, environment, and genetics, we certainly feel the deterioration of our physical temporary "home." I looked at my hands the other day and realized that they looked exactly like my mother's hands, who passed away at age 87; this was not a good feeling! Thus, in the meantime, we groan and moan at the aging process in our weak and wrinkling bodies. Today, in our culture, we fight the aging process in every way we can, so we buy more miracle creams and ointments, go to more doctors, work out until we sweat, and have more plastic surgery just to fight the inevitable.

Visually, these verses may look like this:

> Now, on this earth, our "house" is a "tent,"
> a visible, temporary body,
> which is frail and "wasting away";
> it is our temporary home, and someday it will be destroyed
> (physical death).
> But, one day, God will provide for us an invisible,
> "eternal" home with him (a resurrected body);
> we will be "at home" with him in heaven, in a place not made
> by human hands.

Furthermore, Paul reversed the common adage that we are "swallowed up" by physical death (Prov 1:12) by saying that we will be "swallowed up *by life*"— that is, because Jesus Christ (who fills us and makes us alive, 1 Cor 15:22) was resurrected, what we know as physical death will be "swallowed up" by our resurrected life (1 Cor 15:20–22). This is the transformation of the mortal body to the immortal body (1 Cor 15:42–44). If Christ had not died and been resurrected, our "faith is futile" and we are still "in our sins"; and without the resurrection of Christ, all who die in Christ are "lost." Because he was, indeed, resurrected, we will be also (see 1 Cor 15:12–22), and we will be covered with our new bodies, with Jesus, for eternity. In summation, "resurrection releases from death and reverses its effects."[38]

---

38. Harris, *Raised Immortal*, 162, 219–27.

Being Clothed

Then, Paul added a new metaphor to his descriptions; we can unravel the overlapping imagery to discern a memorable chiasm to help believers live in this life as they wait for their resurrected bodies. Second Corinthians 5:2–4 is very similar to 5:6–8. The new metaphor, the "clothing" image, may look something like this:

> Now we moan and groan,
>> But someday we will be clothed in a new body;
>>> We do not want to be burdened, naked and unclothed,
>> But have the confidence that we will put on new bodies that
>>> God will provide,
> And we will groan no more!

Harris points out that Paul used the same Greek root verb "to put on" (*enduō*) three times in verses 5:2–4 ("to put on clothes"), and that we should understand the uses in verses 3 and 4 to have the same reference as verse 2, which is the resurrected body. The best meaning of "nakedness," or the opposite of being "clothed" (v. 3) is highly debated but may be best interpreted as "bodiless." It is reassuring, then, that after the death of a Christian, his or her existence is not a perpetual void or nothingness, but we are promised that at the human resurrection all believers will receive a new, resurrected body.[39]

On the one hand, the clothing imagery could be understood as the Christian who "puts on" the salvation of Christ; to be "naked" is to be apart from him. Paul used the same imagery in Col 3:9–10, where the believers are to "take off [the] old self" and "put on the new self, which is being renewed in knowledge in the image of its Creator." As they "put on" the salvation of Christ, he tells the Colossians to "clothe yourselves with compassion, kindness, humility, gentleness and patience . . . and over all these virtues put on love, which binds them all together in perfect unity" (Col 3:12–14).

The ancient Greeks considered human death as "stripping the soul and leaving it naked," something that they looked forward to. Paul denied this idea in 5:2–3, insisting that the soul of the believer will be "covered" ("clothed") by the resurrected body. As an example, Jesus's resurrected body was the "clothing" that "covered" his soul; his body was visible to other people and his soul was "intact," not "naked" and separated from his body. Thus, in this passage, Paul spoke of the promised resurrected body of human believers as a "permanent building and an overcoat." As a result, after physical death, believers will not

---

39. Harris, *Raised Immortal*, 222–23.

"lose their personalities or even their recognizable characteristics." Future resurrected bodies will be "redeemed, and will be better than they can imagine."
Perfect and glorious, resurrected bodies will be without pain and sickness.[40]

Physical Death of the Christian

There is no doubt that in the minds of most people, even Christians, that
physical death is a negative experience on every way—it is destruction. When
a person dies, his or her temporal, earthly "tent" (body) is demolished (5:1).
Paul indicated his despair when he faced the "sentence of death" in 2 Cor
1:8–9. Yet, death is undeniable, unavoidable, and inevitable; Paul is quite
confident that all humans will experience it. It was Paul's preference, therefore, to be "away from the body" and "at home with the Lord" (5:6–8). That
is, there is a positive side of death: "for it brings the believer to the promised
land of Christ's immediate presence." Being away from our physical bodies
through death does not leave us "homeless," but it means being "at home" in
the presence of the Lord. Death is, in reality, the end of our Christian faith
journey, a journey like all of life that is lived by faith and not by sight (5:7;
4:18). Furthermore, death does not negate the believer's union with and in
Christ (Rom 8:38–39), so that in life and in death we should "make it our
goal to please him" (5:9; see Phil 1:20–23).[41]

Confidence

As we try to absorb these thoughts about this life and the life to come, it is
easy to miss the purpose of God's big plans and promises: God created people
for eternal life, and while that is guaranteed (2 Cor 5:5), he never promised
that our current life would be easy. God gave us his Spirit to help us in the
life that we live now. Speaker and author Josh McDowell once said that this
life is "boot camp"; we are now being trained for whatever God has planned
for us in the eternal future. Without this perspective, the human body may
have been a contested subject in first-century Corinth, as we can see from
Paul's discussions on sexuality, marriage, eating, and drinking in both 1 and
2 Corinthians. It may have been a topic of dispute between Paul and his
adversaries. Yet, rather than denigrate the physical body, Paul affirms that life
in this body is a gift from God and that the human body is the place where
we are being taught, trained, and tested, and we will be judged accordingly
(5:10). He reminds his readers that their hope and confidence (5:6) rests in
eternal things, not in the worldly wisdom of his opponents. Paul's message

40. Barton et al., *1 and 2 Corinthians*, 339–40.
41. Harris, *Raised Immortal*, 160–61.

of hope did not demand that believers abuse or discard their physical bodies, but their hope rested in the resurrected Christ and in their future, eternal, resurrected bodies to come.

With this in mind, Paul tells his Corinthian readers that they have fixed their focal point on the wrong thing: temporal afflictions, mortality, and physical death. They should refocus on what they know about God's power, his gracious intervention, his Spirit, his gift of life, and the eternal hope of glory. The very same power of God that raised Jesus from the dead is placed within the believer to energize him or her to do what he or she is called to do. Paul was also committed to seeing his present hardships as minimal (4:17) because his gaze was constantly fixed on amazing, eternal, invisible realities (v. 18). The word "eternal" appears in three successive verses, 4:17, 18, and 5:1 and is critical to his argument, implying something that will last forever or exist "without end." The gift of God's glory will last forever, while earthly trials of today that are so visible and so heavy will not. Once more, we see contrasting themes used by Paul not only to defend his own apostolic position, but also to refocus his audience to see the confidence and the hope they have in Christ.

Judgment Seat of Christ

If a person is unaware of the glorious promises of God, 5:10 can be terrifying. Even when we know that we are being reconciled to God as a result of faith in Jesus, it can be very uncomfortable to think about appearing "before the judgment seat of Christ." Perhaps this verse has been used incorrectly by some people to scare others into salvation. It is true that all people will be judged by God on the basis of their relationship to Christ. It appears that Paul's number-one personal goal was to win the approval of Christ, both in life and after his death at judgment (see Gal 1:10; Phil 1:20). Thus, the "judgment seat of Christ" is *not* a reference to one's salvation. It refers instead to "appearance and examination" to reveal the motives of the heart. To "appear" before the Lord is similar to standing before one in authority, like the Roman Caesar, and "give account of ourselves to God" (see Rom 14:10–12). In the same manner, Paul told the Corinthians that ". . . he [Jesus] will bring to light what is hidden in darkness and will expose the motives of the heart. At that time each will receive their praise from God" (1 Cor 4:5). Also, this judgment is limited to believers, and each person will be evaluated as an individual. Again, this is not a question of one's position in Christ, but it has to do with service and stewardship, for "the things done while in the body, whether good or bad" (5:10). In other words, it is a divine judgment that is concerned with the rewards for managing the incredible gifts of God to believers (what did you do with what you have been given?), and not the determination of one's eternal destiny. [42]

Life and Death, Sin and Glory

But why does Paul create this challenging eschatological discussion here? This discussion does tie in to Paul's defense of this ministry and his message. As indicated, Paul's readers had misconceptions about the trials of his life. It is possible that Paul's opponents were using Paul's trials against him, insisting that the hardships were evidence of his weakness and ineffectiveness. Some may have been teaching that there is, in fact, no bodily resurrection as Paul had taught, and Paul was "out of his mind" (5:13), ignorant, or intentionally misleading his readers. Such accusations needed to be addressed by Paul, and corrections were necessary. In reality, few of us embrace and anticipate the amazing, "clothed" body that we will have one day in the final resurrection of believers; it is just too far away, and too unlikely to imagine. Yet Paul knew what it was to face his own death (1:8–11); he also worked through his own hardships and trials (4:8–12) for the sake of his readers. In this passage, then, he layered images of houses and clothing on top of one another to try to illustrate the reality of life and death and glorious resurrected bodies. Christ inaugurated a new reality for believers, and this is Paul's main point of correction: believers are promised that this "earthly tent" (our earthly bodies) will be replaced with a permanent, resurrected body ("eternal house") in the presence of God ("in heaven"). We "groan" or "sigh" in anticipation, waiting for our perfect resurrection bodies, while still existing in our temporal housing and our frail "clothing." Paul punctuates the wonderful hope of believers' future glory (see Rom 8:18–25). [43]

In truth, all Christians know that somehow we must cope with our own sins, guilt, failures, behavior, and attitudes. It is this recognition of sin in our own lives that is so painful, and we recognize that sin in any form keeps us from a close, personal relationship with God. In spite of the believer's position in Christ, Paul makes it very clear that all people, all sinners (that's all of us), must face a time of moral responsibility (Rom 2:16; 1 Cor 4:5) and accountability before God. [44] "Sin inevitably leads to final judgment," yet sin also "brings judgment" in the present time. Sin is pervasive and inevitable. [45] Consistently, Paul wrote that universal human sin is a grave matter and is

---

42. Belleville, 2 Corinthians, 142; Harris, Raised Immortal, 155–58.

43. For much more insight into heaven, believers' resurrection, and "life after life-after death," see Wright, Surprised by Hope.

44. L. Morris, "Sin, Guilt," DPL 877.

45. Morris, "Sin," 880.

ignored at our peril. In his letter to the Romans, Paul deals extensively with the problem of sin and the solution to the human predicament. That is, Paul also is clear that because of the redeeming work of Christ, sin has been defeated so that the believer has nothing to fear in terms of God's judgment; it is by the grace of God that humans can be forgiven. Because of God's grace and reconciliation, believers can prevail over the tendencies to sinfulness by "overcoming evil with good" (Rom 12:17, 21), by putting to death the evil that is within them (Col 3:5), and by condemning evil in the world. The most important key to overcoming the sins of humanity is dependence upon the Holy Spirit of God (see Rom 7:7–8:17).

Therefore, as we live by the Spirit, we please God (2 Cor 5:9), and our "work will be shown for what it is" (1 Cor 3:13). If a person lives selfishly and does not live to please God, he himself will be saved, but only as one escaping through the flames (1 Cor 3:13–15). That is, according to Paul's metaphor, a person living within the will of God will pass the test of God's judgment. Apart from God, even if one is "saved," how we live will be judged by God. Since we live by faith with confidence (2 Cor 5:6, 8), guaranteed by the presence of the Spirit (5:5), we live in righteousness (5:21). As he tried to explain the expected conduct of believers, Paul followed the same "clothing" imagery in Col 3:9–14, where this conduct is expressed in a very practical manner. Thus, the reward is delighting the Lord now and being with him in a "heavenly dwelling" forever and forever.

 LIVE the Story

Suffering

This is a powerful chapter that has more relevance for today's Christians than we have time to consider. There are countless human stories of human sin, as well as human frailty and persecution that intersect with God's story. During times of pain and suffering, it appears to be a weak and fruitless argument to say to the afflicted person, "don't worry, God is in control." Most people have a hard time finding much assurance in the theology of eternal life someday ("pie in the sky by and by"), particularly at the center of tragedy, despair, and persecution. Yet, while Paul is clear in his descriptions of identifiable pain and suffering, he was also adamant concerning the reality and the guarantee of God's power, hope, and glory in the lives of believers. Paul's own personal experiences can be augmented by countless modern-day personal experiences of affliction and "eternal glory."

A personal story enlivens the imagery of the jars of clay. When I was young, my mother was very interested in ceramics as a craft. Like Jeremiah, I learned several lessons about life from watching her work with clay vessels. She would take me with her to a store where she could buy greenware. Straight from the mold, the greenware was just soft clay, raw and ready to be decorated and fired. She would then "clean" the greenware with a small, sharp knife to make it smooth and seamless. Very carefully, she would decorate the piece, using colors that would not fade in the firing process. Then, the piece would be fired at a very high temperature, sitting in the oven for as many as three hours. After it cooled, a clear glaze would be used to finish the process, and the piece would be fired again. If a metallic color was used (gold or silver) on the edging or rim, it had a separate third firing at an even higher temperature. I learned how soft and fragile greenware is, and how nothing becomes stable or usable until it goes through the firing process a number of times. The heat in the kiln hardened the clay and miraculously turned the raw greenware into a beautiful ceramic piece. But the artist had to watch carefully to be sure the kiln did not get too hot for too long, because done incorrectly, the heat could crack, distort, or even completely destroy the vessel.

In the same way, Christian believers today, as in the first century, are familiar with the concept that God is the "potter" and humanity is the "clay." Life lessons were learned, "at the potter's house," through the "heat" of trials, struggles, afflictions, and our own sins that mold us, refine us, and make us who we are. Resembling raw greenware, we may be "fired" in the trials of life, although the Master Potter will not allow life to completely destroy us. The frailty of the human body, mind, and spirit makes us unlikely vessels for the light of the gospel message. Yet God cares enough about us to transform us in this life, in the present, so we can delight in him now. We become vessels filled up with the Holy Spirit, so that we have the courage, the strength, the tenacity, and the passion to serve him, like Paul, tirelessly. As an astute student of mine once said, we are all jars of clay, and we are "unfinished works in many ways."

Persecution for Jesus's Sake

Stories of suffering and persecution for Jesus's sake also intersect with God's big story. We know from his personal testimony that Paul persecuted Christ-followers very early in the movement (Acts 9:1–6). Perhaps these memories never left him, decades later, as he reflected on his own trials and persecution during his ministry (4:8–9). The persecution of Christians did not begin with the apostle Paul, nor has it been abated for more than two thousand years. Specifically, Paul told his readers about the reality of human injustice that is based primarily on contrasting theological and political views (i.e., views about Jesus).

Christian persecution is not restricted to a time or a place. One of the most famous Christians to die for his faith was Dietrich Bonhoeffer. His book, *The Cost of Discipleship,* chronicles his theological reflections that culminated with his death. He met his death at the hands of the S.S. Black Guards in Germany on April 9, 1945. During the Nazi regime, Bonhoeffer and many others were tortured, hanged, and murdered because of their Christian faith.

> [Bonhoeffer's] story has become the story of the victory of the spirit of the loving and truly human person over evil, evil which was not able to break the last stronghold of responsible spiritual freedom. "The life of the spirit is not that which shuns death and keeps clear of the destruction: rather it endureth death and in death it is sustained. It only achieves its truth in the midst of utter destruction."[46]

Worldwide Persecution

Today, a person would have to live in a bubble to be unaware of the persecution of Christians in our world. The persecution of Christians has been revealed, defined, debated, and sometimes ignored since the first century AD, yet many people have no idea how intense, widespread, and horrific it is today. With the advent of social media in our present culture, worldwide persecution of Christians has been emblazoned in our daily news headlines. Today, we can see more than 22 million Internet locations to research this vital topic. While it is impossible to recount all of that information here, it is worth investigating a few examples that open our eyes to the ongoing persecution of Christians in our lifetimes.

The website titled Open Doors is committed to serving persecuted Christians worldwide. From this website, we can "learn more about the persecution of Christians worldwide, and what you can do to help."[47] This website informs readers as to what persecution is, the theology of persecution, where it is taking place, why it occurs, and what we can do about it. At the time of this writing, the most recent available statistics online from the Open Doors website are shocking:

EACH MONTH:

322 Christians are killed for their faith.
214 churches and Christian properties are destroyed.

---

46. Dietrich Bonhoeffer, *The Cost of Discipleship* (New York: Macmillan, 1959), 33.
47. Open Doors, USA, www.opendoorsusa.org. A recent book available from the Open Doors website is called *Why Do You Persecute Me?* It is eight Christians in eight countries who tell real-life stories of incredible persecution because of their Christian faith.

772 forms of violence are committed against Christians, including beatings, abductions, rapes, arrests, and forced marriages.

More than 215 million believers face persecution, intimidation, loss of jobs/income, prison, and even death simply for their faith in Jesus Christ. Beatings, physical torture, confinement, isolation, rape, severe punishment, imprisonment, slavery, discrimination in education and employment, and death are just a few examples of the persecution they experience on a daily basis.

According to the United States Department of State, Christians in more than 60 countries face persecution from their governments and/or surrounding neighbors simply because of their religious beliefs.[48]

There are numerous reasons why Christians are persecuted. Three significant reasons are: authoritarian governments seeking to control all human thought and expression, hostility toward nontraditional and minority religious groups, and few personal freedoms and a lack of basic human rights.[49]

The Open Doors website offers the World Watch List, which names the top fifty nations with reported persecution of Christians. In August 2019 they listed the locations of the worst levels of violence against Christians in the world. At that time the most notable offenders of Christian persecution included:

1. North Korea—communist oppression
2. Afghanistan—Islamic oppression
3. Somalia—Islamic oppression
4. Libya—Islamic oppression
5. Pakistan—Islamic oppression
6. Sudan—Islamic oppression
7. Eritrea—Dictatorial paranoia
8. Yemen—Islamic oppression
9. Iran—Islamic oppression
10. India—Religious nationalism
11. Syria—Islamic oppression.[50]

Iranian Prisoner

Another recent example of Christian persecuted is the story of Pastor Saeed Abedini, who was viciously beaten in an Iranian prison. He was unjustly held

---

48. Open Doors, USA, www.opendoorsusa.org.
49. Open Doors, USA. www.opendoorsusa.org/christian-persecution/world-watch-list.
50. www.opendoorsusa.org. Website article written by Joshua Pease.

as a spy for years and was told his only way to freedom was to deny his faith in Jesus Christ. While Abedini was finally released from prison and returned to the US, he is one of the few who experience reprieve from hostile treatment as a result of his Christian faith and service.[51] In a 2016 Facebook communication, David Curry, Open Doors USA's CEO and president, said, "The last four years have seen the largest growth of persecution in the modern age; this year tops all previous years of attacks and violence. We need to do something about it."

There is so much suffering on account of Jesus, and the persecution continues. Ephesians 6 reminds us that the battle is spiritual (6:10–12). It is important that all Christians recognize and remember the martyrdom and hardships that were experienced, and are still being experienced, by our brothers and sisters all over the globe. We must be determined to stand firm against the domain of evil and to be prayer warriors for mercy and deliverance. Those oppressed, like Paul, show patience, endurance and strength in the face of opposition forces, and are encouraging to all of us on this faith journey. For those in Christian service across the world, it can often feel exactly the way that Paul expresses it: "so then, death is at work in us, but life is at work in you" (4:12). It is critical that churches support missionaries locally and across the globe with prayer, notes of support and love, and financial assistance. We pray in unity against evil, and for the kingdom of God to come—soon.

Aware of the continuing maltreatment, Franklin Graham led the *World Summit in Defense of Persecuted Christians* in May of 2017 in Washington, DC. Graham turns the spotlight on what he calls the "Christian Genocide" across the globe.[52] In search for answers, Graham offers five ways to pray for persecuted Christians:

1. Pray for Christian believers amid persecution (Jas 5:13–16).
2. Pray for those who are *doing* the persecution, that they might repent and come to know the Lord Jesus Christ (Matt 5:43–45; Luke 6:28).
3. Pray for strength and comfort for the families and loved ones of those amid persecution (Heb 4:16).
4. Pray that the church will rise up and bear the burdens of the oppressed (Acts 4:23–26). Support from the body of Christ is crucial. In addition to prayers and financial aid, we can make others aware of the trials and write to our elected officials for their help.
5. Pray that world leaders would do all they can to fight the persecution and oppression of Christians (Ps 2:10–11). Pray that they will draft

51. www.opendoorsusa.org. Stoyan Zaimov, reporter for *The Christian Post*, June 11, 2015.
52. Franklin Graham and the Billy Graham Evangelistic Organization, www.billygraham.org.

and execute procedures and policies that will make a lasting, global difference. At the time of writing, examples of such leaders include Vice President Mike Pence and US Senator James Lankford.[53]

Sadly, in American culture today, we see abuse and ill-treatment of people based solely on religious beliefs. Jewish and Muslim communities have experienced destruction and degradation simply because of their religious worship and practice. As Christians, we must reject any form of prejudice and persecution based on religion, while we remain boldly steadfast and committed, as Paul did, to the truth of the Christian gospel that focuses on loving one another. We live in a progressively unchristian society, and we can see that religious freedoms are being eroded away; the word of God is being defamed, ignored, and dishonored. The distinct separation of church and state in America has affected such freedoms as prayer in public schools and teaching Christian values in public universities, but we must commit to trusting God, loving one another, and being part of the solution, not the problem.

Tender Ministry

One of the most endearing aspects of this letter is the open honesty and unashamed sharing of Paul with his congregation in Corinth. In the same way, in our own neighborhood churches, it is important to recognize that Christian ministers and church leaders can suffer in silence because they are too embarrassed or too afraid to be honest about their painful trials in ministry. Perhaps the trials enumerated by Paul in 4:8–9 may be familiar to many Christian ministers today, especially those who have been called to serve in dangerous territories, unfamiliar cultures, and in disgruntled, unhealthy congregations. Christian leaders can be very effective as they share their own stories, confess their own shortcomings, and humbly relate how Christ Jesus has worked in their lives. Frank, personal stories demonstrating trust in God's calling and provision will be remembered long after the benediction on a Sunday morning. In spite of intense trials, afflictions, and failures, it is encouraging for Christian leaders today to be assured of God's total, unfailing sufficiency that dominates this letter. Paul teaches us that our personal stories can and do touch people and enlighten others to God's big story. We need to be reminded of the words of Jesus:

> Blessed are those who are persecuted because of righteousness,
> for theirs in the kingdom of heaven.

---

53. Franklin Graham and the Billy Graham Evangelistic Organization, www.billygraham.org.

Blessed are you when people insult you, persecute you and falsely say all kinds of evil against you *because of me*. Rejoice and be glad, because great is your reward in heaven, for in the same way they persecuted the prophets who were before you. . . .

You are the light of the world . . . let your light shine before men, that they may see your good deeds and praise your Father in heaven. (Matt 5:10–12, 14, 16 my emphasis)

> Sing the praises of the LORD, you his faithful people;
>   praise his holy name.
> For his anger lasts only a moment,
>   but his favor lasts a lifetime;
> weeping may remain for a night,
>   but rejoicing comes in the morning. (Ps 30:4–5)

LISTEN to the Story

¹¹Since, then, we know what it is to fear the Lord, we try to persuade others. What we are is plain to God, and I hope it is also plain to your conscience. ¹²We are not trying to commend ourselves to you again, but are giving you an opportunity to take pride in us, so that you can answer those who take pride in what is seen rather than in what is in the heart. ¹³If we are "out of our mind," as some say, it is for God; if we are in our right mind, it is for you. ¹⁴For Christ's love compels us, because we are convinced that one died for all, and therefore all died. ¹⁵And he died for all, that those who live should no longer live for themselves but for him who died for them and was raised again.

¹⁶So from now on we regard no one from a worldly point of view. Though we once regarded Christ in this way, we do so no longer. ¹⁷Therefore, if anyone is in Christ, the new creation has come: The old has gone, the new is here! ¹⁸All this is from God, who reconciled us to himself through Christ and gave us the ministry of reconciliation: ¹⁹that God was reconciling the world to himself in Christ, not counting people's sins against them. And he has committed to us the message of reconciliation. ²⁰We are therefore Christ's ambassadors, as though God were making his appeal through us. We implore you on Christ's behalf: Be reconciled to God. ²¹God made him who had no sin to be sin for us, so that in him we might become the righteousness of God.

⁶:¹As God's co-workers we urge you not to receive God's grace in vain. ²For he says,

> "In the time of my favor I heard you,
> in the day of salvation I helped you."

I tell you, now is the time of God's favor, now is the day of salvation. ⁶:³We put no stumbling block in anyone's path, so that our ministry will not be discredited. ⁴Rather, as servants of God we commend ourselves in every way: in great endurance; in troubles, hardships and distresses; [5]in beatings, imprisonments and riots; in hard work, sleepless nights and hunger; [6]in purity, understanding, patience and kindness; in the Holy Spirit and in sincere love; [7]in truthful speech and in the power of God; with weapons of righteousness in the right hand and in the left; [8]through glory and dishonor, bad report and good report; genuine, yet regarded as impostors; [9]known, yet regarded as unknown; dying, and yet we live on; beaten, and yet not killed; [10]sorrowful, yet always rejoicing; poor, yet making many rich; having nothing, and yet possessing everything.

Listening to the Text in the Story: Psalm 19:9; 34:9; 111:10; 118:4; 128:1; Isaiah 40:9–11; 42:67; 49:3–8; Romans 5:10; Galatians 3:26–27; Ephesians 2:11–22.

The book of Isaiah describes the sacrifices God desires: sacrifices of praise and rejoicing, the heart's gifts of commitment and trust, offerings of justice and compassion. God longs for our very selves, our willingness, devotion, humble submissiveness, faithful obedience, confident dependence, eager witness. He wishes that we would love him with all our heart, and soul and mind and strength.

—*Marva J. Dawn*[1]

As we follow Paul through his *"apologia,"* the defense of his ministry and his mission in Corinth (2 Cor 2:14–7:1), it is important to remember that he was primarily concerned about the community in Corinth as a whole. Even in his related discussion concerning a single person who injured Paul personally, Paul's main concern was for the entire church (2:5). Garland suggests that this entire discussion and defense is related to the "tearful letter" Paul sent to Corinth before this letter and after his "painful visit" with the congregation (2:1–4). His *apologia* was, in a sense, an attempt to explain to the church what God had called Paul to do, and to convince them of the truth of his "paradoxical gospel." He wanted very much to win them to Christ and have them leave behind their earlier lives of idolatry. Paul was aware that he was "answerable to God" for all he said and did in ministry; he wanted to assure the church that he was ministering in a straightforward, honest manner.[2]

---

1. Marva J. Dawn, *To Walk and Not Faint*, 2nd ed. (Grand Rapids: Eerdmans, 1997), 98.
2. Garland, *2 Corinthians*, 271.

Indeed, we as modern readers must understand Paul's teachings not only as individuals in the twenty-first century, but also in terms of *his* audience—a brand-new, struggling community of "baby" believers. A cursory reading of many biblical texts in English results in the interpretation of the pronoun *"you"* as a singular pronoun, as "we implore *you* on Christ's behalf: Be reconciled to God" (5:20b). We could interpret this as instructions for each person, but the individual believer is not Paul's main emphasis. Paul is imploring the whole church to be reconciled to God, and to be reconciled to Paul as their "founding father" in the faith. In American culture we tend to be individualistic, focusing on ourselves and hearing the word of God in the same manner. But often when Paul wrote "you," he was implying the plural form; he was addressing the whole community. Certainly, there are passages that are intentionally singular in nature: "[I]f *anyone* is in Christ, *he/she* is *a* new creation; the old has gone, the new has come!" (5:17; my translation and emphases). When Paul is referring to the individual person, he is usually intentional about his pronouns.

What did it mean to be a "church" in the past, and what does it mean in our culture today? In describing the Christian church, Rev. Richard Halverson, chaplain to the US Senate from 1981 to 1994, is quoted as saying:

> Christianity began on Palestinian soil as a relationship with a person. It moved onto Greek soil and became a philosophy. Then it moved onto Roman soil and became an institution. It moved further onto British soil and became a card-carrying church culture. It moved again, onto American soil, and became an enterprise, something to be packaged and sold.[3]

The congregation in Corinth was learning to do a new thing, and it took a number of letters and visits by Paul and his colleagues to teach the people what it means to be a gathering of Christian believers. They were a young cluster of converts, worshiping together, caring for one another, and learning together about a God and a Savior that were unlike any other deities in their culture.

With this letter, Paul's intention was to both edify and correct the young church in Corinth. First, one of the main purposes of this letter was to defend Paul's calling and his character against opposition and denigration from outside intruders in the church. In his own defense, he must explain his ministry to the Corinthians, and explain what a "church" looks like in view of Christ and of his teachings. There are four aims of Christian ministry: transformation

---

3. John Chalmers, "Signposts of a Living Faith," *Life and Work: The Magazine of the Church of Scotland* (December 2017): 24.

(3:18), reconciliation (5:11–21), agency (6:1–4a), and self-sacrifice (6:4b–10). Unfortunately, there were people on the inside who did not fully understand his message and his mission (1:14). There was also pressure from the outside: false teachers and rival missionaries who tried to convince the people that Paul's message was wrong and that he did not have their best interests at heart. To the best of his ability, in a letter (an unfortunate but necessary replacement for a face-to-face meeting), Paul had to convince the believers that their distrust was groundless. He therefore emphasized the fact that he served them and not himself.

Second, Paul pointed to his ministry of reconciliation as an entirely new paradigm of thinking about themselves, about others, and about him as the authentic apostle. Verse 5:11 opens with a transitional word translated "since" or "therefore" acting as an arrow to send readers back to the previous verse (5:10). In view of divine judgment, Paul and his colleagues actively pursued the ministry to which they have been called, despite obstacles and hardships. Paul defends his "ministry of reconciliation" and insists that this ministry gives believers a completely different view of other people and the world around them. Verses 5:11–13 are similar in content to 1:12–14, where Paul writes that his message is a message of God's grace. His readers could understand him because his life and ministry was an open book, and his confidence was in the Lord. His apostolic mission and message were well within the big salvific plan of God and God's people. God's message of reconciliation was proclaimed by Paul and his associates who were given the task of publicly stating it to the world.[4]

Third, verse 6:1 opens with plural words: "co-workers," "we," and "you." Paul was including his missionary associates in his proclamations to the whole church. As "servants of God," they were devoted agents of God, commissioned and commended by him (6:4a). Paul then moves into another list of the hardships of ministry (6:4b–10) to assure the people that he and his colleagues functioned only in a self-sacrificial manner, and not for human position and acclaim. Paul lived a commendable life before his people; in fact, trials and afflictions were a sign of Paul's authenticity as an apostle. His life was utterly different from the lives of his self-seeking opponents who were concerned only about their own comfort and status. The true value of a ministry is not in the material rewards, financial gain, and accolades from other believers.

This complex passage of 2 Corinthians is not unfamiliar to readers today. We have heard familiar verses (5:17 and 20) and, if not the details, we have

---

4. Chalmers, "Signposts of a Living Faith," 268–69.

certainly heard of the extent of Paul's sufferings during his ministry. But we must dig a little deeper to discover what this passage tells us about the early church and about today's Christian community in God's "big story."

EXPLAIN the Story

A Message of Reconciliation (5:11–15)

One key theme in this letter is Paul's "ministry of reconciliation" proclaimed to a church that had doubts about Paul, about his authority, and his aims. When any relationship is struggling, the most important beginning is a step of reconciliation. It is not always easy to reconcile with another; perhaps no one wants to take the first step to resolve disputes or thorny issues. Yet, as Paul proclaimed, it was God who took the first step to initiate reconciliation with humanity. Through the death and resurrection of Christ, God graciously reconciled sinful humanity to himself, removing our sins and making us righteous. Reconciliation is a free gift from God; it is neither earned nor deserved. "For if, when we were God's enemies, we were reconciled to him through the death of his Son, how much more, having been reconciled, shall we be saved through his life!" (Rom 5:10).

Paul explained to his readers what stimulated him to serve as a minister of reconciliation and why he was so devoted to this task (2 Cor 5:11–15); then he reveals the essence of his gospel message (5:16–6:2); and finally, he points out the characteristics of his ministry.[5]

Paul was convinced that he was called to persuade people of three key truths: that Jesus is the Messiah and the Lord of all (both Jews and Greeks); that he, Paul, was "credentialed" as an apostle, called and sent by God, and that he conducted his life accordingly; and that his motives among the Corinthians were pure and sincere. His aim was to seek the approval of God (in Christ) and not that of human beings.[6]

"Fear of the Lord" (5:11)

Paul knew what it is to "fear the Lord," which is an odd phrase, ignored, unused, and misunderstood by some. Fear is not to be "afraid" of God, or to quake in dread of his divine retribution. The concept is ancient (Pss 19:9; 34:9; 111:10; 118:4; 128:1), but Eugene Peterson has done a marvelous job of explaining this phrase to Christians of today.

---

5. Harris, *Second Corinthians*, 411.
6. Harris, *Second Corinthians*, 413.

[The fear of the Lord is] a way to refer to the way we live the spiritual life—not just what we do and say, but the way we act, the way we speak. . . . It is the phrase for the way of life that is lived responsively and appropriately before who God is, who he is as Father, Son and Holy Spirit. None of the available synonyms in the English language—awe, reverence, worshipful respect— seems quite adequate. They miss the punch delivered by "fear of the Lord."[7]

Peterson continues, "Most of the Christian life involves paying attention to *who* God is and *what* he does; but not only the *who* and the *what*, but the *how*, the means God employs to accomplish his ends. If we get too interested too soon in what we do and are, we go off the rails badly."[8]

Thus, we can assume that Paul was very aware of an intentional connection between himself and God. Paul knew, without doubt, that his mission and his ministry was rooted deeply in the "*what*" and "*how*" of God. Paul assured his readers that he was directed by God, a vehicle of his purposes, and was compelled to serve God (5:14).

"Fear of the Lord" is not shrinking back in fear of rules and regulations; quite simply, it is living in reverence before God. The best way to do this is in a *communal* setting. Such a life is nourished by other Christians in community by reading and studying his word, and by prayer. It is a thoughtful, deliberate interruption in the commonness of our own lives, to stop and pay attention to God. This could be in a community worship experience, or in a quiet place and a sacred time, but it could occur at any time or place when God invades our lives and grabs our awareness.[9]

Self-Commendation (5:12–13)

Paul writes that "we are not trying to commend ourselves to you *again*" (5:12, my emphasis), revisiting the same issue he addressed in 3:1 and 4:2. Harris points out that there are two types of "self-commendation": one type that glorifies the self ("self-praise") and a second type that leads to the praise of God ("boasting in the Lord"). The latter assumes the power of God in and through human weakness, especially for his own glory. Paul employed both types of commendation in this letter, and it is a clever play on words that he liked to use in his Corinthian letters. "Commending" or "self-introduction" was not uncommon in Paul's society, and his readers would have recognized the distinctions between the two types.[10] That is, Paul did not want to boast

---

7: Peterson, *Contemplative Pastor*, 41.

8. Peterson, *Contemplative Pastor*, 41.

9. Peterson, *Contemplative Pastor*, 41.

10. Harris, *Second Corinthians*, 470–71.

or brag about himself and his preaching, so he was very cautious about not commending himself (3:1; 10:18). Instead, Paul wanted the people to take pride in him and his associates because of their untainted intentions and motives in ministry (5:12).

In spite of what his adversaries might have said, Paul and his colleagues were ministering in their "right mind" for the specific benefit of the community at Corinth (5:13). The background of this verse is blurry at best. We cannot be certain of exactly what Paul meant by saying that he was not "out of his mind," or that, conversely, he was "in [his] right mind" (5:13). We know that he was in good company, as Jesus was accused by his own family of being "out of his mind" in Mark 3:21. Perhaps the Corinthians really thought that Paul had a mental problem. Was this an accusation by his opponents? Was this a reference to his visions, or a kind of religious ecstasy (1 Cor 14:2, 18; 2 Cor 12:1–7)? The phrase "out of your mind" is from a Greek word that is the root of our English words "ecstatic" or "ecstasy." This phrase could imply a mystical experience, where someone was in a trance or in a state of mind generated by God and used by him for a special communication with a person (i.e., Peter in Acts 10:10; 11:5, and Paul in Acts 22:17).[11] In addition, we do know that the Corinthian believers were very proud of their spiritual gifts, and were highly interested in visions and other ecstatic experiences (see 2 Cor 12:1–6). Their exuberance for the gift of speaking in tongues had taken primacy over other more important matters in the church, such as love and edification of one another (see 1 Cor 13:1–14:5). So, despite the words of others, Paul's point here was that he was not "mad"; he had his proper, rational senses. His experiences were not for show, but were for the sake of God (2 Cor 5:13). Perhaps he was charged by his rivals of being "out of his mind" in his (well-intended) "tearful letter" (2:4), especially if the letter was written as a corrective for the Corinthians.[12] The Corinthians may have been amazed by the impressive words and performances of the false teachers, but Paul clearly refutes the accusations of "craziness" because his intentions toward his readers were good, honest, and sensible. He was driven not by sensationalism, self-interest, acclaim, or selfish gain, but by the love of Christ, to proclaim the Christian gospel for the benefit of the people (5:14).

"Compelled by God" (5:14)

Paul insisted that he was compelled by Christ's love to minister the way he did, even if it meant he had to write a difficult letter to the Corinthians.

---

11. Garland, *2 Corinthians*, 274.
12. Garland, *2 Corinthians*, 276.

The interesting verb "to compel" or "to constrain" is used here in 5:14; in a little different context, it also appears in Philippians 1:23, where Paul is "constrained" or "hard pressed" to choose between two emotions. Here, it can be translated as "to hold within bounds so as to manage or guide; direct."[13] In a sense, Paul said that he and his colleagues were "held together" within their ministry by the love of Christ; they were left with no choice but to be directed and controlled by Christ in their attempt to "try to persuade others" (2 Cor 5:11). It was their habit to present the gospel message of Christ and endure whatever affliction that might come to pass. It isn't a matter of reason; it is a matter of love.[14]

Paul and his associates are completely convinced that Jesus "died for all and therefore all died" (5:14). Because he "died for all," for the Jew and for the non-Jew, Jesus involved all humanity in his death. Likewise, in his letter to the Romans, Paul wrote that "all of us who were baptized into Christ Jesus were baptized into his death . . . [and] will certainly also be united with him in a resurrection like his" (Rom 6:3–5). That is, Jesus did not act out of his own selfish desires, but willingly died on the cross for the sake of all humanity. In the same sense, Paul and his colleagues willingly responded to the love of Christ by ministering *not* for their own self-gratification but for the benefit of the people. Their selflessness before the Corinthians was no doubt in direct contrast to the behavior of Paul's opponents, the self-seeking rival missionaries. "Christ's submission to God's will was a supreme act of self-giving love."[15] This foundational truth is what drove Paul and his colleagues to ministry, whatever the cost.

Second Corinthians 5:15 further explains and qualifies Christ's atoning death. That is, for some people, his death confirms the fact that everyone, someday, will meet death; for others, who by faith are united with him, his death is the end of their old way of life. The latter believers "die to self" and can live with and for Christ. Belleville writes that while Jesus died for all of humanity, "it is only believers who reap the benefits. The scope of Christ's redemptive work may be all-encompassing, but the application is particular."[16] That may be true, as one needs to personally receive the benefits of Christ's redemptive work to initiate any change. When one does "die to self" there is no reason for any Christian to live selfishly. Change means consciously maintaining a lifestyle that is pleasing to God and not to self. "To live for Christ is to serve him," a "transfer of ownership" from my will to his.[17]

---

13. Garland, *2 Corinthians*, 277. See BDAG 971.
14. Garland, *2 Corinthians*, 277.
15. Garland, *2 Corinthians*, 279.
16. Belleville, *2 Corinthians*, 150.
17. Belleville, *2 Corinthians*, 152.

Harris summarizes Paul's reasons for proclaiming his message and executing his ministry as an apostle of God. These *five motivations* should be considered relevant for Christian ministry today; that is, like Paul, why do we do what we do? We should *have a desire to please Christ* in all circumstances (v. 9), and we *need to be conscious of a final accountability to Christ* ("fear of the Lord," vv. 10, 11a). This requires *a deep awareness of God's glory* and a *profound concern for our congregation's wellbeing* (v. 13). We have the example of Christ's sacrificial love for us (v. 14), and ultimately, *we live for Christ because of his death and resurrection* (v. 15). Harris writes that these motivations are the "focus of Pauline ethics"; that is, our conduct, our message, and our ministries are Christocentric, inspired by and governed by Christ himself.[18]

Reconciliation with God (5:16–21)

Thus, Christians who are committed to living for Christ and serving him are transformed (3:18) into people with new thought patterns, new attitudes, new behavior, and new motivations. They consider the world not by worldly standards or worldly paradigms, such as the Romans' views of noble birth, wisdom, outward appearances, and honorable positions. Christians are not to regard the world by the typical Pauline phrase, "according to the flesh" (5:16; see 1 Cor 1:26–27). Many Gentiles may have heard of *Jesus* before their conversion; rumors had it that he was a good teacher, or a "miracle-worker," or even a dreadful Jew. But that was the worldly point of view, and their faith in Christ changed their perspective entirely. This leads us into the familiar passage on being entirely "new creatures."

New Creation (5:17)

Verse 5:17 is memorable, mysterious, and somewhat misunderstood in the church today. By calling them "a new creation," Paul was saying that Christian believers think in a whole new way. Every individual believer is being transformed (3:18), and his or her old view of the world is gone. Because of Christ, the believer has a brand-new view of the world. In Paul's day, religion in the Roman Empire was polytheistic and quite flexible. A new "religion" or a new "god" was just absorbed and folded into all the other myriad beliefs in the culture. Paul is saying that Christianity is different; it is unique and exclusive. A person cannot assent to belief in Christ and just add it to all the other belief systems. This is often called syncretism, or the blending together of numerous religious beliefs. It was not unusual even in the world of the Old Testament, when the ancient Jews tried to live among other people with very

---

18. Harris, *Second Corinthians*, 423–24.

different religious practices. Often, they merely kept the old, pagan cultural ways and adopted a belief in Yahweh as well. At the time of Paul, society was a ". . . vortex of cultures—Greek learning and Roman government and Jewish moral traditions mixed in with gnostic sects, mystery cults, terrorist bands and assorted messianic adventurers and fanatics. The mix changed weekly."[19]

In truth, this diverse mixture of culture could describe our world today. We have so-called "tolerant" thinkers in our society who reject Christianity's exclusivity, and absorb numerous (even contradictory!) beliefs into their worldview to demonstrate their tolerance for all religious views and to "cover all their bases."

Yet, Paul contended that belief in Christ meant that all the old traditions, old worldviews, the old gods and goddesses, and old ways of life and worship were gone. "The new has come," in the form of a baby in a manger. Christianity transforms people into new creatures who follow one God and his only Son (5:14). We can offer recipes as an analogy: we can add new ingredients to an old recipe. We can add chocolate chunks or cut strawberries to vanilla ice cream, but in the end, we still have ice cream. We can add seeds and nuts to an old bread recipe, but we still have bread. Christianity, therefore, is like a whole new recipe, with all new ingredients, a wholly new method, and a whole new treat at the end.

Essentially, this means that changed people have new concepts about other people (5:16), about fearing physical death (5:1–5), and about the old "ministry of condemnation" of his opponents (3:9). Further, worldly wisdom (1:14) does not control believers anymore. The Corinthian community was different, and they were not to value human actions and behavior in the old way. They were not to judge Paul and his missionary rivals in the old way of human inclination, but by the new way, by the standards of God. In Romans 12:2, for example, Paul said that as new creatures, "do not conform any longer to the pattern of this world, but be transformed by the renewing of your mind," seeing all of life in a new and extraordinary way.

Thus, the church is a body of transformed people, living for and serving Jesus in the power of God's Spirit. Paul reminded them that their former lives had changed; they now understood who Jesus is (5:15) and that they were reconciled to God through Christ (5:18). Believers must now "think Christianly, that is, to think 'in Christ,' 'in the Messiah'."[20] In 1 Corinthians 2:16 Paul told the readers that "we have the mind of Christ." He instructed them, "Brothers and sisters, stop thinking like children. In regard to evil be infants, but in your

19. Peterson, *Christ Plays in Ten Thousand Places*, 15.
20. Wright, *Paul Debate*, 1.

thinking be adults" (1 Cor 14:20). As new creatures or "Messiah people," they were to think in new ways with a new mind.[21] Apparently the Corinthians were still thinking about Paul in the manner of their society, and so they had the wrong expectations about him and his message. He was neither a worldly success in their eyes, nor did he speak with flamboyant wisdom. In contrast, Paul proclaimed a simple gospel message: that a "new world was being born; Jesus' resurrection was, he believed, the launch of a new creation, a new world being born from the womb of the old."[22] The God who created the world was "re-creating" a people for himself.

> Something happened through which the world was a different place. Everything has become new. This, for Paul, was the defining Messiah-shaped truth, not simply about the world in general, or about this or that individual in particular, but about the community that found itself formed by the new energy which pulsated through what Paul called "the gospel," the good-news message he announced. The result was a community significantly different from anything previously known.[23]

Garland agrees. He notes that "Christ is the divider of history. There is a radical eschatological break between the old age and the new. More than an individual transformation, God is recreating humans into the new community where there are no artificial barriers (such as circumcision)."[24]

Counting People's Sins (5:19)

A brief summation of Paul's "ministry of reconciliation" is seen in verses 5:19–21. Reconciliation begins with the confession of sin. Thank God that he no longer is "counting people's sins against them" (5:19)! That is, in the world of accounting and bookkeeping, this is like erasing the debit column. Our debt of sin was paid by Christ; that is, Christ, who was entirely righteous, paid the price and became "sin for us" (5:21) so that sinful humanity could be reconciled to a holy, righteous God. To the Jews, the idea of "sin" was "deliberate actions knowingly committed against God." To the Gentiles, "sin" was a "mistake that resulted from ignorance."[25] In effect, sin is an obstacle that stops a person on the journey toward a gracious God. Any human destructive behavior, such as idolatry and greed, are the polar opposite of God's grace and

21. Wright, *Paul Debate*, 2.
22. Wright, *Paul Debate*, 3.
23. Wright, *Paul Debate*, 5.
24. Garland, *2 Corinthians*, 287.
25. Belleville, *2 Corinthians*, 156.

forgiveness, and such behavior moves a person away from Christ. What we owe (our debt) can never be repaid by us to God, so he had to forgive the debt himself through the death and resurrection of his Son.

But Belleville shows the real impact of human sin: "sin is a clenched fist and its object is the face of God." Jesus identified so closely with the plight of humanity that our sins became his sins.[26] Thus, there is an extraordinary exchange that is neither deserved nor achieved: God makes it possible for sinful people to receive his righteousness and be reconciled to himself as a result of Jesus taking on our sins on the cross (1 Cor 1:30). This reconciliation is given to the individual person, to be sure, but it was also granted to the entire cosmos. The identity of the community of believers, composed of those who have received the gift of reconciliation to God, had been altered, and the whole culture of that community was different. Hostile groups (i.e., the Jews and the Gentiles) were unified and reconciled one to another because they were all in Christ.

These verses, 5:16–21, are a bit confusing because Paul moves back and forth between "us" in reference to all believers, and "us" referencing those specifically called to be ministers of God (Paul and his co-workers, 6:1). Paul was making reference to himself and his co-workers in 5:12–15. Then, he said that the "ministry of reconciliation" was "given" to Paul (and his "fellow workers") to teach (v. 18), but every believer ("the world") is reconciled to God through Christ (v. 19). It was God who "committed the message of reconciliation" to Paul (and his "fellow workers"), who were appointed the task of being "ambassadors." Yet, the concluding imperative in v. 20 is for everyone: "Be reconciled to God"; everyone should receive this gift and "become the righteousness of God" in the world (v. 21).

Ambassadors (5:20)

Ambassadors are people sent from one country to another country as message-bearers from one leader to another leader of another country.[27] This implies that, as God's representatives, Paul and his colleagues were in God's "authority and in his service," lending credence to Paul's words and actions.[28] It is also a constant reminder of who is "King" and who is not; neither believers are God, nor are human rulers of the world. All believers are to be humble representatives of God on earth—to be God's hands and feet, to be God's heart and love, to be the blessing to other people that God has been to us. In view of God's

---

26. Belleville, *2 Corinthians*, 157, 159.
27. Barton et al., *1 and 2 Corinthians*, 353.
28. Furnish, *II Corinthians*, 350.

reconciliation with humanity, the community of believers has an assignment: Christians are sent out as representatives of God to transform culture, not be transformed *by* culture (5:20).

The profound message that Christians are to represent God in the world in word, action, and deed is summarized simply in 5:21. God's reconciliation with humanity is both a finished act (that of Christ) and a continuing process, a redemption that is both modeled by and experienced in the church.

Righteousness

Still, not every Christian is called to be an ambassador in the specific sense that God calls individuals (like Paul and his associates) and appoints them to be his "message-bearers" (v. 20). In defense of his own ministry, Paul noted that he and his fellow workers were specially called by God to be spokesmen and ambassadors of God (vv. 18–19). Of his own volition, God reconciled the world to himself through the work of Christ. Then, God entrusted this gracious, gospel message to Paul and his associates, who were emboldened and enabled to pass the knowledge along to others. Paul and his colleagues, then, were the ambassadors of God who were making God's appeal for reconciliation with humanity (5:20). Christ is the only human who was entirely righteous; yet, he took on the sins and punishment on the cross, which humanity so rightly deserved. Thus, through this exchange, Christ made it possible for us to receive his righteousness and thereby be reconciled to God.

Verses 5:20–21, familiar and well-loved, have interested scholars for many years. They are climactic verses to Paul's defensive arguments that have been building since chapter three. N. T. Wright sees these verses as powerful statements in defense of Paul's ministry:

An "ambassador" in v. 20 prepares the reader for what Paul is saying in 5:21. Paul himself is "becoming" the "righteousness" or the "covenant faithfulness" of God. One who works on behalf of Christ (vv. 5–20) should also be such a revelation, especially when the one speaking is also acting out, in his own physical body, the same death (4:10). If Paul as an ambassador has any inadequacies, they are dealt with in the death of Christ. If he has a message to deliver, it is because he has become, by the Spirit, the incarnation of the covenant faithfulness of God.[29]

---

29. N. T. Wright, "'On Becoming the Righteousness of God,' 2 Cor 5:21 (1993)," in *Pauline Perspectives: Essays on Paul, 1978–2013* (Minneapolis: Fortress, 2013), 74.

Wright goes on to say that 5:20–21 forms a "natural climax" to the preceding chapters 3 and 4. These verses also point the reader forward; the appeal for reconciliation with God has been made, and thus, the readers are urged not to receive this gracious invitation "in vain" (6:1). "They now have a significant new motive to heed this appeal: the one who speaks is not simply an odd, shabby, battle-scarred jailbird, but one who, however surprisingly, is a revelation in person of the covenant faithfulness of God."[30]

Reconciliation with Paul (6:1–10)

In view of the weighty description of Paul's call to be both a chosen ambassador of God as well as "the righteousness of God" (5:20–21), the apostle reminded his readers that his message was God-given, true, and authentic. He further reminded them that they were, indeed, reconciled to God only through Christ, and that they must not "receive God's grace in vain" (6:1). The primary way that believers diminish the message of reconciliation is to "live for themselves" (5:15). The reference to "God's grace" in 6:1 implies the entire gospel message delivered by Paul, but "particularly to the reconciling love of God established through Christ's death" (Gal 2:20; Rom 5:2).[31] "The grace of God" is Paul's shorthand for "all of the benefits of the gospel that are secured by Christ and mediated by the Spirit."[32]

Anticipating the readers' questions about God's saving gospel message, Paul noted that God graciously performed acts of salvation in the past for his people, and that "now is the time" that his saving grace finds fulfillment in the gift of Christ to all people (2 Cor 6:2). This is not to say that Old Testament believers were somehow short-changed in salvation because they lived before the saving actions of Christ. God gave his pledge that those who demonstrated faith in him (yet who lived before the time of Christ) would receive his redemptive promises that were ultimately fulfilled in Christ (see 2 Cor 1:20; Hag 2:23).

For the second time in this letter (the first is 4:13), Paul explicitly used part of an OT passage in 6:2 to support his "ministry of reconciliation." Specifically, he quoted from Isaiah 49:8; in this chapter in Isaiah, the nation of Israel was given the ambassador assignment of "displaying [God's] splendor" (49:3). Israel was to be a "light for the Gentiles, that my salvation may reach to the ends of the earth" (49:6). The Lord, who is faithful, promises that "in the

30. Wright, "'On Becoming the Righteousness of God,'" 75.
31. Furnish, II Corinthians, 352.
32. Harris, Second Corinthians, 458.

time of my favor I will answer you, and in the day of salvation I will help you; I will keep you and will make you to be a covenant for the people, to restore the land . . ." (49:8; see also, Isa 41:8–10, 13–14).

It was abhorrent to Paul that his readers might allow the grace of God to be futile in their lives. He borrowed the phrase "now is the time of God's favor" (2 Cor 6:1) from Isaiah, and this can be interpreted in two ways. First, the phrase can mean a person's time of conversion when God graciously granted salvation to that individual. Paul used a memorable parallelism to emphasize that "the time of my [God's] favor" is also "the day of salvation" when God comes to help each person (6:2). Certainly, each believer has benefitted from God's saving grace, and we are all privileged to live in a great "now" when we are favored by his grace.[33]

Second, we can see that Isaiah is making reference to an entire nation of people who are being "saved" for the purpose of being a "light for the Gentiles." In Isaiah 49:8, the "you" is plural; the nation is to be "his people." Verse 6:2, then, is one way of describing the age of the church, which has continued into the current time. The church, formed in the time of God's favor and grace, is the "new creation" and the "new covenant" people, acting as Christ on earth until he physically comes back again. Indeed, we are "favored" people, blessed, protected, and helped by God so that we can demonstrate his love for all creation.

In summation, Paul defended his apostleship by demonstrating that he had been given the ministry of reconciliation by God (5:18). Accepting such an assignment, Paul and his colleagues had fulfilled specific requirements: his apostleship was modeled after Christ's death on the cross (self-sacrifice, v. 19); he spoke as the authoritative spokesman of God (v. 20); he was the mediator of God's revelation (v. 20); and, as one acting in God's service, his activities were done on behalf of others (6:3). This did not give him great privileges, but it did mean great suffering (6:4–10).[34] Thus, if people have accepted God's grace and are reconciled to him, that means, by extension, they must also be reconciled to God's commissioned agent, who is Paul.

Hardships and Endurance in Ministry

Finally, it was important for Paul not to discredit ("to find fault with, to criticize") his ministry and the charge that was given to him. His comment in 6:3–4a reflects back on 5:12 concerning his refusal of self-commendation to

---

33. Harris, *Second Corinthians*, 462–63.
34. Garland, *2 Corinthians*, 290.

the readers. Again, Paul was defending his ministry and his apostleship while rejecting the "boasting" of his opponents. Paul refused to be a "stumbling block in anyone's path" (6:3). A "stumbling block," of course, was a metaphor for any kind of obstacle that might prove to be injurious to someone on a physical or spiritual journey.[35] Purposefully putting an obstacle in someone's way is the opposite of reconciliation. It appears that Paul was saying that, at all costs, he avoided any kind of offense in any kind of way. Furnish translates this verse as, "giving no one cause to take offense at anything, lest the ministry be blamed" (see 5:12).[36] Unlike his rivals, and as servants of God, Paul and his associates were very conscious of their behavior, words, actions, deeds, attitudes, and prejudices so as not to offend anyone. It was his desire that the readers be proud of his ministry (5:12), and he had no desire to stand in their way on the road to salvation (6:2). The gospel message itself may have offended some people (and still does), but the apostle was very cautious about doing anything that would genuinely offend his audience.

Without warning, it appears that a significant shift in topic occurs at 6:3. Paul jumped from asking his readers "not to receive God's grace in vain" to a record of his own hardships in ministry. However, this section does flow out of chapter 5. Paul described what could be considered the basic, fundamental core of apostolic ministry (that is, reconciliation with God, 5:20), then he related the benefit of that ministry to his readers (God's grace, 6:1–2). At the heart of both the giving and the receiving of this message is the "love of Christ" (5:14). In what follows, he then explains the actual implementation of that ministry, both to clarify his "sufferings" and to demonstrate his true apostleship for his readers.[37]

Thus, verses 6:1–3 function as an introduction to Paul's list of apostolic credentials, which ironically are the trials he had faced as God's ambassador. In this one letter alone, Paul records a list of his own hardships four times: 4:8–9; 6:4b–10; 11:23b–29; and 12:10. The tribulations recorded in 6:4b–10 serve as examples of his *great endurance,* which captures the essence of his ministry (v. 4b). This list of tribulations, not unlike those in 4:8–12, also serves as a foundation for what follows in chapter 6—for Paul's emotional request for reciprocal "affection" from the Corinthians (vv. 11–13, and 7:2–3). How could his readers refuse to offer their love and support to Paul in view of what he had

---

35. Garland, *2 Corinthians,* 306.
36. Furnish, *II Corinthians,* 354.
37. Harris, *Second Corinthians,* 464.

suffered in his "catalogue of afflictions"?[38] In fact, Paul implied that he would be "disqualified" if he had attempted to "evade the suffering that comes from apostolic service" (perhaps something his rivals had done).[39]

The list of troubles in chapter 6 are listed in an intentional, antithetical structure. Paul recorded his life and his sufferings in a memorable, poetic, lyrical style:

Outward Circumstances (vv. 6:4b–5). In these verses, Paul listed nine "hardships," or three sets of three trials. The first two sets of three are generally experienced at the hands of other people; the final set of three were at least partially volitional on Paul's part:

> In troubles, in hardships and in distresses (6:4)
> In beatings, in imprisonments and in riots (6:5a)
> In hard work, in sleepless nights and in hunger (6:5b)

Qualities of Character (6:6). These are ethical qualities that characterize Paul's ministry. Interestingly, Paul included the work of the Holy Spirit in the middle of the "moral qualities" of the minister. Yet, "purity, understanding, patience and kindness" are all gifts or "fruit" of the Holy Spirit (Gal 5:22). The Holy Spirit is essential to a consistent godly character. In addition, "sincere love" is literally "*unhypocritical* love," or the opposite of pretending to love (6:6).

Spiritual Equipment (6:7). The "power of God" is a dominant theme in this letter, and Paul's specific focus is on divine power amid human weaknesses. Paul depended on God's equipping him in terms of truthful speech and boldness in his ministry (see 3:12; 6:11). In addition, and using military imagery, Paul realized he was doing battle (see 10:3–5) on the missionary field. The "power of God" is righteousness in both hands, ready for spiritual "war." Christian ministry is a battle against sin, Satan, and lawlessness, but with all the power of God to defeat the enemy.

Unexpected Changes in Ministry (6:8–10). Again, we can see Paul's love of antithesis! These verses were created in a clear antithetical structure to demonstrate some surprising changes that Paul encountered in his ministry. In these nine phrases, Paul created pairs of sharp contrasts that were indicative of his ministry experiences. Harris shows the antitheses in two columns:[40]

---

38. Harris, *Second Corinthians*, 464.
39. Garland, *2 Corinthians*, 307.
40. The chart and detailed explanations are from Harris, *Second Corinthians*, 466–86; see also Garland, *2 Corinthians*, 307–9.

In glory	and dishonor,
In bad report	and good report,
As deceivers	and yet truthful,
As unknown	and yet well known,
As facing death,	and yet, see, we live on,
As punished	and yet not killed,
As sorrowful	but always rejoicing,
As poor	but enriching many,
As having nothing	and yet possessing everything.

These last antitheses (vv. 8–10) seem to be the most poignant of the entire section. Paul expressed his most personal sufferings and shared his most painful experiences (i.e., 1:8–11). His life in ministry was a rollercoaster, from the highest of highs to the lowest of lows. His emotions became raw and tender at the same time. It appears that his goal in writing this section was to open his heart and "spill his guts" (as vivid as the final two verses) to his Corinthian readers in the hope that they would fully understand and fully accept his apostolic commission, and then fully love Paul as he loved them.

It is possible that these verses were written as a direct or indirect response to false allegations and derogatory remarks about Paul put forth by his opponents in Corinth. If so, their lies and deceptions make his troubles even worse. Paul may have found it necessary to discredit those false ministers who were seeking to belittle him and benefit themselves in any and every way. Thus, Paul responded to all kinds of maltreatment with love and moral integrity, with the help of the Holy Spirit and the power of God. His sincere love and truthful speech contrast the malice and insincerity of his opponents.

The virtue of patient endurance (6:4) was well respected in the Greco-Roman world; a true hero endured physical, mental, and emotional suffering and faced the pressures of adversity with incredible bravery. Paul's poetic list of his challenges in ministry and, notably, those of his fellow workers ("we") are examples of human endurance and of God's grace to his own. Yet through the grace and love of God, believers are comforted, encouraged, strengthened, helped, protected, and transformed through suffering (1:3–11; 3:18). This is the irony of being a Christian, and particularly of Christian ministry. We are called out by God, set aside for a wonderful purpose—to proclaim his message of redemption and reconciliation on earth—only to discover that it is a demanding task to live and speak a message that many people do not want to hear.

On the other hand, it is vital to remember that the suffering of one can be a benefit to others. True wealth, for example, is not the accumulation of material possessions; it is "possessing everything" in the Lord of all (6:10). By sharing his ordeals, Paul presented himself as not above his readers, but as one of them; he increased the bonds of affection and understanding. We can share the burdens of sufferings, so if one person suffers in the church, other people can see the example of his or her faith. Prayer strengthens, common bonds are deepened, and God can be glorified in the sharing of suffering. To be reconciled to one another means to share in the good and the bad, to offer and receive support, encouragement, and love in the rejoicing and in the sorrow (6:10). This is what it means to be a church.

LIVE the Story

"New Creation" (5:17)

What does it mean for Christians today to be a "new creation"? If we reflect on the life of the apostle Paul, we see a man who was a "dyed in the wool" Jew. He was "circumcised on the eighth day, of the people of Israel, of the tribe of Benjamin, a Hebrew of Hebrews; in regard to the law, a Pharisee" (Phil 3:5). As a devout Jew, he "persecuted the church of God and tried to destroy it" (Gal 1:13; Acts 9:1–2). So, for Paul to become one of the very people that he had persecuted is a God-ordained miracle. Paul had to completely change his mode of thinking. With new eyes and a new mind, Paul had to fully comprehend how Jesus and his resurrection completed and fulfilled the promises of God. Despite all that he had been taught, Paul had to embrace a new meaning of the "people of God"—not just Jews but Gentiles as well. This transition took time, as we can see in Galatians (1:13–2:2). Furthermore, from the very start of his brand-new ministry to Gentiles, Paul had terrifying moments and was met with adversaries and obstacles (Acts 9:19b–30; Gal 2:5). The tenacity of such a man is incredible, yet the complete transformation of the man was even more remarkable.

Second, we can consider the congregation at the church at Corinth and what those people were like. Consider, for example, the fact that the people of the Roman Empire were generally polytheistic, worshiping whatever gods or goddesses that were the most expedient for their purposes (see Acts 14:8–15).

Many Romans even worshiped the current Roman emperor as a divine dictator and benefactor (17:6–9). The worship of local and regional deities had economic, social, and political advantages as well (see 19:23–41). Large cities like Corinth and Ephesus vied for top honors as major religious cities with extraordinary temples. Attendance at local feasts and festivals for the gods and goddesses at their temples was a requirement for the people. It was a huge transformation of the new believers in Corinth to repent and to totally reject their prominent Greek and Roman culture. It would have been very simple just to add Jesus to their plethora of deities and remain active participants in their society and culture, but Paul would have none of that. Christianity was (and still is) an exclusive faith in "the only true God, and Jesus Christ" (John 17:3).

Thus, the "new creation" is both individual and corporate. Both the believing Jews and Gentiles had to adopt a whole new way of thinking—about themselves, about each other, and about God. Sworn enemies had to become friends and brothers and sisters in Christ. A new community was born; old adversaries became allies. They had to worship together, commune together, and eat together (1 Cor 10:31–33; 11:17–34). They had to learn to care about one another, loving and supporting one another, while still guarding the purity of the congregation. When someone's thinking changes, then his or her actions, behavior, and attitudes change. It was critical that the congregation recognize that, no matter where they came from, as Christians they were all "baptized by one Spirit so as to form one body—whether Jews or Gentiles, slave or free—and we were all given the one Spirit to drink" (1 Cor 12:13).

Today, as in the time of Paul, the entire "new creation" is redeemed by the same Jesus and filled with the same Holy Spirit. Many Christians in our society were born and raised in Christian homes and take for granted their title and position as a "Christian." Some people have been Christians for so long, they have gone to the same church for eons, they have the same set of contented Christian friends, so they are quite comfortable and rooted deeply in their own comfy "American-Christian" lives. Being changed and molded and formed by God (like clay vessels) can be painful and is not on their agendas. We can check off the "salvation" box for security and then go on with life, knowing that we are "saved." Society says it is the acceptable thing to do, but Jesus never really reigns in the temple of our hearts. "Getting saved is easy; becoming a community is difficult—damnably difficult!"[41]

"So from now on," wrote the transformed Paul, "we regard no one from a worldly point of view" (2 Cor 5:16). This verse is key to our understanding

---

41. Peterson, *Christ Plays in Ten Thousand Places*, 250.

of the next verse about being a "new creation" in Christ. If we say that we are Christians, how do we look at the world around us? Do we see the world as the politicians see it? As the media sees it? Do we have the same hopes and fears and anxieties as the non-Christians who live next door? Do we hurt where Jesus would hurt? The true Christian knows that God has changed his or her mind for good; it is irreversible. A transformed mind results in a new and different mindset for a person: new points of view, new feelings, new compassion for others, new heartaches, and a new concern for the world around us. As a follower of Christ, are we so different from the world that other people even notice a difference? Again, Paul directs us: "Do not conform to the pattern of this world, but be transformed by the renewing of your mind" (Rom 12:2).

How are we "transformed"? How does God "renew" our minds? Transformation is a process, and not a single "saving" event. It is God working on our spirit every single minute of every single day to bring us into conformity with his will, not ours. Renewal begins with the individual person communicating with God through his word and prayer; it is augmented by communicating with others in the Christian community. Eugene Peterson writes,

> Spiritual theology is the attention that we give to living what we know and believe about God. It is the thoughtful and obedient cultivation of life as worship on our knees before God the Father, of life as sacrifice on our feet following God the Son, and life as love embracing and being embraced by the community of God the Spirit.[42]

In view of this individual transformation and newness of life, the next question posed is, What does it look like to be a community of believers today? How does this passage inform our understandings about the contemporary church, the Christian community in general, and Christian ministry in particular?

Ministry and the Contemporary Church

The "new creation," the people reconciled to each other and to God, *the church* is to be an agent of transformation within the world (2 Cor 5:17–21; also, 3:18). It was by the teaching and preaching of Paul that the Corinthians heard and responded to the gospel of Jesus Christ. Even today, ministry means delivering a *message of change* to those who receive it. It is the message that God, through Christ, changes people and makes them "new creatures."

42. Peterson, *Christ Plays in Ten Thousand Places*, 6.

In response, the job description of every believer (and therefore, the church) is to be a reconciler in the world. Divisive issues plague our society, and the church is not immune to these debates: racial tension, abortion, sexual and religious preferences, marriage, pornography, immigration, drugs, and poverty, just to name a few. Even within the cloister of the Christian church, there are thorny issues that divide us: ordination, gender issues, celebration of rituals, finances, worship and music styles, and many more. Politics can divide communities, neighborhoods, families, and friends; there is a real need for the church to step out of politics and reconcile human relationships in God.

An old legend illustrates the minutiae that can separate Christians in America: Two families had been the best of friends in a small church in a small community in the Midwest. For some unknown reason, a rift began that made enemies out of folks who had been so tight. Three generations passed, and the families never spoke in the church. They sat on opposite sides of the sanctuary for worship and in the fellowship hall during the church potluck dinners. Neither family helped or supported the other in planting, harvesting, or ranching. Finally, a young boy was determined to find the origin of the dispute. He interviewed people in both families (against his father's wishes), and no one could tell him the root of the issue. "Well, it's just always been like this," they told him. The boy finally went to the pastor and asked for help. The pastor reviewed church records and found the name of an elderly uncle who lived in an assisted living home in another city. He took the boy to the home for a visit, and they were successful in finding an answer. "Oh yeah," the old man recalled, "one Sunday at the potluck the folks in one family got larger slices of the ham than the folks in the other family." He chuckled a little and said, "Caused a big ol' fight that we could never resolve." The consequence of real transformation is real reconciliation. For Paul, the message of reconciliation and the command to be reconciled to God (5:20) and to each other (5:19) is not an option; it is not a suggestion. The ministry of reconciliation is the first and perhaps the most important appointment for the church.

Furthermore, the values of 6:3 are just as applicable today as they were in Paul's day. All Christians must evaluate their lives and determine if they are in any way setting up a stumbling block for others. Harris writes:

> Christian ministry is discredited when the Christian gives offense by un-Christian conduct. For the believer, who is called to embody as well as declare the good news, a lifestyle that is inconsistent with the message proclaimed undermines or at least jeopardizes the credibility of the gospel. Since the message and the messenger belong so closely together,

inappropriate behavior by the messenger reflects adversely on the message. Expressed positively, the upright life of the messenger demonstrates and enhances the power of the message. It is always true that the life of the Christian is the most eloquent advertisement for the gospel.[43]

Following in Paul's footsteps, there is no other position that leaders should assume except as servants of God (6:4) who are ambassadors of Christ (5:20). As Christian leaders, we are to be as bold and yet as humble as Paul. Beyond the incredible, gracious gift of salvation given to all believers, Christian leaders receive a true calling to servant ministry, something Paul experienced deeply (5:14). Leaders are called to love and guide and protect the redeemed, forming them into a godly community as a model for the whole world to see. Leaders are called to guard the word of God (2:17; 4:2), to witness to unbelievers about the gospel of Christ (4:3–6), and to help believers to "be all that they can be" as God's "new creation" (5:17). Hopefully, in the end, we will not "discredit" the ministry, but serve with "endurance" (6:4). Is it really any wonder that Paul asked, "Who is equal to such a task?" (2:16).

We can see Paul's genuine commitment to his calling. Paul indisputably was compelled (5:14) to serve, to become an active reconciler, especially in light of the cultural splits, arguments, and doubts in the Corinthian church. Yet, he did not pretend to overlook sin and injustice in the church (5:19); he also rebuked those who were preaching falsehoods (4:2). Who he was and what he did is an exemplary paradigm for Christian leaders today.

What person reveals in detail all their failures, weaknesses, and hardships on a job application? Yet, it was demonstrated by Paul that sacrifices and suffering are part of the job description of one who ministers in Jesus's name. How we deal with our own shortcomings, disappointments, and breakdowns molds a Christ-like character in a person. Failures and trials put emphasis on our total dependence upon God (3:4–6). Gordon Fee is very insightful as he adds, "That suffering and pain stem from evil is not to be doubted; that they are the direct result of our own evil—or lack of faith, as some would have it—is not only to be doubted but to be vigorously rejected as completely foreign to Paul."[44]

The complete irony of suffering as a part of God's commission was missed by the Corinthians concerning Paul, and it is still misunderstood today in relationship to Christian service. Success is not the absence of suffering; it is the growth through suffering. Fee continues,

43. Harris, Second Corinthians, 469.
44. Fee, Paul, the Spirit, and the People of God, 142.

How can one glory in the power of the resurrection and the life of the Spirit and not have that power applied to one's own physical weaknesses and suffering? [There are those who] never consider that God's greater glory rests on the manifestation of his grace and power through the weakness of the human vessel, precisely so that there will never be any confusion as to the source![45]

The Mission

By God's power, the church is hope and reconciliation to the world. The goal is to make known the transforming power of the Lord Jesus Christ *in and to* the community—that is, among believers *in* the community of Christ, and *to* the nonbelieving community outside the church. By the power of the Holy Spirit and "with sincere love" (6:6), the aim and mission of the church has not changed. It is to mend common brokenness, build bridges, and look beyond assumptions in the world to bring all humanity to a saving relationship with God through Christ. Christian leaders must have a driving dream—sometimes a big dream—to give hope where it can't be found and to bring reconciliation in impossible places.

> God always has a plan for every community if He finds a person to fulfill it. The living Christ has redemptive dreams for Peoria, Phoenix, Parkersburg, Philadelphia, Portland—and all points in between. He has revolutionary strategies waiting to be implemented at rural crossroads, in violent ghettos and in well-heeled suburbs. Take hope from Paul, the dreamer, who broke into ecstasies of praise when he recalled how God fulfilled dreams for him.[46]

On the one hand, "seeker-oriented" churches should be a redundancy—all churches should be seeker-oriented. The church was intended to be neither a social club, limiting its membership to the chosen few, nor to be a security blanket for the believers. These pitfalls miss the point of the church itself. All believers are emissaries of Christ into the entire community and reconcilers in a disgruntled world. A young man was being interviewed for a job as an usher in a movie theater. He was asked, "What would you do in case of a fire?" He answered, "Oh, don't worry about me, I will be all right." In the same way, if the traditional church places too much emphasis on individual salvation ("bringing people to Christ"), and this is its only goal, then those people can

---

45. Fee, *Paul, the Spirit, and the People of God*, 143.
46. London and Wiseman, *Heart of a Great Pastor*, 91.

just smile and say, "don't worry about me, I will be all right," and never give the rest of the world a second thought. The church can swiftly drift away from its initial call to be God's representatives on earth for the benefit of those who are yet to believe. Believers, Paul wrote, are to be caring reconcilers, ushering others into the kingdom, with urgency, before there is a fire.

On the other hand, reconciliation must also be done within the church, as Paul has so vividly demonstrated. It seems paradoxical to say that we must reconcile those who have been baptized into Christ's life, death, and resurrection, which should lead all believers into a new life. The rebirth of believers is visible in their moral and ethical lives. Yet it happens; believers can disagree on major and minor issues. Sometimes legalism rules, and forgiveness is difficult. We can easily fall into the cultural norms of the world around us. Sometimes people want to be a Christian, but they do not want to change. People tend to protect their own worldly points of view, and their own self-interests, especially concerning money, social issues, and relationships. People do not like to be confronted by a minister who sees that change is necessary. This is precisely what Paul is addressing in 2 Corinthians. Leaders must speak freely (6:11) against impurities, concealed sins, dishonor, imposters, prejudice, backstabbing, gossip, and similar transgressions that can tear people's lives and communities apart. The health and the function of the church was more important to Paul than his own reputation in the eyes of those "troublemakers" who opposed him.

Earlier Paul had suggested that a sinner be put out of the church (1 Cor 5:1–2). Yet in 2 Corinthians 2:5–11, Paul insisted on forgiveness by the entire church for an injury done to him. A closer look reveals no inconsistencies; these are two very different cases, and each case is treated differently. That is, in 1 Corinthians, the sin is injurious to the whole church and to the view of the church from the other parts of society. In 2 Corinthians, the sin appears to be slander by one man against another man, Paul. In the best interest of the entire congregation, forgiveness was the best medicine. That is still true of what we need to do in the church today. Each case, each person is distinctive; we cannot treat every case of sin with a "cookie cutter" reaction.

So, what are the stumbling blocks to faith that exist today in your church? What sins have been committed that we are not supposed to count against them (5:19)? Is there legalism, too much tolerance, or too little tolerance? Many hurting people feel rejected and ostracized by what they think of as "the church": the one who has had an abortion, the one who fights alcoholism every day because of grief or failure, the one who cheated on his or her spouse, the one who resorts to pornography to ease his mind, the one facing suicide because things just keep getting worse. Certainly, transformed Christians are creatures who strive for upright behavior, and the church cannot ignore blatant sin and injustice; this discredits the ministry of God. Moreover, as servants of God, Christian leaders should live lives like Paul in his desire to be "commendable" in everything. Christian leaders are not perfect (Paul confessed he was not), as no one is without sin in this life. We should all be honest about our struggles, but it is important that leaders model the desire and the striving for holiness (7:1).

Reconciliation and Church Leadership

In 1963, the Rev. Martin Luther King Jr. wrote a letter from jail to his fellow clergymen in Alabama during a time of racial tension in America. He was attempting to explain his movements and his motives, not unlike what Paul the apostle did in his day. This is only a brief portion of his long and famous letter. It sheds light on the early Christian church, as well as weaknesses of the Christian leadership in his day, which found it difficult to resolve issues and bring together believers into one body of Christ. Dr. King's words can illuminate the failings of some churches today:

> In deep disappointment I have wept over the laxity of the church. But be assured that my tears have been tears of love. There can be no deep disappointment where there is not deep love. Yes, I love the church. How could I do otherwise? I am in the rather unique position of being the son, the grandson and the great grandson of preachers. Yes, I see the church as the body of Christ. But, oh! How we have blemished and scarred that body through social neglect and through fear of being nonconformists.
>
> There was a time when the church was very powerful—in the time when the early Christians rejoiced at being deemed worthy to suffer for what they believed. In those days the church was not merely a thermometer that recorded the ideas and principles of popular opinion; it was a thermostat that transformed the mores of society. Whenever the early Christians entered a town, the people in power became disturbed and immediately sought to convict the Christians for being "disturbers of the peace" and "outside agitators." But the Christians pressed on, in the conviction that they were "a colony of heaven," called to obey God rather than man. Small in number, they were big in commitment. They were too God-intoxicated to be "astronomically intimidated." By their effort and example they brought an end to such ancient evils as infanticide and gladiatorial contests. Things are different now. So often the contemporary church is a weak, ineffectual voice with an uncertain sound. So often it is an archdefender of the status quo. Far from being disturbed by the

presence of the church, the power structure of the average community is consoled by the church's silent—and often even vocal—sanction of things as they are.

But the judgment of God is upon the church as never before. If today's church does not recapture the sacrificial spirit of the early church, it will lose its authenticity, forfeit the loyalty of millions, and be dismissed as an irrelevant social club with no meaning for the twentieth century. Every day I meet young people whose disappointment with the church has turned into outright disgust.[47]

Humbly, Dr. King sought reconciliation within the place where it should all begin—in the church. That is, reconciliation in our world begins and ends with Jesus: Jesus became sin for us, and we are only righteous because he is righteous (5:21). True reconciliation among people cannot take place unless they are first truly reconciled to God (5:20), and then they allow God to "transform" them into "his righteousness." Resuscitated "into" the life of Christ, transformed into "a new creation," believers must continually and intentionally allow the Holy Spirit to control their lives, allowing love, forgiveness, and self-sacrifice to resolve issues. Moreover, we must be accountable to a community of believers, through whom the Holy Spirit can encourage and convict us:

> Since the ultimate goal of salvation is for us individually to belong as a growing, contributing, edifying member of the people of God, others in the body exist for the same purpose, and thus should serve you in the same way. Don't try to be a lone ranger Christian, slugging it out on your own. Seek out those in the community to whom you can be accountable and let them join you in your desire to grow into Christ's likeness.[48]

---

47. Rev. Martin Luther King Jr., "Letter from Birmingham Jail" (16 April 1963). See https://web.cn.edu/kwheeler/documents/Letter_Birmingham_Jail.pdf.

48. Fee, *Paul, the Spirit, and the People of God*, 138.

CHAPTER 8

2 Corinthians 6:11–7:1

 ## LISTEN to the Story

[11]We have spoken freely to you, Corinthians, and opened wide our hearts to you. [12]We are not withholding our affection from you, but you are withholding yours from us. [13]As a fair exchange—I speak as to my children—open wide your hearts also.

[14]Do not be yoked together with unbelievers. For what do righteousness and wickedness have in common? Or what fellowship can light have with darkness? [15]What harmony is there between Christ and Belial? Or what does a believer have in common with an unbeliever? [16]What agreement is there between the temple of God and idols? For we are the temple of the living God. As God has said:

> "I will live with them
> and walk among them,
> and I will be their God,
> and they will be my people."

[17]Therefore,

> "Come out from them
> and be separate,
> says the Lord.
> Touch no unclean thing,
> and I will receive you."

[18]And,

> "I will be a Father to you,
> and you will be my sons and daughters,
> says the Lord Almighty."

> ^{7:1}Therefore, since we have these promises, dear friends, let us purify ourselves from everything that contaminates body and spirit, perfecting holiness out of reverence for God.

Listening to the Text in the Story: Leviticus 19:19; 26:11–13; Deuteronomy 22:11; 32:6; 2 Samuel 7:8, 14; Psalm 27:4–5; Isaiah 43:6; 52:11–12; Jeremiah 31:9; Ezekiel 20:34, 41; 37:27; Amos 3:13.

I will surely gather them from all the lands where I banish them in my furious anger and great wrath; I will bring them back to this place and let them live in safety. They will be my people, and I will be their God. I will give them singleness of heart and action, so that they will always fear me and that all will then go well for them and for their children after them.
—*Jeremiah 32:37–39*

Unrequited love is the heartache theme not only of some sappy, romantic movies but also of many country songs. Someone is very much in love with another person, but that love is not returned. Shakespeare used this theme magnificently in his dramas; in fact, much of human literature throughout the ages reveals a similar plot. We hope it will have a happy ending, where love reigns and "all's well that ends well."

Likewise, Paul came face-to-face with unrequited affection from his people as he attempted to minister to the church in Corinth (2 Cor 6:12). In this letter, he has been defending his apostolic calling and his ministry to the believers in Corinth. In 5:11–6:10, he implored the Corinthian believers to "be reconciled to God" (5:20) and to each other. God first reached out to them and sent his Son to initiate that reconciliation. In response to the self-sacrifice of Christ, Paul proclaimed a compelling message of reconciliation to all the churches (5:11–19). Believers are thus transformed into new creations as they are reconciled to God and *then to each other* in the community (5:20–6:1). Paul then supported his divine ministry calling with, ironically, a record of his own trials and hardships (recall 1:8–10 and 4:8–12). These happened to Paul and his associates because they had spoken the word of God to the Gentiles "for their benefit" (6:4–10; 4:15). The missionaries' "endurance" through trials (6:4) was strong evidence not only of their commitment to God's calling, but it was also evidence of the faithfulness of God through suffering (see 4:7–15). Now in this section, Paul became the caring pastor, focusing on the hope that his relationship with the Corinthians could be restored and that the church could be reconciled to him.

The content and the function of 6:11–7:3 have been argued among schol-ars for decades. There is little agreement as to the origin and role of this section of Paul's letter. Some doubt that this section was, indeed, written by Paul; it may have been inserted by Paul or by someone else. We can see that Paul's primary request of the church was that they would return his affection for them; this plea begins in 6:11–13. Then, Paul takes up the very same request again in 7:2–3. The section in between, 6:14–7:1, seems quite out of place and detached from the two "affection" requests. Moreover, Paul shifts his tone from warm and affectionate in 6:11–13 to a very corrective, instructional, "preachy" tone. Then, he returned to the positive and friendly tone again in 7:2–3. Even if these middle verses are instructional, we hear the voice of a concerned "shepherd" who desired a good relationship with his readers. To exhort his readers, he donned the hat of a loving pastor, even calling his readers "my children" (6:13) and "dear friends" (7:1).

Twice, Paul appealed to the church to show affection to him and to his associates, as they were devoted to the church and were innocent of any accusations (6:11–13 and 7:2–3). His point was that the community was not deprived of Paul's affections (6:12) and he was very much the concerned spiritual father. Perhaps he "brackets this climactic warning with professions of this love for them to make the harsh medicine easier to swallow."[1] In addi-tion, Paul was very much aware of the false teachers, his opponents, who were denigrating Paul and misguiding the church. They may have been accusing Paul of being insensitive and unfeeling because he did not come visit them as scheduled (1:15–17). It is possible that they defied his ethical instructions with smooth, convincing speech. As a result, Paul's motives were misunder-stood as a lack of concern for the people, and his authority was weakened. So, Paul had to answer these thoughts and feelings by emphasizing his love for them.

Positioned between the two appeals for reciprocal affection, there are six verses that appear to be perplexing, if not completely out of place (6:14–7:1). This section could be called a "summons to holiness," because Paul was con-tinuing to address a lack of understanding on the part of the congregation. That is, Paul had more to say about idolatry in 1 Corinthians than in any other letter (see chapters 8–10).[2] So, his warnings applied directly to their behavior as Christian believers, but it seems that they still did not "get it." Mainly, they were still having close connections with those inside a society permeated with idolatry. Garland writes that idolatry may have been the "root

1. Garland, *2 Corinthians*, 323.
2. Furnish, *II Corinthians*, 363.

of the dissension" in the church, as well as the focus of Paul's previous "tearful letter" written to them (2 Cor 2:4).

Paul began with perhaps one of the most recognizable verses in 2 Corinthians: "Do not be yoked together with unbelievers" (6:14); he then followed that command with warnings from Old Testament citations. Finally, as a summary to his argument, Paul instructed his people to be "pure," and to "perfect holiness," commands that are not favorites of Christians today (7:1)! "Like stubborn teenagers who may challenge the limits placed on them by their parents, the Corinthians refuted Paul's prohibitions."[3]

However, Paul's mood and tone changed back to the positive in 7:2–3 when he again made a plea for their affections. The consummate loving pastor, Paul shifted his manner to commend them for their "godly sorrow" and "repentance" in the remainder of the seventh chapter. If the church accepted his admonitions and altered their errant behavior, it would have helped to repair any damage done to their relationships with God and with Paul.

EXPLAIN the Story

Mutual Affection (6:11–13)

At the conclusion of his catalogue of trials (6:4–10), Paul insisted that he and his colleagues were always honest and open with their words to the Corinthians (6:11). This reminds us that because of his hope in the new-covenant ministry (3:12), Paul and his associates spoke boldly to the readers. That is, to "speak freely" (6:11) is also to "speak boldly" (2:17; 3:12), with frankness and without deceit. Paul was completely candid with them, even addressing them directly as "Corinthians" (6:11). He freely revealed his deep emotions, sincere thoughts, and intentions. His heart was wide open with affection for them, but their hearts were closed and restricted toward him (6:12).

Paul stated that whatever thoughts or feelings closed their hearts to him lingered on as an issue on their part. That is, due to their own feelings, they came to mistrust in Paul and his associates. "Earlier in the letter he had sought to assure them his actions had been wrongly interpreted; now he counters that if there has been any lack of concern and understand it has been on their part, not his."[4] Suspicions, misunderstandings, and distrust were making the Corinthians hold back their affections for Paul and his colleagues; it was ruining their relationship. This is not unlike the close relationships within a family,

---

3. Garland, *2 Corinthians*, 323–25.
4. Garland, *2 Corinthians*, 368. See also Harris, *Second Corinthians*, 490.

where withholding sincere affection from a family member (or members) can be a means by which one person exercises control over other people.[5]

Paul's initial request appears in 6:12–13, that they would "open wide [their] hearts also" to the one who founded their church and continued to be devoted to them. If the external sufferings listed by Paul in 6:4–10 were painful, how much more painful was it to be emotionally rejected by the very people for whom he had sacrificed? He had invested a great deal of time and effort for their spiritual welfare (11:28), but his work resulted in their rejection and closed hearts. A fair exchange, of course, would be for the church to return Paul's honesty, openness, and harmony, not their doubt, suspicion, and accusations. When Paul spoke to them "as to my children" in 6:13, he was implying affection, patience, and concern "for their benefit." It was not unusual to address his people as his "children," as Paul thought of himself as a "spiritual father" to his churches, especially in Corinth (see 1 Cor 3:1–2; 4:14–15; 2 Cor 11:2; 12:14b–15a). Perhaps at times the Corinthians were immature in their faith and needed some corrections, but Paul's emphasis here is on reciprocal love and affection.[6]

Like a matching bookend, the second plea to accept and love Paul and his fellow workers (6:1) is reiterated in 7:2–3, where Paul emphasized that he and his colleagues have "wronged no one, we have corrupted no one, [and] we have exploited no one." Again, these may have been implied or direct accusations by his opponents that were proven false by Paul. These verses, while matching previous appeal for affection, also direct the reader forward to the remainder of chapter 7. In addition, they are a preparation for Paul's request for the completion of the financial collection for the believers in Jerusalem, which is the primary topic of chapters 8 and 9. Harris created a visual comparison between the appeals in 6:11–13 and those of 7:2–4, clearly showing their similarities:[7]

6:11–13	7:2–4
We are speaking frankly to you (6:11a)	I am perfectly frank with you (7:4a)
Our heart is wide open to you. There is no restriction in our affection for you (6:11b–12a)	Your place in our hearts is secure (7:3b)
Open wide your hearts also (6:13b)	Make room for us in your hearts (7:2a)

---

5. Barton et al., *1 and 2 Corinthians*, 364.
6. Furnish, *II Corinthians*, 361.
7. Harris, *Second Corinthians*, 515.

In fact, Paul had so much affection for the readers that he was casting no blame. He did not write to the church to bring a charge against them, or "slap their wrists," but instead to pledge great love for them. In fact, Paul humbly pledged that he would "live or die with you" (7:3). With great optimism, Paul hoped that the congregation would see through his opponents, and he received so much "joy" in the hope that they would, indeed, return all of Paul's affection. The language of this section "is that of the optimist who finds an opportunity in every difficulty, rather than a difficulty in every opportunity."[8]

Summons to Holiness (6:14–7:1)

Moreover, there is another plea from Paul to his readers—this time for holiness (6:14–7:1). Again, for many New Testament scholars, this cryptic section represents a strange digression and has little to do with Paul's appeals for healing his relationship with his readers (6:11–13; 7:2–4). Some have suggested that this passage was added later by an editor, or, if Paul did write this section, it could be a fragment taken from another letter and inserted here. The vocabulary and the Greek style are unusual, indicating that perhaps it was not really written by Paul. One suggestion is that Paul was quoting an "early Christian sermon," which in turn had cited numerous Jewish scriptural passages.[9] Furnish points out similarities between this passage and the "forms, themes, concerns and imagery" that were conveyed in the earlier writings found at Qumran. That is, these verses (6:14–7:1) suggest a "separation of what is clean and unclean [that] also pervades the literature" of the Dead Sea Scrolls. We also find in these ancient scrolls the directive for God's people to pursue "righteousness" in the community, to reject "defilement" of "flesh and spirit," and to perfect their "holiness" in an endeavor to secure their "salvation."[10] Furnish arrives at the conclusion that this passage is of "non-Pauline composition, but was incorporated by the apostle as he wrote this letter."[11]

Yet, such a perceived "digression" is hardly unusual in Paul's communications. If we look at 1 Corinthians, we see that Paul began to answer their questions concerning food and idols (1 Cor 8), then he digresses into a discussion about his "rights" as an apostle (1 Cor 9). The two chapters are, of course, related, because in chapter 9 Paul was using himself as an example of putting aside one's own rights for the betterment of someone else. This is exactly what the Corinthians needed to do with respect to their own social status and position, which was in jeopardy if they did not participate in the

---

8. Belleville, *2 Corinthians*, 190.
9. Barton et al., *1 and 2 Corinthians*, 365.
10. Furnish, *II Corinthians*, 377.
11. Furnish, *II Corinthians*, 383.

local feasts for idols.[12] Thus, 2 Corinthians 6:14–7:1 is literarily connected; it could very well have been purposefully placed here in the letter to further his argument and to apply it as an admonition for his readers. It was Paul's ardent desire that the congregation be "reconciled to God" (5:20), "come out . . . and be separate" (6:17), and seek purity and holiness (7:1) so that his readers would not "receive God's grace in vain" (6:1).

The opening verses on "unbelievers" being "yoked" together with "believers" (6:14–16a) are not unfamiliar to Christians today, but they have often been misunderstood. We tend to say that this passage speaks to being "unequally yoked" by individuals in human relationships like marriage, dating, or business partnerships. But it is more than that, and this is not Paul's point; such interpretations do not fit the context of chapter 6 and add to their puzzling position within the text. These verses are primarily a corrective for the entire church: notice his use of plural words in the passage: the collective term "fellowship" (v. 14), and "we" and "them" and "people" (v. 16). This first warning (v. 14) is supported by the following rhetorical questions (vv. 14–16) that should not be separated literally from the opening verse. Paul was encouraging the believers in Corinth to "sever all ties with any form of idolatry and thus become 'wide-hearted' (6:13) in their affection for him."[13] That is, to be fully reconciled with God (5:20) is to be fully reconciled with Paul (6:13), and to completely abandon all compromising associations with the pagan world so familiar to Corinthians.

These verses form a complex structure that shows strong contrasts or antitheses between Christian believers who are recipients of God's saving grace (6:1) and who are therefore "reconciled" to God (5:20), and those people who do not believe in Christ as the Messiah (and remain "unreconciled" to God):

6:14 *a*—An imperative phrase, or strong advice given.

6:14 *b*—Two rhetorical questions warning the readers about the ethical differences between believers and unbelievers.

6:15—Two rhetorical questions cautioning the readers about the religious differences between believers and unbelievers.

16 *a, b*—A question and a statement informing the readers of the stark contrast between the "temple of God" (that is, believers) and idols (worshiped by unbelievers).

6:16 *c*—An affirmation and a scriptural citation that opens with an introduction formula, "*As God has said* . . ."

---

12. deSilva, "Corinthian Correspondence," 568.
13. Harris, *Second Corinthians*, 492.

6:17a—A second scriptural citation that closes with an introductory formula, *"says the Lord."*

6:17b-18—A third scriptural citation that also closes with an introductory formula, *"says the Lord Almighty."*

7:1—Closing advice to believers, encouraging purity and holiness; or "the opening admonition [6:14a] reformulated."[14]

Each of the five rhetorical questions obviously assumes a strong negative answer ("No! Absolutely not!"). There is an unusual "chain" or "collage" of OT quotations, where at least three citations from the Law and the Prophets are interpreted and intertwined. There are also three citation "formulae" ("As God said . . .") placed strategically at the beginning (v. 16), in the middle (v. 17), and at the end (v. 18) of the citation section.[15] Paul quoted the OT here to rouse the Corinthians and to support his claim that there are significant differences between those who are "reconciled to God" and those who are not. In effect, Paul was prohibiting "any relationship with non-Christians which would seriously involve a believer with idolatry and moral defilement."[16] Paul was also placing his own authority within the very words of God. With these intentions in mind, we can divide the passage into three narrower passages: 6:14–16a, 6:16b–18 and 7:1. This allows us to see both the full context and the smaller details of these prohibitions and affirmations more clearly.

Being "Unequally Yoked"

The move from 6:13 to 6:14 is sudden (as is the shift from 7:1 to 7:2). Paul quickly moved from the cool affections of his congregation to his own warnings about the allure of paganism. Their associations with idolatry appear to be very serious. Paul was addressing a "persistent problem of idolatrous relationships that accounted for their embarrassed reserve toward him (6:12–13)."[17] Thus, Paul opened with an imperative command: "Do not be yoked together with unbelievers" (not unlike the imperative in 5:20b). From 5:20 to 7:2, there are six imperative commands given by Paul to his readers (5:20; 6:1; 6:13; 6:14; 6:17; 7:2).[18] These admonitions do not appear to be against Paul's opponents in the church, who were, arguably, Christian believers. Instead, Paul's primary warnings in this section were against the unrighteous unbelievers who did not follow Christ, such as those in the Roman culture who were

---

14. Furnish, *II Corinthians*, 371–75; Barton et al., *1 and 2 Corinthians*, 367–72.

15. Harris, *Second Corinthians*, 492–93.

16. Furnish, *II Corinthians*, 372.

17. Harris, *Second Corinthians*, 497.

18. Garland, *2 Corinthians*, 322.

self-righteous and self-important. This group practiced corruption, immoral behavior, and idolatry, which were so rampant in their society.

In general, Paul was concerned about the unequal partnerships believers form with secular society. This included, but was not limited to, marriage, legal conflicts, pagan cultic meals and rituals, immoral sexual behavior, and the worship of idols. He had addressed these "unequal partnerships" in 1 Corinthians, where the Christian believers "allowed their legal disputes with one another to be arbitrated by the secular courts (6:1–6); they approved of sexual unions with prostitutes (6:12–20), and they participated in cultic meals (10:6–22)."[19] They even ignored a sexual union of a professed believer and his stepmother (1 Cor 5:1–13). Specifically, Paul instructed the Corinthian believers not to participate in pagan feasts and festivals that celebrated pagan gods and goddesses (1 Cor 10:6–32). This section in 2 Corinthians, then, is a reinforcement of the gravity of integrating the pagan culture into their lives. It is also quite possible that the "tearful letter" mentioned in 2:4–5 was an ill-received admonition to believers from Paul to soundly reject their integration with the pagan culture. Paul exhorted his readers to heed his warnings and determine proper limits in their beliefs and behaviors while they were living in such a non-Christian environment.[20] But, as a result of some serious denigration and grumbling, some people in the congregation likely defied the directives given by Paul.

The verb "to be unequally yoked" or to be "mismated" (6:14) has an Old Testament agricultural background, but it occurs only here in the New Testament. Grammatically, this verb implies that Paul was *insisting* that they stop actions already in progress.[21] "The Greek for 'yoked together' was used in the first century for the act of harnessing drafting animals together."[22] For example, God's law (Lev 19:19) says, "Do not mate different kinds of animals. Do not plant your field with two kinds of seeds." This implies an unfortunate mixture of things that do not belong together. If a farmer yoked together two different kinds of animals, one could be stronger or heavier than the other, and the plow would be pulled through the soil unevenly. The ox and donkey cannot be yoked together in front of the plow, as by nature they will battle and struggle and not get the plowing accomplished (see Deut 22:10).

In the ancient Israelite social society, there were numerous prohibitions imposed by God to keep things separate so as to maintain purity and practicality. God knew it would be difficult for his people to "come out" and remain

19. Belleville, *2 Corinthians*, 179.
20. Garland, *2 Corinthians*, 323.
21. Belleville, *2 Corinthians*, 176.
22. Barton et al., *1 and 2 Corinthians*, 366. See BDAG 399.

"separate" (6:17) from the various pagan practices around them. There are other examples in Deuteronomy 22 that are relevant, if not a little odd to modern ears. One example is "do not wear clothes of wool and linen woven together" (Deut 22:11). Any clothing designer or manufacturer will testify that some fabrics blend well together, but some distinctively different kinds of fabrics cannot. They wash and wear differently; woven together, they will pull and furrow and fight each other instead of lying smoothly. Likewise, by their very nature, unbelievers will create dissonance and discord within a community; they can wrinkle and tear a congregation. True believers bring repairs and promote harmony and agreement (2 Cor 6:15). Paul emphasized the "absurdity of Christians continuing to associate with idols and idol worship" associated with the Corinthian culture.[23] His reference to this Levitical law may be a reference to Christians being unevenly joined to the Roman society in general, and not limited to marriage or business partners, as some modern readers have interpreted the phrase.

Rhetorical Questions

The literary device known as a rhetorical question was used to "drive home a point" with the readers; this was a common literary or scholarly technique employed by both Greek philosophers and by Jewish writers.[24] Because each question had an assumed negative answer, Paul was indicating that it is obvious that true Christianity does not mix well with idolatrous ideas and practices. The first two rhetorical questions in 6:14 emphasized the *ethical differences* between Christian believers and the unbelievers. He used two clear, parallel contrasts, "righteousness and wickedness" and "light and darkness," which distinguished between the ethics of believers and unbelievers. "Righteousness and wickedness" (or "lawlessness"), for example, is a sharp contrast in the ethical behavior between changed believers and people who were "slaves to impurity" (see Rom 6:19). We also see another reference to the "light and darkness" imagery as we see in 2 Corinthians 4:3–6; those in darkness are "blinded" and "perishing," while believers have "the light of the gospel of the glory of Christ." Previously, the Corinthian believers had been instructed to cease their relationships with those people who were guilty of immorality, greed, idolatry, slander, a drunkard or a swindler (1 Cor 5:11). In fact, the Corinthians were told not even to eat with such pagans (1 Cor 5:11; 10:19–21). The "light and darkness" imagery was one of Paul's favorites, as we see in a number of his letters (Rom 2:19; 13:12; 1 Cor 4:5; 1 Thess 5:4–5).

23. Barton et al., *1 and 2 Corinthians*, 369n. 178.
24. Furnish, *II Corinthians*, 372.

The next pair of rhetorical questions (2 Cor 6:15) highlight the *religious differences*. The first question pointed out an obvious disparity between "Christ and Belial." The second question revealed the impossibility of things that can never be partnered together religiously, such as the worship of Christ and the worship of Satan. The name "Belial" (in Greek, *Beliar*) is a derivation of the Hebrew word that means "worthless, evil, perversion." In noncanonical literature, "Belial" is associated with the forces of darkness, whereas God is associated with the forces of light. The name "Belial" is not used anywhere else in the New Testament, but in other early literature it is another name for Satan (e.g., Testament of Reuben 2:2; 4:7, 11; 6:3). Paul usually used the name "Satan," as we see in 2 Corinthians 2:11 (where he is pictured as a "schemer"), as well as in 11:14.[25] It is worth noting that in 6:15b, Paul was not commanding a complete severance by believers from all unbelievers. Were that to happen, no unbelievers would ever have been exposed to the gospel message proclaimed by Paul. In this verse Paul was pointing out the radical religious differences in worship, activities, conduct, and inspiration of those people who followed Christ and those people who engaged in wicked (or idolatrous) religious rituals.[26]

The third set of contrasting questions reveal a distinction between the believers who comprise the "temple of God" from those people who worship empty, lifeless "idols" (6:16a). The whole community of believers, who are the temple of God (1 Cor 3:16; Eph 2:21), must reject loyalty to any other gods, goddesses, or temples. In the Corinthian culture, social meals and city festivals took place in and around the temples of idols. Yet, in the OT, the Israelite temple was the residence of the one true God, where he was present with his people. In Psalm 27:4–5, the "beauty" (or benevolence) of the Lord is seen in his temple; God keeps his people "safe in his dwelling," and hides his people "in the shelter of his sacred tent." Furthermore, God promised not only to dwell with his people in the temple, but also to "walk" with them, and "enabled you to walk with heads held high" (Lev 26:11–13). The temple was the stronghold of the Lord, where his goodness and his favor blessed his people. In Ezekiel, God promised to "put my sanctuary among them forever. My dwelling place will be with them; I will be their God, and they will be my people. Then the nations will know that I the LORD make Israel holy, when my sanctuary is among them forever" (Ezek 37:26b–28).

After Christ, the church became the holy "dwelling place" of God, and it should have nothing to do with false gods, idols, or persons of wickedness,

---

25. Furnish, *II Corinthians*, 362. See BDAG 173.
26. Harris, *Second Corinthians*, 503.

dishonesty, and self-interest. How remarkable, to consider the church as the chosen "dwelling place" of the Almighty God; what an honor! Thus, there was no room for a mixture of fidelity; in contrast to the pagan worshipers, the church must remain bound to the one "living and true God" and to his Son, "whom he raised from the dead—Jesus" (1 Thess 1:9–10).

Warnings for the Church from the Old Testament
To expand his use of OT imagery, Paul used a collection of OT passages to stress his words of warnings in 6:16b–18:

> 6:16b—Lev 26:11–12; Jer 32:38; Ezek 37:27
> 6:17—Isa 52:11; Ezek 20:34, 41
> 6:18—2 Sam 7:14; Isa 43:6; 63:16

Paul reminded his Gentile readers that, unlike their neighbors' idols, Christian believers serve a living God (2 Cor 6:16; see Acts 14:15). There is an "essential incompatibility" between the worship of the living God and the worship practices (i.e., prostitution) of "lifeless images."[27] The church, like the nation of Israel, was to "come out from them" (those idolaters and troublemaking unbelievers): "As you come to him, the living Stone—rejected by humans but chosen by God and precious to him—you also, like living stones, are being built into a spiritual house to be a holy priesthood, offering spiritual sacrifices acceptable to God through Jesus Christ" (1 Pet 2:4–5).

The church is summoned to avoid syncretism in their beliefs. In the Greco-Roman world, most people adopted a polytheistic belief system, with the worship of many idols, numerous rituals, temples, ceremonies, feasts, and festivals (2 Cor 6:16). Sacrifices to various gods and goddesses were an important part of their social and religious lives; it was necessary to appease and please the gods and goddesses who controlled their very existence (see Paul's comments in 1 Cor 6:12–17).

"Petitions" were placed (we would call them "prayers") with the appropriate god or goddess; money was given and sacrifices were made. However, the worshiper was never positive if the god or goddess was pleased and the petitions would be granted. In contrast, Christ was not just another god to be placed in the pantheon, another god to be added to the list to be sure a worshiper got what he or she wanted. Christianity negated all other "idol" beliefs and raised the person above the capricious whims of false gods. There is no compromise between the idolatry that they knew and the gospel of Christ Jesus.

---

27. Harris, *Second Corinthians*, 504.

Furnish writes that "the call to turn from idols to serve God was a fundamental part of Paul's missionary preaching (see 1 Thess 1:9; 1 Cor 5:10, 11; 6:9–10; Gal 5:19–21)."[28]

Moreover, Paul instructed his readers to stop touching any unclean thing (2 Cor 6:17; see Isa 52:11). This directive, with the command to be separate, looks forward to 7:1, where believers are commanded to seek purity and holiness. In 6:16c, 17, and 18, Paul employed a recognizable OT formula ("As God has said," . . . "says the LORD") that places these citations squarely within the words of God himself. The formula in 16c and 17a reiterates the words of Isaiah 52:11, where the "unclean thing" probably refers to ritual worship objects from the pagan temples:

> Depart, depart, go out from there!
>   Touch no unclean thing!
> Come out from it and be pure,
>   you who carry the articles of the LORD's house.

The words spoken by the "Lord Almighty" is the third citation formula (2 Cor 6:18), which reflects the title used of God in 2 Samuel 7:8 and Amos 3:13. In the Amos passage, it is the "LORD God Almighty" who is specifically testifying against the sins of Israel and the "altars of Bethel." Here, in 2 Corinthians 6:18, on the positive side, the all-powerful God promised that his own presence would be with his people no matter what. This verse is an allusion to Ezekiel 20:34–36, where God promises both his authority and his judgment on his people. Furthermore, God promises that he would be their "Father" and they would be a family (see Deut 32:6; Jer 31:9). This promise is an adaptation of a divine promise given to David concerning his son, Solomon, in 2 Samuel 7:14. It was modified by Paul, who not only made "sons" plural, but he included "daughters" in the promise as well (see Isa 43:6)![29] Therefore, the Corinthians were to forget their past belief systems, worship practices, all the other temples and gods, customs and fears, and worship only the Father and the Son. They were to totally separate themselves (6:17) from the surrounding pagan culture, be filled with God's Spirit, and be one family in Christ.

In summation, Paul was saying that Christ-followers should be *really* different from their culture: they are "transformed," they are "a new creation," they are "reconciled to God," "separate," "sons and daughters of the living God,"

---

28. Furnish, *II Corinthians*, 363.
29. Furnish, *II Corinthians*, 364.

and the "living stones" of God's metaphorical temple, which is the church. Today, as then, if the church presents itself as identical to the world around it, something is wrong with the church.

Purity

At this point in his discussion, Paul addressed the readers as "dear friends," (7:1, literally, as "beloved"), because he had already pledged his affection for them (6:12), and he will do so again in the following verses (7:2–4). Because he cared so much for the Corinthians, Paul brought to conclusion his case for their separation from the world around them. For those believers who are in Christ, and are in the family of God, it is imperative that they seek to be both purified and perfected by God (7:1). Paul reminded his readers that, while 6:14–18 include warnings, they also feature divine promises (7:1); in fact, there are seven promises in these verses. Thus, in contrast to the culture around them, believers must live out the kind of righteousness and purity given to them by God, and, thankfully, God has promised to be with them in the process (5:21; 6:16c; 7:1).

Verse 7:1 is an extension of the idea from 6:17 that there are things and people in this world that prove to be distractions from the religious commitment believers make to God. In this verse Paul used the unusual phrase "from every defilement," which occurs only here in the New Testament. Specifically, this phrase brought attention to the "pollution of pagan idolatries and impurities."[30] The reality is that any human society has a plethora of things that contaminate body and soul. It is interesting that Paul included himself in the necessity of "purifying *ourselves*." While this directive included unrighteous lifestyles, unholy alliances, and idolatrous associations, Paul's word choice indicated that it is a constant and unyielding battle against temptation and participation, so the Christian should avoid *anything* and *everything* that might be a detriment to a believer. As Paul wrote to another church, "It is God's will that you should be sanctified: that you should avoid sexual immorality . . . for God did not call us to be impure, but to live a holy life" (1 Thess 4:3–8).

Verse 7:1 raises some interesting questions: What are "purification" and "perfection," and who is doing the work? Does God perfect his people, or does the believer accomplish these things "out of reverence to God"? After he borrowed the words of God (the OT quotations) to support his argument, Paul charged his readers to "purify ourselves" from idolatry, which matches his instructions in 1 Corinthians 10:7, 14, 28–29. So this idea was not new territory for the Corinthian believers. They had already been told to steer clear

---

30. Furnish, *II Corinthians*, 365. See Harris, *Second Corinthians*, 512.

of participating in such pagan activities. By avoiding such common events and practices, the readers could begin to cleanse—or to purify—the evil out of their lives.

Moreover, in Greek the idea of "perfecting holiness" is literally "becoming mature or complete." This suggests to us that Paul was not asking believers to work harder toward a sinless life, but toward a maturation of faith. To be "perfect" is to be "exactly right for the intended use." For example, one would not use a feather to pound a nail into a piece of wood, but a hammer is "perfect" for the job. As our faith matures, we are being "perfected," and are far more usable by God. A righteous *position* may be granted by God to the saved believer, but righteous *practice* is appropriately carried out by the believer. Being an imperfect, struggling person in this life (even if you are an apostle) is not an excuse for *failing to* pursue the righteousness and holiness we can find along our spiritual journey. God has given believers all the resources they need—his word and his Spirit—to empower people to move toward Christlikeness (Rom 8:2).

But people can be proud and stubborn. It is often challenging to convince believers to cooperate with and depend upon the Holy Spirit (and not "grieve" him) as he guides and empowers believers toward the goal of purity, righteousness, and holiness. Apparently, the stronger personalities in the church at Corinth were injuring the weaker ones, and some people (siding with Paul's opponents?) had a problem with Paul's ban of idolatry and related social activities and practices. His warnings from previous letters must have festered for a period of time, and some rejected his authority as well.[31] As we will see in chapter 12, Paul had his doubts about some of those in the church who did not want to repent and seek holiness, but continued to practice "impurities" (2 Cor 12:20–21). "Like stubborn teenagers who may challenge the limits place on them by their parents, the Corinthians refuted Paul's prohibitions in 1 Cor 8–10."[32]

Yet, Paul knew that it was crucial that the community unite as a family, knit together by a desire to grow closer to God, with Christ, and thus with Paul. That is, the church needed to "form and maintain appropriate boundaries" that set the community apart from the surrounding society.[33] The believing church, which was reconciled to God, needed to be separate, and reconciled to each other in purity and holiness (see James 1:27). If the community intentionally moved toward holiness and reconciliation in their

---

31. Garland, *2 Corinthians*, 323.
32. Garland, *2 Corinthians*, 326.
33. Garland, *2 Corinthians*, 326.

attitudes and in their actions, empowered by God's Holy Spirit, two results would be evident: first, that there would be a greater recognition of who God is (with reverence, awe, 7:1), as well as his authority over his people (6:16–18). Second, the church would have greater affection, confidence, pride, and joy for their founder Paul, and for one another in the church (7:2–3).

LIVE the Story

There is little need to make readers aware that our society today has many issues and problems, not unlike the issues faced by Paul in Gentile Corinth. Our world is troubled, confusing, disappointing, self-centered, and shallow. What can the Christian church do? What can a pastor do? The only hope may be faith, righteousness, and truth spoken into a world of darkness that is not so different than the one Paul experienced in the first century. Not unlike the Roman Empire of his day, our culture is being destroyed from within; the strength of timeless foundations, like the home and family, are being chipped away.

Why is this happening? Modern Americans can cast the blame on some outside influence—primarily some aspect of the government. But, some brave modern prophets and pastors (like Dr. Martin Luther King Jr.) have called it like it is: the problem is sin, flowing from the deceptive hearts of human beings (Jer 17:5, 9–10). Perhaps it is time for the church to reach out to the deepest needs of people and the deepest wounds of society with the words, the redemption, the authority, and the love of Jesus. Paul, while loving and caring for his people, did not just wink at their sinful ways; he challenged them to separate themselves from all known corruption and do all they could to follow the path toward the purity and holiness and righteousness of God.

The Hunt for Holiness

As I was growing up in the Christian church, it seemed like the main emphasis every Sunday morning was on "bringing people to Christ." Repeatedly, every sermon concluded with an "altar call," for people to "repent," and express their desire to be "saved." This was such a part of my perception of what it meant to be a Christian—Are you saved or not? It was the primary focus and, for many people, the end of the journey, not the beginning. Only later, as an adult, did I ponder these questions: "What is *beyond* salvation?" "What are we saved *for*?" As I matured in my faith and became a church leader and pastor, I gave even more consideration to what it means to be saved. I could see that people needed help in understanding what was expected of them after the initial conversion commitment. This topic is still very close to my heart, as I can see that many "saved" Christians are not reaching their huge potential as people of God. The familiar passage in Ephesians says that we are saved by grace as a gift of God, and a less familiar verse relates that we are saved to be "[God's] workmanship, created in Christ Jesus for good works" (Eph 2:8–10 NASB). That is what we are saved *for*.

I can only imagine Paul attempting to explain the same scenario to the Corinthians: You have been given the grace of God and his righteousness (2 Cor 6:1–2; 5:21), so now act like it! That is, in response to God's undeserved grace given to us, and to Jesus's atoning sacrifice, there are certain obligations expected of the believer. Yes, we are to be "*transformed into his image*" (3:18). Then, in addition to the individual's transformation, we are all saved by God's grace so that all believers can be united in one community by the Spirit of God (see Eph 2:12–22).

This section of Paul's letter includes the long answers to my questions. His six imperative verbs and phrases in 2 Cor 5:20 to 7:1 are to be our keys as to what it means to be "transformed." Beyond being the beneficiaries of God's amazing favor and grace, believers must:

1. Be reconciled to God (5:20, which is the first step in the "salvation" process).
2. Avoid any mismatched union with those people who are known for their deception or their immorality, and who laugh in God's face (6:14). Stop associating with immoral people.
3. Leave behind anything that binds us to our old "dark" way of living (6:17).
4. Be separate from all that is evil and abhorrent to God; do not intentionally choose to become a part of practices and activities that are blatantly against his will (6:17).
5. Avoid being a part of the worship of anything other than the Christian triune God. Run from any spiritual and/or physical depravity, including, but not limited to, other gods and goddesses, the devil and his associates, money, success, position, power, or prestige (6:17).
6. Bring to completion the faith that God has started in us. Practice purity and pursue holiness, not for our own sake, but out of our reverence for God. Honor him who died for us with righteous living and seek to be used by God (7:1).

The chain looks something like this: we receive the love of Christ (5:14) and are reconciled to God (5:20), which changes the way we live. Living as people who have received God's love and righteousness (5:21), we choose to abhor and reject all kinds of worldly evil and deception (6:14–18), only to live a fresh, new, honest life, striving to be Christlike and honor God in all we think and do. Furthermore, we will see how righteousness is connected to actions and generosity in chapters 8 and 9.

This chain of reconciliation is not an easy task for a person to attempt to do alone. What Paul writes elsewhere is what our transformation is all about: our confidence and our competence come from God, who has given us his Holy Spirit to aid in our transformation (3:4, 18). The process (or the chain, above) is directed by and empowered by God's Holy Spirit. He is constantly helping us to remember, helping us to forget, forgiving our failures, and giving us the strength to be changed. If the desire is there on our part, then the Spirit brings us ever closer to the victory over pervasive wickedness. God perfects people, and he can use other Christians to challenge us, to aid us, encourage us, and accompany us on our journey to holiness. God is changing us into light in the darkness (6:14), harmony in the discord (6:15), and into the sweet "aroma of Christ" (2:15).

Being Light in a Dark Culture
Today believers of all ages, from all walks of life, are discriminated against for their Christian beliefs. In schools and universities, in businesses and sports arenas, and in various social circles, the media and related culture are critical of believers as "intolerant," "exclusive," "fundamental," and "old fashioned." I have found that people are generally scared of the Bible and suspicious of Christians. When people ask, I tell them that I taught the Bible at a seminary, or that I have an advanced degree in the New Testament. That ends most conversations, as they either switch topics or just turn away. My favorite reaction is when people laugh and say, "Oh, really? Well, I still go to church— sometimes," as if I am standing in judgment over them and their occasional attendance makes them righteous and holy. Christians can feel heavily burdened, tethered to and yoked with the self-interests and values of a society that would like to make us all go away. We know that, presently, believers are being killed and persecuted across the globe, and that most of our daily media remains silent for fear that they would be accused of promoting Christianity. Thus, we "hide our lamp in a jar" (Luke 8:16), retreat, and try not to raise conflicts on the job, in the workplace, in marriage, with adult children, neighbors, and friends. If we do not stay connected to God's word and to God's community, we can give up, give in, and quickly be led astray.

So, how can Christians be a light in a dark culture if they refuse to touch and connect with unbelievers? Mother Teresa, as many of us know, was a woman with a high calling and high dreams. She dreamed of working for

God among the "untouchables," the lowest people in the society in Calcutta, India. Her love and compassion for the sick, the hurting, the abandoned, the "undesirables" of this world is legendary. Mother Teresa made it clear that "the most dreadful disease in the world is not tuberculosis or cancer, but loneliness and not knowing you are loved." One small, humble woman, following in the footsteps of Jesus, challenged all of modern culture and thinking with a new dream to bring hope to the hopeless, and compassion for everyone.[34]

A young man took on the task of being a missionary to Muslim communities in Italy. His job initially was to teach the people better skiing methods and mountain safety skills. But he was aware that his most important task was to build relationships with the Muslim people, regardless of religious beliefs and differences. He came to love these people in a far-away land and enjoyed their theological and philosophical discussions without conflict or judgment. The love of Christ is expressed (sometimes without words) to other people through the love of his followers.

Another young pastor started a church for street people in a warehouse in Los Angeles. He served people who were without spiritual, emotional, financial, and social assistance. His dream was to "resurrect" these people from that life and bring them into the kingdom of God.

One woman whose husband died and whose children left home attended Bible college in her late 50s. She was called to pastor a small, rural community church in southern Missouri. Her dream was to serve in a church family, to love and be loved, until she physically could no longer fulfill that role.[35]

To love and have affection for the unbelievers without joining their ranks and giving in to Satan's schemes is not an impossible task, with God's help. It can be discouraging, but it takes just one brave, focused, ordinary person, challenged by God to be what God wants him or her to be. It takes just one Paul, who knew from personal experience that "God rekindles hope and energizes dreams so ordinary folks can accomplish supernatural achievements in unexpected ways in tough places."[36]

A number of churches have recently started "Pub Theology" gatherings, led by pastors in local bars or pubs on a weeknight—a strange but effective "church" setting. It is a real way to informally attract unbelievers and "seekers" in a nonthreatening, nonjudgmental situation. Also, such gatherings attract Christians who do not have a church, or who have questions about their spiritual journey; it can be the beginning of reconciliation between pastors and

---

34. London and Wiseman, *Heart of a Great Pastor*, 90.
35. London and Wiseman, *Heart of a Great Pastor*, 90.
36. London and Wiseman, *Heart of a Great Pastor*, 91.

people. Paul too was compelled by the love of Christ to love and serve (and suffer for) other people (2 Cor 5:14), regardless of their situation. His ministry was not confined to a comfortable brick building; in fact, he ministered in dangerous and perilous places (1:8–10; 4:7–12; 6:4–10). Thus, every day on the believer's calendar must be a day of living a life honoring Christ and loving people in some (even small) way. The point is that we are to surrender to the grace of God, who loves all people, and then in his righteousness we are to love other people exactly where they are.

Still, Christians today can get caught up in legalistic rules and forget that an important part of salvation is reconciliation and a relationship with God and with other people. We can read directives in the Bible and interpret them as a new set of rules. If the church puts too much emphasis on human-created rules and regulations, we can miss the mark of reconciliation.

Some Christians refuse reconciliation with other believers who may have different opinions and interpretations of a biblical passage or topic. Years ago, there were southern churches that promoted slavery because it was "in the Bible." Thankfully that has been rescinded.

A "Fair Exchange"

When Paul called for a "fair exchange" in the Corinthian congregation (6:13), he was setting an example for all churches even today. The idea of a "fair exchange" may have been rather unusual for the Greeks, but it emphasized the "reciprocal nature of a transaction—something given in fair exchange for something received."[37] However, what Paul received from his readers was not a "fair exchange" for the "open-heartedness," affection, and sacrifice that he had given to them. Certainly, for Paul and for many modern church leaders, it is very painful to be accused and rejected by one's own congregation. It was painful for him to attempt to defend his authority, his message, and his ministry to a group of people he loved, and who he thought loved him. Their doubts and suspicions (spurred on by outside "false apostles") injured him deeply and was one of the main reasons this letter had to be written. Paul wrote with such emotion in this passage and expressed an ardent desire for mutual openness, harmony, and affection with his readers. That is, "love given should be matched by love returned, especially in family relationships" (6:13).[38] The community is a family—with God as their Father and believers as brothers and sisters in Christ (6:18), "to be saved" means to be a part of a unified body, a temple of God, a family of believers.

---

37. Belleville, *2 Corinthians*, 175.
38. Harris, *Second Corinthians*, 491.

This image supports the idea that the church is unified as a family, and that the leader (the apostle then or the pastor today) is like the "parent," or the "manager of the household" (see 1 Cor 4:1–2). This is an appeal for church-goers to love their pastor, and for pastors to love their congregation—all of them. To create (or to restore) the kind of pastor-congregation relationship that mirrors the character of Christ himself is the desire and the goal. The care, support, and trust in such a relationship is a two-way street. A wise pastor wrote,

> A healthy, loving relationship between the pastor and the congregation is not the only thing that matters in a church, but nothing else matters much without it. Many contemporary pastors do not view developing soul friendships with fellow believers as an important or enabling part of their work. Many want to keep parishioners at a professional arm's length as a physician does with patients or a lawyer with clients or a supermarket manager with customers. When locked into this misconception, a pastor feels isolated in a crowd and friendless at church.[39]

To be a caring pastor means to be given the privilege and the opportunity to enter into the world of incredible human joy and deep human sorrow. The pastor is there to put the faith into practice, to hold hands, to cry and laugh together, and to point to Jesus when he is hard to see. Yet, pastors often need their own healing and restoration. I know a man who spent his first three weeks of a new pastorate lying on the floor in his office, in prayer, arguing with God. His interviews and reception at his new church had been just fine, but the honeymoon was over. All that was left from an important portion of the congregation was criticism—degrading remarks about his appearance, his sermons, and his habits. He prayed for God to remove him away from the church; it must have been a mistake! But it never happened. He is still serving in that church as I write, with unexpected great love and success. Sometimes God has to change the pastor, or he has to change the people, or both.

Living in Community

While Christians may be called out to be separate from the ungodly culture around them, it seems necessary to re-emphasize that believers must live in community, as a family (6:17–18) and not as private individuals. We do not have to face persecution, suffering, hardships, or disparagement alone. God intended for believers to form close bonds, empowered by the same Holy

---

39. London and Wiseman, *Heart of a Great Pastor*, 144.

Spirit, so that the pursuit of holiness is not a lonesome journey. We should desire, then, to gather together to tighten the bonds, and to worship the amazing God who brings us together and loves each of us, regardless of our mistakes. Church, then, should be the "home" of the family of God, a place of acceptance, encouragement, growth, love, and joy. Sara Barton wrote a wonderful blog concerning "Christian Identity and the Church as Family." This is an excerpt from her blog:

> In the ideal, we experience the church as the communion of the Holy Spirit in which our spirituality is not individual but communal. In baptism, we experience *rebirth* into a family that has the unique privilege of addressing the creator of everything as "Abba Father" (or Daddy or Mommy, as we might say in our culture). Our experiences of God as a parent define us, and we can no longer delineate self without relationship to our siblings, whom God has called beloved children. As the body of the risen Christ, the church gives us vocation and calling in relation to other members of the body without whom we each counter-culturally proclaim to be nothing.
>
> So, when it comes to communal practices, the church doesn't merely provide any one the means to become spiritual as an individual through worship experiences, sermons, teaching, works of justice, and service opportunities by meeting individual needs and preferences or catering to learning styles. Sometimes those practices do meet individual needs, and sometimes they don't. In short, we don't grow spiritually through a particular communal practice that floats our individual boats. We're capable of growing spiritually when we experience communal practices, based not on personal preferences but on the growth we experience collectively with our siblings.
>
> A Christian's whole identity, then, is rooted in rebirth into family, and identity is something much more than a personal decision. Identity is not so much about personal ethics or psychological wellbeing (although they are outcomes); instead, identity is radically communal. The experience of spirituality in the church is something akin to a dance with God, Jesus, the Holy Spirit and family in Christ, a dance with which we are in step, apart from the tune of natural birth or society.

Indeed, Barton realizes that not all families are perfect. From television shows to the neighbors next door, we can see that the dysfunctional family today is portrayed as humorous; but in reality, it can be pathetic, destructive, and abusive. The church must firmly reject those characteristics of family dynamics that are critical, caustic, demeaning, and detrimental. She continues,

So, if people are leaving the church, perhaps we need to avoid defensiveness and ask some hard questions about family. Sometimes individuals leave families of origin because of abuse, because of dysfunction that threatens to overtake the entire family system. Could it be that many of our friends and neighbors are leaving church because of dysfunction that needs deep introspection? We can easily cite stories of people for whom the church is functioning. We should celebrate those stories. But, the church is not functioning for others, to such an extent that they are leaving. Instead of being defensive, maybe what we should do for a while is merely listen.[40]

If we live and grow together in a community of believers, then the love shown to us by God and by Jesus does not go unrequited. We return the Father's love by loving one another.

---

40. Sara Barton, "Christian Identity and the Church as Family," *Jesus Creed*, www.patheos.com/blogs/jesuscreed/2014/02/20/christian-identity-and-the-church-as-family-by-sara-barton/.

CHAPTER 9

2 Corinthians 7:2–16

 LISTEN to the Story

²Make room for us in your hearts. We have wronged no one, we have corrupted no one, we have exploited no one. ³I do not say this to condemn you; I have said before that you have such a place in our hearts that we would live or die with you. ⁴I have spoken to you with great frankness; I take great pride in you. I am greatly encouraged; in all our troubles my joy knows no bounds.

⁵For when we came into Macedonia, we had no rest, but we were harassed at every turn—conflicts on the outside, fears within. ⁶But God, who comforts the downcast, comforted us by the coming of Titus, ⁷and not only by his coming but also by the comfort you had given him. He told us about your longing for me, your deep sorrow, your ardent concern for me, so that my joy was greater than ever.

⁸Even if I caused you sorrow by my letter, I do not regret it. Though I did regret it—I see that my letter hurt you, but only for a little while—⁹yet now I am happy, not because you were made sorry, but because your sorrow led you to repentance. For you became sorrowful as God intended and so were not harmed in any way by us. ¹⁰Godly sorrow brings repentance that leads to salvation and leaves no regret, but worldly sorrow brings death. ¹¹See what this godly sorrow has produced in you: what earnestness, what eagerness to clear yourselves, what indignation, what alarm, what longing, what concern, what readiness to see justice done. At every point you have proved yourselves to be innocent in this matter. ¹²So even though I wrote to you, it was neither on account of the one who did the wrong nor on account of the injured party, but rather that before God you could see for yourselves how devoted to us you are. ¹³By all this we are encouraged.

In addition to our own encouragement, we were especially delighted to see how happy Titus was, because his spirit has been refreshed by all of you. ¹⁴I had boasted to him about you, and you have not embarrassed me. But just as everything we said to you was true, so our boasting about you to Titus has proved to be true as well. [15]And his affection for you is all the greater when he remembers that you were all obedient, receiving him with fear and trembling. [16]I am glad I can have complete confidence in you.

Listening to the Text in the Story: 2 Chronicles 7:14; Isaiah 40:1; Matthew 26:47–56, 69–75; 27:3–5; Mark 14:43–46; Luke 22:47–50; John 15:16; 18:15–27; 21:15–22; 1 Corinthians 12:12–13; Galatians 6:9; Ephesians 4:1; 5:25.

Laying down your life means making your own faith and doubt, hope and despair, joy and sadness, courage and fear available to others as ways of getting in touch with the Lord of life.

Henri J. M. Nouwen[1]

I confess that there have been times in my life where I have enjoyed a good pity party. When life is not going well, I admit that a carton of chocolate chunk ice cream, a giant spoon, and a sappy romantic movie are lifesavers. It feels good just to feel sorry for myself for a few minutes, let the tears flow, laugh at the movie, and ignore the serious fat and calories.

When we read about Paul's ministry in Corinth and all the afflictions that he endured, from the first chapter of 2 Corinthians all the way to chapter 7, I cannot help but wonder how Paul could be so joyful (7:7). He makes my pity-parties look pretty pathetic. In spite of all that has happened in Macedonia, how can he be so encouraging, so confident and even happy (7:9)? Regardless of what the readers have done to Paul, or thought about him, he is so pleased with them that he would sacrifice his own life for them (7:3), and would boast about them to others (7:14)! Remember that in spite of all his efforts, care, and love, they have disappointed him, doubted him, rebuked him, took offence at his earlier letter, caused him sleepless nights, and denied friendship with him. Really? Bring on the ice cream.

Yet, instead of whining and complaining about the Corinthians, Paul is able to write to them with perceivable confidence and affection (6:12; 7:3–4). This passage is as convicting as it is encouraging for any of us who have indulged in a chocolate pity-party. How could he renew their fellowship, reignite their faith and trust in him, and move forward in his important ministry with all

1. Henri J. M. Nouwen, *In the Name of Jesus: Reflections on Christian Leadership* (New York: Crossroads, 1992), 43.

the hope and caring of a true apostle? How could he reprimand and overcome the accusations and implications of adversaries who are undermining his fragile ministry in Corinth? How could Paul go on?

Paul did not lose heart in his ministry work because he recognized that he was ministering only by the grace of God, and not under the strength of his own body. He confidently lived by faith (5:7) and ministered by the power of God (4:7). Recall that in chapter 5 Paul gave us his four major purposes of Christian ministry: ministry is transformation, reconciliation, agency, and self-sacrifice (see 5:11–6:10). Paul keys in on the concept of reconciliation; he is confident that through his ministry, God reconciles himself to people, and people have the opportunity to reconcile themselves to God by responding to Paul's proclaimed gospel message (5:20–21). Paul continued in chapter 6 to implore redeemed people to be reconciled to other people. He desperately wanted his readers' hearts to be open to him as their spiritual father, to be reconciled to him, and to return his great affection for them (6:11–13 and 7:2–4). He then wrote an "appeals" or a "warnings" section urging the church to "come out, be separate," and to seek "purity and holiness" distinctly different from the pagan culture around them (6:14–7:1). Thus, Paul's ministry of reconciliation, which was already beginning to blossom among the believers in Corinth, brought encouragement and great joy to Paul (7:4).

Paul's defense of his ministry in this letter to his readers in the church at Corinth has been long, tedious, and a bit disheartening (2:14–7:16). His plan in this epistle was to win the church's allegiance, loyalty, and confidence not only in him, but also in his ministry message. Paul loved these people, cared about them, believed in them, and was clearly upset that they were not returning his affection. In addition, he was anxious about the church's reaction to his "tearful letter" (2:3–4), which was delivered to them by Titus. And, he was aware of strong opposition to his ministry and his character: a number of people were spreading criticisms, falsehoods, and accusations among the believers. His mounting grief and frustrations were perceivable, yet Paul *did not give up on his church.* His letter, and his emotions, have swung from joy and confidence in his people (2:2–3), to a previous "painful visit" and a letter of distress, anguish, and tears (2:1, 4), to deep unrest and depression (7:5–6), and back again to a feeling of confidence, pride, and joy (7:4, 16) for his dear friends (7:1) at Corinth. Through it all, he was fully committed to his church. And graciously, God remained faithful (7:6). Paul wanted his readers to be assured that he and God were totally committed to the wellbeing of the church. If you have ever served as a Christian minister in any manner among any group of human beings, you are probably saying, "That's incredible."

EXPLAIN the Story

A Very Personal Ministry (7:2–4)

This section closely follows the previous section of Pauline appeals (6:11–7:1), where Paul entreats the Corinthians to return his love for them (6:11–12; see 2:4), and to be reconciled to him, to his colleagues, and to each other.[2] In 7:2–3, Paul expressed his integrity and his strong commitment to the congregation, and asked to have that affection and commitment returned. Then, verse 7:4 introduces a new topic; it is a "topic sentence" for the remainder of chapter 7.[3] Key terms in 7:4 (confidence, pride, encouraged, joy) are expanded in the remaining part of the chapter. The central focus in chapter 7 is the comforting news brought to Paul from Titus after his visit in Corinth and the joyful results.

If we look back at 2:1–13, we see the grief and anxiety felt by Paul after the "painful visit" to Corinth (2:1) and after he wrote the "tearful letter" to the congregation (2:3–4). In addition, he related an unfortunate incident with a person in the church that probably took place during the "painful visit." What really hurt Paul was the lack of support for him by the rest of the congregation in obedience to what he had taught them (2:9). This seems to be a three-pronged arrow sent by Satan to disrupt and damage Paul's ministry efforts in Corinth (2:11). But Paul's heart and soul were in his ministry at Corinth, and it was a personal issue with him. He held great affection for the Corinthians; he wanted and needed the community's love and understanding, as any pastor would. Thus, in chapter 7 Paul opened his heart to reveal his conflicted feelings for the church. The deeper the true heart intentions and emotions, the more sharply one can be hurt by slander and false accusations. But finally, Paul received good news from Titus about the Corinthians.

Good News from Titus (7:5–7)

More than a few scholars see 7:4–16 as a "closing section of a letter."[4] It seems to fit literarily, and arguably it brings to conclusion the long apostolic defense that Paul has been presenting since chapter 2. It could be regarded as the end of one letter and 8:1 beginning a whole new letter (see Introduction).[5] Other scholars have noted that 7:5–16 is a continuation of a travel narrative that was suspended at 2:13.[6] That is, we can regard this section as both an epilogue

---

2. Furnish, *II Corinthians*, 375, 383.
3. Furnish, *II Corinthians*, 393.
4. Belleville, *2 Corinthians*, 188.
5. Furnish, *II Corinthians*, 391.
6. Furnish, *II Corinthians*, 392.

to his apostolic defense and a travel plan wrap-up, disclosing the effects of his disappointing travel plans and a severe letter of warning to the people he loved. Things were not going well for Paul and his ministry, and as readers we are held in suspense until chapter 7. Would Satan's schemes destroy Paul's ministry in Corinth (2:11)? Finally, we can find a happy ending, or at least a completion of what was started back in chapter 2:12–13. We see the desired effect of Paul's "tearful letter" and the achievement of Titus in his role as envoy and ambassador. The church's reaction to the earlier letter reaffirmed Paul's confidence in the church (7:16). Paul could breathe a sigh of relief, and verses 7:5–16 now function as a conclusion to the tense narrative and to the long list of appeals asserted by Paul to the church, beginning with the imperative in 5:20.

It is most likely that Paul wrote 2 Corinthians from Macedonia, the northern part of Greece, to the church at Corinth on the northern tip of the Achaia peninsula (see 7:5; 8:1; 9:2). The Christian congregations in Macedonia that were under Paul's care included the church in Philippi and the church at Thessalonica, so it is likely that he was in one of these cities. He was ministering across Asia Minor, from Ephesus to Troas, and it was his intention to then return to Corinth before he visited Macedonia (see Introduction). A travel itinerary in the first century (not unlike travel plans today) had to be flexible; any number of unpredictable, unexpected, unintended events could change it radically. Paul ended up traveling to Macedonia from Asia, which made it necessary to send "my brother Titus" to Corinth instead (2:13; chapters 7–8; 12:18). Paul held Titus in high regard; he had entrusted him to deliver his earlier, "tearful letter" (2:4) and later, this letter we call 2 Corinthians. Even so, Paul was apprehensive and restless about how Titus and the "tearful letter" would be received in Corinth.

Titus is a key character in this Corinthian drama because he was an important stand-in for Paul when it was physically and geographically impossible for Paul to be present in Corinth. We know that Titus was a Gentile Christian, perhaps from the area of Crete (Titus 1:5). In his letter written to Titus, with true affection, Paul called him his "son in our common faith," implying Titus was his spiritual son, having been converted to Christianity through Paul's ministry (Tit.1:4). In chapter 2 we noted that he was a vital "fellow worker" with Paul in the missionary work in Asia Minor (Gal 2:1–3; 2 Tim 4:10). It appears that Titus was gifted at straightening things out and wrapping things up in the established Christian congregations after Paul left an area (Tit 1:5). While Paul listed his requirements for church elders, it was Titus's responsibility to appoint the right people to those positions (Tit 1:5–9). Moreover, we know that Paul trusted Titus explicitly, as he asked him to organize the collection of funds in Corinth for the distressed believers in the church at Jerusalem (2 Cor 8:6). Since he was unable to be in Corinth, Paul was also trusting Titus to use his talents for reconciliation within the troubled congregation.

Paul was called from Ephesus to Troas to preach and teach (2:12), and he was hoping to find Titus in Troas, where he would be returning to Asia from his visit in Corinth. But, since he was not there, Paul crossed the Aegean Sea and left Asia for northern Greece, without connecting with Titus (2:12–13). When Paul arrived in Macedonia, he was very uneasy both in his spirit (2:13) and in his body (7:5). He was deeply concerned about the reception of Titus by the church at Corinth. He was "on pins and needles," waiting to hear about the reaction of the church to Titus's visit following his own "painful visit" and "tearful letter." In the midst of his ministry, Paul was on an emotional rollercoaster, and he was trying to minister in one city while he was anxious about a congregation in another city far away. So, how did such joy and encouragement come out of so much grief, fear, and anxiety for Paul (2:1–4, 12–13; 7:5–7)? Before we can answer that question, it might be helpful to see a timeline devised by Harris to more easily follow the events and the emotions surrounding Paul and Titus in these chapters:

1. Paul wrote the "tearful letter" to the Corinthians from Ephesus (2:4; 7:8, 12); it was delivered by Titus, so Paul had no idea how it would be received.
2. Even before his visit to Corinth, Paul boasts to Titus about the Corinthian church (7:14).
3. Titus traveled to Corinth to deliver the "tearful letter" (7:6). He also was the envoy to encourage the Corinthians to raise funds for the church at Jerusalem (8:16–19).
4. Titus was received with fear and trembling by the church (7:15).
5. When they heard the letter from Paul, some of the people ("the majority," 2:6) experienced "godly sorrow" (7:8–9).
6. The people were sorry that they took no action toward the one who injured Paul;
7. they corrected the situation and punished the wrongdoer, demonstrating deep concern for Paul (2:6; 7:7, 9, 11–12).
8. Because of their remorse, Titus received comfort and encouragement (7:7, 13b).
9. Meanwhile, in Macedonia, Paul found no rest; he was harassed at every turn,
10. with internal fears and external conflicts; he continued to be anxious about the safety of Titus and the church at Corinth (7:5).

11. Titus finally left Corinth and met with Paul somewhere in Macedonia (7:6–7).
12. With praise and thanks to God, Paul was very relieved that Titus arrived safely and was well received by the Corinthians.
13. Titus gave Paul an encouraging report on the Corinthians' "godly sorrow" (7:8–11),
14. "repentance" (7:7–9) and "obedience" (7:15). They realized the error of their ways; Titus was pleased, and his own affection for the church was deepened (7:15).
15. Paul initially regretted the "tearful letter" because it caused his readers sorrow, but then he learned of their repentance, and so he did not regret it (7:8). Paul realized the dreadful letter may have done its job.
16. Thus, Paul is reassured; he finds comfort, happiness, encouragement, and complete confidence in the Corinthians as they respond to his letter and to his representative, Titus (7:6–7, 9, 13, 16).
17. Paul's joy was increased as he heard of Titus's joy (7:13b).
18. Paul was glad that his initial boasting to Titus about the Corinthians was validated by his positive visit with them (7:14). This was such a good experience for Titus to be with the Corinthians that he volunteers to go back to the church to complete the collection task (8:17).
19. In the end, Paul assured the congregation that the whole matter was now behind them (7:11c) and that he had great confidence in them (7:16).[7]
20. Paul was happy that the effects of the "tearful letter" were godly sorrow, repentance, obedience, affection, encouragement, and joy (7:8–16).

Parallels and Similarities

It is very interesting to note the similarities between chapters 1 and 7. The very same emotions captured by Paul in the first chapter, "comfort" (1:3–7), "salvation" (1:6), "boasting" (1:12–14), and "confidence" (1:15) are reiterated in chapter 7. Throughout these first chapters, then, Paul was defending his apostolic position and revealing his heart to his readers.

Yet, the closest parallels we see are between Paul's *words* in chapter 2 and chapter 7. There are similarities in both vocabulary and in content. Verse 7:5 is similar to 2:13 as Paul recounted his arrival in Macedonia. He left a hopeful ministry opportunity in Troas with great disappointment that he had not connected with Titus there. But in Macedonia, Paul experienced "harassment at every turn" (7:5). In 2:13, he found no rest in his spirit, and

7. Harris, *Second Corinthians*, 523–24.

in 7:5 there was no relief in his "flesh." "The former refers to mental anxiety and the latter to bodily fatigue. The two, however, often go hand in hand." [8] He had "conflicts on the outside," which is a picture of a battle, a fight, or a quarrel. In the cities of Macedonia, he had previously encountered quarrels with confrontational crowds (Acts 16:22–24), as well as jealous, unbelieving Jews (Acts 17:5–9). Paul had also experienced compounding fears within. He was concerned about Titus's safety and how he was being received in Corinth. He had fears of continuing opposition in Philippi (see Phil 3:2) and Thessalonica (1 Thess 1:6–8; 2:2; 2 Thess 1:4), for his own safety and for the security of the churches there. However, the plans of God triumphed over the schemes of Satan (2:11), and Paul's downcast spirit and tired body were transformed into joy (7:5–16). Thus, the Titus story that began in chapter 2 is happily concluded in chapter 7.

Paul's meeting with Titus in 7:6–15 is not unlike Paul's meeting with his co-worker Timothy, who brought good news to the apostle from Thessalonica. Paul stated that "in all our distress and persecution, we were encouraged about you because of your faith" (1 Thess 3:6–10). In these verses, three things brought joy to Paul: the Thessalonians' faith, their love, and the fact that they "longed to see us." This brings to light the Thessalonians' proper positions and attitudes toward God, toward each other, toward Paul and his colleagues.[9] In the case of Titus and the Corinthians, Paul was hoping to hear a similar report, and that his stern "tearful letter" caused the congregation to correct the individual who caused grief for Paul and for the entire church (2:5–6). Apparently, this is exactly what Titus reported, along with the Corinthians' longing to see Paul again and the sorrow that was felt over the previous events (7:6–7).

Comfort

Paul was experiencing such a depression in his ministry (7:6) that only God could ease his discomfort. Indeed, his unease was alleviated by comfort given by God in the form of Titus's safe reunion with Paul. Titus's good news about his warm reception in Corinth was another comfort to Paul. In addition, God graciously comforted Titus, which, in turn, comforted Paul (7:6–7a). If this sounds a little repetitive to modern ears, that may have been intentional. Literally, 7:6 reads "but God, the one comforting the humble (or the depressed, or the downcast), comforted us by the presence of Titus." That is, in most English translations the word "comfort," or a derivation of it, appears four

---

8. Belleville, *2 Corinthians*, 191.
9. Belleville, *2 Corinthians*, 193.

times just in verses 7:6–7. This is a reminder of Paul's repetitive words in the first chapter of this letter, where the word "comfort" (or derivations of it) appears 9 or 10 times in 1:3–7 (depending upon the translation). In reference to God, he repeats the same phrase, "the one comforting us" (1:4; 7:6), revealing the source of true comfort, regardless of the human situation.[10] Obviously, then, "to comfort" is an important theme in this letter and something that was very, very real to Paul. After recording his own sufferings and hardships (see 1:8–11; 4:7–9; 6:4–10), Paul insisted that God is a God of "all comfort," a valuable reminder and an encouragement, especially in view of the perceived hurts and injuries that jeopardized the pastor-congregation relationship. "In all our troubles" (7:4) is exactly the same phrase that we see in 1:4, thus implying that God rarely removes us from human trials and hardships, but he comforts us *through* them.[11]

Furthermore, Titus's comforting words demonstrated the congregation's longing and concern for Paul himself, a salve that relieved the sting of the offending person in 2:5–8 (and 7:12). Paul had an ability to see beyond his own hurt, and he saw that the traumatic events during his "painful visit" wounded the entire church (2:5). The intentional backstabbing and discrediting of Christian leaders within congregations injures the entire body of Christ. Yet, in 2:7, he begged the church to forgive and comfort the wrongdoer. Only by the grace of God could Paul overlook the past wounds, forgive, and give comfort to the one who was responsible for so much trouble.

Encouragement from "Godly Sorrow" (7:8–16)

The first part of verse 7:9 is a juxtaposition of a sharp contrast: "[N]ow I am happy, not because you were made sorry, but because your sorrow led you to repentance." That is, Paul was happy as a result of the "sorrow" felt by his church, which is an odd disparity. It is critical to understand the difference between what Paul called "godly sorrow" and "worldly sorrow" (7:8–11). Sorrow over the iniquity of sin is the "good" kind of sorrow because it brings about good results. "The kind of sorrow that God intends results in a change of heart (7:9), and the church had become sorrowful as God intended," says Belleville, calling this "constructive sorrow," which leads to repentance (7:10) and not to regrets.[12] That is, godly sorrow manifests itself by sincere repentance and the experience of divine grace, which leads to salvation (7:10).

---

10. In addition, Paul may be remembering God's tender words in Isa 40:1: "Comfort, comfort my people, says your God."

11. Furnish, *II Corinthians*, 385.

12. Belleville, *2 Corinthians*, 195–97.

In his letter to the Romans, Paul boldly expressed the ravages and the universality of human sin, and the grace of God:

> The wrath of God is being revealed from heaven against all the godlessness and wickedness of people, who suppress the truth by their wickedness, since what may be known about God is plain to them . . .
>
> This righteousness is given through faith in Jesus Christ to all who believe. There is no difference, . . . for all have sinned and fall short of the glory of God, and all are justified freely by his grace though the redemption that came by Christ Jesus. (Rom 1:18–19; 3:22–24)

After the alarming realization that the individual has done something regrettable, godly sorrow brings him or her to remorse. Yet repentance is more than regret. With God's grace and forgiveness, the repentant sinner stands on his or her feet again, determined to rectify the wrong and bring justice to anyone offended.

Indeed, there are "good" consequences of godly sorrow: repentance, salvation, and community welfare. Paul wrote that the sin of one person affects the entire community (2 Cor 2:5). The godly sorrow and repentance of one person leads to justice for others; this means that the appropriate indignation and concern promotes justice within the community of repentant sinners (7:11). On the one hand, the effects of sin in the community can be devastating. Like an infectious disease, it can spread and contaminate the entire congregation. The community cannot be what God intended it to be because of pain, bitterness, and division. All the Corinthian believers should have felt the blow of one person's malicious intentions and should have been sorrowful for the injury to Paul. On the other hand, godly sorrow leads to repentance and then to salvation, not only for the individual, but also for the community. The grace and forgiveness from God can bring restoration to the whole group because each person is aware of his or her human failures and of the grace of God in their lives. If sin multiplies and grows, how much more so does the grace and goodness of God? Sin stops the community from moving forward to be effective in God's kingdom; it stops the church from being what it is supposed to be in the world.

Godly sorrow and forgiveness stand out against the further spread of sin and ungodliness in the community. The forgiveness and grace of God restores the whole person, who in turn restores the entire church, which can, in turn, restore the whole world. Furthermore, Paul did not want any more sorrow placed on the congregation, so he advised forgiveness and reconciliation in the church. Paul also took the opportunity to reiterate to his readers an important purpose of the earlier "tearful letter" (which brought godly sorrow, 7:8–11). It was not a negative purpose—to condemn the offender or the entire congregation, as some imagined. He had a more positive purpose in mind: that they would deeply consider their expressed devotion and loyalty to Paul ("but rather that before God you could see for yourselves how devoted to us you are," 7:12).

In contrast, "worldly sorrow" leads to "death" (7:10). "Worldly sorrow" is devastating; it is a crushing, self-centered kind of sorrow that spirals down into destructive self-pity and regret. "Worldly sorrow" is exceedingly self-centered, not God-centered, or even centered on other people. As a result, it leaves people embittered, unhappy, and hostile. Paul implied that "worldly sorrow" is similar to his use of "worldly wisdom" in 1:12. Paul addressed "worldly wisdom" in 1 Cor 1:18–31. He told the Corinthians that, "the message of the cross is foolishness to those who are perishing, but to us who are being saved it is the power of God. . . . It is because of him [God] that you are in Christ Jesus, *who has become for us wisdom from God*—that is, our righteousness, holiness and redemption" (my emphasis; see 2 Cor 2:15; 7:1).

People think they are wise in their own eyes, but they are foolish to reject the grace and forgiveness of God and the reconciliation of humanity granted through the work of Jesus Christ. Paul told his "spiritual son" Timothy to remember "how from infancy you have known the Holy Scriptures, which are able to make you *wise for salvation* through faith in Christ Jesus" (my emphasis, 2 Tim 3:15). The ruse and deception of "worldly wisdom" can lead to the lament of "worldly sorrow." The consequences of true, "godly sorrow" in Corinth were earnestness, eagerness to clear themselves, indignation, alarm, longing, concern, readiness to see justice done, and they proved themselves to be "innocent in this matter" (2 Cor 7:11). These eight signs of the Corinthians' correct sorrow were a welcome demonstration of their loyalty and commitment to Paul, who was elated to hear this news from Titus (7:7).

Consider the stories of Peter and Judas and the events surrounding Jesus's death. In the Gospel of John we see a distinct contrast between these two characters beginning in chapter 13. From reading all the Gospels we can discern how both men were filled with fear and reacted incorrectly to the unfolding of the tragic events. Judas, of course, betrayed his Master in the garden with a kiss (Mark 14:43–46; Matt 26:47–56; Luke 22:47–50). Peter chose to deny knowing Jesus on three occasions (Matt 26:69–75; John 18:15–27). Later, both men were overwhelmed with grief because of what they had done (Matt 26:75; 27:3–5). Peter was filled with sorrow, but he faced his failure, had the courage to change his behavior, sought forgiveness, and recommitted his life to following Jesus (John 21:15–22). Judas, on the other hand, felt remorse, but did not repent of his sin. Without repentance, his sorrow and guilt destroyed his soul, ultimately leading to his suicide. Judas could not learn from his sorrow and sin; he was too proud to repent and to beg for forgiveness for what he had done. He could not ask for salvation, and his obstinacy led to his own death.[13]

Confidence

In 2 Cor 2:3, Paul explained that he wrote the "tearful letter" so that if he returned to Corinth at some point in time, he would see changed people who were seeking to be obedient to the faith Paul had taught them. Paul had confidence and joy in his people in 2:3, but he lost those positive feelings and was not willing to do a return visit under the same conditions. Instead, he wrote the bold and anguished letter, but was quite uncertain as to how the church would receive it.

Fast-forward to 7:4, where Paul's confidence and pride in the Corinthians have been restored! Like a pair of bookends, the idea of "confidence" appears in 7:4 (NASB), and then again in 7:16, so we begin and end this section with the same idea. Literally 7:4 reads, "I have much *boldness* toward you . . ." Paul repeated the fact that he could speak with boldness, with freedom, and with assurance as he wrote to people he knew and trusted (see i.e., 3:12). An unusual word, Paul uses this expression of "boldness" or "confidence" only in 2 Corinthians (7:4, 16; 10:1, 2), particularly as a contrast to "weakness." The paradox of "weakness" and "boldness" or "power" is central to this entire letter. Probably Paul's rivals accused him of cowardice and weakness in dealing with the Corinthians, so he was rebuking their accusations by using their own language.[14]

In 7:16, Paul was "glad" because he had "every (or complete) confidence" in the people. It is a reiteration of his pride and trust in them that has been the topic since 7:4.

This last verse is clearly a summation of the chapter because Paul has seen evidence of their deep sorrow, their concern for him (7:7, 12), their innocence in the whole injurious offender matter (7:11b), and their desire to live in obedience to Paul's instructions (7:15).[15] That is, Paul was very pleased with their desire to right the wrong, to change their behavior, and to be reconciled to him; he then had the confidence that God could mold them into a holy people (7:1).

Encouragement and Pride

Paul was relieved and grateful that his boasting to Titus about the Corinthians proved justified (7:14). They had received the severe letter in the way that

13. Barton et al., *1 and 2 Corinthians*, 379.
14. Furnish, *II Corinthians*, 271, 391.
15. Furnish, *II Corinthians*, 398.

God had intended and had responded correctly (7:11). It is difficult for anyone to receive criticism cheerfully, much less an entire congregation. The fact that they had received his criticism by accepting Titus was an encouragement to Paul. Thus, Paul was rewarded for his trials, his efforts, and his concern for his people. He had great satisfaction and gratification in the fact that the congregation was responding in an acceptable manner; he had great pride in seeing the evidence of their godly sorrow and their repentance, and how devoted they were to God's messengers (7:4, 12).

In addition to giving joy to both Paul and Titus, the Corinthians "refreshed" the spirit of Titus. Instead of groaning with disappointment that it was not Paul who came to visit them (see 1:15–17), the church received Titus with open arms, and "refreshed" his spirit. He used this expression in 1 Corinthians 16:18, when three men from the congregation brought a letter to Paul, seeking his consultation and advice (1 Cor 7:1). They "refreshed my [Paul's] spirit and yours [the congregation's]." That is, these men supplied the affection and the esteem for Paul that he desired from the entire church. This is a very vivid and precious image used by Paul again in Philemon 7, when the love of his "dear friend" (v. 1) gave Paul great "joy and encouragement" because Philemon had "refreshed the hearts of the saints." Paul must have been so proud of his brother in Christ who "refreshed" both the other believers (v. 7) and then the very heart of Paul (v. 20). This is not unlike an icy cold, refreshing drink given to a thirsty person on a hot and sticky day—ahhh, for Paul, the words of Titus must have tasted so good!

While Paul resisted "boasting" about himself in this letter, he "boasted" to Titus about the church even before Titus's successful visit to Corinth and his report to Paul (2 Cor 7:14). The word used for "boasting" in 7:14 is the same word that is translated "pride" in 7:4. His pride in his churches was reflected in his boasting about them (see 8:1–5). Paul was not "put to shame" by needless boasting about the Corinthians; they had proved his praise justified. Like any parent who is proud of his or her children, Paul was so pleased that they did, indeed, behave as he hoped they would. It had always been Paul's hope and desire that the church could eventually learn to "boast" about him and in his ministry someday, "in the day of the Lord Jesus" (1:13b–14). Yet, while still concerned about their present situation, Paul was able to boast about the Corinthians' warm reception of Titus with true humility and obedience (7:14–16).

Summation

The positive result of this whole discourse, from 2:1 to 7:15, was encouragement (7:13). His beloved congregation repented and turned to longing and concern not only for Paul but for his colleague Titus as well. As a result of all of Titus's good news, Paul was joyously expressing "*complete* confidence" in the church at Corinth (7:16, my emphasis). At this point, Paul offered praise for the Corinthians' loyalty and devotion for Paul as their apostle and "founding father."

LIVE the Story

One bright Sunday morning, a happy pastor stood in front of his congregation. He said that a man and his wife were present in the worship service that day, and it was so good to see them. This brother in Christ had been battling cancer for many months—pain, chemo-therapy, radiation, surgery, and long recoveries. They had traveled all over the country for medical treatments and procedures. It was glorious to see them sitting there in the pew with the rest of us. Then the pastor said something unexpected: he said, "We are so *proud* of you!" The entire church body—staff, women's groups, men's groups, everyone—had been praying for this couple, and he was finally strong enough to join us in worship. It rang again in my ears: "We are so *proud* of you!" Throughout his trials and suffering, we could applaud his tenacity, his faith and faithfulness, as well as his encouraging witness among us. What joy we felt. We were fully rewarded for holding them both up in our prayers. His suffering had served a purpose: prayers were answered, the church body was just a little closer, and we all were encouraged in our own journey with the Lord. No doubt this is the kind of pride Paul felt for his people in Corinth. Perhaps his joy and gladness came as a response to his anxiety, concern, and love that he had for the congregation, and for answered prayers.

Confrontation

As we have seen, Paul was very anxious about his churches; he had a leadership role rife with mental anguish, emotional frustration, strong opposition, and physical suffering. Paul had to confront a strong-willed, errant congregation in love, like a parent disciplining a disobedient child. Confrontation of any kind within a family (even a family of God) is distressing, potentially divisive, and agonizing. However uncomfortable it is, sometimes confrontation is necessary. After their "tearful" confrontation, Paul was thrilled when the Corinthians repented about a disturbing situation. Followers of Christ are called to convey "truth in love" within the community, with the "hope that the strength of the relationship will minimize the inevitable pain of healing."[16]

---

16. Barton et al., *1 and 2 Corinthians*, 377.

Yet, we also must look in the mirror, as well. It is difficult for each individual to face his or her own sin. We resist taking the plank out of our own eyes before we remove the speck from our brother's eye (Matt 7:3–5). That is, our personal pride keeps us from admitting our own mistakes, and we tend to be defensive when confronted. Like the Corinthians, we must accept constructive correction as a tool of growth and do all we can to reconcile, to resolve issues, to rectify misunderstandings, and to mend fences.[17]

The purpose of confrontation or discipline is to help people, not to hurt them. When necessary, there are Christ-like methods of rebuke and confrontation that we can discern from 2 Corinthians that can help us to help each other:[18]

Method	Reference
Be firm and bold.	7:8–9; 10:2
Affirm all that you see that is good.	7:4, 7
Be accurate and honest.	7:14; 8:21
Know the facts.	1:23–27
Follow up after the confrontation.	2:8; 7:13; 12:14
Be gentle after being firm.	7:12, 15; 13:11–13
Speak words that reflect Christ's message, not your own ideas.	10:3, 12–13; 12:19
Use discipline only when all else fails.	2:6–7; 13:2

Leadership

In a day when it appears that the Christian church is struggling in our society, losing its members, fighting commercialism, and dealing with spiritual apathy, what is a Christian leader to do? In the midst of confrontation, trials, and opposition, how can we, as leaders, find confidence, encouragement, and joy? How does a Christian leader stay positive in strenuous ministry situations? Researcher George Barna contends that the church needs "more real leaders." He said that the church is under strain because "the problem is the Christian church is not being led by true leaders." Pastoral leadership is when

17. Barton et al., *1 and 2 Corinthians*, 380.
18. Barton et al., *1 and 2 Corinthians*, 381.

someone "generates positive spiritual achievement in a congregation."[19] There are countless books, magazines, articles, seminars, and blogs available on pastoral leadership, each with its own formula for success. Well-known pastors of highly successful churches and renowned authors outline guiding principles, all of which are extremely helpful. Never in our history have pastors and Christian leaders had so much beneficial, practical information, and so much opportunity to expand their education and experiences. At the touch of a button we can grow and learn about ministry competence.

> Dedication to betterment of personal leadership keeps a pastor blooming anywhere, even in the winters of ministry. Beyond our managing, influencing, directing, preaching, administering and teaching, a growing pastor-leader challenges people to hope, love, believe, compassion, wonder, reverence, and grace.[20]

Moreover, we can assume from this letter that, as a pastor, the apostle Paul took his ministry very *seriously*, but not *personally*. A blog posted by Carey Nieuwhof is quite beneficial as he addresses "5 Reasons You Should Stop Taking Leadership So Personally." His words are wise and timely, not only for pastors, but also for anyone working in a service position:

> One of the problems I struggled with for years in leadership was taking every leadership triumph or set back so personally. I let the dynamics of leadership go to my head and heart too often. My spirits soared when things were good in ministry. They sunk when they weren't. I took too much of the weight home. Well, not just home. It followed me everywhere I went.
>
> Over time, I've learned that there's a world of difference between taking leadership *seriously* and taking it *personally*. Leaders should always take leadership *seriously*. It demands our best, and we should give it. Every day.
>
> But to take it too personally creates a roller coaster that ripples out all over the place.
>
> When you take leadership *seriously*, everyone wins.
>
> When you take it *personally*, almost everyone loses.[21]

---

19. Barton et al., *1 and 2 Corinthians*, 168; George Barna, *Today's Pastors* (Ventura, CA: Regal, 1993), 137.

20. London and Wiseman, *Heart of a Great Pastor*, 170.

21. Carey Nieuwhof, "5 Reasons You Should Stop Taking Leadership So Personally," Carey Nieuwhof, https://careynieuwhof.com/5-reasons-you-should-stop-taking-leadership-so-personally/. Carey is founding pastor of Connexus Church, Ontario, Canada.

Nieuwhof continues to say that in ministry if you let success go to your head, failure will go to your heart. He writes that, too often, leaders tend to see who they are only with respect to what they do. Furthermore, success and failure in ministry can affect all other relationships in the minister's life (marriage, children, parents).[22]

Priest, author, professor, and theologian Henri Nouwen shared that he was tempted to be a "popular" leader in his Christian ministry. He wrote that through his education, he believed that leadership in ministry was "essentially an individual affair": his own methods, his own beliefs and his own time. He carried all the problems and struggles of people on his own shoulders, living and teaching as if he had "all the answers." Then, he went to live and minister in a "community with very wounded people," where he realized that, "I came to see that I had lived most of my life as a tightrope artist trying to walk on a high, thin cable from one tower to the other, always waiting for the applause when I had not fallen off and broken my leg."[23]

Nouwen was right when he surmised that most leaders still desire to do it all and to do it highly successfully. The self-made man or woman is recognized in our society as an achiever, claiming stardom in a competitive society.[24] Yet, Jesus made it very clear that ministry and leadership is a community endeavor, and a mutually inclusive undertaking; it is "shepherding" together (see John 21:15–17). "We are called to proclaim the Gospel together, in community." We need each other to challenge one another, pray for one another, and help one another in purity and in mutual submission to God.[25]

Commitment

This section of Paul's letter to the Corinthians reveals true and heartfelt commitment on the part of a weary pastor toward his beloved congregation. Commitment is the desire and the drive to stay afloat when it feels like the ship is sinking. Leadership, as demonstrated by Paul, is commitment. Like Paul, we don't give up on people, on passions, and on ourselves. We keep going and keep growing. In saying the familiar marriage vows, two people pledge to be committed to one another "until death do us part." Many things can disrupt such vows, and it seems like society puts less and less stock in marital commitments, job commitments, and even friendship commitments. Keeping a marriage together, functioning with maximum love and support for one another, is not a simple task. In the same manner, the pastor-congregation

---

22. Nieuwhof, "5 Reasons."
23. Nouwen, *In the Name of Jesus*, 35–37.
24. Nouwen, *In the Name of Jesus*, 39.
25. Nouwen, *In the Name of Jesus*, 40–42.

relationship can have its trials and its triumphs. Is your church filled with deep affection, pride in one another, encouragement, and joy? Is your family filled with the same qualities? Are you truly committed to one another? Do we cause "worldly sorrow" in our churches and in our homes with selfish ambition, selfish pride, greed, and jealously?

A pastor makes a commitment to love and support the congregation while still trying to teach them and move them toward "perfecting holiness out of reverence for God" (2 Cor 7:1). Like a medical doctor, a minister attempts to heal all he or she serves: "a general practitioner, a father or mother confessor, spiritual obstetrician and faith specialist."[26] A minister helps guide people to Christ, make sense out of this life, resolve conflicts, teach faith to adults and children, help the dying pass from this life, and help the new babes be born into a better world. "Without love for Christ and people, ministry easily turns into uncontrolled ego gratification and a grasping need for prominence and control."[27]

True commitment is very much like both marriage and ministry: "Ideally, ministry and marriage complement and strengthen each other. We can celebrate the fact that marriage and family are microcosms of the Church and the Kingdom of God—a rich source for what is truly satisfying in life."[28]

People in a marriage relationship share both joys and sorrows; the relationship allows them and compels them to face all kinds of issues honestly—from personal spiritual and emotional issues, to family relations, parenting, forgiveness, finances, facing the aging process, even illnesses and death. These are the very same issues faced by people in the "family of God," that is, the church. Strong marriages are the backbone of a strong church. In both cases, we must hold each other's hands and warm each other's hearts. We must forget the past grievances and celebrate the present joy (7:8–16), praising God and the Lord Jesus Christ.

It is both a challenge and an honor to partner with God to affect human lives. Through it all, we have the assurance that God is always faithful to those he has called to serve him, regardless of human time zones, geography, or circumstances:

> Daniel slept peaceably in a den of lions.
> Joseph resisted a seductive woman.
> David overpowered a giant.

---

26. London and Wiseman, *Heart of a Great Pastor*, 116.
27. London and Wiseman, *Heart of a Great Pastor*, 117.
28. London and Wiseman, *Heart of a Great Pastor*, 139.

Elijah defied a heathen cult.
John the Baptist redirected his prominence to Jesus.
Paul sang stress away at midnight in jail.
Jesus modeled God's love on the middle of a cross.[29]

And lest we forget,

Deborah led Israel to victory over the Canaanites.
Ruth, the foreigner, bore the ancestor of King David.
Esther defied a king.
Hannah finally had a son and gave him to the Lord.
Mary survived pregnancy out of wedlock, and then watched her son
  die on that cross.
Mary Magdalene was the first person to experience the resurrected
  Jesus.

Building for the Future

Paul sincerely wanted his church to "brag on him" ("to boast") one day, "in the day of the Lord Jesus" (1:14) when all believers are gathered together at the return of Jesus. This is an incredible goal and vision for Christian leaders: that all the people we diligently serve and save and love will be with Jesus forever because of something we have said or done. Through trials, discouragement, hardships, attacks, and the lack of appreciation, ministers can accomplish great things through God's enabling. "Let us not become weary in doing good, for at the proper time we will reap a harvest if we do not give up" (Gal 6:9).

---

29. London and Wiseman, *Heart of a Great Pastor*, 47.

LISTEN to the Story

8:1And now, brothers and sisters, we want you to know about the grace that God has given the Macedonian churches. 2In the midst of a very severe trial, their overflowing joy and their extreme poverty welled up in rich generosity. 3For I testify that they gave as much as they were able, and even beyond their ability. Entirely on their own, 4they urgently pleaded with us for the privilege of sharing in this service to the Lord's people. 5And they exceeded our expectations: They gave themselves first of all to the Lord, and then by the will of God also to us. 6So we urged Titus, just as he had earlier made a beginning, to bring also to completion this act of grace on your part. 7But since you excel in everything—in faith, in speech, in knowledge, in complete earnestness and in the love we have kindled in you—see that you also excel in this grace of giving.

8I am not commanding you, but I want to test the sincerity of your love by comparing it with the earnestness of others. 9For you know the grace of our Lord Jesus Christ, that though he was rich, yet for your sake he became poor, so that you through his poverty might become rich.

10And here is my judgment about what is best for you in this matter. Last year you were the first not only to give but also to have the desire to do so. 11Now finish the work, so that your eager willingness to do it may be matched by your completion of it, according to your means. 12For if the willingness is there, the gift is acceptable according to what one has, not according to what one does not have.

13Our desire is not that others might be relieved while you are hard pressed, but that there might be equality. 14At the present time your plenty will supply what they need, so that in turn their plenty will supply what you need. The goal is equality, 15as it is written: "The one who gathered much did not have too much, and the one who gathered little did not have too little."

You have found a treasure: the treasure of God's love . . . So many attach-
ments keep pulling you away . . . Having found the treasure puts you on
a new quest for it. The spiritual life is a long and often arduous search for
what you already have found . . . The desire for God's unconditional love
is the fruit of having been touched by that love.
          —*Henri J. M. Nouwen*[1]

My friends, a husband and wife team, were very active in their church, supporting it by attendance, finances, and talents (teaching). Against their wishes,
the church decided to expand and move quite a distance from its original
location, thus entering into a time of fundraising, pledges, and future commitments. My friends suddenly left the church, with grief, saying that "all
they ever talked about was money." Sadly, this is not an unusual story; many
people, even those who love and serve God, generally do not like to be confronted with the "Sermon on the Amount." Another family who served in
a parachurch organization for years complained that they spent more time
trying to raise their financial support than doing actual ministry in the field.

Who wants to hear about money in the church, especially when there are
so many more important *spiritual* things to talk about? Paul does not let us
off the hook that easily; there are things we need to hear about commitments,
giving, and generosity.

From 7:16 to 8:1, we hear a shift in Paul's epistolary tone as well as in
his content, not unlike the ending of one song and the sudden beginning
of another on the same album by the same artist. Typically, two chapters
(8 and 9) of this letter are attached as a unit, quite separate from chapters 1–7
and 10–13. Scholars have even suggested that chapters 8 and 9 comprise a
completely different letter, edited and inserted at some point in time into the
remainder of the material that makes up this letter.

---

1. Nouwen, *Only Necessary Thing*, 29.

Yet, such separation is not necessary. Actually, 8:1 and 9:14–15 are like two parentheses, surrounding these two chapters and binding them together with the theme of "grace." Indeed, we could not understand 9:1–5 at all if we did not have chapter 8 as background.[2] In addition, there are definite connections between chapters 1–7 and chapters 8 and 9. We can hear the clear connections in the references to *people*—in particular, with reference to Paul's colleague Titus, and to the Macedonian believers. We hear Paul making various *petitions* to the church at Corinth in chapters 6 and 7, and his appeals seem to culminate with a very important petition in chapters 8 and 9. While we can hear these connections, we can also see that Paul did change his style to an expository tone while he modified his content. That is, as he shifted to a new topic that needed to be addressed, he altered his tone appropriately to give his full attention to the new concern. It seems best, then, that modern readers hear the two chapters in unison with the rest of the letter to gain a complete understanding of Paul's concerns. His appeal and his exhortation on generosity are complicated, and they can be difficult for us to untangle. Furthermore, we tend to take a verse or two out of context, which can lead to misinterpretation (i.e., 9:6, 7).

Craig Blomberg gives us a brief summation of Paul's pastoral attempts to instruct and to guide the Corinthian church. In our canonical letter 1 Corinthians, Paul addressed numerous problems within the church that plagued the young congregation. 2 Corinthians chapters 1 to 7 indicate that the church was making progress in terms of growth and obedience to the gospel message they had received from Paul, but there was some tension initiated from outside the church. Then, chapters 8 and 9 imply that there was still much work to be done within the congregation, especially in regard to their willingness to finish the relief project to which they had already committed. Finally, in chapters 10–13 Paul reached a boiling point. He fired a burning criticism against the rival missionaries who were disrupting the church and generally provoking mayhem in Paul's ministry in Corinth.[3] All three of these parts of 2 Corinthians are interrelated, as his adversaries were hindering the task of collecting the funds, and the people were questioning Paul's integrity and capabilities. Blomberg also notes that "money matters remain the single most serious obstacle to reconciliation between Paul and the Corinthians."[4]

---

2. Craig L. Blomberg, *Neither Poverty nor Riches* (Grand Rapids: Eerdmans, 1999), 191.
3. Blomberg, *Neither Poverty nor Riches*, 190.
4. Blomberg, *Neither Poverty nor Riches*, 193.

EXPLAIN the Story

The Jerusalem Project

As readers today, we must notice carefully the description of this collection/
service project: we can discern the *what*, the *why*, the *who,* and the *how* of
Paul's appeal to the Corinthians in two chapters of this letter. That is, what
is "The Jerusalem Project," so aptly named by Garland? [5] It was literally a
ministry that focused on supplying the material needs of the poor believers
in the church in Jerusalem. There is a remote reference to this project in Acts
19:21–22, where Paul explained his decision to go to Jerusalem, perhaps with
the funds and the delegates. Outside of this reference, Acts is relatively quiet
on the project; what we specifically know about this collection is found primarily in Paul's letters. All of chapters 8 and 9 are devoted to this undertaking,
and the foundational human mindset behind it. In addition to what we read
in 2 Corinthians, the background information on the collection is found in
1 Corinthians 16:1–4, Romans 15:25–32, and Galatians 2:9–10.[6]

It is interesting to note that the "collection" task is difficult to suitably
name. While it is still a money-raising project, it was far more than that to
Paul. As he explained it and defined it, he used various words and phrases
to identify the nature and purpose of the undertaking. He attributed great
theological significance to a project that is difficult to describe completely. To
begin, Paul used the same Greek word for this project that is employed for
"ministry" or "to minister." In numerous verses, this word is translated into
English as "service," thus, the collection project is a "service" offered to those
in need (see Rom 15:31, and 2 Cor 9:12–13). But it is not just any service
performed. Specifically, it is a "service [or ministry] to the Lord's people" in
Romans 15:25, 2 Corinthians 8:4 and 9:1; it is supplied in English as a "service
to the gospel" in 8:18). Paul called it a "collection" only in 1 Corinthians
16:1–2, where it appears that he was answering one of the Corinthians' questions concerning the matter. It is characterized as a "generous gift" twice in
2 Corinthians 9:5. The project was also regarded as a "grace," or an "act of
grace," or "this grace of giving" in 2 Corinthians 8:1, 6, 7, 9; 9:14.[7] That is,
"grace" appears to be the overall theme of these two chapters. Indeed, verses
8:1 and 9:14–15 are an *"inclusio"* featuring the "grace of God." Christian
giving, then, is a gift from a gracious God, who is the one who enables believers
to serve and bless one another.[8]

---

5. Garland, *2 Corinthians*, 364.

6. Furnish, *II Corinthians*, 409.

7. Furnish, *II Corinthians*, 411. See also Scot McKnight, "Collection for the Saints," *DPL* 143.

8. Blomberg, *Neither Poverty nor Riches*, 191.

Furthermore, Paul used the familiar Greek word *koinōnia* to explain the project in Romans 15:26 (translated there as a "contribution"), while in 2 Corinthians 8:4 it is translated "the sharing in this service" or "the fellowship of the ministry." In 2 Corinthians 9:13, Paul used both the word for "ministry" and the word for "fellowship" in the same verse. The latter word is most recognizable to believers today, as it describes Christian "sharing," "fellowship," or "partnership" (see Gal 2:9). In any translation, Paul created a vivid image of mutual, reciprocal care and concern among "partners" in Christ, both the Jews and the Gentiles, who were unified in an "expression of generosity" to those people in need. Paul declared that the project was an expression of love (2 Cor 8:8, 24), a demonstration of attention and affection for another community. Indeed, it was a lesson on focusing on other people less fortunate than themselves, teaching them "generosity in sharing with [those in Jerusalem] and with everyone else" (9:13). What may appear to be an ordinary fundraising effort takes on the significant meaning of a "ministry" and a "partnership" with other brothers and sisters in Christ. This immense project consumed much of Paul's time and emotions over a long period of time (perhaps AD 52–57). With it, he was seeking to break down all the barriers of Jew and Greek, male and female, as an act of "utter self-giving of Christ for others."[9] So why does Paul plead with the Corinthians to finish the project, and why should they respond with selfless generosity to his request?

The Relief Collection Project among the Gentiles

In view of the crisis in Jerusalem, there is little wonder *why* Paul devoted so much time and gentle persuasion concerning this project. The relief work promoted by Paul had its beginnings in a meeting when Paul was in Jerusalem. The leaders of the Jerusalem church ("the pillars") approved the ministry of Paul and Barnabas, pledging friendship with the men who were about to take on the Gentile world of the first century (Gal 2:7–10). As they agreed on the division of Christian evangelism and ministry, the leaders in Jerusalem asked Paul and Barnabas to "continue to remember the poor," which Paul was eager to do (Gal 2:10). Paul did not forget this pledge, and he wanted to give financial aid to the brothers and sisters in crisis in Jerusalem. "Little did the Jerusalem leaders know that their suggestion would become Paul's *obsession* for nearly two decades."[10]

Harris gives six plausible reasons for the depleted resources in the Jerusalem area: first, numerous Jewish Christ-followers may have migrated to Jerusalem

---

9. Furnish, *II Corinthians*, 412.
10. McKnight, "Collection for the Saints," 143 (his emphasis).

to find other believers. In the city, they would have experienced exclusion socially from other Jews, economic deprivation, and religious persecution (Acts 8:1). Second, the book of Acts mentions an "emergency" voluntary sharing of resources in the budding church, but these provisions were not endless and they may have run short (Acts 2:44–45 and 4:34–35).

Third, and very likely, was the wide-spread droughts and famines across the empire when the Roman Emperor Claudius was in power (AD 41–54; see Acts 11:28). No doubt these were "class famines," affecting the poor people much more so than the rich patrons of the city. Fourth, it was expensive to live in Jerusalem in the first century, just as living in any large, capital city of today. Essentials, such as water and raw materials, were scarce, and food prices became inflated. If a harvest failed because of drought, the prices of food could escalate as high as sixteenfold. Furthermore, there was a heavy house tax levied in the city. In fact, the fifth reason is that Jerusalem residents were subject to smothering taxation; both "civil" (Roman) and "religious" (Jewish temple) taxes were collected. In the time of Paul, these taxes could amount to thirty to forty percent of one's total income.

Finally, the Christian church in Jerusalem was the "mother church" in the region; perhaps there were those in the church who were among the first generation of the followers of Christ. Moreover, the city would draw itinerant teachers, numerous pilgrims, and travelers (Acts 6:1, 7; 1 Cor 9:4–6, 14) who wanted to visit Jerusalem to experience the "holy city" (Dan 9:24; Joel 3:17; Zech 8:3–8; Luke 9:30–31; Acts 1:8).[11]

Another plausible reason why Paul wanted to see the project completed is because it was very close to his heart. During his missionary journeys among the Gentiles, a gnawing issue that plagued Paul was the lack of repentance and faith in Christ by his fellow Jews. It was his desire that the conversion of the Gentiles to Christianity might just "provoke the nation of Israel to believe in the Messiah, for they would see in that act the fulfillment of the promise that the Gentiles would bring gifts to Zion (Isa 2:2–4; 60:6–7; Mic 4:13)."[12] Paul believed that the Gentile Christians owed the Jewish believers material blessings because the Jewish believers first gave spiritual blessings to the Gentile church (Rom 15:27).

Moreover, in this letter Paul was making a concerted effort to separate his ministry from the words and accusations of his opponents. His opponents, the "false apostles" (11:13), promoted wrong intentions, motivations, and prac-tices within the church, just as Paul pointed out in 2:17 and 4:1–6. So another

---

11. Harris, *Second Corinthians*, 88–89; see also McKnight, "Collection for the Saints," 144–45.
12. McKnight, "Collection for the Saints," 146.

reason why this project was so important to him was that Paul found it necessary to defend his authority, apostleship, and mission in opposition to the selfish, self-serving, greedy adversaries who had infiltrated the church. It is quite probable that his opponents were questioning Paul's authentic intentions and purposes for the collection of funds, especially since he did not ask to be paid by the congregation for his ministry work (see 7:2; 11:7–12).

Charity in the Roman Empire

In addition, it is important to give consideration to the attitudes toward material wealth among the Gentiles in the Roman Empire. Paul's proposal to give money to some Jewish people who lived far, far away certainly could have sounded rather strange to Roman ears. What propelled the Greek churches into relief work for people whom they had never met? Did they expect something in return? What did they really think about the whole concept of caring for the "poor"?

We can observe that Paul did not spend a lot of time in his letters addressing the proper use of human wealth, nor did he emphasize the social and ethnic differences concerning wealth in the Roman world. His teachings, for the most part, reflect standards and features of devout Judaism.[13] Scholars have observed that generosity with altruistic, selfless motives was very unusual in the classic Greek and Roman culture. Generally speaking, there was little concern toward the "poor" in the Gentile society, either in thought or in practice. There were, of course, no government programs or assistance for the less fortunate. The whole idea of charity was foreign to them, even to the point of absurdity. Whatever one's status, one just did not give money away expecting nothing in return: "In the vast majority of texts and documents relating to gifts in the classical world, it is quite clear that the giver's action is self-regarding, in the sense that he anticipates from the recipient of his gift some sort of return."[14]

It was far more common for wealthy benefactors to give gifts to civic officials, and they expected recognition and remuneration in return.[15] Little thought was given to how one spent or shared wealth with others: "The Greeks, in particular, were notorious, not least in the eyes of fellow Greeks, for their unreliability in handling money."[16]

Thus, while the Macedonians got on board with Paul's project with full commitment, perhaps the Corinthians were dragging their feet because of

---

13. McKnight, "Collection for the Saints," 144.
14. A. R. Hands, *Charities and Social Aid in Greece and Rome* (London: Thames and Hudson, 1968), 26.
15. Hands, *Charities and Social Aid in Greece and Rome*, 19.
16. Hands, *Charities and Social Aid in Greece and Rome*, 19.

their doubts and uncertainties about such an unusual project. Paul may have recognized the project was countercultural to the Greeks, and that it was only by the grace of God that the Corinthians were able to give voluntarily and unselfishly to the Jerusalem Project.

"The Poor" and the Macedonians (8:1–5)

There has been a fair amount of discussion concerning the true identity of "the poor" in Jerusalem, whether the believers there were materially or spiritually impoverished, or both. *Who* were they, really? Some scholars see a distinct "noneconomic connotation" in Paul's description of the saints in Jerusalem. The title "the poor" was used as a self-designation of the Jews, especially in the Qumran writings, indicating a community of the spiritually "poor" (see Matt 5:3; Luke 6:20). Yet, this may not be Paul's primary designation of the saints in Jerusalem, even though he was concerned about the "spiritual riches of salvation" in this passage. Certainly, if the Christian believers in Jerusalem were experiencing economic deprivation, physical hardships, and poverty, they needed material relief from such adversities. If even half of the above conditions were apparent in Paul's day, the need for outside financial help would be understandable.[17]

Beyond the identity of "the poor" in Jerusalem, and the generally self-serving Greeks, *who* were the people deeply involved in the collecting of funds for Paul's relief ministry?

First, we meet the Macedonians (believers in the northern part of Greece), who were eagerly contributing beyond their ability for the ones in Jerusalem (8:3; see Rom 15:26). They are pictured as an "ideal" church, pleasing Paul, and giving generously in spite of their own adversity and poverty (8:1–5). Perhaps the "severe trial" the church experienced (8:2) was "religious persecution leading to socio-economic hardship (Acts 17:1–15)."[18] We do know from 2:12–13 that Paul adjusted his travel schedule to make a journey from Asia Minor to the region of Macedonia. Christians here included the churches in Philippi, Thessalonica, and perhaps Berea.[19] In chapter 2, Paul traveled to Macedonia with disappointment and a heavy heart, and apparently things improved little after he arrived there. In 7:5, Paul wrote that he was "harassed" in Macedonia, and there he was physically exhausted and mentally apprehensive.

But Paul was comforted by God and by the arrival of his friend and colleague Titus, who encouraged Paul with good ministry reports (7:6). We can

---

17. T. E. Schmidt, "Riches and Poverty," *DPL* 827.
18. Blomberg, *Neither Poverty nor Riches*, 192.
19. Harris, *Second Corinthians*, 104.

also surmise that the severe famine affecting the entire Roman world was crippling areas like Macedonia. In view of this economic and social situation, the believers in Macedonia were experiencing acute poverty (8:2). Nevertheless, the Macedonians "gave themselves first of all to the Lord, and then by the will of God also to us" (8:5). Their foundation was in God, through Christ, not in their own capabilities or their cultural traditions, and they fully recognized Paul and his colleagues ("us") as authentic messengers of the gospel they had received. It was an opportunity to voluntarily share with others (8:4) and be a part of a much larger benevolent project. Paul was able to boast about the attitudes and generosity of the Macedonians in 8:1–5.

Role of Titus (8:6)

The second *who* in this passage is Titus. An important connection point between chapters 7 and 8 is the role of Titus in the story. While the Corinthian church had started the raising of relief funds, it had never completed the commitment of sending aid to their brothers and sisters in Christ in Jerusalem. Titus was assigned the difficult task of helping the Corinthians complete this collection task. In chapter 7, we hear about a significant meeting between Paul and Titus. As Paul's trusted, valued colleague in ministry, Titus brought Paul the good news he so much wanted to hear about the situation in the church at Corinth (7:6–7). Thankfully, Titus was welcomed warmly in Corinth; he was greatly encouraged in his work there and developed a deep affection for the believers (7:13–15). One important note we hear is that Titus was encouraged by the obedience of the church in Corinth (7:15), perhaps demonstrating their willingness to re-commit to the task of raising relief funds, the very task on Paul's mind in chapters 8 and 9.

Appeal to Corinthians (8:7–12)

Furthermore, Paul himself, the dedicated apostle and founder of the church at Corinth, was the primary *who,* the one sending a strong appeal to the church to complete this collection. Paul had attempted to defend his authority, his mission, and his character in chapters 1–7, and may have felt that the foundation had been laid with his readers to make his crucial request to finish the project. Like his Macedonian congregations, Paul was experiencing trials and afflictions, even to the point of life-threatening hardships (1:8; see 4:8–9; 6:4–10; 7:5). One of the major themes of this letter is how God comforts and redeems human affliction and adversity (1:3–7; 7:6). Paul's plethora of sufferings in ministry ("for Jesus' sake") brought "life" to his congregations (4:11–12). In fact, Paul's intense trials resulted in joy and happiness as the Gentiles received redemption and salvation (7:4, 9–10). Likewise, however ironic it may sound, in spite of their severe trial of acute poverty, the Macedonians felt overflowing joy and rich generosity (8:2).

Paul also tackled the tender subject of money tactfully. "Money is always a matter which is difficult to handle with graciousness, sensitiveness and dignity, but Paul does it deftly."[20] Most likely many pastors today would probably agree with that statement. Addressing any kind of topic that has to do with finances, raising funds, giving, and generosity can be intimidating to any Christian leader, in Paul's day and in ours. Yet in chapters 8 and 9, Paul is the quintessential caring, concerned pastor, sensitive to the plight of humanity while still demonstrating great wisdom concerning material wealth. Certainly, Paul was a theologian, but he was also a visionary planner and administrator who did not ignore the stark realities of human life. He complimented his church for what they had started and did not chastise them for what they had not finished (8:7). He handled the situation so wisely, as he delivered "theological pep-talks to those who had grown indifferent to the task, [while] delegating responsibilities and soothing ruffled feathers."[21]

We can consider the final *who* to be Paul's Corinthian readers. Paul's approach was not to condemn his readers but to praise them. The Corinthian believers excelled "in everything—in faith, in speech, in knowledge, in complete earnestness, and in the love we have kindled in you" (8:7; see 1 Cor 1:5–7). Therefore, Paul urged, "see that you also excel in this grace of giving!" (8:7). The Corinthians were richly blessed with material, spiritual, and intellectual gifts, not because of anything they deserved but as a result of the grace of God (8:1). Their participation in this service for others, then, was a reflection of God's unmerited benevolence toward them (8:8–9).

"Grace of Giving"

In his letters, Paul used the word "grace" 63 times, while it appears in the NT about 155 times altogether.[22] Obviously an important part of his theology, Paul regards grace as a gift from God, through Christ, and is granted, unearned, to Christ-followers. The gift of God's grace came through "one man, Jesus Christ, overflow[ing] to the many" (Rom 5:15). It is given so that "grace might reign through the righteousness to bring eternal life through Jesus Christ our Lord" (Rom 5:21). That is, believers are in a position of grace before God through Christ (1 Cor 1:4), and are reconciled to God by his grace, not by anything they did for themselves (2 Cor 5:18–21). Believers are no longer under the

---

20. Garland, *2 Corinthians*, 364.
21. Garland, *2 Corinthians*, 364.
22. Udo Schnelle, *Apostle Paul: His Life and Theology*, trans. M. Eugene Boring (Grand Rapids: Baker Academic, 2003), 482.

condemnation of the powers of sin and death (Rom 5:20–21) but live in the power of God's righteousness and grace (2 Cor 5:21–6:2).

Paul has made it clear to his readers that such grace is "for your benefit," so that "more and more people," will glorify God with thankful hearts (2 Cor 4:15). What God has done, through Christ, is to create a new time in which to live and a "new creation" (5:17) of human beings who are reconciled to himself through his own graciousness (5:18–19). Thus, people can acknowledge the grace of God, given to them as a gift, that places them in a new time—a time of grace. By his grace, they have a new position, a new status, and a whole new way of thinking (see commentary, 5:11–6:10).[23]

Like a pair of bookends, Paul opens and closes this letter with a reference to the "grace from God" in 1:2 and to "the grace of the Lord Jesus Christ" in 13:13 (see also, 1 Cor 1:3 and 16:23). The whole letter, therefore, is an expression of God's grace. It was by the grace of God that Paul was called to ministry and that he endured his numerous trials and hardships (1:9–10; 4:1; 6:4); thus, the very existence of Paul's apostleship and the existence of the church in Corinth were the results of the grace of God alone. The continuation of the church, despite its trials and errors, and the persistence of Paul as an apostle were only by the grace and power of God (3:4–6; 12:9). "It is not the goodwill of Caesar that graces and changes the lives of human beings but the gracious turning of God toward humanity in Jesus Christ."[24]

The Jerusalem Project, then, was to be a manifestation of God's grace in the lives of his people (8:1, 4, 6–7, 19; 9:8, 14–15). The numerous reoccurrences of the word "grace" in chapters 8 and 9 is more evidence of how Paul regarded the relief effort and how he wanted his church to respond to this appeal.[25] Before the Corinthians could give graciously, they needed to fully understand the grace of Christ, who, through his voluntary "poverty," granted spiritual "riches" or "gifts" to the community of believers (8:9). Rather than a warm feeling of sharing (or a human emotion), grace is an act of God that is unexpected and undeserved; simply expressed, grace is an expression of God's love for his people (Rom 5:8). So, in view of God's "overflowing" love and grace, the Corinthians were called to respond in an outpouring of the "grace of giving" (8:7). God filled them up with his grace and love, and they were to "pay it forward" with gifts and service and love for others.

Furthermore, Paul does not "command" them to give, but placed before them the "test" of the "sincerity of [their] love" (8:8). He "intended to verify"

---

23. Schnelle, *Apostle Paul*, 482–85.
24. Schnelle, *Apostle Paul*, 485.
25. Furnish, *II Corinthians*, 399.

or to "test" the congregation to see if their commitment, or their "earnestness," was still present.[26] That is, the relief gift was an examination of their own hearts. Paul intended the project to be a reflection of their love and devotion for Jesus. He reminded the readers who stood in the shadow of the cross of Jesus that they should remember his sacrifice, "who became poor for the Corinthians' sakes by generously giving up his rights as God to become human."[27] Jesus relinquished all his divine position, power, and privileges ("though he was rich"), humbled himself to become a man ("he became poor"), and voluntarily died a brutal death for the benefit of all humanity ("for your sakes"). By his sacrifice, human beings may become spiritually "rich," becoming a part of God's family (8:9) and inheriting the precious gift of eternal life (4:18; 5:1).

"How to" Instructions

But, *how* were they to do it? How were the Corinthians supposed to give generously, show the "sincerity of their love," and grace to the fellow believers in Jerusalem? It appears that these questions were posed to Paul from the congregation, and he necessarily had to respond in this letter. This kind of project was unfamiliar to the Corinthians, and the procedures, as well as the purpose, must have been unclear to them. The "grace of giving" was a totally new concept to the Gentile Corinthians, and they were uncertain as to how to collect the funds, how much should be given, and how it was to be transported to Jerusalem to those in need (8:10–12). Thus, Paul gave them plenty of advice.[28]

Paul's recommendations for the Corinthians began in 1 Corinthians 16:1–3. First, Paul told the Corinthians to "do what I told the Galatian churches to do." This implies that the Galatian churches as well as the Macedonian churches were involved in the relief gift. There is no direct reference to such instructions in our canonical letter of Galatians. But the book of Acts indicates that "Paul and his companions traveled throughout the region of Phrygia and Galatia" on Paul's second missionary journey before they visited Macedonia (Acts 16:1–10). This part of Paul's ministry, then, would have preceded his first visit to Corinth (Acts 18:1).[29] So, whatever they were (and he may be repeating them in 1 Cor 16:2–4), the Corinthians were to follow the same instructions for the project that Paul had already given to the Galatians and the Macedonians.

---

26. Furnish, *II Corinthians*, 404.

27. Barton et al., *1 and 2 Corinthians*, 389.

28. On the collection and other financial matters, see Verlyn D. Verbrugge, *Paul and Money: A Biblical and Theological Analysis of the Apostle's Teachings and Practices* (Grand Rapids: Zondervan, 2015).

29. Kierspel, *Charts on the Life, Letters and Theology of Paul*, 31.

Second, Paul suggested that on Sunday, "the first day of every week," every person should "set aside a sum of money in keeping with [his or her] income" (1 Cor 16:2). Each person was to reserve an amount of money that was appropriate, and then present it as a form of worship on Sunday, not unlike what we find in the Christian churches of today. In Corinth, this was a new day of worshiping together, and a new opportunity to give an offering toward the Lord's work as needed. The amount of money per person was not recommended, nor was an amount demanded (as the tithe is often construed). The key phrase in these instructions is to present money "in keeping with your income" (1 Cor 16:2). This is an amount to be set aside in reserve and given in proportion to a person's revenue. The readers were instructed not to give so much that they put their own economic situation in jeopardy (2 Cor 8:13), but to give generously as evidence of God's rich grace in their lives (8:9) and according to their ability to do so. It was a privilege to be able to participate with God and with other believers in the relief work, and Paul knew that apart from the grace of God, the whole project would be a failure.[30]

Paul's third piece of advice on *how* to do the project implies that the readers had lost Paul's instructions or had just decided to ignore them; regardless, they were not doing as they were told to do on Sundays. He instructs them to "finish the work" they had already started (8:10–12). They began the project with enthusiasm, being "first" to begin the relief work (8:10), but somehow they lost their momentum. Here we see an example of Paul's strategy as their pastor. Shrewdly, he appealed to the Corinthians' competitiveness to urge them into action (8:6–7). He implies that it would be shameful in the eyes of the other churches for the Corinthians *not* to complete their pledge (9:3–4). Thus, to complete the project with strength and enthusiasm would be a demonstration of the nature of the church, which excelled in everything (8:7).

Yet, Paul did not challenge them to meet or beat the amount of the Macedonians' gift; the Corinthians were only to give "according to [their] means" (8:11), which is the same as giving "according to what one has, not according to what he does not have" (8:12). Paul did not "command" the Corinthians to participate in the collection (8:8), but he gave strong, stern advice (8:10) to a church that had lost their initial focus. The challenge, then, was to reignite the fire of gracious giving and complete the project with the other churches in Macedonia and Galatia. "Like a coach in the locker room at halftime, Paul called the Corinthians to finish what they had begun. They had distinguished themselves as winners thus far, but the game wasn't over yet."[31]

---

30. Harris, *Second Corinthians*, 560.
31. Barton et al., *1 and 2 Corinthians*, 390.

Equality and Illustration (8:13–15)

Having clearly addressed the basic *what, why, who,* and *how* of the relief ministry, Paul then explained another less obvious purpose for the service: it was intended to create "equality" among the believers across the empire (8:13). Paul was not asking for a reversal of wealth and poverty—that the believers in Jerusalem would be made materially wealthy while the Corinthians were to embrace poverty.[32] That would become "unequal." So, the idea of "equality" used here implies a sense of "fair dealing," which was not unfamiliar to the Greeks.[33] Paul used a Greek word in this passage, and in only one other place, in Colossians 4:1. The word points to that which is "equitable" and "fair," not to a form of economic socialism, as some might suggest. Since the Corinthians had the resources to help their brothers and sisters in Christ, it was only "fair" that they should do so (8:14). The intent was an *impartiality* of aid (8:14), where there is an "equalization of economic burdens" among all believers. This goal of equity is achieved by "giving that which is proportionate to the resources available at any given time (vv. 11–12)."[34] Blomberg calls this "a graduated tithe: the more money one makes, the higher percentage he or she gives."[35]

Given the unusual nature of Paul's appeal for the Jerusalem Project, he may have thought that it was necessary to support his request from Scripture (8:15). Verse 15 is the fourth citation Paul has used in this letter, and there are only a total of five citations from the OT.[36] "As it is written . . ." is one of Paul's favorite introductory phrases, and the readers' signal that a citation follows. Here, Paul quoted Exodus 16:18; the story of the "manna and the quail" was used to illustrate how Christians are to share with one another whatever they possess. It was God who provided sustenance, the "manna" bread, for his wandering people. Some gathered much, some little, yet in the end, everyone had enough. There was an equal distribution of food; the excess of some served the deficiency of others. "God made certain that no one had more or less than their fair share."[37]

It was critical, therefore, for Paul to remind his Gentile readers of his urgent petition to be generous and charitable. Many scholars suggest that this portion of the letter focuses on the theme of generosity. Certainly, these two chapters address that topic, but the focus should rather be on God's grace to his people.

---

32. Blomberg, *Neither Poverty nor Riches,* 194.
33. Harris, *Second Corinthians,* 590.
34. Belleville, *2 Corinthians,* 592.
35. Blomberg, *Neither Poverty nor Riches,* 194.
36. Harris, *Second Corinthians,* 590. See 2 Cor 4:13; 6:2, 16–18; 9:9.
37. Belleville, *2 Corinthians,* 224.

God is gracious, so Christian believers can be generous. That is, the grace of God is poured out on all believers, and in turn, believers should pour out the "grace of giving" to one another (8:7). As we saw above, the emphasis should be placed on the unmatchable divine "grace," "service," and "blessing" that fills the hearts of those who follow Christ, in view of what he did for humanity (8:9). Believers should demonstrate a strong "eagerness" and "willingness" to share material wealth, however much they may possess, because of their heartfelt gratitude. There is an essential unity and partnership in the church, regardless of ethnicity or citizenship, and there is a demonstrated equity or "fairness" among the believers.

LIVE the Story

Faithful Giving Today

Thus, how do we translate the gift of God's "overflowing" love and grace into our giving and serving in the church today? If Paul called the Corinthians to respond to God's gracious giving in an outpouring of the "grace of giving" (8:7), what does that look like today? Like the ancient church, Christians today are filled with God's grace and love, so they are able to pour out gifts and service and love for others. In fact, generous giving is the "test" of the "sincerity of [our] love" (8:8).

Most of us think that we give God his share of our money when we drop a check in the offering plate on Sunday morning, or simply click the button that electronically sends money to the church of our choice. Yet,

> The Bible challenges that perspective by declaring that God owns everything (Ps 24:1). Everything we own and earn belongs to God! We have simply been entrusted with its use. God is just as concerned about the money we keep for ourselves as he is about the money we give away. Our check-books and credit card statements more accurately reflect our priorities than the money we put in the offering plate.[38]

Several principles concerning Christian giving can be deduced from 8:1–12, but perhaps the most helpful verse for readers today is 8:12. This is a compact but critical verse that promotes the concept of "proportional giving," which can be appropriated by Christians in our own culture. Harris gives us five clear principles from this chapter:

---

38. Connelly, *Wisdom from a Pastor's Heart*, 119–20.

1. It is the *motivation* behind the gift that is important. God knows the heart of the giver. Giving should be voluntary as an expression of gratitude for the grace of God.
2. The *acceptability* of a gift is not based on the amount given; it is based on a person's true eagerness and willingness to give. In contrast, God also knows if a person is giving reluctantly or begrudgingly (see 9:7).
3. Gifts are given in *proportion* to one's resources. This does not allow anyone to claim an exemption from the responsibility of giving. Even the most impoverished Macedonians gave as much as they could (8:2). Another example is the "poor widow" in Mark 12:41–44. God can multiply even the smallest gifts.
4. We should be *responsible* givers. We need to be *wise and discerning* about our gifts. I know my family receives requests for monetary support from literally hundreds of worthy causes: political, religious, and social. If we gave to every one of them, the funds would eventually run out. We must examine and evaluate to whom we give money, as we all know of some shady people and organizations that only want to satisfy their own greed. Nothing should be given without strong consideration by a consensus of family members, and (most important) seeking the Lord's will in prayer.
5. "If Paul had advocated the practice of tithing, this would have been the appropriate place for him to mention or defend it." Instead of advocating the OT Jewish obligation to tithe, Paul promoted "proportional giving." In reality, it would be easier for someone just to tell us exactly how much to give, like a tax, so we do not have to think about it. That way, we would not have to seek direction from the Lord or evaluate our own hearts. True charity and gracious generosity cannot be demanded or commanded.[39]

Even so, there are still questions to be considered and excuses we can find that complicate the matter of giving to the church. For example, I remember that our church featured a Christian "financial adviser" who supported the OT tithe and gave many practical suggestions as to how believers should handle their finances: income, expenses, savings, contributions, and retirement. Yet, odd questions arose from the large audience:

Are we supposed to give to the church from our gross income, or our adjusted net income?

---

39. Harris, *Second Corinthians*, 586–87.

If we give to other charitable organizations, does it count toward our
   required tithe?

We have had a lot of medical expenses; it makes it hard to still give
   to the church this year. Can we "catch up" on our commitment
   next year?

Must we give to the church on cash we receive from sources outside of
   our regular paycheck (like a garage sale)?

Can I give of my time and talents to the church instead of my money?

A portion of my taxes to the government go to welfare—does that
   count?

So, is the tithe the best answer for our response to God for his gracious
generosity, and is it supported by chapters 8 and 9 of this letter? Is the tithe
the best solution to the duty (or the joy!) of giving to the church?

The Tithe in the Old Testament and New Testament Giving

The concepts of financial giving and sharing of material wealth have their
roots in the OT. The OT "*tithe*" began in the agricultural culture of ancient
Israel. The Israelites presented gifts of the "firstfruits" (or the best) of the land
back to God in the form of a tithe (oil, fruit, livestock) because their prosperity came from the land God had given to them (Lev 27:26; Deut 26:1–4).
The tithe was commanded by God as part of the holy offerings and sacrificial
system (see Deut 12:7, 17; 26:12–15). Gifts brought in to the temple were
given to the temple priests, the Levites, as their portion of the inheritance of
the land (Num 18:21, 24). Outside of the commands of the OT law, Proverbs
gives us insight into human nature and the divine aims concerning the act of
sharing the wealth. That is, while God gave commands concerning the tithe
in the OT, they were to point the people to his divine intentions about riches
and poverty:

> One person gives freely, yet gains even more;
>   another withholds unduly, but comes to poverty. (Prov 11:24)

> A gift opens the way
>   and ushers the giver into the presence of the great. (Prov 18:16)

> Those who give to the poor will lack nothing,
>   but those who close their eyes to them receive many curses.
>   (Prov 28:27)

Perhaps the most familiar passage in the Old Testament concerning the tithe is in Malachi 3:8–12. Even today, this passage is used to instruct Christians about the tithe—to give ten percent of one's income to the church (or, to the "Lord's service," however that is interpreted). This passage has been used in scathing sermons to produce feelings of sufficient guilt because we have all "robbed God" and did not "bring the whole tithe into the storehouse" (Mal 3:9–10). On the other hand, the guilt comes with a "guarantee": if we tithe to the church, God will bless us and give us so many blessings we cannot count them all. This message, then, is not God-driven or God-honoring; it is self-driven. If we want to receive God's bountiful blessings, we have to give at least ten percent of what we earn. If we don't, we live in sin and disobedience, even "robbing" God of what is certainly already his. Out of fear, sometimes people give the whole tithe; but just as often, and even if they do, they do not see the excessive "pouring out" of material and financial blessings in their lives (Mal 3:10).

Nevertheless, with the advent of Christ and his atoning sacrificial death and resurrection, the Old Testament laws have been superseded. Is there a scriptural basis in the New Testament for continuing to follow the rule of the tithe? Andreas Köstenberger and David Croteau considered the Christian tithe in an in-depth study of three biblical passages in the New Testament that are often used to support the giving of the tithe: Matthew 23:23, Luke 18:9–14, and Hebrews 7:1–10. In summary, they concluded:

> If anyone were to prove the continuation of tithing based upon the NT, he must produce a passage that has this goal as its *primary purpose*. . . . Of the three passages that mention tithing in the NT, none can be appropriately used to argue for the continuation of tithing in the new covenant period . . . The fact remains, however, that despite the dubious exegetical grounds on which such an argument rests the continuation of tithing is often argued not on exegetical but on larger systematic theological grounds.[40]

The continuation of the tithe into the New Testament and the reward of God's blessings are often supported by Jesus's words in Luke 6:38: "Give, and it will be given to you. A good measure, pressed down, shaken together and running over, will be poured into your lap. For the measure you use, it will be measured to you."

---

40. Andreas J. Köstenberger and David A. Croteau, "'Will a Man Rob God?' (Malachi 3:8): A Study of Tithing in the Old and New Testaments," *Bulletin for Biblical Research* 16.1 (2006): 71, 76–77 (emphasis original).

Yet, the context of this verse implies that Jesus was *not* talking about financial prosperity. The preceding verse mentions judgment, condemnation, and forgiveness (Luke 6:37). These three critical aspects of human relationships are what Jesus is addressing. The more judgment and condemnation we give out, the more we get in return; the more we forgive one another, the more forgiveness we will receive.

Thus, nowhere in the New Testament are Christians commanded to tithe. Jesus went *beyond the tithe*, revealing the true human nature of generosity and a concern for other people. Generosity is not a law; it is an attitude. Jesus moved from legalism to the human heart (as in the "rich ruler" story, Luke 18:22–25). Harris is right—if Paul wanted to continue the demands of the tithes and offerings in Corinth, he could well have said so in these two chapters of 2 Corinthians, but he didn't. This may be an "argument from silence," but it is worth consideration. Paul's readers were Gentiles, who had never followed the OT cult system, and Paul did not want to burden the Gentiles with all the OT Jewish laws (see Gal 3:1–14; 2 Cor 3:7–18). In his view, salvation is through Jesus Christ alone and not through sacrifice; Christians are free from the bondage of the OT law: "[We] maintain that a person is justified by faith apart from the works of the law" (Rom 3:28; see Rom 3:19–31; Gal 3:26–4:7; 5:1–6; Jas 1:25). Therefore, the tithe is an obsolete OT law that is not commanded again in the NT, much like OT food laws and purification rites.[41]

If giving is the law in the OT, it is a *privilege* in the NT. There is a huge difference between giving out of obedience—begrudgingly—and giving out of one's heart and willingness so as to express a love of God who gives graciously to us (we will see more of this in 9:7–8)! In the Gospels Jesus cuts through the outer garment of human selfishness, excuses, and intentions and gets to the real heart of the matter. He never commands people to pay the tithe, only to "love one another" (John 15:12, 13, 17). Giving generously to other people is a manifestation of Jesus's love for us and of our love for other people, just as he commanded. It is more difficult, of course, to love others and give freely than it is to follow a set rule, give out of obligation, and ignore the results. Selfishly, we may hope that God pours out many material blessings on us, while we ignore all the heaps of spiritual blessings he has already given us. Jesus's words should not be the basis for "prosperity religion," where some speakers teach that God *guarantees* a grand return on our money if we give to the church. We give to God not for our own benefit but because he first gave so much to us. We would benefit by recalling other memorable, proverbial sayings by Jesus, including:

---

41. Köstenberger and Croteau, "'Will a Man Rob God?,'" 53.

Freely you have received; freely give. (Matt 10:8)

It is more blessed to give than to receive. (quoted by Paul in Acts 20:35)

Woe to you Pharisees, because you give God a tenth of your mint, rue and all other kinds of garden herbs, but you neglect justice and the love of God. You should have practiced the latter without leaving the former undone. (Luke 11:42)

This is how it will be with whoever stores up things for themselves but is not rich toward God. (Luke 12:21)

So if you have not been trustworthy in handling worldly wealth, who will trust you with true riches? (Luke 16:11)

No one can serve two masters. Either you will hate the one and love the other, or you will be devoted to the one and despise the other. You cannot serve both God and money. (Luke 16:13)

"Proportional Giving"

The concept of "proportional giving" (see Harris's comments above) can be applicable to Christians today. Simply stated, this is giving in proportion to what one has. That is, Paul suggests that we give out of a willing heart, and that we give according to our means (8:12). Further, Paul told his readers that they should "set aside a sum of money in keeping with [his or her] income" (1 Cor 16:2). The more blessings we have, the more we can give to others. We should give in proportion to what we have been given. But how do we decide what to give? Why is it so hard to give? Like a child trying to get out of doing house chores, we are constantly trying to think of excuses for why we do not graciously give to others.

Hindrances to Giving

In many families, it is hard enough to make ends meet without giving dollars away. The assortment of obstacles to generous giving are as numerous as the places where we could give our money. The other side of American culture is one of selfish material gain and selfish material accumulation; this is as prevalent in the church as it is in the rest of culture. We want what we want. Two things contribute to our inability to willingly share with other people: priorities and fear. First, when we have our priorities in the wrong place, God is the last one to receive any recognition or gratitude. Often even struggling families somehow find enough money to fund their priorities—new cars, new furniture, new electronics and technology. Giving to the church (and thus to God) is not a priority in America, and it hasn't been for years:

> In 1916, the year before we entered World War I, Protestants in the United States gave an average of 2.9% of their income to their churches. In 1933, the deepest point of the Great Depression, Protestants gave 3.3% of their income to their churches. By 1955, the percentage given to church was again a little more than 3%. However, since the 1960's, while American incomes have risen steadily, giving by church members has taken up a decreasing proportion of those incomes. Although the average American is over 200% richer than in 1933, the percentage of income given to churches has shrunk from 3.3% to 2.6% in 1989, a decrease of over 20% from the 1933 base.[42]

The second hindrance to generous giving is fear. We do not trust God to take care of us; we must take care of ourselves. Our sense of security may come from having a big, secure bank account, or a secure identity-theft system, a burglar-alarm system on our big homes, or a new car with all the airbags possible. If a person is raised in poverty, often there is a fight to accumulate and hold on to wealth for fear it could be lost forever. Jesus told another story of a "fool" who built the biggest barns and wanted to "take life easy." He intentionally stored up things for himself, but was not rich toward God (Luke 12:16–21). Furthermore, Jesus reminded his listeners not to "worry about your life," your food, or your clothing (Luke 12:22–34; Matt 6:25–33). God is concerned about the "birds of the air" and the "flowers of the field," so how much more so does he care about his children? "The pagans run after all these things, and your heavenly Father knows that you need them" (Matt 6:32), so we are not to live in fear regarding "these things." Instead, we are to "seek first his kingdom and his righteousness, and all these things will be given to you as well" (Matt 6:33). We are to care about other people just as much as we know God cares about us.

Finally, in 2 Corinthians, Paul set no "rules" for the Corinthians in terms of why or how much to give. He did not emphasize their personal fears or guilt, or their financial gain, but he insisted on their "overflowing joy" (8:2) in grateful, generous sharing with others. People are to give themselves "first of all to the Lord" (8:5) and then give materially "according to your means" (8:11; 9:7).

---

42. John Ronsvalle and Sylvia Ronsvalle, *The Poor Have Faces: Loving Your Neighbor in the 21st Century* (Grand Rapids: Baker, 1992), 39–40.

That is, our material gifts should be in response to God's unfathomable grace, should be proportional giving, and should be completely voluntary (8:3).

Christianity Is Expensive

Today we need to recognize that it takes a lot of money to do God's will on earth. We note all of the good, godly organizations that need financial support: pastors, missionaries, churches, schools, and hospitals, just to name a few. There is never an excuse that we cannot find a worthy organization to which we can contribute. However,

> . . . if most affluent Western Christians were to be honest about the extent of their surplus, they would give considerably higher than 10% to Christian causes. They would make sure that a substantial percentage of their giving went directly to individuals and organizations that offered holistic salvation of body and spirit to the desperately poor throughout the world.[43]

Always the concerned pastor, Paul approached the delicate subject of money with grace and fortitude. He repeatedly expressed approval of the congregation, expressing his confidence in them (7:4, 16), and pointed out the positive aspects of their behavior (7:5–15). They were the first to begin the relief-fund project, and Paul bragged about their eagerness to the other churches, thereby setting the whole project into motion across the region (9:1–2). However, the Corinthians had difficulties understanding the role and importance of materialism in their world, not unlike some believers today. They did not comprehend that a person's attitude about money is a gauge of Christian maturity. The importance of the relief fund was first and foremost a voluntary gift for the desperate believers in Jerusalem, but it was so much more than that. It was an outward expression of a recognized unity between the Jews and the Gentiles (at one time sworn enemies). It was expensive because Jesus died for everyone; the life and death and resurrection of Jesus was for all of humankind, not just a privileged few. It was the glue that bonded the Jewish Christians and the Gentile mission, of which Paul was such a part. In the church today, we must grow and blossom beyond our social, ethic, racial, gender, and economic differences, bound together as brothers and sisters in Christ, ready at any moment to share with another person who is in need.

---

43. Blomberg, *Neither Poverty nor Riches*, 198–99.

Human Generosity and God's Grace

Perhaps it may be time, then, to evaluate our hearts instead of our bank accounts. It is so easy to overlook God's gracious provisions, and we forget his daily material and spiritual gifts to us (Matt 6:24–33). We can begin with a shift in our attitudes. If everything belongs to God (Ps 24:1; 102:25) and is given to us by his grace, we should accept his gifts and use them responsibly, sharing with others and promoting his kingdom. In these chapters, Paul has given us guidelines for generous giving. First, everyone can be a generous giver, no matter what one's income may be. The Macedonians gave richly despite their "severe trials" and poverty (8:2). It is easy to delay our generosity, not unlike the Corinthians, and excuse ourselves by saying, "Someday, when we have enough, we'll give." Like that will ever happen! God knows better, and we cannot fool him. We are only managers of all that God has given to us, and sometimes we manage his gifts poorly. We should gladly give back to God our very best, and not just the puny leftovers. The problem is not insufficient funds; it is incorrect priorities and fear.

Second, generous giving is sacrificial. For many people today, this principle is uncomfortable. How do we balance planning for our future and for the future of our families while still sacrificially giving to the Lord today? Sometimes we have to trust God to provide material blessings, and it brings great joy when we see him do it.

Third, generous giving is completely voluntary ("entirely on their own") and not compulsory (8:3). God does not demand a "church tax" or salvation fees.

Therefore, the fourth principle follows, which is that our generosity should be an expression of our love for him and a commitment to God and to his people (8:5). The basis of all biblical giving is primary commitment to Christ and to his kingdom (8:5; see Luke 12:15, 14:33). Giving should be an act of worship.

Fifth, committed giving should be planned, promised, and fulfilled. The Corinthians had planned their giving the year before this letter, but they had not fulfilled their promise (8:10). Biblical giving is not impulsive or an afterthought, but a privilege to be considered prayerfully and wisely. Think about what happens when a monetary "pledge" is given to a missionary family, and then the giver decides to renege on that promise. The missionary, his or her family, the organization, and the entire mission are harmed by a broken promise.

Duty or Delight

Although all that we have is given to us by the grace of God, we can still recognize two ways in which we have lost sight of that grace. We know we have forgotten the grace of God when giving becomes a duty and not a delight. It is his unfathomable grace that motivates us to give generously in response to his gracious, undeserved gifts. If giving is a chore, and we give begrudgingly, it is time to rethink how much God has given and sacrificed for us. We are not under the law of the tithe, but if we do far less than our "proportional giving" simply out of selfishness, then true grace has escaped us. We give out of love for God, and we can never "out-give" his grace to us.

The Remarkable George Müller

A most unusual man and a great man of God, George Müller is said to have supported more than 2,000 orphans. It is also estimated that God generously gave Müller the English equivalent of about $7,200,000. Born in Kroppenstedt, Prussia (now Germany) in 1805, Müller has been called the "prince of intercessors." He opened the Ashley Down Orphanage in Bristol, England, which became known as the "miracle of the nineteenth century." Everything Müller did was rooted and watered in prayer. He searched the Scriptures daily for promises from God, and praying with his Bible open he trusted God to supply all his needs. He never made requests for financial support to people, nor did he ever go into debt. Yet he cared for 10,024 orphans in his lifetime and started 117 schools to provide Christian education for over 120,000 young students. He and his wife personally traveled across the globe as missionaries to preach and teach the Christian gospel.

Even so, over a 60-year time period, he gave away over 80 percent of what he received as personal support, helping to sustain foreign missionaries in China. Müller lived in a "spirit of prayer," and neither he, nor his family, nor any of the orphans lacked for any good thing: "How good the Lord has been to me!" As an example, this is a recorded story:

One morning the plates and cups and bowls on the table were empty. There was no food in the larder, and no money to buy food. The children were standing waiting for their morning meal when Müller said, "Children, you know we must be in time for school." Lifting his hand he said, "Dear Father, we thank Thee for what Thou art going to give us to eat." There was a knock on the door. The baker stood there, and said, "Mr. Müller, I couldn't sleep last night. Somehow I felt you didn't have bread for breakfast, and the Lord wanted me to send you some. So I got up at 2 a.m. and baked some fresh bread, and have brought it." Müller thanked the man. No sooner had this transpired when there was a second knock at the door. It was the milkman. He announced that his milk cart had broken down right in front of the Orphanage, and he would like to give the children his cans of fresh milk so he could empty his wagon and repair it.[44]

People like George Müller love God first, then are prudent, loving stewards of God's resources. This servant joyfully gave away all that he could, and he was such a blessing to a hungry, lonely world. In his words:

It is the Lord's order, that, in whatever way He is pleased to make us His stewards, whether as to temporal or spiritual things, if we are indeed acting as stewards and not as owners, He will make us stewards over more. Even in this life, and as to temporal things, the Lord is pleased to repay those, who act for Him as stewards, and who contribute to His work or to the poor, as He may be pleased to prosper them. But how much greater is the spiritual blessing we receive, both in this life and in the world to come, if constrained by the love of Christ, we act as God's stewards, respecting that, with which He is pleased to intrust us![45]

---

44. "George Müller," EAEC, www.eaec.org/faithhallfame/georgemuller.htm.
45. "Appendix N: The Wise Sayings of George Müller," www.biblebelievers.com/george_muller/g-m_appendix-n.html.

2 Corinthians 8:16–9:15

 ## LISTEN to the Story

¹⁶Thanks be to God, who put into the heart of Titus the same concern I have for you. ¹⁷For Titus not only welcomed our appeal, but he is coming to you with much enthusiasm and on his own initiative. ¹⁸And we are sending along with him the brother who is praised by all the churches for his service to the gospel. ¹⁹What is more, he was chosen by the churches to accompany us as we carry the offering, which we administer in order to honor the Lord himself and to show our eagerness to help. ²⁰We want to avoid any criticism of the way we administer this liberal gift. ²¹For we are taking pains to do what is right, not only in the eyes of the Lord but also in the eyes of man.

²²In addition, we are sending with them our brother who has often proved to us in many ways that he is zealous, and now even more so because of his great confidence in you. ²³As for Titus, he is my partner and co-worker among you; as for our brothers, they are representatives of the churches and an honor to Christ. ²⁴Therefore show these men the proof of your love and the reason for our pride in you, so that the churches can see it.

^{9:1}There is no need for me to write to you about this service to the Lord's people. ²For I know your eagerness to help, and I have been boasting about it to the Macedonians, telling them that since last year you in Achaia were ready to give; and your enthusiasm has stirred most of them to action. ³But I am sending the brothers in order that our boasting about you in this matter should not prove hollow, but that you may be ready, as I said you would be. ⁴For if any Macedonians come with me and find you unprepared, we—not to say anything about you—would be ashamed of having been so confident. ⁵So I thought it necessary to urge the brothers to visit you in advance and finish the arrangements for the generous gift you had promised. Then it will be ready as a generous gift, not as one grudgingly given.

⁶Remember this: Whoever sows sparingly will also reap sparingly, and whoever sows generously will also reap generously. ⁷Each of you should give what you have decided in your heart to give, not reluctantly or under compulsion, for God loves a cheerful giver. ⁸And God is able to bless you abundantly, so that in all things at all times, having all that you need, you will abound in every good work. ⁹As it is written:

"They have freely scattered their gifts to the poor;
their righteousness endures forever."

¹⁰Now he who supplies seed to the sower and bread for food will also supply and increase your store of seed and will enlarge the harvest of your righteousness. ¹¹You will be enriched in every way so that you can be generous on every occasion, and through us your generosity will result in thanksgiving to God.

¹²This service that you perform is not only supplying the needs of the Lord's people but is also overflowing in many expressions of thanks to God. ¹³Because of the service by which you have proved yourselves, others will praise God for the obedience that accompanies your confession of the gospel of Christ, and for your generosity in sharing with them and with everyone else. ¹⁴And in their prayers for you their hearts will go out to you, because of the surpassing grace God has given you. ¹⁵Thanks be to God for his indescribable gift!

Listening to the Text in the Story: Exodus 25:1–2; Deuteronomy 15:10; Psalm 1:6; 112:9; Proverbs 22:8–9; Isaiah 55:10; Romans 4:21; 11:23; 1 Corinthians 16:1; Galatians 6:7–9; Ephesians 3:20–21; Philippians 4:19.

Real training for service asks for a hard and often painful process of self-emptying. Training for service is not a training to become rich but to become voluntarily poor; not to fulfill ourselves but to empty ourselves. . . . To help, to serve, to care, to guide, to heal, these words were all used to express a reaching out toward our neighbor whereby we perceive life as a gift not to possess but to share.

—*Henri J. M. Nouwen*[1]

---

1. Henri J. M. Nouwen, *Reaching Out* (New York: Doubleday, 1966), 108–9.

As a teenager, our son went on a mission trip with his church youth group to El Salvador. It was a life-changing experience for him. He saw poverty in the country unlike anything he had seen in America. While his own friends were salivating over the newest forms of video games and digital technology, the children in San Salvador were laughing and playing kickball in the dirt and on cracked concrete streets. Our son was so surprised that, in the midst of their deprivation and hardships, "they were so happy!"

The "law of the harvest" (9:6) promises that a person will reap the same kind of fruit that he or she sows. On farms and in fields, the reality of this law is clear. The farmer plants corn kernels, and the ground yields more corn. Yet even the richest of soils must be faithfully tilled and plowed; abundant seeds must be planted, watered, and cultivated before the harvest can take place. This metaphor can be applied to the Christian church and to her leaders. Ministry is hard work. Often it is a 24/7 kind of job, frustrating, uncertain, and thankless. As Paul experienced in Corinth, there can be threatening factions within an organization that challenge and discredit the leadership, spread controversy, and wreak havoc. The "spiritual farmer" in Christian ministry can encounter barren, rocky fields, problems, troubles, persecutions, and obstacles in this life. Conversely, ministry can also be a joy, an adventure, and a huge blessing. There may not be a higher calling in this life than to plant the seeds of the Christian gospel; there may not be more satisfaction than harvesting a bumper crop of Christian believers.

Then again, the agricultural metaphor is not limited to Christian pastors and leaders. God has planted a seed of the gospel in everyone who has received his salvation. With continuous cultivation, fertilization, and lots of watering, the young Christian can grow into a mature, blossoming believer who blesses others and produces new and bountiful "fruit." As Christians, what we plant with our words, our attitudes, and our sacrifices will doubtless affect what we harvest around us. When a Christian sows in love, generally love is returned. In fact, the "law of the harvest" even applies to people who do not consider themselves to be a Christian. Often the behavior and actions of people do come back to haunt them. When immorality, selfishness, and evil are sown, too often the same is harvested.

Business organizations have successfully used a model of team building for decades. Employees are linked together on projects and are encouraged to think together, create together, and check one another for miscalculations and omissions. The same model is used in the church; as churches grow larger and church staffs become necessarily more sizable, lead pastors are finding that creating a team of employees strengthens the staff and distributes the work accordingly. In many ways Jesus set an example for us; he formed a "team" of twelve disciples who were commissioned to continue his ministry after he left the earth. In fact, one of the most important jobs of Christian leaders is to develop other leaders and empower the people around them. A strong leadership team in the church is so basic to the ecclesiastical structure that we ignore it at our own peril. Even small churches can enlist the talents of laypeople to team up with the paid staff to distribute the work and build closer relationships within the church.

Second Corinthians is far less known to today's readers than Paul's previous letter we call 1 Corinthians. Yet, in chapter 9 we can hear some verses that are not only familiar to today's audience, they are actually quoted by fathers and mothers and preachers in the pulpit. No doubt we have heard verses 6 and 7 before, and they are as relevant today as they were in the first century. We can hear it in a fitting, modern translation (MSG): "Remember: A stingy planter gets a stingy crop; a lavish planter gets a lavish crop. I want each of you to take plenty of time to think it over, and make up your own mind what you will give. That will protect you against sob stories and arm-twisting. God loves it when the giver delights in the giving."

EXPLAIN the Story

The "Advance Team" (8:16–9:5)

In the latter part of chapter 8, we see Paul's concern for his own integrity and his trust in other Christian leaders. He enlisted three volunteers to send to Corinth to complete the mission and explained why this "advance team" was necessary. In 8:16–24, Paul continued to give more details about *how* the relief work in Corinth would take place. In these verses, he is highly concerned about the responsibility of the collection of the funds and the qualifications of the people sent to help the church finish the project. It appears he took extra precautions to explain exactly who would carry the funds to Jerusalem and why they were qualified to do so. It is likely that Paul was intentionally removing himself from the organization of the project even before his opponents could accuse him of absconding with the funds personally (8:20). That is, Paul was planning ahead, knowing that there might be false allegations against him concerning his motives for the collection of funds from the church. Paul was a "vigorous defender of his own financial independence" (see 1 Cor 9:12b, 15, 18; 2 Cor 11:9–12), so he wanted to be above suspicion of "embezzlement with respect to the collection."[2] His integrity was at stake,

---

2. Harris, *Second Corinthians*, 605.

and Paul wanted to be sure that everything was done correctly to ensure that his credibility was unquestioned (8:21).

This passage brings to the readers' minds the earlier passage concerning "letters of recommendation," which, essentially, is exactly what Paul is doing in chapter 8 (see 3:1–2). He was introducing and highly recommending three men he intended to send to Corinth to collect and transport the relief funds. "Letters of recommendation" in the Roman world were sent before or with speakers and teachers and were used to cull out the imposters and the charlatans. This is why such a letter was unnecessary and inappropriate in the case of Paul, because the converted Christians in Corinth knew him well and knew he taught the apostolic truth. Paul sent his eminent recommendations of these men for three reasons: his first reason is personal. Paul was sending very qualified, committed, "zealous" men in whom Paul had complete confidence (8:16–24). The second reason is ecclesial, because the two delegates joining Titus were representatives from their own churches, probably in Macedonia. As such, they were duly appointed by their home churches to help accomplish the mission (8:23). Third, sending the two associates with Titus was christological; the task of these three men was not just to collect the money, but also to honor Christ in "service to his gospel" (8:23, 18, 19).[3]

Verse 8:16 opens the section with an exclamation, "Thanks be to God . . . !" While Paul's outburst of gratitude begins a new section, it also reflects back on the gracious God who supplies the needs of his children (8:15). This expression of gratitude is not unusual for Paul, who exclaimed his gratitude to God on three occasions in this letter; in fact, 8:16 and 9:15 form a bookend with the identical expression "Thanks be to God!" (see also 2:14). In 8:16, he was very grateful for God's involvement in the life of his colleague, Titus.

Titus was the clear leader of the delegation to Corinth.[4] It was he who volunteered to return to Corinth to see the project through to completion and who shared Paul's excitement and zeal for the project (8:16–17). This is remarkable, considering the fact that most people are not normally excited to be a part of a team of fundraisers in a church! Titus was a key player in the reconciliation process between Paul and the Corinthians, as we saw in chapter 7 (vv. 6–7; 13–17). Not only had he reorganized and reenergized the relief project that had been started the previous year, he also cemented an affectionate, trusting relationship with the Corinthians (7:13–15). It appears that, with Paul, he really did care about the people in Corinth (7:14–16) and not just the project (12:14). Further, Titus may have been Paul's number-one

3. Harris, *Second Corinthians*, 595–96.
4. Harris, *Second Corinthians*, 599.

associate, his "partner" and "co-worker" (8:23) who had suffered with and sustained Paul in the trenches of Christian ministry.

The second person on the team is an "unnamed Christian brother" who must have been well-known and highly respected across the region. He is "*the* brother who is praised by *all* the churches" and renowned for his faithfulness in ministry (8:18–21, my emphasis). This could mean that he was well-regarded in all the Macedonian churches (8:1), or in all the network of churches across the empire. Regardless, he was a man chosen by the churches to accompany the funds from Achaia to Jerusalem (8:19). Unfortunately, we do not know exactly who this man was or why Paul intentionally did not name him. Be that as it may, he had Paul's complete trust and confidence that he could do the job with integrity.

In view of possible opposition in the church, it was incredibly important to Paul that the collection be done correctly, without doubt, suspicion, or criticism (8:20). There were many reliable people involved in the collection process and the delivery of the money so that both God and the people could see the careful, correct handling of the money (an example for us today in our churches). Verse 8:21 restates in a positive manner the negative statement about criticism in verse 20; that is, Paul was very concerned about "doing what is right" not only in the eyes of God, but also in the eyes of all the people in all the churches involved in the project. In verse 21, it is possible that Paul may have been remembering Proverbs 3:4: "Then you will win favor and a good name in the sight of God and man." It is critical that all of God's work should be done in an honest and ethical manner before God and before other people.[5]

The third person of the delegation is also unnamed, but he is referred to simply as "our brother" (8:22). Again, this man was a chosen representative from the contributing churches who had proven his enthusiasm in participating in the mission. He may have been known to the Corinthians, as he had "great confidence" in them. Although Paul called him "our brother," he may not have been as well-known as the previous unnamed church delegate. He had two things in his favor: he had proved his worth to Paul in many ways, and he believed in the Corinthians and in their ability to complete the task at hand. Paul sincerely hoped that the Corinthians would not let them all down. Titus and the two other delegates were giving of their own time and risking their lives to carry their funds to help fulfill Paul's important appeal to aid "the poor" in Jerusalem, all to "honor the Lord himself" (8:19).

In 8:24 Paul summarizes his commendation of these three church representatives. Proud of these qualified men, Paul admonished the Corinthians to

---

welcome his associates with love, which would validate Paul's boasting about the Corinthians. Paul also complimented the church to urge them on to the finish line; their accomplishment would be an inspiration for all the churches to see.

Explanation of the "Advance Team"

Before the great evangelist Billy Graham would speak in a city auditorium or sports venue, his organization would send an "advance team" months in advance to the city to prepare the local churches, choirs, leaders, and lay volunteers for his engagement. It is not unusual for teams of qualified technicians, public relations people, and marketing strategists to do the groundwork in advance for large events or concerts. Likewise, Paul was committed to a third visit to Corinth, and he wanted to have everyone on board with his agenda when he got there. Thus, the "advance team" (9:5) of Paul's trusted colleagues was sent to do the groundwork for Paul's anticipated visit (8:16–9:5). Chapter 9, then, proceeds directly from chapter 8. While Paul's emphasis on completing the project may have been perceived as a bit excessive to the Corinthians, he was anxious to let them know that he had confidence that they could finish well, with "eagerness" (9:1). In spite of this, he continued on for the next paragraph (9:2–15) to do exactly what he said he really didn't need to do—that is, to speak about the eager willingness of generous giving. Yet, he gave his explanation in 9:5 for why he "thought it was necessary" to send his advance team, and to strongly advise them to use that "eagerness" (9:2) to accomplish their goal.

Here, Paul wrote about the collection process as both a "ministry to the saints" in Jerusalem (9:1), and a blessing to those in need (9:5). Such an important project necessitated additional help in Corinth. The reason why Paul sent his "advance team" in 8:16–24 was two-fold. It was not that he did not trust the Corinthians to complete their commitment with enthusiasm (9:1–2); it was first to validate Paul's "boasting" about the Corinthians in "this matter" (9:3). He was bragging on the congregation to inspire them to do as he requested with eagerness and enthusiasm (v. 2). Once again, Paul recounted his "boasting" about the Corinthians—the first time he boasted about them to Titus (7:14). He admitted to boasting about their enthusiasm to their neighbors, the Macedonians (9:2). Since he told the Macedonians how great the Corinthians were, how could the church renege on their commitment?

Second, Paul wanted the church to be ready when he arrived to pick up the gift and accompany the other representatives to Jerusalem (9:2). The team was sent ahead of Paul to motivate the congregation to be prepared so their gift would be ready to go (9:4). The team would finish the arrangements, and the generous gift would be ready when Paul arrived in Corinth. Titus's advance team would make certain that the preparation of the funds was complete when Paul arrived, and that it was done in an honorable manner.

Yet, verses 9:3–5 imply that the Corinthians were not yet ready to send their gifts to Jerusalem. It would be so embarrassing if key representatives arrived in Corinth and the relief fund gift was not ready as it was in Macedonia (9:4). Was Paul playing another competitive game, bragging on one church to get another church involved in the project? Harris helpfully notes that there is a distinction between their "readiness of desire or intention" and their "readiness of completion."[6] Initially, Titus had urged the Corinthians to begin the relief fund "last year" (8:10), and the congregation seemed eager and ready to proceed. They were willing to get involved, but they were delayed, as they had questions about *how* and *when* to do it (1 Cor 16:1). Yes, the Macedonians and the Corinthians did play off of one another, motivated each other, and spurred each other to complete the task.

Paul "urged the brothers" (the whole advance team) "to finish the arrangements" in 9:5, just as he had "urged" Titus in 8:6 to help complete the collection commitment. Certainly, with Titus and the aid of these qualified assistants, the church would respond with generous hearts and get ready for Paul's visit. Of course, Paul would then follow the advance team to Corinth as soon as he could, while still allowing some time for the church to collect a "generous gift" (9:5).

Not to be overlooked is the word "grudgingly" in 9:5. Other appropriate English words in this verse include "by compulsion" or "greediness." In sharp contrast to the eagerness, willingness, and enthusiasm Paul mentioned in 8:2–3,11, and 9:2, no one should give to the Lord unwillingly, resentfully, or with reluctance. More than just a monetary collection, the "gift" was to be a generous blessing from the hearts of the Corinthian believers to other believers in dire need (9:5). Thus, the Jerusalem church would understand the gift was voluntarily given by their Gentile brothers and sisters, thereby strengthening the relationships between the Jewish and the Gentile believers. It was to be a "love-gift" that would bless others and encourage the recipients to give thanks to God and to glorify him (see 9:12).[7] It is this contrast of heart attitudes that spurred Paul into writing the following section of the letter, 9:6–15.

The Effects of Generous Giving (9:6–15)

While most English translations begin 9:6 with the word "remember," directed at the Corinthians, literally this section begins with Paul's words, "I am saying

---

6. Harris, *Second Corinthians*, 620.
7. Harris, *Second Corinthians*, 628.

this . . ." or "This is what I mean . . . ," reflecting back to his words in 9:5.[8]
What he was declaring was that ultimately, in receiving such a "generous
gift," those believers in Jerusalem would honor God. Paul reinforced the idea
of genuine, generous giving, for it is God who provides the means by which
the Corinthians could be generous (9:6–10). The corollary idea is that eager,
willing generosity demonstrates the glory of God (9:11–15). In 9:6–15, then,
Paul concluded his appeal concerning the gift of blessing for the Jerusalem
believers. If 8:1–9:5 addressed the *what, who, why* and *how* of the Jerusalem
Project, then in 9:6–15 Paul broadened his appeal to all of humanity. While
most modern readers understand this section of chapter 9 to be about money
and human generosity, the real focus of these verses should be on the *effects* of
generous giving, which are a demonstration of God's grace (i.e., 9:8). "Generous giving" describes not just what the readers were able to share out of their
own material blessings, it is also an outpouring of God's undeserved, gracious
giving for which believers are thankful (9:12) and, in turn, share with others
unselfishly. Believers are to be merely a conduit of God's grace, through which
both his material and spiritual blessings are granted to his people.

The Law of the Harvest (9:6–11)
Verse 9:6 was likely a familiar proverbial saying. Perhaps he had an old Hebrew
saying in mind, found in Proverbs 22:8–9:

> Whoever sows injustice reaps calamity,
>   and the rod they wield in fury will be broken.
> The generous will themselves be blessed,
>   for they share their food with the poor.

The "harvest" principle of 2 Corinthians 9:6 is also found in Galatians
6:7–9, where Paul instructed the Galatians concerning the Holy Spirit and
that, indeed, they would "reap what they sow": "The one who sows to please
his sinful nature, from that nature will reap destruction; the one who sows to
please the Spirit, from the Spirit will reap eternal life. Let us not become weary
in doing good, for at the proper time we will reap a harvest if we do not give
up." A basic reality in the world of agriculture, a person "reaps" or "harvests"
according to his or her initial sowing. If I plant only a few scrawny little seeds,
I will not reap a bountiful harvest. If I plant corn kernels, I will not harvest
beets. Paul used this common metaphor to emphasize what we may call the
"law of return," or "what goes around, comes around."

---

8. Furnish, *II Corinthians*, 440. See 1 Cor 7:29; 15:50.

Furthermore, in terms of human relationships Luke 6:38 reminds us to "give, and it will be given to you. A good measure, pressed down, shaken together and running over, will be poured into your lap. For with the measure you use, it will be measured to you." An extension of the material metaphor, the "law of return" (as it pertains to judgment and forgiveness, for example) is not unlike the "law of the harvest": what we give *emotionally and spiritually* is what we get back. For example, during the grim days of World War II, and despite her own suffering, the minister Esther Ahn Kim asked God every moment of every day, "Who do you want me to love today?" And that love that she gave was returned to her many times over. "Even jailers and government officials noticed how Esther shone in a dark place."[9]

Thus, verse 9:7 implies that a person should give material blessings as a result of the correct heart attitude, not out of reluctance or compulsion, which is an expansion of 9:5b. Paul has articulated both the positive and the negative posture of the human heart: to give with sorrow or reluctance, or to give with a sense of joy and thanksgiving. This echoes Deuteronomy 15:10: "Give generously to them and do so without a grudging heart; then because of this the Lord your God will bless you in all your work and in everything you put your hand to."

In Exodus 25:1–2, the people are directed to give *voluntary* offerings to God for the ancient Tabernacle, according to one's "heart": "Tell the Israelites to bring me an offering. You are to receive the offering for me from everyone whose heart prompts them to give." Furthermore, only the person giving without resistance, without reluctance, can be a "cheerful giver" (2 Cor 9:7). The joy of giving to other people is an expression of the joy of receiving the grace and love of God. In fact, God freely gives special gifts of grace to believers to use in the church, so if one's gift is "to encourage, then give encouragement; if it is giving, then give generously" (Rom 12:8).

On the other hand, life does not always go according to our plans, even if a person is generously giving of their material blessings. Generous giving does not automatically guarantee a huge return on one's money any more than the "faithful tithe" will result in a guaranteed ten-fold return. Second Corinthians 9:8 explains the answer to this situation: the outcome of generous giving is up to God. This is an unusual verse, as the Greek word for "all" appears four times in one verse, while the word "every" appears once: all grace, all things, all times, and all that you need, in every good work. First and foremost, "God is able." We could just stop the verse right there and try to absorb the fact that

---

9. Francis Chan, *Forgotten God: Reversing Our Tragic Neglect of the Holy Spirit* (Colorado Springs, CO: David C. Cook, 2009), 98–99.

God has the power to do all things, no matter what our needs (see Rom 4:21; 11:23). While we are not able, God is; what we cannot do, God can. Second, in spite of "all" of our anxiety, God is quite able to provide "every benefit to you, and every good work, in every good way, having everything you need," through his abounding grace![10] For some people, financial security, a title, or a position in society is the result of "self-sufficiency," but the word Paul used in verse 8 ("having all that you need") is more like "complete sufficiency," which is found in Jesus Christ, not in one's own achievements.[11] Likewise, in his letter to the Philippians, Paul offered this promise: "And my God will meet all your needs according to the riches of his glory in Christ Jesus" (Phil 4:19).

Indeed, the apex of Paul's letter to the Ephesians is this prayer: "Now to him who is able to do immeasurably more than all we ask or imagine, according to his power that is at work within us, to him be glory in the church and in Christ Jesus throughout all generations, for ever and ever!" (Eph 3:20–21).

We know that God may not meet all our "greeds," but we have the confidence that he is able to meet all of our "needs," materially and otherwise, and that allows believers to be generous with what they have. Such promises given to the churches by Paul should have bolstered the believers' faith and hope, as they experienced God's amazing, "abounding grace."

Once again, Paul reinforces his words with an OT passage (see 2 Cor 8:15). In 9:9 he borrows from Psalm 112, which is a poetic comparison between godly, righteous people ("those who fear the Lord," v. 1) and "the wicked" (v. 10). The righteous people have wealth and riches and are gracious and compassionate, they are generous and lend freely, and "their hearts are steadfast, trusting in the LORD":

> They have freely scattered their gifts to the poor,
>   their righteousness endures forever;
>   their horn will be lifted high in honor. (Ps 112:9)

Thus, the godly, generous person will be held in high honor, and

> The LORD watches over the way of the righteous,
>   but the way of the wicked will perish. (Ps 1:6 NRSV)

All such promises in 2 Corinthians 9:6–9 are summarized in 9:10. It was God who provided the material means by which the Corinthians could

---

10. Furnish, *II Corinthians*, 441. Also, see Blomberg, *Neither Poverty nor Riches*, 196.
11. Furnish, *II Corinthians*, 442.

give generously; then, it was God who supplied the results of that giving, which is the "harvest of [their] righteousness" (9:10; see Isa 55:10). This is because they obediently, voluntarily, graciously gave in service to others. In fact, Paul assured his readers that they will be "made rich" *so that* they could be "generous" (2 Cor 9:11). Through the Corinthians, God was answering the prayers and supplying the needs of his people in Jerusalem (9:12). This leads to "overflowing in many expressions of thanks" to God (9:12) because he chose to use the Corinthian believers in this service. The brothers and sisters in Jerusalem are the harvest of the Corinthians' righteousness. Moreover, the thanks to God were not limited to the believers in Corinth and Jerusalem; praise was also from "unbelieving Jews in and around Jerusalem [who] will come to faith in Christ when they see how generously the Gentile Christians share with their Jewish brothers and sisters" (9:13).[12] The growing, expanding, enlarging "planting and harvesting" metaphor thus concludes with praise and thanksgiving, and with recognition of the "surpassing grace" that God gave to all his people (9:14).

Thus, generosity glorifies God. The principles set out by Paul in chapter 9 can apply to all people in all financial situations and in all times. Generous giving results in prayers of praise to God by both the givers and the recipients, thus uniting all the believers in common gratitude for God's grace (see 1:11 and 9:14). "It is giving instead of gaining, thanks instead of interest, confidence instead of credit, trust instead of security, community instead of market, spiritual worship instead of temple cult, charisma instead of property."[13]

The Indescribable Gift!

Seldom in his letters do we see Paul get so excited that he uses an exclamation point, but it has been inserted in our English translations in 9:15 because a sudden exclamatory phrase of thanksgiving concludes Paul's preceding thoughts (in contrast, see 2:14, where his exclamation of thankfulness opens a new section of his letter). The Greek word for "indescribable gift" occurs only here in the New Testament. It is surely a culmination point and the goal toward which Paul has been moving since the beginning of chapter 8. It is God's exceeding grace that enables the Corinthian church to be a part of this service of relief for the other believers (9:14). Such an "indescribable gift" as God's grace denotes "something that is beyond human description." Some have noted that this "gift" is the "miracle of Jew-Gentile unity," while other

---

12. Blomberg, *Neither Poverty nor Riches*, 197.

13. Dieter Georgi, *Remembering the Poor: The History of Paul's Collection for Jerusalem* (Nashville: Abingdon, 1992), 154–58, cited in Blomberg, *Neither Poverty nor Riches*, 198.

scholars note that it is the gift of his own Son, Jesus Christ, selflessly given to all believers. Because of verse 14, we can deduce that the "gift" is "the surpassing grace God has given you," which concludes the theme of grace found in both chapters 8 and 9. The effect, then, is that all true Christian giving from the heart is a human response of gratitude for God's gracious gifts, which are beyond human comprehension.

What Happened?

The story of the Jerusalem Project does not have a definite ending in the New Testament; neither the letters of Paul nor the account in Acts completely satisfies our desire to know what happened in Jerusalem. Romans 15:25–28 reveals the most about the results of the relief fund story. It is easy to understand that after all his work and worry, Paul wanted to personally present the funds to the believers in Jerusalem. His "service of the saints" was the treasured gift, representing the unified concern of the churches in "Macedonia and Achaia" (which included Corinth). Paul related that the Gentile churches were "pleased" to offer contributions to the relief fund, since all the Christians, regardless of ethnicity, were united in the sharing in the "spiritual blessings" that began with the Jewish believers (15:27). No doubt the gift needed some interpretation and explanation from Paul to be sure that the Jerusalem believers understood the love and care being sent in the form of material blessings.

However, some scholars doubt that the relief funds accomplished what Paul had in mind. Paul was aware that controversy could ensue regarding the collection effort and gift delivery. He asked the Romans to pray for him (15:30), that his presence and the gift would be well received in Jerusalem (15:31). Certainly, he wanted nothing more than to see an excellent response from the church in Corinth, and no doubt many people gladly participated in the Jerusalem Project. But when Paul wrote to the Roman church about his future plans, we do not see the optimism about the Jerusalem Project that we see in 2 Corinthians 8–9. After Paul delivered the gift, he gave no indication that the funds radically changed the circumstances of the poor in the city. Relations remained strained between the Jewish and the Gentile Christians, and of course the conversion of Israel to Christianity did not take place (see Rom 9–11).[14]

Furthermore, there is no explicit mention of the relief gift or of the church representatives who accompanied Paul to Jerusalem in Acts 21:10–30. In the Acts record, we see strife and turmoil in the city. It appears that the believers in Jerusalem greeted him "warmly," received his good reports, and perhaps accepted the relief gift (Acts 21:17–19; cf. 24:17). In the end, he was right to

---

14. McKnight, "Collection for the Saints," 146.

fear the Jewish unbelievers in the city who brought charges against Paul that eventually led to a beating and to his arrest (Acts 21:27–36).[15]

Finally, the last four chapters of 2 Corinthians reveal a frustrated Paul, even before he visited Corinth for a third time (9:4; 12:14; 13:1–3). That anticipated visit should have been a joyous occasion when Paul and his colleagues collected the relief funds and victoriously started off for Jerusalem with the precious gift. But it may not have turned out to be as successful as Paul had anticipated. The "false apostles" exposed by Paul had invaded the church and were increasingly influential within the congregation. These rival missionaries disrupted the church, demeaned Paul's authority, and may have sabotaged the relief project to some extent (11:13–15). We can only speculate about the final outcome of the project. What a bittersweet ending to such an ardent attempt by the tenacious apostle to help the needy, unite the churches, and demonstrate God's love and concern for all his people.

LIVE the Story

> Money is the most overrated commodity on today's market of values.
> It can buy a house, but it cannot make a home.
> It can pay for medicine, but it cannot purchase health.
> It can acquire things, but things do not satisfy the soul.
> —James McGraw[16]

For people in the Western world, it is easy to ignore or discount the obvious poverty and want across the globe. A book called *The Poor have Faces: Loving Your Neighbor in the 21st Century* by John and Sylvia Ronsvalle opened my eyes; it awakened me to incredible statistics concerning poverty and wealth and the American way of life. Their data is rather dated now, reflecting statistics from the late twentieth century. However, if we project this data into the twenty-first century, we can surmise that any updated statistics would still reflect tremendous need:

Worldwide, 38,000 children, ages five years and younger, die each day from preventable poverty conditions. Between 1700 and 1987, there have been 471 wars in which 101,550,000 people were killed. In the past ten years alone, at least 136,000,000 children have died from preventable

---

15. Furnish, *II Corinthians*, 453.
16. Connelly, *Wisdom from a Pastor's Heart*, 120.

poverty conditions—more children in ten years than all the people in all the wars in 287 years. For every one child who dies in poverty, six more will live on, permanently damaged by the deprivations they have faced. For example, each day 500 children become permanently blind from a lack of Vitamin A.[17]

Reading these and similar statistics can lead to anger, despair and frustration on the part of some committed Christ-believers. What is to be done about a worsening poverty situation, all over the world? What can we do?

For the Ronsvalles, the answer is found in one of the most striking verses in this passage, 2 Corinthians 9:8: "And God is able to bless you abundantly, so that in all things at all times, having all that you need, you will abound in every good work." This verse is an important promise to us today that is often overlooked. *God has provided us with all we need* (locally and globally), and in our *abundance*, it is possible for us to "abound in every good work" for the kingdom. Can we do this? Can Americans give abundantly to the good work of abating poverty in the world? If we can, why don't we? Again, the Ronsvalles give us startling statistics about how Americans spent their money at the close of the twentieth century:

- $3.5 billion was spent on cut flowers
- $8 billion was spent on pets
- $2 billion was spent on the lawn industry
- $350 million was spent on microwave popcorn
- $2.9 billion worth of quarters were spent on video games
- $2.6 billion worth of quarters were spent on pinball machines
- $2.7 billion was spent on skin care
- $2 billion was spent on golf equipment
- $2.5 billion was spent on chewing gum
- $5 billion was spent on new pools and accessories
- $29 billion was spent on diets and diet-related products
- $12 billion was spent on candy
- $44 billion was spent on soft drinks
- $1.5 billion was spent in the fingernail industry, including nail art

In contrast, in 1987 American Protestant agencies received $1.73 billion for overseas ministries.[18] That means that if we add up the money expended as

---

17. Ronsvalle and Ronsvalle, *Poor Have Faces*, 35–36.
18. Ronsvalle and Ronsvalle, *Poor Have Faces*, 42, 53–54.

above, for a total of $118 billion dollars, .01 percent of that total was donated to overseas ministries. This is just one example of the gap between intentional "self-spending" and purposeful "God-spending."

Yet, there is good news! Think about what could be accomplished if people cut back only a few percentage points of what we spend on these types of items. It would be a small sacrifice for a large need. The West could meet the most essential human needs around the world: clean water, sanitation, mother and infant care, basic education, immunizations, and efforts for long-term developments that are affordable. These funds could overcome many of the poverty conditions that continue to exist.[19] It is doable.

We live in a world of "covetousness," which is self-interest, self-centeredness, and self-promotion. In our day, just as in Paul's, the principles of selfless, generous giving are more appealing to those who are threatened by economic conditions:

Paul's gospel held a special place for those whose burdens were usually neglected by ancient configurations of power throughout the Mediterranean basin—that is, the economically poor. No wonder "faith working practically through love" is the only thing that matters to Paul; it encapsulates the gospel in a nutshell.[20]

What remains, then, is the idea that "Christlike burden-bearing is the antithesis of competitive covetousness."[21] Contrary to this world of self, the community, the church, the "new creatures" in Christ must demonstrate the "obedience that accompanies your confession of the gospel of Christ" (9:13) by their sharing and generosity that can change the ethos around them.

The Evening News

The statistics about world hunger are so horrifying that we try to forget the numbers. Hunger is not just across the globe; it is right in our urban and suburban neighborhoods. Thousands of victims are children, who may get only one meal a day thanks to a free lunch program at their schools. But what happens during summer breaks from school? Just around the corner from large, affluent homes are homes where families must decide whether to heat their home or feed their children. And homelessness—people, families, have had to resort to sleeping under viaducts or on the streets of our cities. Even if

19. Ronsvalle and Ronsvalle, *Poor Have Faces*, 45.
20. Bruce W. Longenecker, "Faith, Works and Worship," in *The Apostle Paul and the Christian Life* (Grand Rapids: Baker, 2016), 54.
21. Longenecker, "Faith, Works and Worship," 55.

they are taking up space on sidewalks or camped on church steps, they are displaced, forgotten, and ignored. What we decide to do about it, how we support worthy causes, and how much of our time and resources we choose to give "is of such great importance that we are not just saving the world, we are saving our own souls."[22]

Furthermore, after the big, catchy headlines in the news, we see small stories of ordinary, everyday people trying to survive from day to day. Some stories are private aches and pains, losses, and emptiness; a small clip may be about human heroism or sacrifice. We may be acquainted with people who fight inner battles, who are lost, lonely, in despair, and struggling with great demons in their minds. What does it mean to be a Christian amid such chaos? What can I do? Jesus said,

> Woe to you who are rich,
> for you have already received your comfort.
> Woe to you who are well fed now,
> for you will go hungry.
> Woe to you who laugh now,
> for you will mourn and weep. (Luke 6:24–25)

Woe to us if we forget them when we turn out the lights at night.[23] For Paul, the gracious giving of the Father and the selfless giving of the Son are the foundation of self-giving Christians.

Simplicity

Second Corinthians 8 and 9 may be even more relevant today than in Paul's day. Perhaps in our day there is a greater need to enter into a simpler life and into a common community (like the church) that cares about others. In his book *The Radical Disciple*, John Stott writes that "[one] characteristic of radical disciples, especially in relation to the whole question of money and possessions, is simplicity."[24] If, indeed, Christians are new creatures in Christ (5:17) and if God can make all grace abound to you so that we can "abound in every good work" to others (9:8), then how is that reflected in a new way of life or a new lifestyle? Stott and other concerned leaders studied "simple living" in terms of evangelism, relief, and justice in the world. Their conclusions concerning wealth and poverty are fitting for us today:

---

22. Frederick Buechner, *Secrets in the Dark: A Life of Sermons* (New York: HarperCollins, 2006), 245–46.

23. Buechner, *Secrets in the Dark*, 249–50.

24. John Stott, *The Radical Disciple* (Downers Grove, IL: InterVarsity Press, 2010), 60.

We affirm that involuntary poverty is an offense against the goodness of God. It is related in the Bible to powerlessness, for the poor cannot protect themselves. God's call to rulers is to use their power to defend the poor, not to exploit them. The church must stand with God and the poor against injustice, suffer with them, and call on rulers to fulfill their God-appointed role. We believe that Jesus still calls some people (perhaps even us) to follow him in a life-style of total, voluntary poverty. He calls all his followers to an inner freedom from the seduction of riches . . . and to sacrificial generosity (1 Tim 6:18). Indeed, the motivation and model for Christian generosity are nothing less than the example of Jesus Christ himself, who, though rich, became poor that through his poverty we might become rich (2 Cor 8:9).[25]

Further, Stott made a commitment to simply take care of God's creation, a world so abundantly given to us and meant to be shared for the benefit of all people. Some people suffer in poverty because others misuse the resources given to all of us, such as clean water and air and fertile soil. We are stewards of the earth, and believers today must take an active role in changing the literal and figurative landscape of our society. If each person cared and did his or her part, we could literally change the world. Also, we can *pray*—pray for peace and justice and a shift of power in our world. We may need to make a personal commitment to a simpler lifestyle or enter into the struggle for a more Christlike culture in a more active manner. We can be good stewards of our possessions and be aware of the great needs around us. We must be willing to sacrifice and to suffer, just as Paul suffered for his faith. And "the call to a responsible life-style must not be divorced from the call to responsible witness." The truth and authenticity of the Christian story is questioned when we contradict it with lives of fear, greed, and selfishness. "When Christians care for each other and for the deprived, Jesus Christ becomes more visibly attractive."[26]

In summation, Paul was telling believers that *we are blessed so that we can be a blessing to others*. I am blessed so that I can bless you; by blessing you, I am blessed. We can seek opportunities to bless other people with God's richest blessings—not just with material things, but also with simple kind words, thoughtful deeds, encouragement, sincere care, and concern. Priceless.

---

25. Stott, *Radical Disciple*, 72–73.
26. Stott, *Radical Disciple*, 78–81.

LISTEN to the Story

¹⁰:¹By the humility and gentleness of Christ, I appeal to you—I, Paul, who am "timid" when face to face with you, but "bold" toward you when away! ²I beg you that when I come I may not have to be as bold as I expect to be toward some people who think that we live by the standards of this world. ³For though we live in the world, we do not wage war as the world does. ⁴The weapons we fight with are not the weapons of the world. On the contrary, they have divine power to demolish strongholds. ⁵We demolish arguments and every pretension that sets itself up against the knowledge of God, and we take captive every thought to make it obedient to Christ. ⁶And we will be ready to punish every act of disobedience, once your obedience is complete.

⁷You are judging by appearances. If anyone is confident that they belong to Christ, they should consider again that we belong to Christ just as much as they do. ⁸So even if I boast somewhat freely about the authority the Lord gave us for building you up rather than tearing you down, I will not be ashamed of it. ⁹I do not want to seem to be trying to frighten you with my letters. ¹⁰For some say, "His letters are weighty and forceful, but in person he is unimpressive and his speaking amounts to nothing." ¹¹Such people should realize that what we are in our letters when we are absent, we will be in our actions when we are present.

¹²We do not dare to classify or compare ourselves with some who commend themselves. When they measure themselves by themselves and compare themselves with themselves, they are not wise. ¹³We, however, will not boast beyond proper limits, but will confine our boasting to the sphere of service God himself has assigned to us, a sphere that also includes you. ¹⁴We are not going too far in our boasting, as would be the case if we had not come to you, for we did get as far as you with the gospel of Christ. ¹⁵Neither do we go beyond our limits by boasting of work done by others. Our hope is that, as your faith continues to grow, our sphere of activity among you will greatly expand, ¹⁶so that we can preach the gospel

in the regions beyond you. For we do not want to boast about work already done in someone else's territory. [17]But, "Let the one who boasts boast in the Lord." [18]For it is not the one who commends himself who is approved, but the one whom the Lord commends.

Listening to the Text in the Story: 1 Samuel 17:47; 2 Chronicles 20:15; Psalm 50:16–22; 103:8–17; Proverbs 11:2–5; 21:22; Isaiah 2:4; 1 Corinthians 4:14, 18–21; 9:1–2; 15:3–8; Galatians 1:15–16; 2:7–10.

Wisdom is better than strength . . .

> The quiet words of the wise are more to be heeded
> than the shouts of a ruler of fools.
> Wisdom is better than weapons of war,
> but one sinner destroys much good.
> —*Ecclesiastes 9:16–18*

It was time to look for a new automobile; we really needed a new car. With that in mind, I watched cars on the street, studied them on the highway, examined them in parking lots, shopped on the Internet, and pretty much made up my mind about which one I wanted to buy. All the advertisements on the television, the statistics on the web, and the words of the salesperson at the dealership were glowing. Everything looked good, and we were confident in our choice. We were ready to seriously consider one model until a mechanic who attended our church put a halt on our aspirations. He told us about documented mechanical issues, gas mileage issues, and the problems he had seen with this particular model. We changed our minds in a flash. This was not the car for us. It is amazing how just a little news—pertinent revealed truth—can completely change one's mode of thinking.

Scholars have struggled for decades to account for the obvious shift in content and tone from chapter 9 to chapter 10. How do we explain the definite cloud that settles over the remainder of this letter, especially in view of the affectionate, confident, joyful Paul we see in 7:2–4, 7:13–16, and even 9:15. What happened?

Linda Belleville writes that the existence of chapters 10–13 may be

> the most challenging critical issue that the interpreter of 2 Corinthians faces. It is impossible to read Paul's stern words in 10:1–2 after the conciliatory

tone of the previous chapters and the diplomatic and restrained argumentation of chapters 1–7 (not to mention the appeal for funds in chapters 8–9) and not wonder what is going on.[1]

Murray Harris observed, "After the warmhearted appeals of chs. 8 and 9, the change of tone in 10:1–2 to vigorous and sustained self-defense, self-assertion, and polemic comes as 'a bolt from the blue.'"[2]

On the one hand, scholars have proposed as many as nine explanations for this remarkably distinct interruption in the text. It is odd that there is no definite Hellenistic epistle closure at the end of chapter 9, although it does sound like Paul is "reintroducing" himself in 10:1, with his name, typical of an opening of an epistle. It is not unusual to find scholars like Victor Furnish who suggest that these chapters are a new letter, apart from chapters 1–9, composed because Paul learned that "certain rival apostles are succeeding in their attempt to demean and discredit" him within the congregation.[3]

On the other hand, "there is no manuscript evidence to support the notion" that the first seven or nine chapters circulated without the latter four chapters (see the Introduction).[4] Garland supports the integrity of the letter, demonstrating its unity through the repetition of vocabulary, themes, and topics. The concept of "confidence," for example, is repeated in 1:15; 3:4; 7:16; and 10:2. The theme of "commendation" is woven throughout the letter, in 3:1; 4:2; 5:12; 6:4; 10:12, 18; and 12:11. We can observe that the "painful visit" of 2:1 is exactly what Paul wanted to avoid in his "upcoming visit" to Corinth (9:4), which must necessarily be given more emphasis in the latter chapters. Preparation for his third visit is outlined in 10:1–11, and his warning about his visit punctuates 12:14 and 13:1–10. Moreover, the theme of Paul's defense of his own character and ministry in the church at Corinth builds from 2:14 through chapter 7, then crescendos in the last four chapters with great force.[5]

Thus, we have rejected the theory that chapters 10–13 were written as a completely separate letter from the first nine chapters and delivered at a later time.[6] Harris contends that the first nine chapters were written by Paul in stages over an unknown period of time, and after he had written these chapters, "he received distressing news of further problems at Corinth that prompted him to write chs. 10–13 and then send all thirteen chapters as a

1. Belleville, *2 Corinthians*, 30.
2. Harris, *Second Corinthians*, 661.
3. Furnish, *II Corinthians*, 454.
4. Belleville, *2 Corinthians*, 32.
5. Garland, *2 Corinthians*, 419–20.
6. Belleville, *2 Corinthians*, 32. See also, Harris, *Second Corinthians*, 661.

single letter."[7] We can be certain about neither the content of such news nor who delivered it to Paul. Yet, we can guess that the intrusive rival missionaries who were demeaning and discrediting Paul (see Introduction) were increasing their threats in the church, while the congregation appeared to be more and more open to their deceptive and destructive teachings. The last four chapters were Paul's response to the intensifying, damaging behavior of his opponents.

In agreement, Belleville sees a "gap" of time that passed between the "dictation" of chapters 1–9 and 10–13, especially if we contend that enough time passed in the interim for someone (perhaps trusted Titus?) to inform Paul of crushing news regarding expanding and deepening threats in the church against Paul's authority and apostleship.[8] If we listen to chapter 10 very carefully, we can hear Paul's pointed answers to false accusations to his discredit, as well as his growing impatience with those who were contesting his ministry and his very person. As a result of the slander and deception, the susceptible church was falling prey to the ravages of false teachings and allegations; they were declining in their commitments and loyalties, and Paul was very concerned (see 12:20–21). Garland suggests that the change of tone in chapters 10–13 is an intentional "rhetorical strategy" to lend great emotional impact, used by Paul to persuade his readers to alter their attitudes and behavior. The "conciliatory posture" that we see in the first nine chapters changes to a "combatant one."[9]

What cannot be argued is the fact that in chapters 10–13, Paul was ardently defending his own character and his calling as God's authorized apostle and teacher to the Gentiles. These four chapters are the third division of the letter, revealing a progressive disintegration of the relationship between Paul and the Corinthians, and an increasing threat to the stability of the church. We know from 1 Corinthians that splits and factions were a serious issue within the congregation, in spite of Paul's attempts to unite the people (1 Cor 1:10; 3:1–5). Such conditions were fertile ground for rival missionaries to deepen the divisions and the distrust for Paul.

In view of the influence of these troublemakers, in the first seven chapters (the first division) Paul attempted to give a full understanding of his life and his ministry (2 Cor 1:13–14) and to protect his apostolic calling and character among the Corinthians. After securing this groundwork, Paul then made a number of appeals to his readers in chapter 6, while encouraging them in chapter 7. Perhaps many people in the congregation were being persuaded to accept

---

7. Harris, *Second Corinthians*, 661.
8. Belleville, *2 Corinthians*, 33.
9. Garland, *2 Corinthians*, 417–20.

and receive Paul and his colleagues, despite strong opposition. His requests culminated with the significant plea to finish the relief project in chapters 8–9 (the second division). He shared the details of this very important request in the eighth chapter, emphasizing the *what*, the *why*, the *who*, and the *how* such a "service" should be accomplished (see commentary, 8:1–15). Then, it appears that Paul broadened his appeals and explanations about human generosity in general in chapter 9. Verse 9:6 is a universal axiom that is not limited by time or culture. He worked up to the climax of the first nine chapters of this letter, which is expressed in 9:15: overcome with gratitude for everything that had happened, Paul exclaimed, "Thanks be to God for his indescribable gift" of overwhelming grace!

Theme: Power and Weakness

While most modern scholarship has focused on chapters 10–13 with respect to Paul's apostleship defense, Dustin Ellington has added a new dimension to these chapters. He contends that while the defense of Paul's ministry is very much apparent, modern readers should not miss the fact that Paul was using his self-description and personal examples in these chapters for the purpose of correcting and instructing the Corinthians (i.e., 11:16, 21b). Paul was speaking of himself not to enhance his own reputation; before God, his primary concern was to strengthen his "dear friends" in Corinth (12:19).

His purpose in the last four chapters was to share his own experiences of ministry with the readers, intentionally teaching them that power and weakness are intrinsically connected in the Christian life and in leadership—his and theirs. That is, foundationally, Christian believers participate in the life and death of Christ (as they are "in Christ," 2:17) through Christ's power and suffering. The congregation at Corinth had misunderstood Jesus's divine power and weakness in contrast to that of the arrogant human rulers of the Roman Empire. So, it was necessary for Paul to set the standard for Christian leadership and be the example of true power and weakness in such a way that his readers would have a criterion for evaluating not only their own lives, but also the lives and leadership of those in the church who so clearly opposed Paul's thinking and teachings.[10]

Theme: "Verbal Crucifixion" of Paul

We can listen to another side of the story, overhearing the people in the Corinthian congregation instead of hearing the apostle who was sent to them.

---

10. Dustin W. Ellington, "Not Applicable to Believers? The Aims and Basis of Paul's 'I' in 2 Corinthians 10–13," *JBL* 131.2 (2012): 325–40.

His adversaries who had infiltrated the church were set against Paul, and they created disorder and division among the believers. The specific issues they held against Paul are revealed in chapters 10–13 in this letter. His opponents focused on criticizing the very core of Paul's being, on his God-given gifts, as well as his speech and personal appearance. They questioned Paul's financial integrity, his authority, and his calling as a true apostle. The compounding accusations against Paul created an opportunity for him to express his real and true emotions to the church, much more so than in the previous nine chapters. Further, their abuse gave Paul the occasion to defend himself and his ministry, and to request the proper responses to their accusations from his readers.[11]

In chapter 10, Paul was accused of timidity, of living by different standards, of not belonging to Christ, of frightening them in his letters while he was unimpressive in person, and of going beyond his limits in his career and in his boasting. Oddly enough, Paul was accused of boasting too much, and at other times, he did not boast enough (10:8, 13–15). He could not win for losing. More accusations are outlined in chapter 11: he was inferior to the "super apostles," untrained in speech, and lacking in knowledge. They alleged that he did not truly love the people. He was weak because he did not enslave, exploit, or take advantage of the congregation. He "foolishly" dared to boast about himself and his labor of love in Corinth.

But the indictments continued; in chapter 12, Paul was blamed for making a fool of himself. He repeats again that he was not inferior to those he called the "super-apostles," as he demonstrated his authority through the "required" signs and wonders that authenticated his apostleship. He was not trying to reap a harvest of funds from his readers; in fact, he would have financially given whatever was necessary to further the gospel message with them. They may have charged him with being a burden on the church and may have claimed that he was a shrewd and cunning man who tricked them into following his message.

Finally, in chapter 13 Paul was dismayed that his opponents demanded more evidence and proof that Christ was speaking through him. Through the power of God, Paul could rebuke his enemies with grace and dignity while he subtly turned back the accusations onto them. Ultimately, it was Paul's intention that all these indictments and rebuttals were reckoned to strengthen and encourage the congregation and to raise them up, not primarily to bolster his own reputation.[12]

---

11. McKnight, *Pastor Paul*, 133.
12. McKnight, *Pastor Paul*, 132–33.

Literary Tools

This letter contains a variety of beautiful literary imagery employed by Paul to paint pictures with words for his readers. A familiar example is the "triumphal procession" image in 2:14, with all the sights and smells that accompany such a Roman display of power and victory. Chapters 10–13 display Paul's literary genius at its best; in these chapters we see rhetorical devices, familiar imagery, and clever use of irony to illicit a response from his readers and to teach them lessons. Chapter 10 opens with another familiar Roman image, that of warfare, then chapters 10–13 are rife with literary devices. In addition to wordplay, mock humility, and strategic repetition, Paul abundantly used metaphors (i.e., 10:4–5; 11:2, 7–11, 13; 12:14), hyperbole (12:7), parallelism (i.e., 11:17–18, 22–23, 29–30), an oxymoron (a contradiction, 12:10), and meiosis (a belittling of one thing to magnify another, 11:1, 16, 21; 12:11).

Perhaps more than anywhere else in Paul's letters, we hear his use of irony and sarcasm. Irony, by definition, is a figure of speech where a thought is expressed in a manner that uses its complete opposite. For example, Paul ironically must speak "like a fool" in his own defense, when in reality, it was his opponents who were the real "fools" (11:1, 16, 21). Instances of irony in these chapters include 11:8, 16–17, 19–21; 12:5, 11 and 13.[13] It also appears that Paul even created new words, such as his term for the "super-apostles" in 11:5, and the "false apostles" in 11:13.

These numerous rhetorical devices and figures of speech barely mask Paul's frustration and irritation with his enemies' slander and accusations, as well as with his readers, who were being charmed and deceived. The true state of affairs in Corinth was so concerning to Paul that he had to use a literary boldness to get past the surface of things (10:7) and awaken his readers to their erroneous misconceptions and fallacious teachings in their midst. Meanwhile, in these chapters Paul remained the quintessential encourager and teacher, attempting to build up the believers in the authentic gospel faith (10:8; 13:10).

EXPLAIN the Story

If the first nine chapters are a defense of Paul's authority as a Jewish Christian missionary to a Greco-Roman Gentile region, then chapter 10 begins the implementation of that God-given authority. With his defense, Paul inherently taught, instructed, and corrected his readers as to the proper way to be a Christ-follower. He increased his "boasting" in the final chapters, because

---

13. Kierspel, *Charts on the Life, Letters and Theology of Paul,* 89–90.

the Corinthians had "misplaced confidence" in human strength, oration, and knowledge. Instead of "boasting in the Lord" alone (10:17), the "false" leaders boasted in their human talents and abilities, comparing themselves only to one another (10:12).[14] Furthermore, numerous modern scholars have noted a major theme that runs throughout this letter, and that is the *visits* of Paul to Corinth. He was at this point an "absentee pastor" (13:10), but Paul had visited Corinth on two previous occasions: his first visit was his founding visit when he established the church (see Introduction); his second visit was less than successful, as he himself called it a "painful visit" (2:1). While the first nine chapters were concerned about Paul's *past* experiences with the Corinthians, the last four chapters of this letter were in anticipation of his *future* third visit with this church (9:4–5; 12:14; 13:1).

We note that from 9:15 to 10:1 Paul suddenly shifted gears after his closing appeal concerning the Jerusalem Project. Even as Titus and his colleagues prepared to travel back to Corinth to collect the aid for the relief project (8:16–24), it is possible that Paul's opponents may have been accusing Paul and his worthy colleagues of "exploiting" the church by organizing the relief fund for the poor. In reality, they suggested, Paul was lining his own pockets with the funds (12:17–18). Despite some very good signs within the congregation (i.e., 7:5–9:15), these "deceitful workers" (11:13) in the church were not backing down in their false teachings and allegations. These opponents were "boasting in the flesh" of their own accomplishments and spirituality, as well as in eloquence of speech and rhetoric. They demeaned Paul as a weak and ineffective leader and were corrupting the church.

These intruders were not only "poaching" on Paul's missionary field (10:15–16) but were "seducing" the Corinthians not unlike the way Satan deceived Eve (11:2–3).[15] It was horrifying to realize that the congregation was allowing counterfeit "apostles" to pollute the congregation with their "boastfulness," false authority, and their self-interest. Their deception and attacks had to be halted in order to save the church from ruin, and so Paul prepared it for his third visit (10:2).

The War of Words (10:1–6)

To change metaphors (so typical of Paul!), we can see that the gauntlet was thrown down. Let the battle begin! Let the boasting begin! With more boldness and firmness (in contrast to their accusations of "weakness"), Paul entered a fierce battle to combat the groundless allegations leveled against him.

---

14. Ellington, "Not Applicable to Believers?," 329.
15. Garland, *2 Corinthians*, 424.

Rather than being defensive, even as we see in chapters 1–7, Paul took the offensive, not only to save his own authority but also to teach his people and secure the very survival of the church. In doing so, verses 10:1–6 introduce his refutation of his opponents' attacks and his anticipated third (and future) visit to Corinth.

He began gently with another "appeal" to the Corinthians (10:1), which he does not really complete until verse 6. Conversely, the intervening verses (vv. 2–5) are an image of warfare and victory employed by Paul to characterize his apostleship. It was an honest appeal urging the believers to return to Paul's gospel and completely obey Christ (10:5–6). The supremacy of Christ and his work on the cross seemed to be lost in the arrogant words and behavior of the intrusive "false apostles." His readers may have forgotten Paul's initial introduction to his mission and the proper Christian gospel message taught by Paul himself—one on which he staked his life:

> When I came to you, I did not come with eloquence or human wisdom as I proclaimed to you the testimony about God. *For I resolved to know nothing while I was with you except Jesus Christ and him crucified.* I came to you in weakness and great fear and trembling. My message and my preaching were not with wise and persuasive words, but with a demonstration of the Spirit's power, so that your faith might not rest on human wisdom but on God's power. (1 Cor 2:1–5, emphasis added)

Christ was the center of everything Paul said and did. If a believer is "in Christ," then that person is a "new creature," and that usually means a great deal of change in manner and lifestyle. N. T. Wright points out that the "larger world of Pauline mission" was the formation of a "new creation" (2 Cor 5:17):

> His work, founding communities loyal to Jesus and learning to think messianically, was designed to produce signs of new creation in the middle of the old world . . . In 2 Corinthians 10 [:4–5] his mission envisages both confrontation and cooperation. . . . The world is full of folly but also of good and useful things—good and useful if they can be liberated from the enslaving thought-forms and life-ways of the pagan world and brought into the new-creation world of the gospel.[16]

Acceptance of the gospel of Christ can and did disrupt the world as they knew it. For example, the concept of the "ideal" leader was a person of human

---

16. Wright, *Paul Debate,* 96.

strength, power, and authority, not a weak, indecisive, timid individual. These human standards were unacceptable to Paul (10:2). Therefore, in this letter he was resolved to make Christ the central message of his preaching, to allow the Holy Spirit to make his words effective in the congregation, and to correct faulty teaching. The appeal he made in 10:1 reflects the character of Christ and of Paul's basic message. The integrity of the appeal rested in the "gentleness and kindness of Christ"—the one who suffered and died for them (see 5:14)— and not in anyone else. That is, complete obedience to Christ is even more important than Paul's own reputation; this will be repeated and concluded in 12:14–13:10.[17]

The military imagery in 10:3–6 is suitable for the war of words that follows all the way through to the end of the letter. Paul was prepared for warfare. He ramped up his defense in the last four chapters, doing battle against the strongholds of his opponents and their deceptions. Paul identified himself with the qualities of Christ (10:1a), and he knew that in the end Jesus and his apostle would be the victors. That is, the "divine power" becomes an irresistible force against the fortress of thoughts erected against the knowledge of God (10:4–5).[18] Furthermore, he wanted the congregation to be obedient to the lordship of Christ. There was a sense of urgency in the appeal, as Paul was preparing the congregation for his next visit.[19] Like a concerned parent, he was saying to his "children," "You need to shape up, be obedient, and do it now, because I'm coming!" Should that be accomplished, his next visit with the church would not be a "painful" one (2:1).

However, Paul got sidetracked. The appeal was presented, but why should the people conform to his request? He then had to counter the allegations thrown at him by his rivals in order to answer that question. With malicious intent, they implied that he presented two different sides of his personality: "Paul the bold and Paul the timid."[20] His rivals alleged that, removed from the people geographically, Paul presented a strict authority in his letters; but in person, he was weak and indecisive (10:1–18). They accused him of being an amateur speaker who rejected their friendship (11:5–6, 7–11), and of having little spiritual experience (12:1–10).

Ironically, Paul then made a "strong" appeal to the readers through "the meekness and gentleness of Christ" (10:1). He set up this antithesis between strength and weakness as an echo of the words of his opponents, such as "timid." No doubt his opponents who wished to discredit him set up their

---

17. Furnish, *II Corinthians*, 459, 461.
18. Ellington, "Not Applicable to Believers?," 329.
19. Furnish, *II Corinthians*, 460–61.
20. Harris, *Second Corinthians*, 664.

own antithesis of accusation: that Paul was "bold" from a distance (by letter), but "timid" in person ("face-to-face," 10:1). Typical of Paul, he used their absurd charges to highlight the unfounded accusations brought against him. The sharp imagery of positive and negative will influence the remainder of Paul's instructions and vindication (i.e., his "weakness" and "boasting," 11:30; the "fool" and the "wise," 10:12; 11:1; 12:10). It was his desire that the readers fully understand who he was (see 1:14) and why his claims to apostolic authority were valid in spite of the opponents' indictments.

By worldly standards, both in the time of the Roman Empire and in our own time, the idea of a person being "meek," "weak," and "gentle" is far from desirable or admirable. The two concepts of meekness and gentleness (10:1) work together in what is considered a *hendiadys*, where two ideas are so linked that they act as one concept; often the second concept "qualifies" the first element.[21] Meekness denotes a humble and gentle attitude that is "the quality of not being overly impressed by a sense of one's self-importance; gentleness and humility."[22] In a similar sense, "gentleness" implies patience or "constant forbearance; clemency, graciousness, tolerance, indulgence," such as the gracious forbearance of God.[23] Paul realized that his character as an apostle was rooted in the character of his Lord. In demonstrating their trust in God, and in spite of opposition and disparagement, both Jesus and the apostle Paul are quintessential examples of these two words taken together.

Unfortunately, the word "timid" was a familiar Roman pejorative term, used by his rivals to create an image of a low social status. It was used of a person who was in a deprived position, "being servile in manner, of no account," miserable, and hopeless. In particular, this quality would make a person "lose face" in the Greco-Roman culture, and was certainly a judgment cast on Paul by his opponents.[24] The opposite of "timidity" is "boldness," and Paul insisted that his self-assuredness, confidence, and strength came from the Lord, not from the judgment of other people; this is a concept that is repeated throughout the letter (i.e., 1:12; 3:4, 5; 5:6–10).

The Corinthians had an ill-conceived notion of "strength" and "confidence" from a human viewpoint; but, Paul's "boldness" or confidence in 10:2 was an expression of his own confidence in the Lord, and not in himself. His rivals evaluated Paul as being subservient, cowardly, and not self-assured enough in his person-to-person communications (10:1–2). In the Corinthian culture, "boldness" was especially associated with one's speaking, or oratory

---

21. Harris, *Second Corinthians*, 668. See Furnish, *II Corinthians*, 455.
22. BDAG 861.
23. BDAG 371.
24. BDAG 989.

talents (see comments on 3:12). Separated by time and space, Paul's threats appeared to be empty, and his letters lacked real force. And yet, the appeal that Paul made to the church in 10:1 was spoken with the true humility and selflessness of Christ himself. Paul entreated his readers to turn away from the demeaning rebels in the church, fully understand and embrace Paul, and live by the standards of Christ instead of the standards of the world.

To fully understand this paradox of "meekness and boldness," we can recall the life of Jesus on earth and remember his words found in Matthew's Gospel. Jesus said of himself, "Take my yoke upon you and learn from me, for I am *gentle and humble in heart*, and you will find rest for your souls" (11:29, emphasis mine).

Clearly, there is a sense of Jesus's gentle expression and a lack of retaliation despite great adversity during his passion and crucifixion (1 Pet 2:21–23). In terms of "gentleness," Paul wrote a very memorable passage to the Galatians, "But the fruit of the Spirit is love, joy, peace, patience, kindness, goodness, faithfulness, *gentleness*, self-control" (Gal 5:22–23 NASB). To the Philippians, Paul wrote, "Let your *gentleness* be evident to all. The Lord is near. Do not be anxious about anything . . ." (Phil 4:5–6a). And he reminded the Colossians that they were "God's chosen people": "Holy and dearly loved, clothe yourselves with compassion, kindness, humility, *gentleness* and patience. Bear with each other and forgive one another if any of you have a grievance against someone" (Col 3:12–13).

Yet, for the Corinthian believers, gentleness was not a virtue. Instead, they had the spurious assurance in the power of faulty human leaders. Their confidence should have rested in God, through Christ, and in his appointed apostle. Admittedly weak in himself, Paul was strong in his faith in the Lord—as this whole letter explains (2 Cor 3:4–5; 12:5). Assured of that strength, Paul was certain that the critics who were trying to discredit him in Corinth could expect to feel the force of his divinely given authority with the gentleness and humility modeled by Christ.

Waging War God's Way (10:2–6)

Verses 10:2–4 employ repetitions that are often overlooked in our English translations. We see the phrase "live by the standards of this world" or "in the world," or "of the world." But in Greek, Paul used different words to create phrases that translate "in the flesh," "according to the flesh" or "of the flesh" in these verses. These phrases contrast the "divine power" in verse 4. That is, in the original language, verses 3 through 6 are all one sentence, with the repetitions, and are therefore one long, compact Pauline thought:[25] "For though we walk *in the flesh*,

---

25. Harris, *Second Corinthians*, 681.

we do not war *according to the flesh*, for the weapons of our warfare are not *of the flesh*, but divinely powerful for the destruction of fortresses" (10:3–4 NASB).

The dichotomy of flesh and spirit are prominent in Paul's letters. Paul taught that we are all now living "*in* the flesh" in this physical, worldly existence. But to live "*by* the flesh" or "*according* to the flesh" is to live only on the finite, physical level, acting in a merely "sinful" human manner under limited human strength. Paul addressed this sharp contrast earlier with the Corinthians, when he rebuked them for placing too much emphasis on "human wisdom" or "wisdom of the world," and not enough emphasis on his gospel message that revealed the righteous wisdom and power of God (1 Cor 1:18–25; see 2 Cor 6:7). Probably the Corinthians were slipping back into their old habit of placing greater value on "human wisdom" (*the "flesh"*) as they listened to the lies of false teachers. They were disregarding what they knew about God's wisdom, power, and Spirit (1 Cor 1:21–24; 2 Cor 6:7).

Therefore, by the standards of the world, Paul was accused of being timid and weak, and he did not have apostolic authority that he claimed he had. He utilized the "war" image to inform and to warn his readers (10:3–6), certainly appealing to an image familiar to his readers in the Roman Empire. The image of war is common in Paul's communications, and his chosen vocabulary in verses 4–6 created a vivid picture of battles, walls, and towers, using the words "weapons," "fight," "demolish," and "strongholds" (all in v. 4). To "demolish arguments and every pretension" of his rivals, which set themselves up against the true "knowledge of God," is a picture of the utter destruction of the foolish words and false reasoning of his enemies (v. 5). Not only that, Paul intended to "to take captive every thought" (v. 5), and "to be ready," as well as to "punish every act of disobedience" (v. 6), again using a strong military image. It is possible that Paul had an OT proverb in mind as he waged his battle of words:[26]

> One who is wise can go up against the city of the mighty
>   and pull down the stronghold in which they trust. (Prov 21:22)

It was time to squelch the rebellion, and Paul was ready to put them in their place. He had "weapons of righteousness" in both hands and the "power of God" to strengthen him (10:4; see 6:7), such that despite "dishonor," "bad report," and "imposters" (6:8), Paul was certain that his weapons were stronger than anything his opponents could handle.

The arrogance of his opponents (10:4–5) had to be "demolished"; they were attempting to promote themselves as they crushed Paul's character and mission

---

26. See Harris, *Second Corinthians*, 676–78.

in Corinth. The divine power of God destroys such contention, which sets itself up against the true gospel of Jesus Christ (the knowledge *about* God, as preached by Paul). We see the contrast between "building you up" and "tearing you down" (see 10:8; 13:10). It is God's power that "demolishes" "arguments" and "pretentions" that oppose the "knowledge of God," while believers "take captive every thought" in obedience to Christ (10:5; see Rom 8:39).[27]

Thus, in the battle between flesh and Spirit, God's power will overcome the rebellious enemy (10:4–6; 6:7). His "weapons" were the reversal of the malicious tactics of the rivals in Corinth (10:3). Such "weapons" were not even acknowledged in a world so filled with human arrogance and pride. This is the nature of the pure, true gospel message: the real authority is always God, not human beings. Paul was like a military commander who was a "strategist in God's service."[28] Human leaders and resources can set up false "strongholds" of reasoning and thinking that can lead people in the wrong direction and are in opposition to God's truth (see Rom 1:18–23). Therefore, in this battle of knowledge, true believers must "take captive every thought," and *consciously evaluate* the veracity of what is taught or modeled in relation to God's standard, then be obedient to what they know is true (10:6).

In 10:6, Paul pushed his readers to a new level of obedience: rejecting the false wisdom of the world. He was ready to "punish" those who were on the wrong side of the war. Why would Paul be prepared to "punish every act of disobedience," when the people's "obedience is complete"? Furnish explains that Paul must have been thinking about the congregation's "obedience" to Christ ("your obedience," in v. 6), which was being completed by their faith. The "acts of disobedience" he was ready to punish were those of his opponents or those who undermined the gospel of Christ and the work of Paul.[29] Thus, Paul could no longer tolerate such disobedience that perverted the gospel of Christ (see 11:4), as well as those who were causing others to accept the same. The appeal, then, that was started in 10:1 is finally completed in 10:6: Paul admonished the congregation to be obedient to Christ, to the gospel as presented by Paul, and only to his message, regardless of the "war of words" conducted by his opponents.

The Support of His Authority (10:7–11)

Perhaps the troublemakers in Corinth accused Paul of being weak and cowardly; one who did not have apostolic power should therefore not attempt

27. Furnish, *II Corinthians*, 458.
28. Harris, *Second Corinthians*, 679.
29. Furnish, *II Corinthians*, 458, 464.

to exert apostolic authority. But Paul had a different concept of power and authority, which rested in his faith in Christ. He chose not to express his God-given authority as a despotic dictator like the Roman Emperor. This may have been hard for the Corinthians to understand, since in verses 7–11 he addressed the issue of authority, indicating that the Corinthians were concerned only about external claims and appearances.

Thus, Paul challenged his readers in verse 7 to be aware of the danger right in front of them. That is, in listening to his adversaries, and typical of human nature, his readers were only observing the surface of things (10:7) and did not see a real threat right before their eyes. Harris translates 10:7 as an imperative: "Look at what is staring you in the face!"[30] It seems that one dominant person (the singular "he" in v. 7) was leading the doubts about Paul's fundamental relationship with Jesus Christ, and others were just following along. Belleville wrote, "Paul faces a catch-22 situation at Corinth. When he downplays or makes little of his credentials, the genuineness of his apostleship is questioned (v. 7). But when he emphasizes his apostolic authority, he is accused of being overly "boastful" (v. 8).[31]

His rivals claimed to be spokesmen for Christ while they disparaged Paul's "unimpressive" speech (10:10). This gave them grounds to proclaim their authority was superior to that of Paul.

But, as their founder and pastor, his readers should have known that Paul "belonged to Christ" perhaps more than anyone else, including (and in particular) his opponents. He asserted that his relationship with Christ, as well as that of his ministry colleagues ("we," i.e., Titus), was at least equal to his rivals, if not greater. Furnish contends that there may have been two groups of adversaries: one group were the "false apostles" (11:13) who invaded the church from the outside; and perhaps under their influence, there was another group of people within the congregation who were recognizing the outsiders as legitimate. If this is so, Paul was being attacked from outside and from inside the church by those who were questioning Paul's motives and "spiritual relationship with Christ."[32]

This must have been especially painful for Paul. They may have claimed that Paul never actually learned at the feet of Jesus, as did at least twelve other "authentic" apostles. Yet, this was a man who had experienced a dramatic encounter with the risen Christ on the road to Damascus, and who had received his gospel message directly from Jesus Christ himself (see 1 Cor

30. Harris, *Second Corinthians*, 686.
31. Belleville, *2 Corinthians*, 258.
32. Furnish, *II Corinthians*, 466.

9:1–2; 15:3–8; Gal 1:1, 15–17). Thus, Paul stated that his apostolic authority was derived from the Lord and not from other people.[33] Furthermore, Paul's position and authority in Christ was verified and supported by the other Christian leaders in Jerusalem (Gal 2:6–9), who recognized his appointment to minister to the Gentiles.

In 2 Corinthians 10:8, Paul began his "boasting" with great hesitation and awkwardness, which is apparent throughout the remaining portions of the letter (see 10:13, 15; 11:16, 18, 30; 12:1, 5, 6). Paul insisted that the power of his authority was given to him so he could be an encouragement to the believers, to be constructive instead of destructive in their midst. Unlike his adversaries, Paul's true boasting was being called by God to "build up" the believers, and not to "pull you down" (10:8).

Paul changed his metaphor again to illustrate that he was like a contractor, working for God, to build a gathering of people who would glorify God through Christ. This "building up" image is critical for Paul, as it reinforces the idea that his authority is from God, and not from anyone who desired to injure the Gentile churches. He repeats this again in verse 13:10, where the words are nearly identical to 10:8. In spite of erroneous surface claims, the believers should have known that he was a genuine apostle who belonged to Christ, who served the Christian community in an attempt to unify the church and build the believers up, just as others were intentionally trying to destroy and divide it. He is not ashamed of boasting about his authority because it was from the Lord, and not something achieved by human effort. Again, a passage from the Old Testament serves as a support for Paul's use of the "building" imagery and his assignment to preach the gospel message: "I [the Lord] have put my words in your mouth. See, today I appoint you over nations and kingdoms to uproot and tear down, to destroy and overthrow, to build and to plant" (Jer 1:9b–10).

That is, Paul was not trying to intimidate the readers or frighten them with his letters, as some rivals must have implied (see 1 Cor 4:14; 2 Cor 2:3–4; 7:8–9); in fact, he was trying to encourage and edify them! His rivals sneered that his writing was strong and impressive, but his speeches were weak and contemptible (10:10). Perhaps the same people who made the "timid and bold" accusation in 10:1 were also accusing Paul of writing letters that were intended to threaten and scare his readers "to death."[34]

However, he clearly addressed his letter intentions in 2:3–4 and 7:8–9. They maliciously misconstrued his communications with the church to their advantage (1 Cor 4:18–21; 2 Cor 10:10–11). In that culture, oratory was a

---

33. Harris, *Second Corinthians*, 662.
34. Furnish, *II Corinthians*, 468.

recognized talent and trade, and clever speech was designed to make money. Yet, Paul's manner of speaking and his godly intentions were quite different from that of his rivals. His speech was free from artificiality and self-interest but was filled with the wisdom of God (see 1 Cor 2:1–5). While Paul was determined to speak (and write) under the guidance of only God's Holy Spirit, his Corinthian readers were being deceived and were missing the underlying truth. Both in his writing and in his speaking, Paul presented a gospel "in truthful speech and in the power of God, with weapons of righteousness in the right hand and in the left" (2 Cor 6:7).

His readers and his enemies needed to realize that the very same Spirit guided Paul and his fellow workers both in letters and in person (10:11). Verse 11 stands as a refutation of the idea that there were two of him, a "timid" Paul and a "bold" Paul (10:1). The argument that he was weak as an "absent" pastor and a strict authoritarian in the presence of the congregation simply was not true (10:10–11). The frequent phrases "some people" (v. 2) or "some say . . ." (v. 10) or "such people" imply that there were a number of people in the congregation (who knows how many?) who were participating in the demeaning and denigrating of Paul. In addition, because he intended to visit Corinth again (i.e., 13:1), Paul wanted to make sure that the church understood completely that his character and his motives were totally godly and consistent, whether revealed in his writings or in his face-to-face speaking.

Paul's Legitimate Boasting (10:12–18)

Moreover, Paul and his colleagues in ministry did not evaluate themselves or compare themselves to other rival speakers by human, worldly standards (10:12; see 3:1–2). This was a sharp contrast to the speech and behavior of Paul's enemies in Corinth, who highly recommended themselves and were measuring Paul by their own worldly standards. They assumed that there was no means of comparison higher than themselves; but in reality, Paul wrote that this was really not a wise thing to do! Paul and his colleagues, in contrast, "boasted" properly about their ministry within the region to which they were assigned (10:8, 13). Paul was "not ashamed" of his righteous gospel (10:8; see Rom 1:16–17), and he gladly preached it by the authority of the Lord, regardless of the "boasting in the flesh" of his disobedient opponents.

"Boasting" is a word that is very common in this latter section of this letter. It appears in every verse from 10:13 to the culminating verse of 10:17 (see also, 11:17–18, 30; 12:1, 5, 6). For Paul, "to boast" has two aspects; one is positive, and one is negative (see commentary, 1:12, 14 and 7:14). More often, the word implies a "good thing," bragging about people who have earned Paul's affection and pride (2 Cor 1:12). But it is also used in a negative way of Paul's enemies who think too highly of themselves and who brag about their wisdom and their work (see 1 Cor 5:6). His rivals had no doubt "boasted" to the church about their influence, their oration, and their wisdom, and in the process degraded Paul and his authority. Paul appears to be using his enemies' own words ironically, right back at them, to emphasize their true motives of self-interest, false superiority, and power. In effect, Paul was turning "foolishness" upside down so his readers would perceive the ridiculous standards ("measurements") of his opponents' selfish "boasting."

Second Corinthians 10:13–18 develop an inclusive thought unit. Paul was demonstrating his authority and justifying his style of ministry in the church at Corinth. He knew it was right to "boast within proper limits," implying that his boasting was not about himself, but about what God has done (10:15, 17). Paul refused to overstep his boundaries when it came to time and location of his ministry. He did not encroach on another missionary's geographic area or calling. That is, Paul was called to take the gospel of Christ to the Gentiles (Gal 1:16; 2:7–8), a calling and a commission that was confirmed by his Jewish ministry colleagues in Jerusalem (Gal 2:9).

We know that Paul would launch his ministry in a city at a Jewish synagogue and then move into Gentile circles as the people responded to his message (Acts 13:4, 14–48). Given that Paul was a planter of new churches, he was active wherever the gospel had not been proclaimed. However, his letter to the Romans is an example of Paul communicating with a congregation well after it was initially established by other godly missionaries. What we see in the book of Acts is that Paul never overstepped his limits and consistently served in areas to which he was led by the Holy Spirit (see Acts 16:6–10). He never took credit for someone else's service, and it was his ardent desire that the expansion of his ministry would be achieved by the Corinthians themselves (2 Cor 10:15, 16).

Harris translates the word as "domain" as a reference to one's "assigned area" ("limits," 10:13, 15, 16).[35] In the same way, often pastors today are assigned to or hired by one church, or called to serve a specific limited circuit of a few churches (as in a rural area). It would be unethical and unprofessional for a pastor to preach, teach, and minister to people outside of his or her assigned area unless specifically invited to do so. Paul also implied that Corinth was at the edge of his assigned area at that time (10:14), but he wanted to deliver the gospel message even farther across the vast unreached areas past Greece (Spain might have been on his mind; Rom 15:24, 28).

God has called people with different gifts to serve in different locations and

---

35. Harris, *Second Corinthians*, 713.

areas of work, not unlike competitive swimmers confined to their own "lane" of movement. Paul declared that the rival missionaries invaded the territory that was assigned to Paul—that is, Corinth. Paul repeats his familiar mantra, reminding his readers that proper "boasting" is about God's work and not human achievement: "Let the one who boasts boast in the Lord!" (1 Cor 1:31; 2 Cor 10:17; also see Jer 9:24).

Likewise, Paul returned to his original thought in 2 Corinthians 10:12— that it is the Lord who commends his workers and not the workers themselves (10:18). Finally, we can see the irony of the whole state of affairs in Corinth: Paul was criticized for living a very worldly life (10:2), but in reality he was called and directed to serve within God's "limits." His critics, however, were indeed out of bounds, swimming in the wrong lane, arrogantly "boasting in the way the world does" (11:18).[36]

LIVE the Story

Chapter 10 is the beginning of Paul's last push to squelch a rebellion in Corinth before his intended third visit to the church. We observe a clearer picture of his adversaries in the final chapters of this letter—internal strife among the believers, and external strife from outside intruders who were arrogant and "boastful," disobedient to God, and injurious to the church.

The question is, did the readers, the members of the congregation, know that they were being duped and that they were wrong to accept as truth the words of the corrupt and antagonistic "false apostles"? Did anyone put up a hand in Corinth and say, "Wait a second—what you are espousing is not what we learned from Paul!"? Apparently not.

Granted, the Christian teachings and ethics that Paul taught in Corinth were very unusual in that Greco-Roman culture. As we see in 1 Corinthians, he introduced a set of new ideas to common daily life in Greece, including (for example) marriage and sexual morality (1 Cor 5:1–5; 6:13, 15–20; 7:1–40), eating and food (1 Cor 6:13; 8:1–8; 10:31), freedom and rights (1 Cor 8:9; 9:3–18), and idolatry and sacrifice (1 Cor 10:6–22). Thus, Christianity became a whole new way of life for the Corinthians, and of course it would have been very easy to fall back into the old culture and the old way of life.

In the same way, are some believers today so lacking in the "knowledge of God" (10:5) and biblical wisdom that they cannot recognize sinful, destructive, self-promoting teachings when they happen? If so, this is a cause for alarm.

---

36. Harris, *Second Corinthians*, 716.

Are we so numbed to the perverse rhetoric all around us that we do not see—cannot see—the deceptions, even in those who presume to be in service to the Lord? Are people afraid to hear the strong truths of the Bible? Perhaps we choose to ignore the immorality and vice promoted around us and just hope that someone else will do something about it. In our postmodern culture, the word *tolerance* is a significant term. If a person is too tolerant, then that implies that "anything goes" and one has no conscience or backbone. Yet if someone is not tolerant enough, then that person is narrow, restrictive, exclusive, and unforgiving. "The world" (10:2) blames Christians for being "intolerant" of other beliefs and views; biblical Christian ethics are "old fashioned" and "out of date." Therefore, and most important, who is "bold" enough to rebuke this charge? Who is willing in our day to stand up and take the suffering and verbal abuse for the gospel of Christ as Paul did in his day?

Perhaps even more than in Paul's day, today we have "false teachers" and preachers full of self-interest and self-aggrandizement. Instead of preaching the word of God, they appeal to people's emotions, loneliness, and a lack of self-worth, and rob people of their hard-earned money. They promise material prosperity to those in poverty, and spiritual riches to those who lack the knowledge and/or the will to "see through" the claim. It is a crime what some finely dressed, smooth-tongued speakers promise to susceptible, well-meaning folks from a pulpit and/or on the TV screen. These phonies even try to find a scriptural passage (usually from Proverbs) to appear biblical and support their claims. Ultimately, what is important to them is the size of the church, the size of the offering, and the size of the speaker's paycheck. Thus, we as Christians must use caution and discernment so we are not deceived, and so we do not crumble in weakness before the power of the enemy (Satan; see 2:11). On the other hand, certainly not all devoted Christian workers fall into this category—the vast majority of pastors, chaplains, leaders, and counselors are hard-working, self-sacrificing people of God, and they deserve our respect, our "boasting," our support, and our love.

Let's Talk about Sin

In fact, Paul was most gracious as he rebuked some rebellious people in the congregation and the antagonistic, intruding leaders about their sins. Like a fearful parent, he warned the congregation about sin and disobedience with love and concern instead of threatening animosity. Today, we don't like to discuss sin, but we secretly love to watch it in movies and on TV. Yet, even the most committed Christians are vulnerable to self-interest and to the temptations of Satan—the more invisible the sin, the greater the opportunity (like pornography). We may knowingly drift into a mental attitude of "only sinning a little," and relatively speaking, whatever it is, it is certainly not as great as the sins of other people! It is a battle, and it cannot be denied or overlooked or swept under the carpet. Any counselor or counseling pastor can attest to the fact that the church today is rife with sin.

A few young boys were playing baseball in the front yard of a home when a ball went sailing through a window, shattering the glass. One boy's father made the event into a "teaching moment," telling his son that it was a mistake and a sin to have broken the window. The boy was horrified and said, "No, it was not a sin! I didn't mean to do it! It was an accident!" This illustrates what many of us believe: that actions or behavior are not a sin when they are unintentionally committed. Adultery is not a sin if "we didn't intend for this to happen!" Certainly, intended injuries are worse than accidents, but doing wrong is still doing wrong. We are all sinners, and even as believers, we are still subject to the temptations of sins of thought, words, and actions.

> The kingdom of self is heavily defended territory. Post-Eden Adams and Eves are willing to pay their respects to God, but they don't want him invading their turf. Most sin, far from being a mere lapse of morals or a weak will, is an energetically and expensively erected defense against God. Direct assault in an openly declared war on the god-self is extraordinarily ineffective. Hitting sin head-on is like hitting a nail with a hammer; it only drives it in deeper.[37]

A pastor friend had a lady, a believer, come into his office for a conversation. Sadly, her story was not unique: her husband had been very unfaithful in their marriage, and for years he had abused her emotionally and psychologically. This was a couple who had been attending his church for a long time, but the pastor had no idea of the situation. The marriage could not be saved, and they divorced. Almost immediately thereafter, the women met a nice man who "wooed" her and "wowed" her with dinners, flowers, and compliments. They ended up in bed together on a regular basis. She said she had never been so happy; he appreciated her, and she felt loved for the first time in a long time. Yet, she still felt that she wanted and needed the approval of the pastor concerning this new relationship. It was a blessing from God and an answer to prayers following all the torture and abuse. Doesn't God want us to be happy? So, it was a sexual relationship outside of the boundaries of marriage, but how could it be a sin, when she so deserved such happiness and affection? How could it be bad when it was so good?

---

37. Peterson, *Contemplative Pastor*, 41.

My friend did not endorse the relationship; he could not accept it as a gift from God. Despite all the sins of the past, it was still not biblical. It was not right to enter into a union that was not part of the plan of God. The old adage is "two wrongs do not make a right." Actually, this was not really a love relationship, the pastor said; it was retaliation. Only God can truly redeem the past and promise a brighter future. It pained the lady greatly to hear his words, but it pained the pastor even more to point out what the woman already knew in her heart. She left his office in tears. The pastor could not sleep that night; he prayed and searched the Scriptures for something positive to say to her, but nothing could reverse the truth. In the end, about three months after the "rebound" relationship began, the man confessed that, indeed, he had a wife and children living in another state. Searching for a strong "drug," she wanted the pain to go away; but like a drug, the addiction actually removed all reason and strength. It was just more pain, more guilt, and more depression than what she had had before.

"Vandalism of Shalom"

What is sin? Is it just "missing the mark"? Some may think that worshiping the right god, meditating in the right position, owning the right material goods, or thinking the highest intellectual thoughts can raise one above the swamp of sin . . . until they fall into it.

Cornelius Plantinga writes that sin is the "vandalism of shalom"; it "violates shalom and breaks the peace, because it interferes with the way things are supposed to be."[38]

> The webbing together of God, humans and all creation in justice, fulfillment, and delight is what the Hebrew prophets call *shalom*. We call it peace, but it means far more than mere peace of mind or a cease-fire between enemies. In the Bible, shalom means *universal flourishing, wholeness, and delight* . . . Shalom, in other words, is the way things ought to be.[39]

Sin, therefore, is not merely law-breaking; sin is the "smearing of a relationship" with God and with the One who died on a cross to break the bondage of human sin. "All sin has first and finally a Godward force." Any "act, thought, desire, emotion, word, or deed" that would be displeasing to God is sin. Or, it is the "*power* of human beings that has the effect of corrupting human thought, word and deed" that produces displeasure in God and guilt in the

---

38. Plantinga, *Not the Way It's Supposed to Be*, 14.
39. Plantinga, *Not the Way It's Supposed to Be*, 10.

human being. Sin seems to be so *present*—what is happening in the here and now. And yet, "human sin is a violation of our human *end*, which is to build shalom and thus to glorify and enjoy God forever."[40]

"Not incidentally," Plantinga writes, "the pride that resists God and God's superiority also resists objective moral truth."[41] That is, human beings think they can create their own morals and values and accept moral relativity. Furthermore, "all sin is equally wrong, but not all sin is equally bad." In both the Protestant and the Roman Catholic traditions, there is clear right and wrong behavior; some actions are within God's will, or they are not. But some good deeds are better than others, and among bad actions, some are worse than others.[42] Thus, "moral evil is social and structural as well as personal." In summation, Christianity has traditionally viewed sin as being "culpable evil," voluntary, blameworthy, and self-deceptive.[43]

The rival missionaries, opposing and demeaning Paul's character and mission, *knowingly* sinned by speaking lies and accusations against him. While they pretended to be followers of Christ, they were in strong disobedience to God. Their Christian witness was badly tarnished with lies and hatred. Some members of the congregation were likely *unknowingly* sucked into this deceitfulness. Yet if we read 1 Corinthians and acknowledge that Paul clearly informed them about the Christian gospel, ethics, and expectations in other letters as well (1 Cor 2:4; 11:4–6), it is reasonable to believe that some people in the church were *knowingly* accepting the opponents' sins. They should have known better than to believe these "false apostles," whose intentions, we can assume, were evil in nature and were pulling the church down (2 Cor 10:8).

Clean, Rinse, Repeat . . . or We End Up in a Spin Cycle!

So, what is the answer for us today? What can be done about human sin, both individual and corporate? If we truly understand the universal nature of sin, and hate it within ourselves, then it leads to the importance of human forgiveness. Our prayer is that we can forgive others just as we have been forgiven (Matt 6:12; Luke 11:4). One of the most poignant and emotional prayers concerning sin is Psalm 51, where the poet David offers a contrite heart for forgiveness and cleansing. Like our weekly laundry, this plea ends up as a cycle of "cleansing," "rinsing," and getting "dirty" again and again. Dirty laundry cannot be covered up, ignored, or forgotten—it gets smelly!

---

40. Plantinga, *Not the Way It's Supposed to Be*, 13–17.
41. Plantinga, *Not the Way It's Supposed to Be*, 17.
42. Plantinga, *Not the Way It's Supposed to Be*, 21.
43. Plantinga, *Not the Way It's Supposed to Be*, 25.

In the same way, lingering, unrecognized and unconfessed sin can ruin lives and split relationships. It can leave us corroded and stained in our marriages, families, jobs, and ministries. Above all else, sin ruins our relationship and communication with God (see Ps 51:4). How we long for renewal! There is a deep inner conviction of our own sin and spiritual poverty, and a great need for personal cleansing. Further, there is no real worship as a corporate body of Christ without the forgiveness, grace, mercy, and unfailing love of God:

1. We take responsibility for our own sin (Ps 51:1–2).
2. We confess our "uncleanness" (vv. 3–6).
3. We allow God to cleanse and forgive us (vv. 7–9).
4. We seek renewal and restoration and recognize the Holy Spirit that God has placed in us (vv. 10–12).
5. We testify to others about the forgiveness of God's grace in our lives, which renews our new heart for worship and witness (vv. 13–17).
6. God's church is built up because individuals have been reconciled and reunited with God and with others (vv. 18–19).

In addition, David teaches us that there is no renewal apart from pain (Ps 51:7–8). In other words, we must face the reality of our own sins, confess them before the Lord, and feel the pain of repentance; this leads to confession before other people to make things right. Sometimes being in "hot water" tends to "shrink" us. What David asks of God was answered through the Messiah, and Jesus suffered great pain in order to forgive us of our sins (John 3:16). Therefore, the deepest renewal is spiritual, within the boundaries set by a loving God. When we break those boundaries, it is painful. Since God is holy, and since he has given us a conscience and his Holy Spirit, we cannot be renewed apart from dealing with our moral failures before him first.

Paul wrote about "boundaries" and "limits" set by God in terms of ministry and taking credit for something where credit may not be due (2 Cor 10:13–18). The same is true of sin. When we enter into a sinful situation (even unintentionally), we are moving beyond the limitations and boundaries set by God for human thoughts and behavior that are ordained for our benefit! Christian leaders are especially vulnerable to stepping outside of divine limitations of power and authority. That is, Paul teaches us that deceitful, sinful leaders who perform under their own power, outside of the ministry boundaries set by God, can ruin lives and fracture and break a congregation. For years some leaders spoke in favor of slavery in America; even today, there are those who speak against godly women serving in leadership positions in churches. Those who intentionally mislead, misinform, and misguide other people, and mishandle the word of God to their own advantage, will have to face severe consequences (see Ps 50:16–22).

Deliverance from the power of sin and evil is available to the person, like David, who is contrite and humble before God. On the personal level, we must make things right with God, and then make things right with others. Give forgiveness even more than you have been forgiven, and be reconciled with everyone as much as possible. Keep a very short "laundry list." Let God forgive you, and then forgive yourself. Forget the past and move forward, knowing that you are cleansed and have learned from brokenness. On the corporate level, restored people can restore a church, a community, and a nation. Proper worship is the outcome of renewed hearts. A renewed pastor can lead a renewed congregation. Finally, we know that we serve a compassionate and gracious God who does *not* "treat us as our sins deserve or repay us according to our iniquities" (Ps 103:8–10).

> For as high as the heavens are above the earth,
> so great is his love for those who fear him;
> as far as the east is from the west,
> so far has he removed our transgressions from us. (Ps 103:11–12)

> As a father has compassion on his children,
> so the LORD has compassion on those who fear him. (Ps 103:13)

CHAPTER 13

2 Corinthians 11:1–15

 LISTEN to the Story

¹¹:¹I hope you will put up with me in a little foolishness. Yes, please put up with me! ²I am jealous for you with a godly jealousy. I promised you to one husband, to Christ, so that I might present you as a pure virgin to him. ³But I am afraid that just as Eve was deceived by the serpent's cunning, your minds may somehow be led astray from your sincere and pure devotion to Christ. ⁴For if someone comes to you and preaches a Jesus other than the Jesus we preached, or if you receive a different spirit from the Spirit you received, or a different gospel from the one you accepted, you put up with it easily enough. ⁵I do not think I am in the least inferior to those "super-apostles." ⁶I may indeed be untrained as a speaker, but I do have knowledge. We have made this perfectly clear to you in every way.

⁷Was it a sin for me to lower myself in order to elevate you by preaching the gospel of God to you free of charge? ⁸I robbed other churches by receiving support from them so as to serve you. ⁹And when I was with you and needed something, I was not a burden to anyone, for the brothers who came from Macedonia supplied what I needed. I have kept myself from being a burden to you in any way, and will continue to do so. ¹⁰As surely as the truth of Christ is in me, nobody in the regions of Achaia will stop this boasting of mine. ¹¹Why? Because I do not love you? God knows I do! ¹²And I will keep on doing what I am doing in order to cut the ground from under those who want an opportunity to be considered equal with us in the things they boast about.

¹³For such people are false apostles, deceitful workers, masquerading as apostles of Christ. ¹⁴And no wonder, for Satan himself masquerades as an angel of light. ¹⁵It is not surprising, then, if his servants also masquerade as servants of righteousness. Their end will be what their actions deserve.

Listening to the Text in the Story: Genesis 3:13; 6:1–4; Deuteronomy 22:13–21; Psalm 82; 148:2; Isaiah 1:20; 29:14; 49:2; 62:5; 1QM 17; 1QS 3:22–23; Romans 2:20, 28–29; 3:8; 8:15; Galatians 1:6–9; Ephesians 1:17–23; 4:2–3; 1 John 4:1–3; Revelation 1:12, 16, 19; 2:2, 7, 9–10, 13, 17, 29; 3:6, 8–9, 13, 22; 20:10.

Be alert and of sober mind. Your enemy the devil prowls around like a roaring lion, looking for someone to devour. Resist him, standing firm in the faith, because you know that the family of believers throughout the world is undergoing the same kind of sufferings.

—*1 Peter 5:8–9*

Not too long ago, there was a scheme that played tricks on elderly people that reaped a tidy sum of money for thieves. My neighbor was 87, and her landline phone rang one day. The voice at the other end of the line was rushed and choppy, making it hard for her to understand. The caller said that he was her grandson on a sudden trip to Guatemala.

"Grandma, I'm in trouble!"

He said that he had been arrested and was in a pathetic jail awaiting trial. He had not done anything wrong, but he needed money for his release so that he could get home and settle the dispute.

Anxious, my neighbor said of course she would do anything to help her grandson.

The caller then gave her specific instructions: he said that she should go to her bank (yes, he knew the name of her bank) and put $5,000 on a Visa card. She was to put the card in an envelope, then she was to take it to the ATM just outside of her local grocery store (yes, he knew the name of the grocery store right in her neighborhood).

Dazed and confused, my neighbor drove to the bank, and she was shaking when she approached the teller. She asked for the money to be put on a Visa card, and the teller went to work to find the right account to make the transaction. Fortunately (thank God), my neighbor's daughter was a co-signer on the account, and the bank called her to verify the transaction. It did not take long for the daughter to "smell a rat," and she hurriedly went to the bank to halt the phony request and to calm her mother. Her grandson was fine; he was in school and not in prison in Guatemala. The tricksters came very close to getting money from that kind, concerned grandma, and the whole incident made all of us sick. My poor neighbor told us that she felt like such a fool to almost be "suckered in" by that man on the phone. There must be a special place for people who cheat, lie, and deceive elderly adults, and God knows where that is.

Certainly, at one time or another, we have all felt like a fool for believing the wrong person or a very unlikely story, accepting someone's feeble excuse, or giving money to dubious organizations. Sometimes when something sounds too good to be true, it really is. Perhaps the Corinthians were "suckered in" to believing charming words from unscrupulous teachers that were more appealing than the gospel message preached by Paul. And they fell for all the tricks of his rivals' trade. These intruders were eloquent speakers, teaching with boldness, perhaps polished in their appearance, and self-confident beyond words. In reality, they were self-righteous frauds, and their only interest was in themselves, not the congregation (see Introduction).

Figures of Speech

Indeed, if the "war of words" began in 2 Corinthians 10, in chapter 11 the battle rages on between Paul and these rival adversaries. These outsiders who had invaded the church at Corinth were determined to disparage Paul as an inadequate apostle and damage the community of believers. Yet Paul did not give in to his opponents; in fact, in this chapter he increased his offensive tactics and stripped his enemies of their masks and shields. He revealed the true nature of his adversaries and uncovered their hidden motives and intentions.

As in chapter 10, we can again perceive of Paul's liberal use of figures of speech and rhetorical devices—irony, sarcasm, and meiosis ("the belittling of one thing to magnify another," 11:16; 12:11).[1] Paul's words almost drip with irony throughout this chapter of the letter. We can hear so many antitheses in Paul's declarations, including "wise" and "foolish," "boasting in the Lord" and "boasting as the world does," "truth" and deception, "superior" and "inferior," "weak" and "bold" (or "strong"). He even makes a parody (an amusing imitation of the speech or writing of someone else) out of the words of his opponents when he lists the "accomplishments" of his adversaries in Corinth, which are really just the opposite (11:19–21). He uses this kind of discourse to catch his readers' attention, but also to persuade them to see the reality of the situation as he sees it, to recognize the intruders for what they were, and to correct the conflicting conduct.

---

1. Kierspel, *Charts on the Life, Letters and Theology of Paul,* 90.

EXPLAIN the Story

Deception and Foolish Opposition (11:1–15)

Paul opened this section of this letter with "a little foolishness" (11:1). In chapter 10 he described the situation in Corinth figuratively as a "war of words"; in this chapter his description is more literal. If chapter 10 is a corrective for his readers (i.e., 10:7), then chapter 11 is an assault on his rivals (i.e., 11:13). He contrasted the manner of ministry of his rivals, which was deceptive, to his own style of ministry, which was clear and accurate (11:6). To distinguish himself from his enemies, in chapter 11 Paul humbled himself so that his people in Corinth may be exalted (11:2, 7). Some commentators begin Paul's "Fool's Speech" (11:1–12:13) with this opening verse, but we will wait to begin Paul's speech discourse until 11:16.[2] In verses 11:1–15 Paul was defining the battle lines, showing clearly and sternly the differences between himself and his opponents. Furnish labels these verses a "prologue" to the actual speech itself.[3] That is, Paul had to differentiate his remarks from those of the rival missionaries who have deceived the Corinthians with their arrogance and false accusations. He had to clearly separate his missionary style from that of his opponents so his readers would see the pretense under which they were trusting. Reluctantly, but out of necessity, Paul adopted the tactics of his opponents to justify his own "boasting" and "foolishness."

Paul already taught that the only good boasting was "boasting in the Lord" (10:17), but he suddenly found himself doing exactly what he could not bear: "Boasting in the way the world does" (11:18). This is so unlike Paul, but he had good reasons for doing this kind of "self-confident boasting" (11:17). The Corinthians continued to misunderstand the truth of "strength in weakness," which is a key theme of chapters 10 through 13. The dreadful situation in Corinth pushed him to an extreme, so Paul found it necessary to defend himself and his ministry in a way that would highlight the real "foolishness" of his rivals. He was a "fool" to be stooping to the level of his enemies, but he had a plan. To illustrate how foolish his rivals were, and how silly the Corinthians were for believing them, he would employ their own words and schemes to "fight fire with fire." He gave his readers fair, advanced warning of his intentions, and asked them to bear with him (11:1).

Therefore, in chapters 10 through 13, Paul had three main objectives: to defend himself and his apostleship against his adversaries, to teach the

---

2. Furnish, *II Corinthians*, 486.
3. Furnish, *II Corinthians*, 498.

Corinthians the reality that "power and weakness cohere," and to build up the congregation in their Christian faith.[4]

"Foolishness" (11:1)

"Foolishness" and related words appear seven times in chapters 11 and 12; elsewhere in his letters, this word appears only in 1 Corinthians (1:18, 25; 2:14; 3:19). In 1 Corinthians, the primary meaning of the word is used as the antithesis of "wisdom," and certainly that is implied ironically in these chapters as well.[5] In 1 Corinthians, Paul clearly contrasted the wisdom and foolishness of humans (cf. Isa 29:14), and he even ended 1 Corinthians 1:31 with exactly the same Old Testament quotation as he used later in 2 Corinthians 10:17 (Jer 9:24). Yet, under the influence of Paul's enemies, the community continued to align themselves with "human wisdom" and the "wisdom of the world." People who cannot evaluate themselves with veracity are, in reality, "fools." Such people depend on their own "wisdom" and put themselves at the center of the universe, whereas Paul saw reality entirely in terms of Christ.[6]

Thus, Paul resorted to playing their game. Four noteworthy reasons stand behind why Paul chose to use a kind of ironic rhetoric that appears on the surface to be foolish and boastful: Paul's "jealousy" for the church, his opponents' erroneous teachings, an accusation of inferiority, and Paul's unusual rejection of remuneration for his ministry services.

Jealousy (11:2a)

First, he explained that he was "jealous" for the church with "godly jealousy" (11:2), meaning that he cared very deeply for the congregation. Some translations use the word "zealous," thus implying that Paul cared for them as much as God cared about them.[7] Specifically, Paul cared a great deal about the spiritual well-being of his people. In contrast, his opponents had little concern for the congregation—physically, spiritually, or otherwise. Expressing his deep love for the church, he had to "boast" about them and their faith in Christ (2:2–3; 7:2–4, 15–16), in contrast to the foolish, selfish "boasting" of his opponents. Thus, his "boasting" actually reflected his pride in and his worry for the congregation. In fact, Paul restated his love for this congregation four times in this letter to demonstrate his affection and pastoral anxiety for the people (2:4; 8:7; 11:11; 12:15b).[8]

---

4. Ellington, "Not Applicable to Believers?," 339.
5. Furnish, *II Corinthians*, 485.
6. Garland, *2 Corinthians*, 459.
7. Furnish, *II Corinthians*, 486.
8. Furnish, *II Corinthians*, 493.

Marriage Metaphor (11:2b–3)

Paul explained why he was so concerned about the Corinthians. He had taught the Corinthians to be "pure and faithful" to Christ; the union of Christ and the believer is an eternal bond not unlike that of betrothal and marriage (11:2). He used a betrothal and marriage metaphor to show his abhorrence that anyone else would capture the hearts of the Corinthians. We noted that Paul's teachings among the Gentiles in Corinth were new and unusual in that culture.

Paul adhered to Jewish traditions that required one man and one woman be pledged to each other, marry, and then remain married for a lifetime. Ancient tradition used the marital "betrothal" as we use the time of engagement. A bride was promised in marriage to only one husband, and the agreement was as binding as the marriage itself. The union is a common Jewish image, denoting the relationship between Yahweh and his people (see Isaiah 62:5). Later the wedding/marriage image was used in John's Apocalypse to picture the union of Christ and his church (see Revelation 19:7–9; 21:2, 9; 22:17). In this way, Paul had promised the congregation at Corinth to be the bride of Jesus, faithful to *only* Jesus ("one man"). Like the father of the bride in ancient traditions, it was important for Paul to guard and protect "the bride" (the community) to present her as a "pure virgin," undefiled, chaste, and blameless to Christ at "the wedding," or his return (2 Cor 11:2; see Deut 22:13–21).[9]

However, Paul had fears that the Corinthians had been disqualified as an innocent bride. They were corrupted and deceived by his adversaries, just as Eve had been betrayed by the "serpent"—that is, Satan (11:3). This is an allusion to Genesis 3:13, where Eve realized she had been tricked by the serpent into disobeying God's instructions. Satan is characterized by craftiness and deceit, as one who leads others astray. That is, Satan leads people away from their "pure devotion to Christ." He does so with "craftiness," the same word that Paul used in 4:2, which can be translated "cleverness" or "shrewdness," always in a negative sense.[10] Paul used this word again, of himself (ironically!) in 12:16. Here, Satan is presented as one who uses *alluring pleasure* to mislead people *in their minds,* away from God. This description of Satan in verse 3 is a preface to Paul's evaluation of his adversaries that follows in 11:14–15.

A Different Gospel, a Different Christ (11:4)

The second reason Paul resorted to their "foolish" rhetoric was in response to his full awareness of the erroneous teachings of the false apostles, and

---

9. Garland, *2 Corinthians*, 460.
10. Garland, *2 Corinthians*, 218, 487.

how quickly the church received and accepted their lies (11:4). They readily accepted such fools among them, so why would they not also readily accept the "foolish" Paul, too? In verse 4 Paul summarized the specific counterfeit teachings of his opponents. While he uses the singular form, "someone," he is surely writing about any number of false teachers who were delivering the wrong message. They were preaching some other Jesus, a different spirit, and a different gospel that contradicted what Paul had taught. Not only had these rogues "sown" in Paul's field (that is, his geographical ministry region, 10:13–16), they also had "sowed the field with tares of a false gospel which led away from Christ."[11] We do not see the combination of the "Jesus, Spirit, gospel" concepts knitted together anywhere else in Paul's letters other than in this verse.[12] But obviously they are tied together and should not be separated. The "false gospel" no doubt proclaimed a "false Jesus" and a "false spirit." This is a picture of "abusive power" and influence, as well as a deceitful manner of ministry.[13]

Surely there were differences between Paul and other Jewish Christians in the first century, as we see in 11:4. Central to their disagreements was the rejection by some Jewish Christians of the validity of Paul's message to the Gentile audiences, as well as the conditions upon which the Gentiles were to be "treated as full coreligionists by Jewish believers."[14] Moreover, between Christian and non-Christian Jews was strong disagreement about Jesus himself and his unique status before God. For the Christian, Jesus was to be "glorified" and worshiped in an identical way to the Father, a disagreeable notion to an orthodox, monotheistic Jew, and a difficult concept to fully embrace by a converted Jewish Christian.

We know that Paul held to a very high view of Jesus and his divine Sonship; this is reflected in his letters and in the devotional practices of his planted churches.[15] The different "Jesus" may have been a bogus figure who did not die, humiliated, on the cross, but was more akin to the Hellenistic gods of power and control; of course, gods and heroes do not suffer and die (but, see 1 Cor 15:3–4, 12–17). On the other hand, his rival missionaries in Corinth may have been proclaiming a belief in a "Jesus" who was not so radically different from their former Jewish belief system, and therefore Jesus was not so highly exalted. Perhaps the false teachers promised comfort instead of the cross, and selfishness instead of sacrifice.

---

11. Garland, *2 Corinthians*, 463.
12. Garland, *2 Corinthians*, 463.
13. Ellington, "Not Applicable to Believers?," 330.
14. Hurtado, *God in New Testament Theology*, 106–7.
15. Hurtado, *God in New Testament Theology*, 106.

A false gospel appears again in Paul's letter to the Galatians (1:6–9) and may be similar in a few aspects. However, the false teaching in Galatia may not have been the same as that in Corinth. In any event, both the Galatians and the Corinthians fell for false teachings, and Paul chastises them for rejecting what they already knew to be true from Paul's message (2 Cor 11:4).

A different "spirit" may have been a spirit of bondage, fear, and worldliness, instead of the "spirit of sonship," of freedom, joy, peace, and love granted to believers (Rom 8:15; 1 Cor 2:12–13; 2 Cor 3:17; Eph 4:2–3). The Corinthians had a problem with fully understanding the purpose and role of God's Holy Spirit in their lives. Paul had previously addressed their misunderstandings and self-edification in 1 Corinthians, and he will address it again in chapter 12 of this letter. His readers assumed that the power of the Holy Spirit was for their own benefit, so their incorrect assumptions resulted in an air of superiority over others and divisions in the community.[16] Thus, the different "gospel" may have been a composite of misconstrued, dishonest, "perverted" messages that commended the false teachers and denigrated not only Paul's true gospel message, but also those who believed it. In his letter to the Galatians, Paul wrote that the corrupted gospel is really "no gospel at all" (Gal 1:7), and the one who teaches such falsehoods should be eternally condemned! (Gal 1:9).

Garland records the fundamental errors in the preaching of Paul's enemies, as observed in the last chapters of this letter, and we can observe how they are very unlike the preaching of Paul:

1. Boastfulness and arrogance, self-aggrandizement;
2. Spiritual authority over others;
3. Berating humble servants of God;
4. Human standards as a way of judging others;
5. Rhetorical showmanship;
6. Pride in racial heritage;
7. Personal ecstatic visions;
8. Interpretation of Jesus as not a weak, suffering, humiliated servant (see 13:4);
9. Faulty doctrines of self-serving and not self-denying.[17]

In truth, Paul was less apprehensive about what his opponents were doing to his own reputation, and more about what they were doing to the congregation. Their arrogance and false doctrines were harming the peace and unity of

---

16. Garland, *2 Corinthians*, 465.
17. Garland, *2 Corinthians*, 463–64.

the community. The Corinthians were "putting up" with deception and false proclamations "easily enough" (11:4), which was corrupting their thinking and their faith.

"Super Apostles" (11:5–6)

Third, Paul "boasted" that he was hardly inferior to the adversaries, despite what they thought of themselves! In truth, Paul did have an impressive Jewish education and background, and he was granted knowledge of Christ that was true, powerful, and God-given (Gal 1:13–2:10); this made Paul distinctly different from his rivals' human wisdom. His enemies probably accused Paul of being a poor speaker; Paul replies that he made his gospel message very clear and very understandable to those in Corinth (11:6). His lack of oratory skill was not an excuse for the people to easily forget Paul's message and accept the words of the false teachers. Obviously, their salvation through faith in Christ was evidence of the clarity of Paul's message (3:2–3). In addition, there was no "secret" knowledge encrypted or spared from his readers (11:6). How could being totally honest and up-front with his readers make him an inadequate and inferior apostle?

In response to their accusations and denigrations, Paul twice insisted that he was *not* "the least inferior" to these adversaries. Justifying his own apostleship, he ironically labeled his opponents "super-apostles" (11:5; 12:11). In our vernacular, these were "hyper-" or "uber-apostles," or, in their own eyes, "exceedingly great." Perhaps Paul coined this label, which is full of irony and sarcasm, because it appears nowhere else in the New Testament. Surely it was what they must have considered themselves; yet in reality, of course, they were the "uber-fools." They put on their Superman capes, flexed their theological muscles, and demeaned Paul as being weak and "timid" (10:1), not belonging to Christ (10:7), and "inferior" (11:5; 12:11).

To label his opponents as "super-apostles" was a bold move of sarcasm. The superlative form of speaking is overdone in our culture today, but it was rare in Paul's culture. To use this title implied "over-inflated self esteem, pretentious claims and hero-worship by the Corinthians."[18] The title has vexed modern scholars because it is so unusual. Are the unnamed "super-apostles" the same as the demeaning opponents we have encountered throughout this letter? Are the "super-apostles" the same as the "false apostles" in 11:13–15? Are the "super-apostles" actually the "original twelve" apostles, the "pillar apostles" from Jerusalem?[19] The latter is highly unlikely, as it is a disparaging

---

18. Garland, *2 Corinthians*, 466.
19. Furnish, *II Corinthians*, 490; Belleville, *2 Corinthians*, 274.

title used for Paul's opponents, not for his legitimate colleagues in ministry (see 11:4). Paul's intruding, denigrating, boastful rivals who invaded his church at Corinth and were leading the people astray were both the "super-apostles" (sarcastically), and the "false apostles" (11:13, see introduction). They were filled with arrogance and self-importance and were deceptive, flawed, and manipulative.

The "Free" Gospel Message (11:7–9)

The fourth reason Paul chose to speak with "foolishness" was in response to his opponents' reprimand for not taking a fee for his services to the church. Paul explained why he did not take wages from the Corinthians as a payment for his services (11:7–9). Again, we can jump back to 1 Corinthians to see how Paul had set an earlier foundation for his financial situation with the congregation. First Corinthians 9 is an explanation of Paul's standards and model for missionary work. It is a passage on the material "rights" of an apostle (1 Cor 9:11–12). Yet, despite this he voluntarily gave up some of his "rights" simply to benefit his churches (1 Cor 9:12, 15, 17–19). He maintained an ardent desire to preach the gospel of Jesus Christ "free of charge": "we put up with anything rather than hinder the gospel of Christ" (1 Cor 9:12), and his "reward" for his ministry was "that in preaching the gospel I may offer it free of charge, and so not make use of my rights as a preacher of the gospel" (1 Cor 9:18). That is to say, Paul wanted to be neither a financial burden to his listeners, nor be in debt to someone (a patron) who, by supporting Paul financially, would have had some control over what he had to say in the community (1 Cor 9:19).

However, this was not enough explanation for the Corinthians. Another slanderous attack made by Paul's adversaries was that his refusal to accept payment for his ministry was evidence that his preaching was inadequate and amounted to nothing. In the first-century Roman Empire, traveling teachers and philosophers earned a living by charging payment for their professional instructions. By not doing so, his opponents suggested that Paul "lowered" himself to an amateur status and that he had broken the rule of payment for performance! The ridiculousness of these accusations is emphasized by Paul's use of irony and his formation of his rebuttal into a rhetorical question. Of course he was not sinning as he attempted to "build up" the congregation and bring them into a meaningful relationship with God through Christ Jesus (2 Cor 11:7)!

So, how did Paul earn a living that allowed him the opportunity to travel, preach, and serve in various cities across Western Europe and Greece? First, Paul was a "bi-vocational pastor." He worked as a tentmaker in various cities, including Corinth, to produce some income (Acts 18:1–5). Working as a common laborer was looked down upon in that culture; it caused more criticism and was not a good thing to put on his résumé. Primarily, however, he was "compelled to preach" (1 Cor 9:16), and he was devoted to this task to the point of self-deprivation. His "payment" for faithful, self-giving teaching was the salvation of the Corinthians themselves (1 Cor 9:1–2; 2 Cor 3:2–3).

Second, other churches donated material blessings to Paul so that he could continue his missionary work in the region. Of course, he did not "rob" other churches for support so that he could minister in Corinth, and he was *not* a financial "burden" to any church while he was working there (11:8–9). In fact, believers in Macedonia and Philippi supplied what Paul needed *after* he had served in their communities, so that he could minister in other places free of charge. In this way, his missionary efforts could continue in other areas (11:9, see Phil 4:15–19). Paul never wanted to be a "burden" (a financial liability) to new Christian communities who were already suffering (see 8:1–2), so he continued his ministry no matter what, and the false critics could not stop his efforts (11:10; see 1 Cor 9:16–17). No doubt his opponents had collected quite a tidy sum of payment for their services in Corinth and so considered themselves "superior" to Paul. His mode of ministry made his rivals look greedy for gain, and so they would have preferred for him to take a payment for services. They would have been Paul's "equals" (11:12).

Moreover, Paul's refusal to accept payment from the Corinthians was misconstrued as a lack of love and friendship for them (11:11). It was dishonorable to turn down friendship and an insult to a donor. The congregation failed to grasp the self-sacrifice of Paul in order to preach the plain truth of the gospel of Jesus Christ. It was because he loved them that he had to "boast" about them and their faith in Christ (7:14), in contrast to the foolish, self-centered "boasting" of his opponents.

Receiving gifts and remunerations in that culture had a number of "burdens" attached, including the reality that "friendship" could be bought, that benefactors only wanted prestige for themselves, and that there was a social obligation to return gratitude in kind. This is not the kind of "love" that Paul wanted (11:11; see 6:11–13; 7:2–4). Paul intentionally removed himself from the burdensome web of favoritism and financial obligations (see 12:13). The gullible Corinthians failed to recognize that the gracious gift of God, the salvation of human believers, does not have a price tag. To preserve and protect this amazing gift, Paul had to be different from the self-seeking, counterfeit apostles and swindlers who sought payment and prestige only for themselves. They were "crawling parasites who expected payment to serve their own private ends."[20] The same

---

20. Garland, *2 Corinthians*, 479–84. The wonderful, final quote of "crawling parasites" is on p. 484.

is true today: the price of salvation has already been paid, and paid with great suffering, so that it cannot be purchased by human wealth (6:10; 8:9).

False Apostles vs. the True Apostle (11:10–15)

One final motive for Paul's "foolishness" is a summation of the previously listed four, and is found in 11:12. He pledged, therefore, to continue his ministry and his "boasting" (1 Cor 9:15) and to literally cut off those pesky parasites who indicted him, demeaned him, and disparaged his ministry in the Corinthian church. They may have been very convincing in their speech, but they were charlatans who were putting on "religious faces" to further their own private objectives. Paul's argument of 11:13–15 continues from verse 12, where we see Paul's determination to eradicate such unscrupulous characters from the church. Now, Paul "unmasks" his opponents, the "super-apostles" (11:5; 12:11) and reveals their true nature using another coined name ("false apostles") for the same group of adversaries.

The idea of "masquerading" (11:13) is rightly understood as "disguising oneself" or "an alteration of outward appearance," especially with "deceptive intent."[21] The term "worker" implies some kind of missionary of the Christian gospel, as we see in Matthew 9:37–38 and 2 Timothy 2:15.[22] These rival missionaries posed as believers, but were actually "undercover agents," professing to be Christians, though doing the work of Satan.[23] Paul unleashes his rhetoric to compare and contrast the true, *authentic* apostle of Christ (that is, Paul) and the fake ("masquerading") "apostles" of Satan who were *inauthentic* in every way. They were "false apostles, deceitful workmen" and "servants of Satan," and only pretended to be "apostles of Christ" and "servants of righteousness":

Paul	False Apostles
Authentic apostle	Deceitful workmen
Apostle of Christ	Servants of Satan
Servant of righteousness	Servants of false Jesus, false spirit, and false gospel (11:4)

Paul exclaimed that it was "no wonder" they were trying to cover up their genuine character, because they were on the wrong team (11:14), and Satan is a deceiver and the father of lies.

---

21. Furnish, *II Corinthians*, 494; Belleville, *2 Corinthians*, 282.
22. Furnish, *II Corinthians*, 494.
23. Garland, *2 Corinthians*, 484.

The infiltration of counterfeit teachers and deceitful teachings were not unusual in the first decades of Christianity. There was a diversity of "Christian" interpretations, proclamations, and doctrines, many of which were erroneous and heretical. First-century Christians experienced intense persecution and strong opposition from two sides—from the Jews and from the Gentile unbelievers in their communities. So, Satan's work was centered on the new Christian communities, who were struggling to follow Christ and exist and prosper in the Roman Empire. Although he was defeated at the cross of Jesus Christ, Satan persisted in combating the people of God on earth (and continues to do so even today). His main "weapon" against humanity is deception, so within the church, Satan instigated false and deviant teachings; that is, "unacceptable and dangerous teaching becomes a prominent topic in the postapostolic generations of Christianity."[24]

For example, the Johannine community experienced "false prophets" (or teachers), and they were instructed to "test the spirits to see whether they are from God" (1 John 4:1–3). Peter calls Satan "a roaring lion," an image that speaks to the fear of the believers (1 Pet 5:8). We see in the book of Revelation that the new communities of Christians in Asia Minor were suffering under the influence of Satan (Rev 2:10). There were people in the Roman Empire (in Smyrna and Philadelphia) who masqueraded as devout Jews, but who were really not Jews at all; they were in the "synagogue of Satan" (Rev 2:9; 3:9). Satan was the power and deception behind the cult of other religions, as well as magic and sorcery among the Greeks and Romans. Satan "sat on his throne" in the city of Pergamum, where the temple of Zeus was central to the city (Rev 2:13).[25] The believers in Ephesus had a similar experience to that of the Corinthians: "I [Jesus] know that you cannot tolerate wicked people, that you have tested those who claim to be apostles but are not, and have found them false" (Rev 2:2). In fact, such false teachers may have convinced the believers in Ephesus to forsake their first love (Rev 2:4), turn their backs on Christ, and forget what Christ had done for them.

Furthermore, much of the peril and persecution of the Christian church in the first century was in the form of speech and "slander" (Rev 2:9). That is, the pretend Jews in Smyrna, in Pergamum, and in Sardis (see Rev 3:9) were slanderous "liars" who rebuked "the name of Jesus" and told his followers that he did *not*, indeed, love them. It is easy to criticize something one does not understand. It is also worth noting that in Revelation 2:12, it is Jesus who is the one using the "sharp, double-edged sword" of words to address his churches. This image is found in the prophecy of Isaiah:

24. C. E. Arnold, "Satan, Devil," *DLNTD* 1079.
25. Arnold, "Satan," 1078.

If you resist and rebel,
>   you will be devoured by the sword,
>   For the mouth of the Lord has spoken. (Isa 1:20)

Before I was born the Lord called me;
>   From my mother's womb he has spoken my name.
> He made my mouth like a sharpened sword . . . (Isa 49:1b–2a)

As a description of Jesus, the same wording is found in Revelation 1:16: "out of his mouth came a sharp double-edged sword." Thus, using direct words, Jesus both compliments and condemns ("double-edged") the seven Asia Minor churches (Rev 1:19–3:22). Repeatedly, Jesus insisted that the believers must "hear what the Spirit says to the churches" (Rev 2:7, 11, 17, 29; 3:6, 13, 22). The offensive words of the slanderous opponents of the young Christian churches were rebuked by the assuring words of their Savior.

In the same way, the "wicked men" and "false apostles" had seduced the "foolish" Corinthians with their slanderous words (note the word "preaches" in 2 Cor 11:4). Those believers had quickly turned their back on Paul's teachings and accepted the false apostles and their teachings, thus fragmenting the church itself. Had they "tested" the intruders? Did they simply "tolerate" their dishonesty and selfishness? In short, Paul was talking as his enemies had talked—as fools (11:17). Even more than their "actions" (11:15), the lies and deceptive speech of his rivals (11:4) were intended to bring Paul down.

Paul labels Satan a "masquerading angel of light" (11:14). An "angel" is generally used as a term for a messenger of God, and angels are described in the New Testament as "lightning" (Matt 28:3), shining (Luke 2:9), and gleaming (Luke 24:4).[26] Therefore, the exterior guise of Satan is bright and shining while it hides his dark, true nature. In reality, he is the "prince of this world" (John 12:31; 14:30; 16:11), and the archenemy of God/Jesus. In the Old Testament, "there are holy angels (Ps 148:2), fallen angels (Gen 6:1–4), and corrupt angels (Ps 82)."[27]

Angels became more important in the later apocalyptic and pseudepigrapha literature, especially in the literature from Qumran. In the Dead Sea Scrolls we meet "Belial, the prince of darkness," and "Michael, the angel of light" (1QS 3:22–23; 1QM 17). Note Paul's use of "Belial" in his discussion of light and darkness, believers and unbelievers, in 2 Corinthians 6:14–16. According to Jewish legends, found in the extracanonical writings called

---

26. Belleville, *2 Corinthians*, 282.
27. S. F. Noll, "Angels, Heavenly Beings, Angel Christology," *DLNTD* 44.

The Life of Adam and Eve (9:1) and the *Apocalypse of Moses* (17:1–2), Satan transformed himself into the brightness of angels when he appeared to Eve, pretending to be concerned about her.[28] In the New Testament, then, the evil powers have the authority to corrupt and condemn only "in the present age," and yet are ultimately defeated by Christ who is "above all rule and authority, power and dominion" (Eph 1:17–23).[29] The true, authorized apostles of Christ are his servants of righteousness (see 2 Cor 5:20–21). Thus, Paul assured his readers that Satan is doomed to destruction with all of his "servants" (his false apostles or "false prophets," 11:15; see Rev 20:10). Amen!

In the first half of chapter 11, then, the reader perceives the truth through viewing personal experiences of Paul. One who was an authentic apostle of Christ sarcastically evaluated his opponents in such a way that would capture his readers and help them fully grasp the ridiculousness of their false thinking. This is, in fact, genius. Paul did not rebuke, criticize, or belittle his audience. He did not reprimand or correct them. He simply established the truth about his rival missionaries and about their felonious gospel message. The titles that he gave them ("super-apostles," "false apostles") were descriptive enough.

How ironic that the supreme persecutor of the earliest Jesus-followers, the Pharisee Saul, became Paul, the receiver of severe persecution and denigration by the very people who should have valued and supported him the most—those who shared his field of Christian missionary work. How ironic that the one who dearly loved the church at Corinth was being replaced by selfish, slanderous, deceitful, and arrogant teachers. In spite of this, Paul warned the church that his adversaries would certainly get what they "deserve" (11:15; see Rom 3:8; Phil 3:19). He continued his ironic rhetoric and defense as he engaged in what is now known as the "Fool's Speech" (2 Cor 11:16–12:13), which takes us to the next section of the letter.

LIVE the Story

"Different Jesus"

In the middle of the twentieth century, especially during the 1960s, there was a popular "Jesus Movement" that swept across America. It was accompanied by slogans of "peace and brotherhood," topics that were attributed to Jesus's teachings. But the reframed Jesus was an awkward picture, one of a man who wore headbands, comfy sandals, sang love songs, played the sitar, and who was

---

28. Belleville, *2 Corinthians*, 283; Furnish, *II Corinthians*, 495.
29. Noll, "Angels," 44.

surrounded by flowers and incense. It was an amalgamation of Jesus Christ, the Buddha, and whatever Hindu god that was in fashion at the time. This Jesus was all about self-realization, loving one's neighbor (at least for one night), and pacifism. One could get to know him better not by reading the Bible, but by mediation and drug-induced contemplation.

This is not the biblical Jesus; it is certainly not the Jesus Paul preached (11:4). The Bible teaches a Jesus who was misunderstood, accused, threatened, rebuked, spat upon, denied, and suffered and died a cruel death. What a difference! It seems that a "warm and fuzzy" Jesus is much more desirable than the reality of the biblical Jesus. However, what would life be like if Jesus were just another influential speaker, a kind and compassionate man, a miracle worker, or a promoter of human goodwill? Eliminate the terrible passion of Jesus, and what is left? No crucifixion, no resurrection, no redemption? This may sound incredible, but this is the Jesus that some people follow today. No rules, no judgment, just "love and brotherhood."

If an erroneous Jesus is taught, then the results are erroneous ideas about the Spirit and the truth of the gospel. As it was for Paul, is it the responsibility of Christian leaders to guard the truth, present the whole, complete, and authentic message of the Bible, and help believers mature with the veracity of all of God's Word—love and grace, obedience and judgment. John Stott says it beautifully:

> Away then with our petty, puny, pygmy Jesuses! Away with our Jesus clowns and pop stars! Away too with our political Messiahs and revolutionaries! For these are caricatures. If this is how we think of him, then no wonder our immaturities persist. Where, then, shall we find the authentic Jesus? The answer is that he is found in the Bible—the book that could be described as the Father's portrait of the Son painted by the Holy Spirit. . . . Nothing is more important for mature Christian discipleship than a fresh, clear, true vision of the authentic Jesus.[30]

What kind of Jesus are we teaching today? Are we preaching a "half-Jesus" who is much more appealing to our culture without all the suffering? As Christian leaders, do we love our congregations so much that we want them to know the *whole* Jesus? Our society is suffering, so would it help to know that Jesus suffered, too? Again, Stott says, "Nothing is more important for mature Christian discipleship than a fresh, clear, true vision of the authentic Jesus."[31]

---

30. Stott, *Radical Disciple*, 44–45.
31. Stott, *Radical Disciple*, 45.

"Different Spirit"

In addition, it is still confusing to hear or sing about the "Holy Ghost," a name which scares young children and bewilders adults. But it is imperative that believers fully understand the role and the function of God's Holy Spirit. First, it is important to realize that it was "Paul's eschatological vision of personal and communal transformation empowered by the Spirit" that drove his ministry.[32] That is, the transformation of each believer (3:18) as well as the growth and transformation of the church can only be accomplished by and through the Holy Spirit.

Second, Paul believed that we live in the "new age" of the Spirit, in contrast to the "old age" of the law, so the Christian is empowered by his Spirit to obey and enjoy our God. While the roots of Paul's faith in the Holy Spirit were found in the Old Testament, in his letters he reframes the human life in relationship with God *through* his Spirit. Paul was greatly concerned about the moral and ethical lives of his people and how they were to "walk by the Spirit" (Gal 5:16–18). Christians are to be different; we are to be living life *according* to the Spirit, and not according to the flesh (or our worldly desires, Rom 8:9, 11). For Paul, "life in the Spirit is dominated by the cross as well as the resurrection"; it is now defined by faith in Jesus Christ and obedience to him through his Spirit (Gal 2:20).[33]

Third, with the writer of 1 John, believers today need to learn to "test the spirits" to be certain that it is God's Spirit that directs their lives. Christians today are still in a spiritual battle between the evil in the world and God's good Spirit. To remain faithful to God through all kinds of adversity is not easy, but the Spirit is present and remains faithful. To mock or ignore this battle leaves a person open to peril.

Fourth, the Spirit is the promise, the "deposit, and guarantee" (2 Cor 5:5; Eph 1:13) of a life never separated from God. That is, the Spirit grants the believer that "eschatological vision" and hope of the eternal life to come. Unlike the guarantee for my refrigerator, the Spirit's promise lasts forever, and gives hope and security for believers in the face of life or death.

Finally, as we have seen in 2 Corinthians 10–12, Paul was acutely aware of his own weakness and the power of the Holy Spirit. The power of the Spirit may be omitted or ignored by many Christian leaders today, perhaps because they fear the consequences of promoting the vague, misunderstood aspect of "spiritual" Christianity.

All things considered—transformation, empowerment, an advocate, a guarantee for the future, and strength in weakness—the ramifications of this for

---

32. Mitchel, "New Perspective and the Christian Life: Solus Spiritus," 74.
33. Mitchel, "New Perspective and the Christian Life: Solus Spiritus," 97.

believers today are massively significant. While we recognize the Spirit in our trinitarian confessions, most Christians tend to function in view of an impersonal, powerless, phantom Holy Spirit. We need to shift our thinking and be energized by the presence of God in and among us in the person of the Spirit.[34]

It is the Spirit who both converts and convicts; the Spirit inaugurates conversion of a person to the Christian faith and then empowers and convicts believers (see John 14:15–27; 16:5–16). Thus, the Spirit brings about the ethical Christian life. For Paul, Christian ethics, the way that we live and behave as Christians, is life in the Spirit. Furthermore, the Spirit brings diversity into unity in the community of Christian believers. The "people of God" are those who are "brought to life by the Spirit so as to live the life of heaven on earth, also by the Spirit—walking in the Spirit, being led by the Spirit, sowing to the Spirit. The whole of life under the new covenant is now lived in and by the Spirit, including worship, one's relationship to God, and everyday life itself."[35]

"Different Gospel"

Literally the word "gospel" means "good news"; for Paul, it was the message of God's saving work through Jesus Christ (1 Cor 15:1–4). The "good news" is a timeless expression of the grace of God that generates a positive response of human faith. Paul was concerned about those teachers who proclaimed a "different gospel" (Gal 1:6–9), and the same should be concerning to Christians today. Paul makes it clear that an alteration of the essential gospel message is to "desert" the God "who called you by the grace of Christ" (Gal 1:6 NASB). There are those teachers who achieve fame and fortune by declaring a "prosperity gospel" to vulnerable audiences. Preachers tend to deliver a message that the congregation wants to hear—Jesus is love, peace, joy, and financial security. Who wants to hear a Sunday morning message about oppression and suffering? But maybe that's exactly what we need in our world today.

How do we determine if the correct "gospel" is taught? How do we "test" our teachings to be sure they are the pure, unadulterated gospel? Not unlike the church in Galatia, the church today must evaluate teachings to see if there are any additional requirements for salvation or justification beyond a simple belief in Jesus Christ. It is by grace through faith alone that justifies a person; other rules or fees or practices that "help people get to heaven" are erroneous. Jesus released his people from the bondage of legalism, especially those rules and regulations established by people who could profit professionally and financially from their teachings and instructions. Paul's gospel was the

34. Fee, *Paul, the Spirit, and the People of God*, 34.
35. Fee, *Paul, the Spirit, and the People of God*, 98–99.

proclamation of Jesus Christ, so that all nations might believe and obey him (see Rom 16:25–27). Furthermore, Paul was not "ashamed" to preach the true gospel message (Rom 1:16), and he fought to protect the truth of the gospel (Gal 2:5, 14); these are paradigms for the Christian church today.

Early in my Christian life I was taught that I was saved because of my profession of faith in Christ, but I was also taught that there was an imperative second step. I had to make sure that Jesus was *Lord* of my life through the sacrificial giving of my time, talents, and tithes. This was a bit perplexing because I could never figure out exactly what that involved. What was the minimum or the maximum amount of myself that I should give? How much was necessary to be sure I was being obedient and making him Lord of everything? I was taught a "slanted" gospel. I thought I had to be obedient to God to be accepted by him; in truth, I am accepted by God, and then I choose to be obedient out of love for him. It is not all about my efforts and my earning God's love. I neglected to appreciate the grace of God in my life and the power of the Holy Spirit that was in me.

The history of the Christian church over the last two millennia is one that bears the scars of courageous missionaries who put their own lives into peril for the sake of the gospel (2 Cor 4:5, 10–12). The correct, God-given gospel message that was delivered so boldly resulted in the spread of the faith all over the globe, and it continues today. To promote an incorrect gospel message would be an insult to those who put their own lives into jeopardy for the sake of Jesus and the correct message.

John Stott gives an example of missionary work in China. When the Communist government took over China, all the foreign missionaries were instructed to leave the country. There were, perhaps, only a million Protestant believers in China. A decade into the twenty-first century, there were about 70 million Christian believers thriving under the Communist regime. How does that happen? It happens when the true gospel message is proclaimed. Stott quotes Tony Lambert as saying:

> The reason for the growth of the church in China and for the outbreak of genuine spiritual revival in many areas is inextricably linked to the whole theology of the cross. . . . The stark message of the Chinese church is that God uses suffering and the preaching of a crucified Christ to pour out revival and build his church. Are we in the West still willing to hear? . . . The Chinese church has walked the way of the cross. The lives and deaths of the martyrs of the 1950s and 1960s have borne much fruit.[36]

---

36. Stott, *Radical Disciple*, 122–23; Tony Lambert, *The Resurrection of the Chinese Church* (London: Hodder & Stoughton, 1991), 174, 267.

Indeed, "are we in the West still willing to hear" a gospel message of a crucified Christ and to willingly, faithfully follow in his footsteps? Are we willing to be silent and listen to the still, small voice of the Holy Spirit in our midst? Do we manipulate the message every Sunday morning to make it "more relevant" and more pleasing to the comfortable Christians of today?

Pastoral Ministry and "Sinners"

The battle of sin and righteousness is not only in the secular world, it is also in the church. No doubt Satan is very pleased to have "false Jesuses," feeble views of the Holy Spirit, and defective gospel messages preached in our churches today. Sin is rampant in the church, even among church leaders. Satan loves it; he is pleased that we all have learned to cover up our sins effectively and present faces of good, moral people. Conceivably, he can destroy the church from within.

Yet, constantly confronting sins and disobedience in a congregation can be discouraging to pastors and leaders. Efforts to reform a church, not unlike Paul's task in Corinth, can be distressing and depressing. I heard of a pastor who spent the first three months of a new charge on his knees in his office, pleading with God to remove him from the new assignment. Some influential members of the congregation hated his preaching style; they called him unrepeatable names and even criticized his wife. The pastor quickly filled with resentment and frustration. His perseverance won the day, and he is still in the same church today, but ministry can be an unbearable struggle against sin—both our own and that of others.

Since he is the "father of lies," Satan takes pleasure in human deception and dishonesty (11:13–15). Seldom do human beings, even Christian believers, take sin and Satan seriously and regard themselves through a lens of sincere, honest evaluation. Yet, is it the job of the pastor, the Christian teacher, or leader to correct and combat all the gnawing sins in the Christian community? How do we address sin in the church with honesty, tact, and truthfulness? Eugene Peterson writes that "a tug of war takes place every week between pastor and people."

> The contest is over conflicting views of the person who comes to church. People see themselves in human and moral terms: they have human needs that need fulfilling and moral deficiencies that need correcting. Pastors see people quite differently. We see them in theological terms: they are sinners—persons separated from God who need to be restored in Christ. These two views—the pastor's theological understanding of people and the people's self-understanding—are almost always in tension.[37]

---

37. Peterson, *Contemplative Pastor*, 125.

Peterson explains that "sinner" is a "theological distinction" and *not* a "moralistic judgment." It places the human being in relation to a holy, just God and reveals a gulf of separation between humanity and God. Most people are really nice people, and not evil, conniving, unhappy, and anxious axe murderers. Calling someone a "sinner" is not a condemnation on a person's morals or ethics; it is a condition common to all human beings that places every one of us in need of forgiveness and grace. "If the pastor rigorously defines people as *fellow* sinners, he or she will be prepared to share grief, shortcomings, pain, failure, and have plenty of time left over to watch for signs of God's grace operating in this wilderness, and then fill the air with praises for what he or she discovers."[38] As Paul wrote to the Romans, "But where sin increased, grace increased all the more, so that, just as sin reigned in death, so also grace might reign through righteousness to bring eternal life through Jesus Christ our Lord" (Rom 5:20b–21).

Moreover, Paul wrote that believers are "new people," "new creatures," reconciled to God, with new thoughts, actions, and desires. Remarkably, our sins are not counted against us, and we can become "the righteousness of God" (2 Cor 5:16–21)! Since we are all in this thing together, the gracious pastor or leader helps us to understand *forms* of sin (*why* is it there?) and how we can come out of its bondage. With prayer, love, discernment, and words of faith that are appropriate for each human frailty, we can journey on the road to Christian maturity together.[39] In addition, we must allow the heartbreaking results of sin to be avenged and rectified by God (11:15).

Finally, Peterson writes that "the happy result of a theological understanding of people as sinners is that the pastor is saved from continual surprise that they are, in fact, sinners."[40] Sin is no surprise; grace is. There is seldom a good reason for complaining about anyone in the congregation, because the Christian leader is just as much of a sinner as the worst person in the community. In conclusion, then, Peterson contends that "grace is the main subject of pastoral conversation and preaching."[41] In all aspects of Christian ministry and service, it is not about superior judgment, or condemning people, or even "missing the mark." It is about "indescribable," undeserved grace, reconciliation, and redemption for all of us.

---

38. Peterson, *Contemplative Pastor*, 126 (emphasis mine).
39. Peterson, *Contemplative Pastor*, 128.
40. Peterson, *Contemplative Pastor*, 127.
41. Peterson, *Contemplative Pastor*, 127.

LISTEN to the Story

¹⁶I repeat: Let no one take me for a fool. But if you do, then tolerate me just as you would a fool, so that I may do a little boasting. ¹⁷In this self-confident boasting I am not talking as the Lord would, but as a fool. ¹⁸Since many are boasting in the way the world does, I too will boast. ¹⁹You gladly put up with fools since you are so wise! ²⁰In fact, you even put up with anyone who enslaves you or exploits you or takes advantage of you or puts on airs or slaps you in the face. ²¹To my shame I admit that we were too weak for that!

Whatever anyone else dares to boast about—I am speaking as a fool—I also dare to boast about. ²²Are they Hebrews? So am I. Are they Israelites? So am I. Are they Abraham's descendants? So am I. ²³Are they servants of Christ? (I am out of my mind to talk like this.) I am more. I have worked much harder, been in prison more frequently, been flogged more severely, and been exposed to death again and again. ²⁴Five times I received from the Jews the forty lashes minus one. ²⁵Three times I was beaten with rods, once I was pelted with stones, three times I was shipwrecked, I spent a night and a day in the open sea, ²⁶I have been constantly on the move. I have been in danger from rivers, in danger from bandits, in danger from my fellow Jews, in danger from Gentiles; in danger in the city, in danger in the country, in danger at sea; and in danger from false believers. ²⁷I have labored and toiled and have often gone without sleep; I have known hunger and thirst and have often gone without food; I have been cold and naked. ²⁸Besides everything else, I face daily the pressure of my concern for all the churches. ²⁹Who is weak, and I do not feel weak? Who is led into sin, and I do not inwardly burn?

³⁰If I must boast, I will boast of the things that show my weakness. ³¹The God and Father of the Lord Jesus, who is to be praised forever, knows that I am not lying. ³²In Damascus the governor under King Aretas had the city of the Damascenes guarded in order to arrest me. ³³But I was lowered in a basket from a window in the wall and slipped through his hands.

¹²:¹I must go on boasting. Although there is nothing to be gained, I will go on to visions and revelations from the Lord. ²I know a man in Christ who fourteen years ago was caught up to the third heaven. Whether it was in the body or out of the body I do not know—God knows. ³And I know that this man—whether in the body or apart from the body I do not know, but God knows—⁴was caught up to paradise and heard inexpressible things, things that no one is permitted to tell. ⁵I will boast about a man like that, but I will not boast about myself, except about my weaknesses. ⁶Even if I should choose to boast, I would not be a fool, because I would be speaking the truth. But I refrain, so no one will think more of me than is warranted by what I do or say, ⁷or because of these surpassingly great revelations. Therefore, in order to keep me from becoming conceited, I was given a thorn in my flesh, a messenger of Satan, to torment me. ⁸Three times I pleaded with the Lord to take it away from me. ⁹But he said to me, "My grace is sufficient for you, for my power is made perfect in weakness." Therefore I will boast all the more gladly about my weaknesses, so that Christ's power may rest on me. ¹⁰That is why, for Christ's sake, I delight in weaknesses, in insults, in hardships, in persecutions, in difficulties. For when I am weak, then I am strong.

¹¹I have made a fool of myself, but you drove me to it. I ought to have been commended by you, for I am not in the least inferior to the "super-apostles," even though I am nothing. ¹²I persevered in demonstrating among you the marks of a true apostle, including signs, wonders and miracles. ¹³How were you inferior to the other churches, except that I was never a burden to you? Forgive me this wrong!

Listening to the Text in the Story: Deuteronomy 25:1–3; 31:6, 8, 23; Joshua 1:1–2:1; Isaiah 6:1; 8:18; 20:3; Jeremiah 1:1–3; Ezekiel 1:1–3; Hosea 1:1; Amos 1:1; Acts 16:9–10; 18:9; 20:22; 22:6–13; 26:12–19; Galatians 1:11–12, 16; Ephesians 3:2–3.

Unfriendly waters do a friendly
Thing: curses, cataract-hurled
Stones, make the rough places
Smooth; a rushing whitewater stream
Of blasphemies hate-launched,
Then caught by the sun, sprays rainbow
Arcs across the Youghiogeny.

Savaged by the river's impersonal
Attack the land is deepened to bedrock.
Wise passivities are earned
In quiet, craggy, occasional pools
That chasten the wild waters to stillness,
And hold them under hemlock green
For birds and deer to bathe and drink
In peace—persecution's gift:
The hard-won, blessed letting be.
　　　　　—*Eugene H. Peterson*[1]

I love to travel—anywhere, anytime—I am ready to go explore new places, new cultures, and new experiences. Yet, most extensive travel involves thoughtful preparation and careful planning. Even after the most vigilant planning, unexpected circumstances (like a blizzard) can alter or cancel the very best travel intentions. Imagine, for a moment, the travels of the apostle Paul in the first century. He had no online reservations or airline miles in his favor; he had only ancient ships, donkeys, and sandals on his feet. It has been suggested that Paul traveled over 20,000 miles in his lifetime, over hazardous land and tumultuous seas. It was unfortunate that Paul was forced to change his travel plans to visit the Corinthian church (1:15–17), and when he finally did arrive in Corinth, it was not a pleasant visit (1:23–2:1). The result of that visit was a "painful" or "severe" letter (2:3–4).

At this point in the letter, Paul was preparing to visit the church at Corinth for a third time (12:14). He had planted the church on his first visit to the area in Greece (Acts 18). After that initial visit, Paul penned a letter that has been lost to us (see Introduction), followed by our canonical *1 Corinthians* letter, in response to deep divisions in the community and to questions that arose among the believers. Then, following that unsuccessful second visit, there was a "tearful letter" sent to the congregation (2:3–4; 7:8–12). Indeed, this was a tough assignment for Paul. The travel was grueling, and the successes in ministry were fading. He could not be there with the believers on a permanent basis because he was called to be a traveling missionary and a church planter in the region. In his absence, divisions, tension, suspicion, and accusations in the church were present and growing. No one looks forward to the repetition of a painful visit or a confrontational communication with "many tears" (2:4), so 2 Corinthians is a letter that was written with the intent of preventing another unhappy visit with the believers in Corinth. Paul needed to resolve the tension,

---

1. Peterson, *Contemplative Pastor*, 147.

the false accusations, and false teachings to prepare the church for a better, more productive third and final visit.[2]

We have already noted that chapters 10 through 13 feature Paul's "foolishness" and "boasting," just the opposite of what we would expect from a teacher correcting his readers. Yet, this was Paul's tactic; he was combating malicious opponents, false teachings, and deceptive slanderers corrupting and hurting the church. He was using his opponents' own scheme of "worldly boasting" to emphasize their deception and self-interest in the hope that the congregation would recognize that they were being duped by these false teachers. In chapter 10 he described the situation in Corinth figuratively with a "war of words," and in the first part of chapter 11 he described his opponents more literally. He contrasted the deceptive, misleading manner of the ministry of his rivals to his own style of ministry, which clearly centered on Jesus Christ and on the best interest of the church. Paul made a commitment not to be a "burden" on the congregation financially, so that the people in Corinth might be exalted (11:7–12). In verses 11:1–15 Paul was defining the battle lines, clearly differentiating between his message and his missionary style and that of his opponents, so his readers would see the fallacy of his adversaries' knowledge, words, and actions. Thus, what some modern commentators call Paul's "Fool's Speech" opens with 11:16 and continues to 12:13.

Figures of Speech

We are able to hear Paul's use of varied figures of speech, which continues through chapters 11 and 12. He turned the idea of "boasting" upside down to emphasize the kind of worldly boasting employed by his opponents (10:2). He never disparaged his opponents' theology; he simply points out their true motives and destructive behavior (11:20). He maintained the use of antithesis to challenge his readers' thinking, particularly in contrasting weakness and power. In 11:23–28 we see the third and final catalogue of hardships listed by Paul (see 4:8–9; 6:4–10). Ironically, Paul used his human weakness to illustrate God's power and strength (11:30; 12:5, 9, 10; 13:4). By concentrating on his human weakness in these chapters, he challenged the readers' misguided confidence in human power and strength (10:1–2). Again, we observe Paul's prolific use of irony as he humbly called into question the "wisdom" of his readers: he chided the Corinthians that they were "so wise" for "putting up with the fools!" (see 1 Cor 4:10–13; 2 Cor 11:16–17, 19–21, 29; 12:5, 11, 13). Perhaps Paul's most famous metaphor appears in 12:7, expressed as a "thorn in my flesh," a constant physical pain that God chose

---

2. Belleville, *2 Corinthians*, 21–22.

not to remove from Paul's body. The succinct contradiction (or paradox) in 12:10 is memorable: "For when I am weak, then I am strong." Additionally, Paul's memory of the incident in Damascus (11:32–33) serves as a *metonymy*, where one idea is substituted for an original idea to which it is connected. The story illustrated his "weakness" (11:30), and he used it as an example of God's power and grace.[3]

Finally, we can also hear Paul effectively arguing for his life and his ministry in the final chapters of this letter; he is also contending for the life of the Christian church in Corinth. It appears as though he was selecting every word carefully and positioning every argument strategically, constructing a strong case for the church he loved and for the spiritual lives of people about whom he cared deeply. Paul moves from numerous "I" statements in chapters 10 through 12 to "you" statements in chapter 13 (vv. 7–10). He was finished using himself as an example of God's presence in times of weakness and hardship in an effort to reinforce his final instructions to his readers concerning the reality of power and grace of God in all believers.

EXPLAIN the Story

Paul Boasts about His Sufferings (11:16–33)

All this silly boasting by Paul (11:1–15, 16–18) was very much against his nature, but was done to prove a point that his readers needed to learn. The tone of the "Fool's Speech" is clearly ironic; he was using the technique employed by his adversaries ("foolish" or "worldly boasting"), tossed back at them, to illustrate how foolish they really were. Verse 11:16 is not unlike 11:1, where his readers were accepting the foolishness of his opponents, so they could certainly tolerate the same from Paul. He asked for their patience, and then he told his readers what he was about to do—that is, speak like a fool. Some commentators have entitled Paul's words the "Fool's Speech" (11:16–12:13) because Paul was "forced to play the fool."[4] In addition, and contrary to Paul's normal discourse, we observe the abundant use of the singular pronoun "I" in 11:16–12:13. Of course, it was Paul's rival missionaries who had invaded the community and who had started the whole business of "foolish boasting," so Paul chose to continue using their method, reluctantly turning the spotlight on himself. He quickly pointed out that this kind of

---

3. Kierspel, *Charts on the Life, Letters and Theology of Paul*, 89–90.
4. Belleville, *2 Corinthians*, 284, whereas Furnish begins the speech "proper" at v. 21b (*II Corinthians*, 512).

"self-boasting" was not the habit of godly apostles, because true apostles only "boasted in the Lord" (11:17; 10:17). Thus, the readers were warned that Paul would continue to "boast as the world does" (11:18), even hesitantly, in order to make the readers listen and fully understand why they were, indeed, the foolish ones, for listening to the words of his adversaries.

Verse 11:19, then, is a repeat of Paul's point in 11:4; ironically, his readers "easily enough" accepted the foolish boasting of his opponents, the "false apostles." Also, the rival teachers/preachers were addressed in a neutral manner in 11:4, as "someone," but in 11:19, they are characterized as "fools." His words progress to make the point more clear—here, the people "*gladly* put up with the *fools*" who were actually "taking advantage" of the congregation! (11:19–20). Of course, they are not wise at all, just the opposite (v. 19), because the congregation was being abused by the very ones who were "boasting in the way the world does" (v. 18). How could they reject Paul, their founder in the faith, and foolishly follow the "fools" who enslaved them, exploited them, took advantage of them, put on airs or slapped them in the face (11:20)?

He had mock pity for the readers because they were really "slaves to deception" and allowed themselves to be exploited, or "devoured" by his enemies. The "false apostles" had even resorted to physical and mental abuse, treating the people as their inferiors and pushing them into submission. The picture of Paul's adversaries comes into alarming focus as aggressive, authoritarian, greedy leaders who "took advantage" of the congregation in every way imaginable.[5] Instead of arguing against his adversaries' theology and rhetoric, Paul merely points out their abuse of power and their deceitful manner of ministry in Corinth (11:20).[6]

Furthermore, and with another ironic statement, Paul confessed that he would never be so "weak" (certainly an accusation made by his enemies) as to hurt the people like that (11:21). It is strange to modern ears that a group of people would accept and follow leaders whose intentions were to hurt them and take advantage of them, but it happens. Their self-importance was acceptable in that culture, and it was fine (perhaps expected) for people to be arrogant, egotistical, and proud, giving themselves all the glory.[7] With deep disparity, Paul continued to speak "foolishly" as he launched into his own boasting to counteract the pride of his rivals. They may have made many claims to demonstrate their "superiority" over Paul (and others), but Paul rebuked them all, and lists his own real reasons to "boast" (11:22–23).

---

5. Garland, *2 Corinthians*, 489.
6. Ellington, "Not Applicable to Believers?," 330.
7. Garland, *2 Corinthians*, 487–88.

Hebrew Heritage (11:22)

First, his adversaries were proud of their heritage (11:21b–22). They were card-carrying, nationalistic Jews from Palestine. This was a position worth bragging about. "Hebrews" indicated a native language and a way of life indigenous to the Palestine area (Acts 22:3; Phil 3:5). It is a title of honor and demonstrates respect for their nation.[8] "Israelites" implied that they were members of God's chosen people from the time of their ancestors. They were people of Israel, "adopted as sons" by God, adhering to God's traditions and laws (Rom 9:4–5). "Abraham's descendants" (or in the OT vernacular, the "seed of Abraham") were Jews who followed the ancient covenants of God, so they were "children of the promise" (Rom 4:13–18; 9:6–8).[9] In addition, the Greeks and Romans put a great deal of emphasis on one's family line; honor and prestige were granted based on one's heritage, so this made sense to the Corinthians. Yet, point by point, Paul matched his opponents' boasting and reiterated, "I am more" (2 Cor 11:22–23). Paul was a bit embarrassed to boast of his background, but his rivals had little to go on in comparison to Paul's "pedigree."

Hardships (11:23–29)

The second reason Paul "boasts" about himself is because his opponents considered themselves "servants of Christ" (11:23), and probably supported this statement by claiming a trouble-free life. It may appear to be a title of devotion, but while they wore "sheep's clothing, . . . inwardly they are ferocious wolves" (Matt 7:15). Ironically, and in clear contrast, Paul used his own hardships to convince his readers that his opponents' claims were hollow (2 Cor 11:23–29). The nature of his ministry and the persecution he experienced demonstrated that he was far more of a "servant of Christ" than any of the others. This is the third time in this letter that Paul was boasting about his sufferings. His tribulations listed here were intense, even life-threatening, in the same vein as the trials he listed earlier in the letter in 4:8–11 and 6:4–10. Eight floggings are recorded here, five at the hands of the Jews (see Deut 25:1–3; Matt 10:17–18), and three at the hands of the Roman authorities, who used rods in some circumstances (11:24–25; see Acts 16:22–23). The latter beatings took place despite the fact that Paul was a Roman citizen and was legally protected from such punishment (see Acts 16:37–39; 22:23–29). Stoning (2 Cor 11:25) was the traditional method of Jewish execution (Acts 14:19–20). The three shipwrecks are not detailed in the Acts accounts of

---

8. Furnish, *II Corinthians*, 514.
9. Garland, *2 Corinthians*, 493–94; see Belleville, *2 Corinthians*, 288.

Paul's travels, but probably took place on his missionary journeys (e.g., Acts 9:30; 13:4, 13; 14:25–26).

Why would Paul receive floggings from the Jews as he ministered among the Gentiles? Professor Hurtado sides with author Paula Fredriksen in a description of why Paul, the apostle to the Gentiles, would be punished by his fellow Jews:

Paul required his pagan converts to withdraw from worshipping the gods of the Roman world. Given the place and significance of the gods in Roman-era life, this would have generated serious tensions with the larger pagan community. As he identified himself as a Jew and linked up with Jewish communities in the various diaspora cities where he established early assemblies of Jesus-followers (*ekklesias*), these Jewish communities could have feared that they would bear the brunt of these tensions. So, Paul was meted out synagogue discipline in the form of the 39 lashes as punishment on several occasions (he mentions five).[10]

No doubt, then, that the cruel Jewish punishments inflicted on Paul were used as a clear statement for all the local Gentiles to see (Matt 10:18) that his ministry was false and blasphemous, and he did *not* have their stamp of approval. In reality, one's ethnic heritage and national background are irrelevant in the eyes of God, and Jesus's work on the cross was to redeem all of humanity, Jews and Gentiles alike, and Paul arranged his ministry around that truth (see Rom 11:11–21).

More broadly, Paul constantly experienced physical dangers and deprivations in his ministry (2 Cor 11:26–27), as well as emotional pain and pressure (11:27–28). As an anxious pastor, he recalled his sleepless nights and the apprehension about his co-worker Titus in this letter (7:5–7). The list of physical dangers set the tone of all of Paul's ministry, following in the shadow of Christ's suffering. Paul described his own life and leadership as being "in Christ," or in union with Christ, in such a way that "power and weakness cohere."[11] That is, participation in being "in Christ" means that a believer is a part of both Christ's power and suffering. Thus, the nature of Paul's ministry cost him dearly with such trials and suffering, but tribulations were evidence that Paul was, indeed, an authentic "servant of Christ." It is interesting that he specifically mentioned three groups of people—"my fellow Jews," "Gentiles," and "false believers"—as

10. Thanks to Larry Hurtado for his review of Fredriksen's then-forthcoming book in "Paul's 'Persecution' of Jewish Jesus-Followers: Nature & Cause(s)," November 11, 2014, http://wp.me/pYZXr-DP; see Paula Fredriksen, *Paul, the Pagan's Apostle* (New Haven: Yale University Press, 2017).

11. Ellington, "Not Applicable to Believers?," 339.

people who placed him in grave danger (11:26). He felt danger everywhere, and from every side, from people to natural disasters. Wherever he went, Paul was always on guard (Matt 10:17). In ministry, he was on the job and under scrutiny 24/7. Moreover, Paul knew that he was merely a human being, with common faults and flaws, and he acutely felt the ache of all human flaws and sins. Therefore Paul explained that his "boasting" was not in himself but was in "the God and Father of the Lord Jesus Christ" (2 Cor 11:30–31).

God's Strength (11:30–33)

Third, what made Paul "superior" to his adversaries was not a painless life, or his oratory skills, or his own strength; it was the power of God. The boasting continued, and God could attest to Paul's truth in his speech (11:31). He always put his churches first in his concerns (Rom 15:1–3). In his human limitations and weaknesses, the strength of God was demonstrated (2 Cor 11:30–31).

As an example, Paul related the incident in Damascus when God saved him from certain imprisonment or death (11:32–33). This was a daring escape from a politically charged city in a "bag of braided rope."[12] The brief account of this incident in Acts 9:23–25 indicates that the Jews planned to kill Paul (2 Cor 11:26). The Damascus incident took place about three years after Paul's conversion to Christianity. Paul had returned to Damascus after his conversion (see Gal 1:17–18), where the governor under Aretas ordered his arrest (2 Cor 11:32). No doubt his words about Jesus were becoming more and more powerful, and the Jews were angry and "baffled" (Acts 9:20–22). "His followers" saved him by smuggling him out of the city through "an opening in the wall, by night" (Acts 9:25). Although this event sounds like a James Bond adventure, it was a humiliating experience for Paul. For him, it was humbling to run from danger, and dishonorable not to face his opponents. He may have placed the story here as evidence of his humble spirit, as he boasts "of the things that show my weakness" (2 Cor 11:30).[13]

Throughout his life, Paul experienced such trials as if he were encountering death at every turn (1:8–9). Yet, it was God who rescued him from all the "dangers," and Paul learned not to rely on himself, but on God (1:9). It was God who "delivered us from such deadly peril" (1:10), and it was God who displays his power through human weakness (see 12:9–10). His "boasting in his weakness" allows Paul to expound on God's grace.[14] Eventually, of course,

---

12. Belleville, *2 Corinthians*, 296.
13. Belleville, *2 Corinthians*, 298.
14. Garland, *2 Corinthians*, 488.

God will destroy the "wisdom of the world," and the Corinthians needed to be reminded of that (1 Cor 1:19–20). The power and prerogative of God leads to another reason for "boasting" in response to the arrogant words of his opponents.

Visions, Revelations, and More Boasting (12:1–13)

There was a fourth reason why Paul continued "boasting" (2 Cor 12:1). If his enemies boasted about their special, extraordinary spiritual events, and that they received their teachings directly from God, Paul could declare that this was even more true in his life and ministry. Paul was afraid that even this testimony about "visions and revelations" would be insufficient to convict his rivals, but he realized it was necessary to counteract their accusations. In response to his adversaries, who may have placed too much emphasis on their ecstatic visions, Paul recorded one such personal experience (12:2–4). He had experienced other divine revelations and personal ecstatic visions, beginning with his dramatic conversion to Christianity which he called a "vision from heaven" (see Acts 26:12–19; Gal 1:11–12, 16). No doubt he had numerous such experiences, although he was reluctant to mention them. The Greek word for "vision" in 2 Corinthians 12:1 is found only here in Paul's letters, and he denies the idea that "visions" were a criterion of apostolic ministry.[15] In fact, how one serves, instructs, and edifies a church is a better claim to true servanthood. The very fact that Paul reluctantly told of this vision in this letter is a "sort of parody of the practice of his rivals."[16]

So, how does one describe the indescribable? How do you record words and sounds that you cannot express in human language? The vision in chapter 12 has been analyzed by modern interpreters in numerous ways; scholars have perceived similarities to Old Testament prophetic powers, to rabbinic parallels, to Jewish mysticism, to Greco-Roman or Stoic philosophies, or a combination of any of these. "Heavenly ascent" stories were not uncommon in ancient literature, and each culture placed great emphasis on visionary occurrences. While we can speculate about his vision, Paul simply does not "feed the appetite" of the Corinthians with juicy details of a supernatural event. And, the nature of Paul's account is unusual in that it is so connected to the narrative of the "thorn in the flesh" that follows.[17]

Paul is, perhaps, the "theologian of the Spirit," as he gives a fuller, more integrated understanding of the Holy Spirit than we find in other literature

---

15. J. Camery-Hoggatt, "Visions, Ecstatic Experience," *DPL* 963.
16. Furnish, *II Corinthians*, 543.
17. Camery-Hoggatt, "Visions," 964.

from the first century. The Holy Spirit is the initial mark of a Christian believer, and the filling of the Spirit in a converted person had "discernible effects."[18] Thus, Paul had visions and revelations from God, whose Spirit saved him, taught him, and directed him. This experience was remembered as the supreme height to which Paul was raised by God (see Acts 16:9–10; 18:9; 20:22; 22:6–11; Gal 1:11–12; Eph 3:2–3). Such an astounding event is juxtaposed next to the crushing, humiliating depth of one particular difficulty Paul was given to bear (2 Cor 12:7–10).

The way Paul related such an experience seems odd to us today. He shifted suddenly from first-person "I" (12:1) to a vague third-person approach ("a man . . . he . . . ," vv. 2–4). Then he separated himself from "a man like that" in verse 5 so that he could "boast" about such a man, who was, in reality, himself (did you get that?)! Then he shifted back to the first-person "I" again in verse 6. This is all so confusing that some modern scholars deny that Paul is really talking about himself in these verses. Yet, 12:1, 5, 7 would imply to the readers that the occurrence was surely one experienced by Paul. Again, he "boasted" about his experiences reluctantly, as he was meeting his opponents head-on; no doubt they had bragged about their own "visions and revelations" as evidence of their (patently false) apostolic authority (12:1).

Garland suggests that at first glance, it appears that Paul was relating an experience that happened to someone else, but he was actually recalling a very personal event that emphasized not his supremacy, but his weakness (11:30; 12:5). There may be at least three reasons why he chose to relate in it this way: first, "pseudonymity" was part of the Jewish tradition when it came to visions and revelations. The later rabbis were skeptical of supernatural visions, and people were not allowed to talk publicly about such events. Second, this may have been the nature of the event itself. In other words, Paul may have experienced the vision as if he were a spectator. Third, Paul was aware that, historically, only the greatest figures in the biblical past were "snatched up" to the "heavens" by God. He did not want to place himself on the same level as heroes like Enoch and Elijah, or especially the risen Jesus. Paul wanted to steer clear of any praise or glory for himself. He was not that special; whatever happened to Paul happened to a man who was "in Christ" (12:2), so boasting about such a revelation was truly a boast about Christ and not about himself.[19]

The event may have happened "fourteen years ago" (12:2), a long time before he planted the church in Corinth, but it must have been very memorable to Paul. He calls it a "vision." "A vision is always seen, whereas a revelation may

---

18. J. D. G. Dunn, "Spirit, Holy Spirit," *NIDNTT* 701.
19. Garland, *2 Corinthians*, 510.

be seen or may be received in some other way; all visions are also revelations, but not all revelations come through visions."[20] Like a person waking from a trance or from sleep-walking, the specific facets of the vision were unclear in Paul's mind or difficult to narrate. However, it was a life-changing experience, never to be forgotten.

In this vision, Paul employed the concept of being "caught up" as a description of being raised or lifted up (at least temporarily) and taken to a different place (2 Cor 12:2). This Greek verb in various forms has a number of nuances: in Acts 23:10 it is rendered "to seize, take away by force." In this verse, it denotes "to take away suddenly and vehemently" (see also, Rev 12:5).[21] In fact, Paul used the same verb in a different form to describe how believers "will be caught up [or raised up] together with them in the clouds to meet the Lord in the air" (1 Thess 4:17). In every case, it is God who is doing the "snatching," and his actions cannot be resisted by humanity. This is the image of an eagle who "swoops" down on his prey with such force that the poor rabbit has no chance to escape.

Thus, the vision Paul recorded was not imagined, but was truly of God and by God. He could not be certain whether it was "in the body" or separated from his earthly body, but God did it, and Paul was merely the receiver of the message. Perhaps Christ was not only the giver of vision but also the main subject matter of this one (12:2, 9).[22] Perhaps Paul saw the exalted Christ, and yet, in this explanation, we have only what he *heard*, and not *saw* (12:4). Be that as it may, the impact on Paul was great. Not unlike his conversion experience on the road to Damascus, this vision changed Paul's life completely; it was a very personal and cherished event that he seldom discussed.

Paradise (12:1–6)

Paul was raised to the "third heaven" (12:2), to a place he also called "paradise" (v. 4). The two terms refer to the very same place. We find both terms in ancient Jewish literature, thus revealing Paul's background. In the Greek Old Testament, "paradise" is a word used for a "garden" (Gen 2:8–10), a place of delight. The Persians also used the word "paradise" to denote an enclosure, park, or garden. In the New Testament it is a place or a position of happiness, harmony, and rest between human death and resurrection (see Luke 16:22–31; 23:43). The word "paradise" appears in only two other places in the New Testament: Luke puts the word in Jesus's mouth on the cross as a promise of

20. Harris, *Second Corinthians*, 831.
21. BDAG 133–34.
22. Furnish, *II Corinthians*, 524.

reward to righteous believers (Luke 23:43), and in Revelation 2:7 those believers who remain faithful and overcome adversity are given the right to eat from the "tree of life" (see Gen 2:9, signifying eternal life) in the paradise of God.

A related term, "heaven," is "that portion of the universe that is distinguished from the planet earth."[23] This is a picture of the final state when God and human believers are restored in perfect fellowship with one another; it is a common word for the dwelling place, or the realm, of God (Matt 6:9). It is also the dwelling place of the Father and the Son (i.e., Mark 16:19; Luke 24:51; Heb 9:24; John 14:2–4). Mentioned together, "heaven and earth" is a picture of all of creation, ruled by the Creator God. However, it is difficult to derive with certainty the origin of the concept of more than one "heaven" ("heavens," i.e., Ps 19:1; 57:5; 139:8; Eph 4:10; Rev 12:12). Thus, Paul's use of the parallel terms "caught up to paradise" and "caught up to the third heaven," (12:2–4) indicate that he was somehow transported to another "abode" through his vision where divine pronouncements originated.[24] The implication is that Paul was granted an astonishing vision of the glory of God (or Jesus, or both) beyond earthly reality, and he heard words that were beyond human vocabulary. The purpose of this revelation was to strengthen him in his weakness and suffering, and to give him a brief glimpse into an unknown but extraordinary future. Indeed, if an uncommon religious experience and an encounter with the living God could not legitimize Paul's apostleship, what would convince the Corinthians?[25]

In sharing his revelatory experience, Paul was teaching the Corinthians a new and different way to understand power and weakness. That is, what humans perceive as power is nothing compared to what God can do, and did, through Christ. Paul's experience was a paradigm of God's power, authority, and control, and that force that moved him beyond the realm of human understanding, to instruct his readers about true power and glory. Paul was not just telling a good story, he was narrating an event for the purpose of teaching an important lesson: self-exaltation is the enemy of a person's union with Christ.[26] This was basic criteria for recognizing true and false apostles; the life of a true apostle was "marked by hardship, dangers and deprivations, and not by personal acclaim, a winning personality or sensationalism" (2 Cor 11:23–12:10).[27]

God had graciously given so much to Paul—incredible insight and wisdom, apostolic authority, direction and position, physical and spiritual salvation, even special visions to direct, encourage, and strengthen him (Acts

23. Furnish, *II Corinthians*, 526. See BDAG 737.
24. BDAG 737–38; see also Belleville, *2 Corinthians*, 302; Furnish, *II Corinthians*, 525–26.
25. Furnish, *II Corinthians*, 545.
26. Ellington, "Not Applicable to Believers?," 332.
27. Belleville, *2 Corinthians*, 23.

16:9–10; 18:9; 2 Cor 12:2–5). God had blessed Paul so much that all the beyond-human-understanding blessings could have made Paul very prideful. Like a successful quarterback in a football game, it is easy to elevate one person after a successful season. Yet, Paul further rejected boasting about himself and his amazing experiences because the church's acceptance of arrogant leaders was a false sense of confidence in the wrong people. He would rather boast about his weaknesses (12:5–6) because his readers needed to learn that strength and weakness coalesce in life and in leadership.[28]

"Thorn in my Flesh" (12:7–10)

Immediately following the account of Paul's stunning, glorious experience (12:2–4), Paul revealed the other side of the coin, which was an infuriating weakness that plagued him relentlessly (12:7b). We do not know the exact nature of this affliction, but we do know its purpose, which was to keep Paul from "becoming conceited" because of the special revelations given to him by God. "Extraordinary religious experiences often come at personal cost."[29] The "throne in my flesh" metaphor indicated acute pain, and a severe, physical difficulty that somehow affected his body. He further describes the affliction as "a messenger of Satan," which may imply a spiritual struggle as well (v. 7). Thus, it is both a gift from God and an "instrument of Satan," used by God to humble his servant.[30] In this letter, Satan was very much on Paul's mind, as one who "schemes" against the church (2:11), the "god of this age" (4:4), masquerading as an "angel of light" (11:14) and directing his malevolent "servants" against the church (11:15). Here, Satan appears to be the one who intended to use the affliction to bring shame, defeat, torment and collapse to Paul's ministry (see Job 2:3–5).

For ages, scholars have discussed and debated both the translation and the meaning of Paul's "thorn." Literally, it can also be translated as "stake," used especially for execution or impalement. This highlights the severity of the ailment. But it can also mean "thorn," as most translations agree, or "splinter," which lessens the harshness of the situation.[31] While it could be associated with the persecution Paul endured for many years, the most widely accepted scholarly view is that Paul experienced some kind of a serious physical illness. He may have had a fever, or migraine headaches. Very possibly, he had problems with his eyes, with some kind of "defective vision" that made it difficult for him to read or write.[32] In fact, he mentioned his ailment to the Galatians

---

28. Ellington, "Not Applicable to Believers?," 333.
29. Belleville, *2 Corinthians*, 305.
30. Harris, *Second Corinthians*, 857.
31. Furnish, *II Corinthians*, 528; Belleville, *2 Corinthians*, 306.
32. Harris, *Second Corinthians*, 859.

(4:14–15), and he ends that letter by writing, "See what large letters I use as I write to you with my own hand!" (6:11). Furthermore, we know that at his conversion experience, Paul was blinded by a heavenly light (Acts 22:11–13). It was a physical experience that convinced Paul of the truth of the gospel and revealed to him his assignment from the Lord Jesus (Acts 22:21; 1 Cor 9:1; 15:8). During this unforgettable experience his eyes may have been damaged such that, later on in life, he gradually had difficulties with his sight. Perhaps it is better that we do not know exactly what it was; if it remains a general condition rather than a specific affliction, believers throughout the ages can identify with such a situation and associate with Paul's hardships.[33]

Whatever it was, it "tormented" Paul. Even arduous prayer (2 Cor 12:8) did nothing to relieve the agony of the affliction. Such affliction affected his work, his ministry, and his life for a long time. God's response to Paul's prayers for relief may have been in the negative, so that Paul learned to rely on God's grace. Instead of removing the thorn, God provided enough grace for Paul to continue on in ministry (12:8–9). Quite naturally, Paul wanted the thorn to be removed, not so much for his own pleasure, but for the advancement of the gospel message. On the one hand, this passage does not in any way imply that Christians should seek afflictions in order to please God. On the other hand, it does not suggest that God must guarantee a "happy and healthy life" to all believers because they pray for it. Paul's prayer was answered; he was assured that in spite of whatever pain is experienced, "God's grace is sufficient." Divine grace is adequate because "God's power is made perfect in [human] weakness" (12:9).

Further, Paul listed four cases in which he "delighted" in adversity, in insults, in hardships, in persecutions and in difficulties (12:10; see 4:8–9). That is, human weakness and trials are a "means to the knowledge of Christ and fellowship with him" (Phil 3:8–11).[34] God's power does not eliminate human suffering; "it comes to its full strength *in* it."[35] This was a lesson for the Corinthians because they had false reliance on the "strength" of their self-assured leaders. In addition, from the perspective of today's readers, we are grateful that even while Paul was in pain, persecuted, and placed in prison, he was still able to write letters to his churches through an assistant (*amanuensis*), so that we can still have his words today. Second Corinthians 12:9 is endearing and enduring to all believers who suffer from any kind of affliction. "Grounding his thorn in God's activity, a thorn-stricken apostle becomes no longer an oxymoron but a paradigm for believers and their leaders."[36]

---

33. Ellington, "Not Applicable to Believers?," 335.
34. Ellington, "Not Applicable to Believers?," 336.
35. Belleville, *2 Corinthians*, 309 (her emphasis).
36. Ellington, "Not Applicable to Believers?," 333.

Signs of a True Apostle (12:11–13)

Paul concluded his "Fool's Speech" by summarizing the nature of a true, godly apostle (12:11–13). The Corinthians had driven him to write about himself in such a "boastful" manner because of their approval of the false slander and accusations from his opponents (12:11). They had misplaced their trust in the "super-apostles" who had deceived and misled them with a different Jesus, different spirit, and different gospel altogether (11:4–5). In fact, "misplaced confidence, such as self-exaltation, is the foe of the believers' participation [and union] in Christ" (11:2–3).[37] He emphatically repeated that he was not to be judged "inferior" to these "false apostles," because in reality he was the true apostle to the Corinthians. The things that "mark" (or "signs of") a genuine apostle are listed in 12:12: "signs, wonders and miracles," which were done in their midst on more than one occasion. The implication, then, is that the "false apostles" did *not* demonstrate such extraordinary strength and gifts in the congregation, but only bragged verbally about their supremacy. Further, Paul reminded the people that he had not been a financial burden to them, and he therefore in jest asked for their forgiveness (12:13; see 11:7–9).

In truth, the power of the correct Spirit of God was shown in the life and ministry of Paul in Corinth, as well as in his patient endurance with the church (12:12). Forms of the phrase "signs and wonders" is not unusual in the OT, where it was connected with the work of Yahweh God in the congregation of his people (Isa 8:18; 20:3). It also occurs in the book of Acts (4:30; 5:12). The triad of "signs, wonders and miracles" is probably a reference not to specific marvelous events, but to a general display of divine power "belonging to or characteristic of an apostle." This may have included such occurrences as healings and exorcisms performed by Paul that revealed the power of God through Christ and authenticated his apostleship (see Acts 13:6–12; 14:8–10; 16:17–18; 19:11–12; 28:3–6, 8). Certainly, such occurrences were not unusual as Paul founded churches in the Gentile regions. But Paul himself does not make a great distinction between the miraculous signs; they were simply different expressions of "one and the same Spirit" (1 Cor 12:11).[38] Moreover, Paul clearly made the point that "religious experiences, no matter how extraordinary, cannot legitimate one's apostleship, but only weakness and suffering," which were personally experienced by Paul.[39]

In 2 Cor 12:13 Paul again appears to be countering an accusation directed against him by his opponents. Their point of attack may have been a presumed

---

37. Ellington, "Not Applicable to Believers?," 333.
38. Harris, *Second Corinthians*, 875–77.
39. Furnish, *II Corinthians*, 546.

comparison made between the Corinthians and other local congregations, in which the Corinthian church was placed at a disadvantage. Yet Paul poses the question, "In what respect, then, are you worse off than the other churches?" This was especially relevant because they were privileged to witness the supernatural events that validated his apostolic position (12:12). Then, he conceded that there might have been one area where the people might have felt imposed upon, and that was in the area of financial assistance (12:13). His refusal to accept payment for his ministry had been twisted by his adversaries. Again, dripping with sarcasm, and using a very serious tone as if he had harmed them dreadfully, he begged for their forgiveness. This rhetoric leads into the final section of the letter, where he promised not to be a "burden" on the church (12:14).

LIVE the Story

"Be Strong and Courageous"

When a reader today takes in all the hardships and persecution experienced by the apostle Paul recorded just in this letter, it can be quite overwhelming (see 4:8–9; 6:4–10 and 11:23–29). We can rarely compare our present trials to those of Paul. He had amazing courage in the face of adversity. How did he face such hard times and respond to these servants of Satan (11:15) with grace and mercy? Following in his footsteps, Christian leaders today must deal with verbal and emotional criticisms from the very people they are trying to serve, and disappointments are so much a part of the ministry of the gospel of Jesus Christ.[40]

Upon the death of Moses, Joshua was tagged the leader of the Israelites, and the one who had to lead them across the Jordan River and take possession of the "promised land" (Josh 1:1–9). This was a daunting task, and perhaps Joshua felt ill-prepared to lead all his people into the great unknown. While the Lord repeatedly urged Joshua to "be courageous" (1:6, 7, 9, 18; see Deut 31:6, 8, 23), he also promised Joshua great success. By trusting in the Lord and obeying his commands, Joshua and the nation (God's people) would be triumphant despite tremendous obstacles (Josh 1:8). What we see in the story of Joshua are two key concepts: obedience to God and courage in carrying out his commands. It is difficult for a believer to be strong and courageous unless he or she is in step with the will, the laws, and the commands of God. God promised to be with Joshua, to direct him, sustain him, and help him

---

40. McKnight, *Pastor Paul*, 133.

to complete the very task God asked him to do. Joshua did not delay but immediately devised a plan to set the commands in motion (Josh 1:10–2:1). "Be strong and courageous" became the nation's motto, led by Joshua and his faith in the Lord God (1:9).

In the same way, do we have the courage to face the adversities in our lives—spiritual, physical, and emotional? Contrary to other self-centered leaders (2 Cor 11:15), are we truly committed enough to be selfless "servants of Christ" (11:23)? Despite obstacles, criticism, and mocking from the "world," do we have the courage to stand up for our faith in Christ and be obedient to our Lord?

My friend and former lead pastor Art Greco wrote about courage in his own life and in his ministry. He notes that "Courage is the willingness to make sure that fear never dictates actions."[41] He related the story of Vicki Soto, who never saw herself as a hero:

> Vicki grew up singing in the choir at Lordship Community Church in Stratford, Connecticut, where, according to the *Hartford Courant*, her pastor, Meg Williams, recalled Soto as being full of energy and always having a bright smile. When a gunman entered her first-grade classroom at Sandy Hook Elementary School on December 14, 2012, that smile left her face forever. It was on that day that Soto taught her final and most powerful lesson. . . . Newspaper reporter Josh Kovner wrote, "She ushered special education teacher Anne Marie Murphy and several children under her desk. She moved other children behind a bookcase or barrier. When the killer came in, Soto was the only one he saw. She faced him. He killed her, and then he killed the children and Murphy under the desk. Murphy died shielding children in her arms. Other children escaped the classroom. Soto's actions saved children's lives. Only God knows what guided her."[42]

This account is an example, Greco writes, of "true courage," which is "always an outcome of true love, and the power of love in active resistance to evil." This is the kind of courage that is necessary for being a Christian, and especially for being a Christian leader, in the world today. It is "knowing what to listen to and what to ignore":

> It's the wind in us that penetrates the cracks it finds in our doubts and, while being fully aware of them, refuses to allow them the last word.

---

41. Art Greco, *God Kills* (Petaluma, CA: Roundtree, 2014), 149.
42. Greco, *God Kills*, 149.

Courage isn't the absence of terror; it's the presence of love. It's not some super-cowboy lack of angst, but a supernatural immersion into the only thing that can put angst in its place.[43]

In fact, strength and courage do not exist *without* the presence of fear; they are the victory over fear. It is the "measurable conviction that fear doesn't get to call the shots."[44]

Often courage comes out of pure conviction, as in the case of Joshua, who was submitted to God and placed his confidence in the promises of God. "By faith," people can overcome their fears and have the courage to persevere. The Corinthians, for example, excelled in faith (2 Cor 8:7), yet Paul urged them to increase their faith (10:15). Faith, then, is never static; it must grow and mature. The seeds of Christian faith are planted by a gracious God who confers faith as a gift (Eph 2:8–10). Then, as we "live by faith" (2 Cor 5:7), being obedient to God, faith begins to fill the life of a Christian. "By faith" we carry on in life, living with the assistance of God's Holy Spirit, to combat fear, evil forces, opposition, and conflict. Our confidence and our courage are not in ourselves and our abilities, but in our faith in God through Christ. Paul famously wrote that the "abiding" qualities of the Christian life (and leadership) are "faith, hope and love" (1 Cor 13:13).[45]

Proper Manifestations of the Spirit

One of the most controversial passages in 2 Corinthians has to do with Paul's revelatory vision in 12:1–4. Do spiritual visions and revelations still happen to Christians today? What constitutes a proper manifestation of the Spirit in gospel ministry? Are ecstatic visions still part of our Christian culture in this age? Linda Belleville begins this discussion by writing,

To be sure, there is a place in preaching the gospel for persuasion and the working of "signs, wonders and miracles." Paul himself sought to reason with his listeners (Acts 9:29; 18:4). And he did preach a word accompanied by power, conviction and the Spirit (i.e., Rom 15:19; 1 Cor 2:4; 2 Cor 2:12). But the role of the miraculous was to validate, not displace, the gospel; and persuasion functioned to convince that "the Christ had to suffer and rise from the dead (Acts 17:2–3). It is all too easy for an audience to fasten on an outward show and miss the intended message.[46]

---

43. Greco, *God Kills*, 151.
44. Greco, *God Kills*, 153.
45. L. Morris, "Faith," *DPL* 289.
46. Belleville, *2 Corinthians*, 274–75.

Belleville correctly makes two key points about miraculous events: first, they are a validation of Christian truth, and second, they are intended to turn the spotlight on the real Christ. Paul's primary focus was not on himself or on his abilities, but on "Christ and him crucified" (1 Cor 2:2). It is the Spirit of God, and only him, who grants visions and revelations to believers today, in appropriate and unusual circumstances, and for these two purposes. Paul's ecstatic experiences were valuable only as they validated his work among the Gentiles and as they demonstrated the power of God in his life. Surely this is still the case in our culture today.

Ecstatic experiences are neither a requirement for a higher level of spirituality, nor a requirement for salvation in Christ. A person is no less of a believer if he or she has not experienced unique, ecstatic experiences.

From Death to Life, Weakness to Strength

Paul's message is still true today: the life of a maturing, growing Christian is not centered on extraordinary experiences and unusual revelations. Against all traditional convention, the life of a Christian is characterized by weakness, suffering, death, and grace. "Jesus does promise true self-discovery, at the cost of self-denial, true life at the cost of death." That is why Dietrich Bonhoeffer wrote that "when Christ calls [a person], he bids him [or her] to come and die" (see Luke 9:23; 14:27).[47] That is, we must "put to death" the fallen human nature, which seems so innate to most of us in our culture, and that is consumed with self-interest and self-indulgence. Thus, there is a life that leads to death, and a death that leads to life (see 2 Cor 4:10–12). The only way to live a full and godly life is to die, which is to renounce all sin and evil, and selfish, fleshly desires.[48] The way to enduring strength is through human weakness empowered by God (11:30–31). Weakness is the hallmark of Paul's apostleship because it was only by the grace of God that he was commissioned and accomplished the task. "By accepting his tribulations as real weaknesses he is led by them to acknowledge his ultimate dependence on God (see 1:8–9)." This must be true for all Christians today, especially those in leadership: our trials and human weaknesses become the means by which God's copious power is manifested (4:7–15).[49]

In the words of John Stott, "radical discipleship" is the "death and burial" of our own fleshly human nature and the power of God in our weaknesses.

---

47. Stott, *Radical Disciple*, 117, 118.
48. Stott, *Radical Disciple*, 118. See also an excellent book on ministry and Micah 6:6–8: Walter Brueggemann, *To Act Justly, Love Tenderly, Walk Humbly: An Agenda for Ministers* (New York: Paulist, 1986).
49. Furnish, *II Corinthians*, 550.

It is a real "death," putting to death the self to trust and serve God. This is especially true for cross-cultural missionaries like the apostle Paul. Even today, missionaries often leave home and comfort, peace and ease, family and friends, jobs and opportunities, to give and serve, and to build up fellow Christians under unfamiliar, difficult circumstances:

> Josif Ton is a Romanian Christian leader, born in 1934, who became a pastor of the Baptist Church in Oradea, which today is a world-famous Baptist center. After four years of faithful pastoring, the curiosity of the authorities was aroused and he was arrested and interrogated. He was then given the opportunity to leave the country and settle in the United States, where he pursued doctoral studies and was awarded a doctorate by the Evangelical Faculty of Belgium. His research topic was "Suffering, Martyrdom and Rewards in Heaven," which was later published as a book. During the oppressive regime of Nicolae Ceaușescu, Josif Ton in one of his published sermons told how the authorities threatened to kill him. He responded: "Sir, your supreme weapon is killing. My supreme weapon is dying."[50]

That is, Stott points out six areas where all Christians discover the "paradoxical principle of life through death: salvation, discipleship, mission, persecution, martyrdom and mortality." In each area, human weakness gives way to the power of God, and human death gives way to life. "This is the radical, paradoxical Christian perspective."[51] This is what Paul shared with his readers as his own experiences in his Christian life. As he experienced each of these six areas, he realized more and more that he could only boast about the superabundant power of God and his grace. It is not about what I have done, but it is all about what God has done *through* me.

---

50. Stott, *Radical Disciple*, 127.
51. Stott, *Radical Disciple*, 132, 133.

CHAPTER 15

2 Corinthians 12:14–13:14

¹⁴Now I am ready to visit you for the third time, and I will not be a burden to you, because what I want is not your possessions but you. After all, children should not have to save up for their parents, but parents for their children. ¹⁵So I will very gladly spend for you everything I have and expend myself as well. If I love you more, will you love me less? ¹⁶Be that as it may, I have not been a burden to you. Yet, crafty fellow that I am, I caught you by trickery! ¹⁷Did I exploit you through any of the men I sent to you? ¹⁸I urged Titus to go to you and I sent our brother with him. Titus did not exploit you, did he? Did we not walk in the same footsteps by the same Spirit?

¹⁹Have you been thinking all along that we have been defending ourselves to you? We have been speaking in the sight of God as those in Christ; and everything we do, dear friends, is for your strengthening. ²⁰For I am afraid that when I come I may not find you as I want you to be, and you may not find me as you want me to be. I fear that there may be discord, jealousy, fits of rage, selfish ambition, slander, gossip, arrogance and disorder. ²¹I am afraid that when I come again my God will humble me before you, and I will be grieved over many who have sinned earlier and have not repented of the impurity, sexual sin and debauchery in which they have indulged.

¹³:¹This will be my third visit to you. "Every matter must be established by the testimony of two or three witnesses." ²I already gave you a warning when I was with you the second time. I now repeat it while absent: On my return I will not spare those who sinned earlier or any of the others, ³since you are demanding proof that Christ is speaking through me. He is not weak in dealing with you, but is powerful among you. ⁴For to be sure, he was crucified in weakness, yet he lives by God's power. Likewise, we are weak in him, yet by God's power we will live with him in our dealing with you.

⁵Examine yourselves to see whether you are in the faith; test yourselves. Do you not realize that Christ Jesus is in you—unless, of course, you fail the test? ⁶And I trust that you will discover that we have not failed the test. ⁷Now we pray to God that you will not do anything wrong—not so that people will see that we have stood the test but so that you will do what is right even though we may seem to have failed. ⁸For we cannot do anything against the truth, but only for the truth. ⁹We are glad whenever we are weak but you are strong; and our prayer is that you may be fully restored. ¹⁰This is why I write these things when I am absent, that when I come I may not have to be harsh in my use of authority—the authority the Lord gave me for building you up, not for tearing you down.

¹¹Finally, brothers and sisters, rejoice! Strive for full restoration, encourage one another, be of one mind, live in peace. And the God of love and peace will be with you.

¹²Greet one another with a holy kiss.

¹³All God's people here send their greetings.

¹⁴May the grace of the Lord Jesus Christ, and the love of God, and the fellowship of the Holy Spirit be with you all.

Listening to the Text in the Story: Deuteronomy 19:15–21; Job 38:1–42:6; Psalm 17:3; 24:1–2; 26:2; Proverbs 11:24, 25, 28; Jeremiah 17:10; 20:12; Lamentations 3:40–42, 55–57; Malachi 3:5, 8–12; Matthew 23:11–12; Luke 14:11; 18:9–14.

Create in me a clean heart, O God,
    and renew a steadfast spirit within me.
Do not cast me from Your presence
    or take Your Holy Spirit from me.
Restore to me the joy of Your salvation
    and sustain me with a willing spirit.
The sacrifices of God are a broken spirit;
    A broken and contrite heart, O God,
You will not despise.
            —*Psalm 51:10–12, 17 NASB*

Nobody likes an exam. Ask any student, any professor, any driver's education instructor—nobody relishes taking an exam. But tests must be taken, usually under created pressure, and then they have to be graded. I know they are a necessary evaluation of what is learned and absorbed, but I confess that I am a poor test taker. College entrance exams like the SAT made my stomach churn. In college one of my literature classes had only a midterm exam and then a final exam. The grade for the whole semester rested on two exams. As a student, I would rather write four papers for a class than take two exams. Then as an instructor, I realized that was not such a great idea, because I had to grade all those papers. In addition, students want instructors to believe that their whole lives depend on one grade on one exam in one class (and, it might!). So, what did the people in Corinth think when Paul told them to "examine yourselves to see whether you are in the faith; test yourselves" (2 Cor 13:5)? Did they break out into a cold sweat? Did their hearts break because they mistakenly accepted the groundless doubts and false accusations about Paul? Where was their faith in Jesus Christ—and in Paul? Did they see the importance of Paul's command? For any of us, an honest examination of one's spiritual faith and relationship with Christ might just be a life-changing test.

This is the final section of this complex, heart-wrenching letter written by Paul to people he loved in Corinth. If a reader rereads chapter 1 and then jumps to chapter 13, the closing chapter sounds like a completely different author. As the letter progressed, certainly Paul's tone shifted from explanatory to instructive, confident to condemning. Yet, careful observation of the words and the topics in the last chapter show connections to the rest of the letter. Some readers have considered chapter 13 an epilogue, but it is so connected to chapter 12 that it would be misleading to isolate it from the rest of the letter. In chapter 13, Paul's use of figures of speech (like irony and sarcasm) found in chapters 10–12 have ceased; he wrapped up his letter with boldness, truth, clarity, and apostolic authority.

We see more clearly now how the letter sounds like a courtroom trial (see introduction). And it appears that Paul, the accused, turned the tables on his opponents and became Paul, the accuser. In first-century Jewish culture, it was possible for the defendant in a trial to turn the charges against the accuser, especially when falsified charges brought dishonor and discredit to the one incriminated (Deut 19:16–19). In the Roman world, accusations brought against a person were brought before a governor of the state, and it was the official duty of the governor to examine the one accused to learn the truth. Paul was called to do this, to defend his case—without excess flattery or bribery—in Acts 24:1–27. In 2 Corinthians 12:19 and 13:1, we see how the roles are reversed. Paul was not the "fool" anymore as he put the people in Corinth on the defensive. Paul spoke the truth, "in the sight of God" (12:19; see 2:17) who was his true and primary judge.[1]

---

1. Garland, *2 Corinthians*, 535.

EXPLAIN the Story

The Intended Third Visit to Corinth (12:14–18)

The ironic words in 12:13 made evident the greed and deception of Paul's accusers. Paul answered his opponents and taught the Corinthians a thing or two about their misplaced loyalties in chapters 10 through 12. As he began to close his letter to the Corinthian church, he asked the church to prepare for his final visit two ways: they needed to repent (12:20, 21; 13:2), and they needed to thoroughly "examine" and "test" themselves (13:1, 5, 11). Should they complete those tasks, it would be unnecessary for Paul to implement severe discipline in the community during his third visit (10:6; 13:2, 10). His deep concern was less for himself and more for the church, so Paul, too, intended to make preparations for his upcoming visit (12:19). He would pray mightily for the repairs to be made to their true devotion to Christ and to his relationship with the people (6:12–13; 13:7, 10). The church was guilty of failing to love and honor the God-appointed apostle Paul, of accepting other false accusations, and of failing to defend Paul against his opponents. They needed to accept their responsibility in the restoration of broken ties with Christ and with Paul, the true apostle (13:7–8).[2]

"Now," he began; this Greek word that opens 12:14 is a distinct divider and punctuates the beginning of the last section of this letter. It may be better interpreted as "Look!" with greater emphasis, as Paul wanted to grab the readers' attention: "Look here, readers, now that you know the truth about my opponents, I am ready to visit you for a third time!" Now that the deception of the "false apostles" was exposed, Paul was anticipating a better visit, while he was giving the people fair warning of his intentions and his parental apprehension (12:14a, 20–21; 13:1–2).

Immediately, Paul restated his position on financial matters, indicating that he would again avoid being a financial burden on the church (12:14b, 16). That is, he refused to be a part of the patron/client relationship so common in the Corinthian society, and he chose to relinquish his apostolic rights of payment. Thus, he chose *not* to be a financial "burden" to the church, and the proclamation of the gospel message was debt free (see 11:9, 10, 12).[3] He based his clear position on finance for two specific reasons.

The first reason is that he had little concern about money and possessions; instead, Paul was totally concerned about the spiritual well-being of the congregation (12:14). Unlike his rival teachers, Paul was not interested in wealth,

---

2. Harris, *Second Corinthians*, 880.
3. Harris, *Second Corinthians*, 882.

but in people. He had "invested" wisely in the believers at Corinth, and his "dividend" was their spiritual growth in the gospel (see Phil 4:17–18). The expression Paul created in 2 Corinthians 12:14 is a beautiful idiom of how a church leader should regard his or her congregation: "what I want is not your *possessions* but *you*" (my emphasis). In reverse, people should not just donate lots of money to a church or to a mission out of guilt in place of a true faith in Christ and genuine spiritual growth. Eugene Peterson writes:

> Being a pastor who satisfies a congregation is one of the easiest jobs on the face of the earth—if we are satisfied with satisfying congregations. Why aren't we content with it? Because we set out to do something quite different. We set out to risk our lives in a venture of faith. We commit ourselves to a life of holiness. . . . In the process, we learned the difference between a profession, a craft, and a job. . . . With professions, the integrity has to do with the invisibles; for physicians, it is health; with lawyers, it is justice; with pastors, it is God.[4]

The second reason is that Paul was the Corinthians' spiritual "father," as he founded the church and felt responsible for its growth and maturity (see 1 Cor 4:15). He referred to the believers as his "children," indicating sincere love, care, and concern for them. Continuing his financial arguments, he used the metaphor of the parent/child support (2 Cor 12:14) to show a reason for not accepting payment from the Corinthians. Certainly, a small child is not responsible for supporting a parent financially; it is the responsibility of the parent (Paul) to support a growing child (the church). This imagery is tender and moving, as Paul considered the believers in Corinth his "dear children" (1 Cor 4:14). Proof of this love and concern for his people appears in the next verse. He was devoted to his people because he would "gladly" spend whatever money or possessions he had on them, even to the point of expending all of *himself* on their behalf (2 Cor 12:15). He was willing to sacrificially give all that he had and all that he was to them, no strings attached—and if that is not love, what is? I would bet that his rival missionaries would never say *that* to the Corinthians.

Paul slipped back into a mode of sarcasm in 12:16. He called himself a "crafty fellow" and wrote, "I caught you [the believers] by trickery!" This plausibly echoes a slanderous rumor or a direct accusation made by Paul's enemies. In the New Testament the word "crafty" always has a negative sense. His opponents (those "crafty fellows!") may have accused Paul of "tricking"

---

4. Peterson, *Contemplative Pastor*, 139–40.

the congregation into taking up a collection that would actually not be sent to Jerusalem, but instead would be put in Paul's pocket. Of course—*this* was how Paul was being paid! Such lies, such deception, forced Paul to threaten disciplinary action against those who considered him "weak." Paul challenged the opposition by arguing that neither he nor any of his colleagues (i.e., Titus) had ever exploited the church (12:17–18; see 7:14–15). He did not "shrewdly" send representatives to Corinth to receive the collection funds in place of his own presence.

Fears for the Third Visit (12:19–21)

His reputation in Corinth was certainly at stake, yet Paul insisted that his primary concern for writing to the church and in speaking about himself was not for personal gain or selfish desires (12:19). In truth, Paul placed his own self-defense well below the building up, "strengthening" and edification of the church. This is not unlike his confession in 2:1–4 as he explained his reasons for writing another letter. On the one hand, Paul would have been fully aware that his readers/audience might have received this letter as a lengthy self-defense focused on himself and on the charges leveled against him (12:19). On the other hand, Paul's real audience, of course, was God, and God was the only one Paul was trying to please in his ministry efforts (12:19).[5]

"All along" or "for a long time now" (12:19) implies that it took some period of time for Paul to compose this entire letter, and it had also been some time since he had physically been in their presence.[6] Then, the next phrase "We have been speaking in the sight of God" emphasized that Paul's entire ministry was done in the sight of God (see 2:17). Indeed, Paul spoke and stood in front of God as his judge as he proclaimed the true, free-of-charge gospel. With his term of endearment ("dear friends") in 12:19, Paul provided proof that he was putting his congregation first. They were in need of strengthening, as one day, too, they would stand before God, as (hopefully!) people "in Christ." His entire ministry in Asia and Greece, as well as his copious sufferings, subsisted and persisted to this end.

However, there was significant fear that some of the people in Corinth were not in right standing with God. In 11:3 Paul recognized the deception that was leading the church away from their true devotion to Christ. Here in chapter 12, he lists additional fears of immorality that might stand in the way of the Corinthians appearing "pure" before God (7:1) and before Paul on his next visit. Verses 12:20–21 catalogue his real doubts and fears based on information

---

5. Harris, *Second Corinthians*, 894–95.
6. Harris, *Second Corinthians*, 894.

he received related to the activities and accusations in the congregation (see a similar list in Gal 5:19–21). His language ("might," "perhaps") implies that he still held on to the hope that his fears were no longer grounded, and that the church would be found reformed in their ways on his third visit.

First, the contentiousness in Corinth is expressed in four sins, or "deeds of the flesh" (1 Cor 1:11–12; Gal 5:219–21) that are the opposite of the "works of the Spirit." Continuing quarreling, jealousy, anger, and factions led to sharp rivalries dividing the church (2 Cor 12:20). "Quarreling" (eris) is "strife, discord and contention, engagement in rivalry." In addition, our English word "factions" is a derivative of the previous word in Greek (eritheiai). Similar in meaning, then, "factions" implies "strife, selfishness and selfish ambition."[7] We find evidence of this contentiousness in 1 Corinthians 1:10–13 when the church was "quarreling" and suffered from "divisions" early in its existence. Paul's opponents either ignited or fueled such disagreements, animosity, and divisions in the assembly.

Second, Paul listed four vices, or "verbal sins": "slander, gossip, arrogance and disorder" (2 Cor 12:20). "Slander" could be translated as "to speak ill of, to defame or to speak degradingly of"; this may have been the primary sin that plagued his relationship with the congregation. "Gossip" is actually translated "whisperings" or "derogatory information about a person that is offered in a tone of confidentiality," which may be very descriptive of what was happening in the assembly. Further, "arrogance" is literally "puffing up," or the "groundless inflation" of oneself in his or her "fleshly mind." The "exaggerated self-concept" was quite acceptable in the Roman culture. "Disturbances" is a general term for "an unsettled state of affairs," but it also carries the connotation of "opposition to established authority."[8] Ironically, the Romans abhorred disorderly conduct and events, and were careful not to be involved in any kind of insurrection. Yet, through their speech and behavior, the Corinthians were in direct conflict with Paul and his authority. A "disorderly" church is bound to disintegrate or divide if left unrestrained or uncontrolled. In our vernacular, Paul was very much afraid that he was the victim of a "politically motivated smear campaign by arrogant rivals," who were successfully captivating the congregation and driving a wedge into the church.[9]

But this was not all. In 12:21, Paul expressed further uneasiness about the impending third visit. The failure of the church was his personal failure; the disorderliness and sinfulness in the church would be humiliating to Paul.

---

7. BDAG 392.
8. BDAG 519, 1098, 1069, 35. See also, Harris, *Second Corinthians*, 899–900.
9. Garland, *2 Corinthians*, 536.

"His God" might choose to "bring him low" with a new dose of humiliation ("again," 12:21). Details of this potential "humiliation" are not given, but it might be the huge disappointment Paul would experience if the Corinthians were not reformed and were not in a better place morally and spiritually. He would be totally "down-cast" if the church failed to change, and the end result would be as agonizing (if not more so) as his experiences during the second, "painful" visit (2:1). Furthermore, Paul would "mourn" or "grieve" any continuing "sexual sins," "impurity, immorality and debauchery," by those people who indulged in such evil behavior previously. Such sins may have been connected to worship rites at idol temples, making them even more dissolute and treacherous (see 7:1).[10] Indeed, "their disobedience to God's will is as humbling to him as a stake in his flesh."[11]

Interestingly, there is no repetition in the list of sins/vices in 12:20–21. Harris contends that this may indicate that there were two groups of people in the church. One group was easily affected by the "false teachers" and was susceptible to disagreements, divisions, and factions (1 Cor 3:1–4). Another group of people were still practicing idolatry and sexual sins that were socially acceptable before they became Christian believers (see 2 Cor 6:16–7:1; 1 Cor 6:18). This might be debatable, but certainly the *entire* congregation was heavily influenced by the "false apostles," the representatives of Satan (11:13) who led the church in the wrong direction with their deceitful teachings and their permissive immorality (1 Cor 5:1–2; 2 Cor 11:4, 13–15).[12] Corinth was a morally lax sea-port city with a great deal of opportunity to indulge in "sins of the flesh." While the church seemed to excel in many areas (1 Cor 8:7), they were failing in basic Christian theology, ethics, and loyalty. Indeed, while this criticism had to be said, Paul pledged not to "tear down" the church (2 Cor 10:8; 13:10), but with grief and words of encouragement his intention was to "build it up." Like a parent, Paul felt guilty that his "children" were not behaving as they should have been.

Final Warnings and Exhortations (13:1–10)

Again, Paul noted that this would be his third visit to Corinth, emphasizing his full intentions. But this time, the congregation would be on trial! In 13:1, Paul briefly cited an Old Testament passage by which he brought the court into session: "One witness is not enough to convict anyone accused of any crime or offense they may have committed. A matter must be established by

10. Harris, *Second Corinthians*, 903–4.
11. Garland, *2 Corinthians*, 537.
12. Harris, *Second Corinthians*, 904.

the testimony of two or three witnesses" (Deut 19:15). Jesus supported this Old Testament standard in Matthew 18:15–17, and Paul's third visit was a time of judgment and reckoning.[13] Furthermore, it is interesting to note that Paul cites this Old Testament text immediately after he reiterates that he was about to visit Corinth for a *third* time. Certainly, he must have been aware that this strong Deuteronomy passage goes on to establish judicial guidelines:

> If a malicious witness takes the stand to accuse a someone of a crime, the two people involved in the dispute must stand *in the presence of the LORD* before the priests and the judges who are in office at the time. The judges must make a thorough investigation, and if the witness proves to be a liar, giving *false testimony against a fellow Israelite*, then *do to the false witness as that witness intended to do to the other party.* You must purge the evil from among you. The rest of the people will hear of this and be afraid, and never again will such an evil thing be done among you. Show no pity: life for life, eye for eye, tooth for tooth, hand for hand, foot for foot. (Deut 19:16–21, my *emphasis*).

Despite his Torah knowledge and background, Paul did *not* seek vengeance for his lying, false accusers! While he could have attacked his opponents with vicious and justified rebuttals, he did *not* seek an "eye for an eye, a tooth for a tooth." In the end, vengeance was not in the best interest of the congregation. Paul's deepest concern was for his "dear friends," and not for his own private justice; to attack his opponents as he had been attacked would have only increased the division and the animosity in the church. And yet, perhaps Paul was implying to his readers that on his *third* visit, he could, and indeed would, bring charges against his opponents because of their lies and false accusations.[14] In accordance with the Old Testament passage, Paul could call at least *three* witnesses against the Corinthians' indictments and in his own defense: Timothy, Titus, and Sosthenes (1 Cor 1:1), Aquila, and Priscilla (1 Cor 16:19), or any of the other unnamed fellow workers in 2 Corinthians 8:18–24. In addition, he had warned the church at least twice before on other occasions, and patiently waited for them to repent and return.

Still, Paul was so confident that when he appeared "in the presence of the LORD," and if a full investigation was conducted, it would be revealed that he truly was the blameless, authentic apostle of Christ. With this in mind, Paul was willing to threaten strict disciplinary action against his enemies and

13. Barton et al., *1 and 2 Corinthians*, 462.
14. Garland, *2 Corinthians*, 540.

to those in Corinth who continued to commit the blatant sins of 12:20–21 ("those who sinned earlier or any of the others," 13:2). We don't know exactly what discipline Paul had in mind under such conditions, but excommunication from the church or the prohibition of certain people to participate in the congregation (see 1 Cor 5:11) may have been in order. If drastic measures had to be taken during his final visit, Paul was aware that he had "co-workers" (6:1) such as Titus and the Macedonian Christians to stand beside him and defend his ministry (8:16–19; 9:4).[15] Ultimately, Paul could have called God as his witness (1:23–24).

"God's Power" (13:3–4)

Paul's rivals, the "false apostles" (11:13), and some of the people were still demanding proof of his God-given authority (13:3), but Paul had given the Corinthians ample proof of his commission. Paul reiterated that "Christ is speaking through me" (13:3; see 2:17; 12:19), and he was, indeed, a voice for God and an ambassador for Christ (5:20). Paul repeated the antithesis of "weakness and power" to prove beyond doubt that God does empower his "weak," willing servants, and God stands behind them for service to the church (13:3b–4).

Paul never failed to proclaim the crucifixion of Christ (1 Cor 1:23), which, in human terms, was considered Christ's weakness (in death). The resurrection was a display of God's power at work in the most wretched of human weaknesses—death—even death on a cross (see 1 Cor 1:20–25). Because of the death and resurrection of Christ, Paul and his associates were empowered to serve the churches, to correct their behavior, and exercise their authority (2 Cor 13:4). Divine power is not to be snubbed; the false rivals would be judged correctly, and God's power would be exhibited in the punishment of those who refuse to accept Paul's authority. The church was being misled by the false teachers' teachings, motives, "strength," and behavior. Thus, mutiny against Paul was really mutiny against Christ, because Paul's mission was the same as Jesus's mission: self-sacrifice and servanthood to God to the church, no matter what (compare 4:5; 6:4; 11:23 with John 13:12–17).[16] The church's failure to recognize the full effect of Christ's crucifixion and resurrection was a serious flaw in their faith. This was a key theological difference between Paul and the congregation—they could not grasp the paradox of power in weakness.[17] Despite all the obstacles, persecutions, and opposition in ministry,

---

15. Barton et al., *1 and 2 Corinthians*, 462.
16. Barton et al., *1 and 2 Corinthians*, 464.
17. Garland, *2 Corinthians*, 544.

it must have been a great comfort to Paul to state that "yet he [Christ] lives by God's power. Likewise, we are weak in him, yet by God's power we will live with him in our dealing with you" (2 Cor 13:4). This is precisely the same concept we hear from Paul in 11:30–31 and 12:9–10.

"Examine Yourselves" (13:5–6)

Instead of questioning Paul's authority, as prompted by his rivals, the people should have been looking into their own hearts. Paul reversed the indictments and demanded the people prove *they* did, in fact, belong to Christ (13:5). The verbs "examine" and "test" in 13:5 are both written in the imperative form in Greek, indicating that this is not a suggestion or an option, but an order. The word "test" is repeated in 13:5, 6, and 7, indicating that there are really three tests to be taken.

The congregation was to first give themselves a test to be certain that they were true believers; that is, the church was challenged to prove that Christ was really in them. This test Paul expected them to pass (13:5). Then, Paul offered to test his apostleship, which he intended to pass with flying colors (13:6). Next, the test in 13:7 was "wrong vs. right"; indeed, the corrected behavior of the people was evidence of his apostleship, even if some opponents still had doubts. In fact, if he was forced to impose corrective measures during his third visit, such a move would suffice as the authentication of his true apostleship.[18] These verses were tests of *their* revealed faith. If they "passed the test" of committed faith, then so did he (13:6). That is, did the readers really know themselves? Were they standing firm, or would they be found to be "unproven" or counterfeit in their faith? Knowing his faith was "proven," Paul was not defending his own authority and apostleship as much as he was questioning their genuineness as followers of Jesus Christ.[19] While it appears in 13:6 that he was defending himself, he was exhibiting more interest in the health and welfare of the church than in his own defense.

Prayers for the Corinthians (13:7–9)

If their lives were changed because of Paul's authentic gospel, then, indeed, they were his best witnesses of a legitimate, successful ministry (see 3:1–3). Therefore, in spite of his doubts and admonitions, Paul offered two important prayers for the Corinthians. First, he trusted and "prayed" that they would "not do anything wrong," but choose to "do what is right" (13:7). "Doing what is right," or virtuous, noble behavior, was an important theme in Greco-Roman

---

18. Harris, *Second Corinthians*, 924–25.
19. Furnish, *II Corinthians*, 572.

ethics.[20] Paul sincerely hoped that they would "see the light," reform their moral behavior, and turn in obedience to his teachings, "even though we may seem to have failed" in the eyes of some of the people (13:7). This prayer was a subtle plea for the people to mend their ways, avoid punishment, and turn their lives around to the positive. With Christ speaking through him (13:3), Paul spoke only the truth (13:8). He had refused to proclaim a "false gospel" to satisfy his own fame and fortune. In contrast to their sins and disobedience, if the Corinthians were "doing good," then the veracity of his gospel was demonstrated, and his apostleship was authentic. To be sure, the congregation had to allow Paul's gospel to become operative in their midst.

Paul was committed to working for the truth of the gospel (13:8), and in his own weakness, because it produced strength in the believers (13:9). Through his weakness, the power of God was experienced and proven to be effective for others (13:3–4; 4:7; 12:9–10).[21] The church itself was the "proof" of his true proclamation and his divinely appointed authority. Yet, how can weakness and strength occur at the same time? Paul reiterates that his strength and weakness are not incongruent (see 11:30; 12:10). If he had appeared to be weak to the congregation, it was only for their benefit that he appeared as such; this was a hard concept for the Corinthians to grasp. In truth, he had delayed using any kind of corrective discipline in the hopes that because of his sacrificial, servant ministry, he would find the church strong in their Christian faith.

Furthermore, his second prayer was one for the "full restoration" of the people (13:9, cf. v. 11). Certainly there was a need to mend what was broken in Corinth, to fully "restore" the committed faith of the people, and "put in order" their beliefs and their behavior. Prayers for the restoration and the moral integrity of the people as an active congregation of Jesus-followers were far more important to Paul than his own vindication in Corinth.

"If 13:1–4 is basically a warning about impending discipline, then 13:5–10 is essentially an exhortation to avoid that discipline."[22] Verse 13:10 succinctly reveals Paul's true heartfelt intent in Corinth: although he could not always be present with the believers, when he was able to be with them, he wanted an amicable relationship. He truly loved and cared about them; thus, to avoid any more painful face-to-face encounters with the congregation, or necessary "harsh" discipline, Paul wrote this letter. This important purpose for writing echoes what he wrote in his opening comments concerning his change in

---

20. Furnish, *II Corinthians*, 573.
21. Furnish, *II Corinthians*, 578–79.
22. Harris, *Second Corinthians*, 928.

travel plans (1:15–17). Letters were a necessary alternative when personal visits were not possible, as Paul expressed at the beginning of this letter (1:12–2:4, 9). While Paul spent a great deal of time and effort in this letter dealing with the church's concerns and allegations, he continued to encourage and affirm the believers (2:3; 7:4, 10–16). He rebuked and challenged his adversaries whose teachings and ministry were deceptive and injurious to the church (11:4, 13–15). He imagined that Corinth would be a strategic hub in his missionary work in the region (10:15–16), and it would have been a bitter disappointment to see the church crumble under the weight of "false apostles," internal immorality, and dissention.

Conclusion (13:10)

While Furnish contends that this concluding purpose verse does not fit the earlier chapters 1–9, in fact it can be considered a conclusion to the whole letter.[23] The key to this summation is the theme of Paul's God-given apostolic authority, which necessarily covers the entire epistle. His competency and his authority in Corinth have been called into question from the first chapter, while his sufficiency in God is also clear from the start (1:9, 12, 21). Verse 13:10 is parallel to 10:8; in both verses, Paul uses identical words for "authority," "edification" (or "building up"), and "overthrow" (or "destroying"). No doubt this repetition was for emphasis; Paul's authority in the church was given to him by God, and his authority was for the purpose of edifying the church, not for destroying it (10:8; 13:10; see 1:24). His purpose emphatically stated that, in contrast to his opponents (and especially in his absence), Paul's rivals *were* attempting to obliterate the church (see introduction). Paul was not flaunting his position or selfish power or taking advantage of the church. Nor was he trying to threaten them in any way, or even seek revenge.

Granted, some discipline was necessary, but it was never Paul's intention to disparage and "tear down" the people, despite painful misunderstandings, false accusations, and teachings instigated by his rivals against Paul (see 1 Cor 15:33–34). After a lengthy letter and an honest appraisal of the situation in Corinth, Paul was ready to "rest his case." Should they choose to reject his authority and his instructions, they would face God as their final judge (13:5, 7). Like a seasoned defense attorney, Paul longed to see a complete victory in Corinth—full restoration in the church, and full obedience with the gospel of Christ. He wanted a church full of holy people, full of the Holy Spirit, and active in building up one another. Then the people would be trained to be God's people in Greece and all over the western region of the empire.

---

23. Furnish, *II Corinthians*, 574.

His final argument in defense of his ministry was penned to prevent further severe actions and bruised feelings, so he could go to Corinth in the "humility and gentleness of Christ" (10:1) rather than in a showdown of wills.

In these summary verses, then, we see the same two emotions Paul expressed when he wrote the "tearful letter" in 2:1–4: sincere hope that the Corinthian church could be restored and their relationship with him would be mended (7:9–11), but with nagging fears that they would not receive his epistle with love and repentance (12:20–21).[24] In "resting his case," Paul might have recounted his earlier statement in 5:10: "For we must all appear before the judgment seat of Christ, so that each of us may receive what is due us for the things done while in the body, whether good or bad."

Benediction: Greetings and a Blessing (13:11–14)

Paul brought his letter to a close with a blessing and a greeting. The tone of his writing shifts again from warnings to warmhearted, not unlike the shift from chapters 9 to 10.[25] Final greetings were typical of Paul's communications, and his closing verses are not unlike other letters. It seems that he was determined to close the letter on a positive note, using common literary elements: exhortation, greeting, and benediction.

Thus, Paul told his readers to "strive for full restoration," which is echoing 13:9. But in this verse the verb is reflexive, meaning they are to do it themselves. Thus, the people are to restore themselves and to encourage themselves. The fellowship was also to "be of one mind" (or "agree in the Lord"), a phrase also found in Philippians 4:2. As a family, as "brothers and sisters" in Christ, they were to "live [together] in peace."

More than just a cessation of quarreling, Paul wanted an intentional effort on the part of the Corinthians to secure unity and common concern in the church. The corrections and repentance were to be made of their own volition, and not just because he instructed them to do so. The whole Corinthian congregation (the same "dear friends" he addressed in 12:19) should be thinking about caring for one another—building up one another, comforting each other, mending their ways, and pursuing the "full restoration" with one another and with him mentioned in 13:9. Thus, conscious preparation for Paul's third visit was realized in the completion of these essential, summarizing requests to be followed by the church.

All of this was to be accomplished through the "God of love," the giver of true "peace" (13:11). The final promise in 13:11, "and the God of love and

---

24. Harris, *Second Corinthians*, 930.
25. Garland, *2 Corinthians*, 552.

peace will be with you," is unique even if "love and peace" are common expressions in the New Testament epistles. "God of peace" is found in other Pauline epistles, as well as in Hebrews 13:20 (see 1 Cor 14:33; Phil 4:7; 1 Thess 5:23), but the "God of love" is found nowhere else in the New Testament. This duo of "love and peace" was not just a cliché for Paul. The Corinthians were in serious need of both love and peace within their body of Christ. Harris suggests that "God actually imparts these virtues to empower believers to fulfill what is required of them," and this divine help was Paul's final promise to them.[26]

A "holy kiss" (2 Cor 13:12) was a sign and symbol of trust and affection, not unlike a hug or a warm handshake in our culture (see 1 Pet 5:14). "All God's people" also occurs in the closing of Philippians (4:22), indicating that this phrase recognized a union of everyone belonging to Christ (see Rom 1:7; 1 Cor 1:2; Titus 3:15). Generally, Paul was writing that the same Holy Spirit united (and still unites) all believers, no matter the geographical distance between them. Specifically, if indeed he wrote this letter from Macedonia, he must have been pleased that the believers in that church sent expressions of greetings, connection, and love for their fellow believers in Corinth.

The Trinity (13:14)

The last blessing or benediction in this letter is Trinitarian in nature, naming the three Persons of the Trinity. While the word "Trinity" does not appear in the NT, this is one of a number of passages where the three names of the triune God are linked together (see Matt 28:19; Luke 1:35; 1 Pet 1:1–2). As Christians deepen their relationship with the Father, the Son, and the Holy Spirit, their human relationships deepen into a unity of faith (see Eph 4:3–7). This demonstrates how Christians experience these Persons: we encounter the "grace of the Lord Jesus Christ," we feel and experience the "love of [Father] God," and we participate in the "fellowship of the Holy Spirit."[27]

In view of what was written in this letter preceding this benediction, this is quite a summary promise. He blessed the very people who revolted against Paul, denigrated him, told lies about him, flaunted flagrant sins, and rebuked his authority. He was under no obligation to treat them with mercy and forgiveness. How can he now trust these people, bless these people, and talk about the love of God with them? Yet, his relentless love for the church was what Jesus had shown to him (see 1 Tim 1:12–14).[28] He had vividly experienced the reality of the Trinity in his own life. He knew firsthand all the grace, love, and

---

26. Harris, *Second Corinthians*, 35.
27. Garland, *2 Corinthians*, 555–56.
28. Barton et al., *1 and 2 Corinthians*, 470.

fellowship of the triune God, and he sincerely wished such love and blessings on the struggling church at Corinth.

LIVE the Story

Self-Examination

It is difficult to ignore the directives in these last verses to "examine and test ourselves" in light of our faith in Jesus Christ (2 Cor 13:5–6). But in the church today, how is that accomplished? How do we turn the spotlight on our own lives, and to what do we compare ourselves?

What we are on the inside is demonstrated by our actions and behavior on the outside. Here, I mention just three specific areas ripe for examination mentioned in the Pauline letters that can help us assess our lives: relationally, financially, and in terms of service. Are we "doing right" (13:7) in these three areas?

First, if we are "in the faith" (13:5a), it is demonstrated in our relationships. We need to test our *vertical* relationship with God through Christ, aided by the Holy Spirit, and *horizontal* relationships with other people. Vertically, are we growing and maturing in our relationship with God on a daily basis, or do we forget about God until a crisis happens? The test is, why *aren't* we spending more time with God to enrich our relationship with him? Horizontally, Paul was seeking complete restoration of broken human relationships provoked and fueled by deception, greed, arrogance, and self-interest. How do we treat people—even those who persecute us? Human sin causes rifts between people today, just as outlined by Paul in 12:20–21. The test is, what divides us? Where do we need to build up human relationships—Marriages? Families? Friendships? Neighbors? Between a person and a pastor? Between members of the same family of God? Even so, in our world, we need to strive to build bridges of understanding between human races, genders, and cultures. We must examine our own prejudices and predispositions and see if they are fair and just. Do we criticize people, or do we comfort people (1:5–7)? If Christ is in us (13:5b), then we will endeavor to restore relationships and serve one another with the power of God. If restoration is possible and the needs of others are placed before our own, relationships are enriched. When we try to build up one another instead of tear each other down, then, and only then, will we experience real peace in our world (13:11).

Second, and so critical for Paul, we can test ourselves financially. We can go back to Paul's words in 9:6–15 to test our attitudes about generosity, gratitude, and the grace of God. This is a test of the heart. Paul taught as Jesus taught, that "where your treasure is, there your heart will be also" (Matt 6:21). Jesus spoke about the evils of greed in the parable of the rich fool, emphasizing that a person's life "does not consist in an abundance of possessions," and "this is how it will be with whoever stores up things for themselves but is not rich toward God" (Luke 12:13–21). In fact, Jesus taught a great deal about riches and poverty, and the New Testament lessons are based on God's purposes and intentions spoken in the Old Testament. A loving, generous God expected his people to be loving and generous. Wealth was intended to be shared among God's people, and the wealthy were to help those less fortunate:

> One person gives freely, yet gains even more;
> Another withholds unduly, but comes to poverty.
> A generous person will prosper;
> whoever refreshes others will be refreshed. . . .
> Those who trust in their riches will fall,
> but the righteous will thrive like a green leaf. (Prov 11:24–25, 28)

The ancient Israelites had many social responsibilities to care for one another, especially those people in need. The covenant stipulated that the poor, the widow, and the defenseless were special objects of God's care and concern (for example, Lev 19:9, 13–15, 32–33). They were to be treated fairly and were to receive material aid from those with plenty. In fact, to mistreat a poor man was a "sin" (see Deut 24:10–15, 17–18).

The Old Testament book of Malachi has a similar "courtroom scene" and a justice theme not unlike 2 Corinthians. In Malachi, the Lord is the judge of his rebellious people: "'So I will come to put you on trial. I will be quick to testify against sorcerers, adulterers and perjurers, against those who defraud laborers of their wages, who oppress the widows and the fatherless, and deprive the foreigners among you of justice, but do not fear me,' says the LORD Almighty" (Mal 3:5).

That is, God challenged the people to a *test*, a test to demonstrate his promised, gracious gifts to them, and their selfish hearts (Mal 3:8–12). In the same way, Paul challenged his readers to "test yourselves" (2 Cor 13:5), to examine their own hearts and to "do what is right." Our possessions are not our own, and generosity is an expression of our faith in a good God. Then as now, blessings given by God to his people were to be used as blessings for other people (Deut 26:8–15). Today, we may call this "pay it forward!"

So, when Paul taught the Corinthians about giving and grace in 2 Corinthians 9:6–15, he informed all of us that our generosity is proof of our "obedience that accompanies your confession of the gospel of Christ" (9:13).

People will "praise God" for our "generosity in sharing with them and with everyone else" (9:13). Thus, we are called to test ourselves in our giving of our income, our time, and our talents. More than just an obligatory tithe, Christians should *love* to give, should give from their heart, and should rejoice in the opportunities to do so (9:7). It is a heart matter, not a "tax" matter. Wealth is not a bad thing; there is a huge difference between a wealthy person and a greedy person. Even people in poverty can be greedy and unconcerned about the needs around them. The Christian knows where his or her wealth comes from and recognizes who is ultimately in control of it. In truth, God has so richly blessed us that we should always be ready to bless others. It is God who "supplies the seed" for our prosperity (9:10) and, "You will be enriched in every way so that you can be generous on every occasion . . . overflowing in many expressions of thanks to God" (9:11–12). Thanksgiving should always be on our lips because of what God did for us through Jesus Christ (see 9:15), in contrast to the accumulation and hoarding of all of our material blessings. Grace generates generosity.

Here's a test: Who is your G[g]od? The answer to that question is the demonstration of what is the most important thing in your life—The next job or the next raise? The house(s), the boat, or the car? What idol does your bank account say you worship? The year 2017 was a very tragic one for many people, and a test of human resources across America. There were horrific and unyielding hurricanes and floods, ravaging wildfires, and senseless mass murders of innocent people. Yet, people across the nation opened their hearts and their bank accounts, giving financially and sharing selflessly in the rebuilding of the lives of those victims of tragedies. An outpouring of despair was met with an outpouring of material blessings.

Third, we can test ourselves in term of our service. Are we actively using our spiritual gifts (1 Cor 12:4–11) to edify and build up his church (Eph 4:11–13)? Are we doing our part in advancing the kingdom of God, or merely complaining about the culture as we know it today? The Holy Spirit, who saves us and indwells us, also empowers each one of us to serve in the body of Christ as God has determined. Christian ministry is not limited to ordained pastors and apparent church leaders. Every believer is called to serve in Christ's church. The presence of the Spirit is that divine energy evident in acts of service that promote the common good for all. The spiritual or motivational gifts are recorded by Paul in Romans 12:4–8, 1 Corinthians 12:1–11, and Ephesians 4:1–6, 11–13. No two biblical lists of gifts are identical, and each list expresses a great diversity of gifts but unity in the Spirit. Perhaps Paul was listing *categories* of the various gifts given to believers. The spiritual gifts that God has given to us fit perfectly with our passions, abilities, personalities, and past experiences. The reason why it is so important to know one's spiritual gift is that many Christians try to serve in areas for which they are not designed; the result is frustration, minimal effort, burnout, or worse. We are accountable to God for the gifts he has given us, and it would be an insult to God to ignore or neglect his gracious gifts!

I have used the analogy of a hairdryer: I have a great hairdryer that is 1200 watts. It is a powerful tool, so functional, and an incredibly important piece of my morning ritual. Yet, if I do not plug the hairdryer into an electrical outlet, it is a worthless hunk of plastic. If we do not "plug into" the power of the Holy Spirit, our lives are not useful to God to accomplish his purposes. One time an older woman came to me after a lesson on spiritual gifts and said that she did not have one. I asked her what she liked to do. She said she crocheted; she was in a group of ladies who met regularly to crochet layettes for babies in Africa. Bingo! Crocheting is not mentioned in the New Testament as a spiritual gift, but she was serving God with an expressed gift of mercy. She had tapped into the power and was enjoying every minute of it!

Finally, a good Christian leader is one who creates and encourages opportunities to empower everyone in his or her community. As leaders, we need to equip and to edify people. Each leader has a unique set of gifts to serve, but other people in the church have gifts the leader does not have. We need to mine the gold found within everybody in Christ. Thus, a unified, growing, functional church is one where people have been honest with themselves, have assessed their gifts and abilities, and joyfully, lovingly serve alongside one another in the kingdom of God.

Prayer

It is not unusual to end a communication—a letter or a sermon—with a "prayer to God," just as Paul did (13:7, 9). In fact, in worship today, a closing prayer is almost expected. Reference to the Holy Trinity is also such a part of our worship tradition today that we seldom think about who we are addressing in prayer.

A pastor in the Church of Scotland, Rt. Rev. Derek Browning had some interesting thoughts about prayer and the church:

> Have we not been bombarding the Almighty with our endless petitions, confessions, and intercessions for centuries, and occasionally remembering good manners and offering our adoration, thanksgiving and praise? I sometimes imagine God enthroned in splendour with hands firmly over ears and muttering, "Won't they simply shut up for a moment and get on with what they already know they ought to be doing?"

Paul was asking his church to get on with it! Get on with what they already knew they should be doing! We can, and often do, misuse prayer as a way of telling God what he already knows or instructing God to do something our way, like we have it all figured out. It is easy to tell God how we have been mistreated and how he should handle our enemies, forgetting what we know to be true about forgiveness and mercy and the restoration of human relationships. The fact that Paul was able to pray sincerely for his enemies and for this contentious congregation is astounding. He prayed not for himself, or for revenge, but for the "building up" of the church. We are humbled by Paul's humility to consistently think of others before himself.

Rev. Browning sees prayer as "open communication between God and God's people today." But, are we listening, or just talking? Perhaps prayer is first listening to God, and then talking, and then listening again. Most of us have little time for listening to God, and our hurried prayers are self-centered pleas and a "grocery list" of things for God to do. Yet, Browning says prayer is "essentially about discernment"—discerning when to talk and when to listen, when to act and when not to act, what is best of others and what is most beneficial for everyone. In fact, don't we already know what we really need to do?[29] So, what are our strategies as a church, and what are our priorities? Yes indeed, prayer is godly discernment, and this is a day and age of discernment, a time to carefully move through a world of evil, injustice, and sin. It is time to discern how God wants each of us, and all of us together, to be a positive force in his work on earth.

---

29. D. Browning, "Catching Up with God," in *Life and Work: The Magazine of the Church of Scotland* (September 2017): 15.

Scripture Index

Acts

Galatians

Ephesians

Subject Index

afflictions, 68, 80–84, 152, 175–77, 181–82, 191–92, 369–70
  catalogue of, 214
  human, 80, 275
  momentary, 181
  present, 182
  temporal, 189

believers
  assembly of, 34, 43
  false, 356, 363
  fellow, 66, 164, 245, 278, 391
  human, 187, 345, 368
  individual, 116, 146, 200, 206
  true, 234, 323, 387
blessings, spiritual, 272, 285, 291, 300, 304
boasting, 36–37, 91–93, 259–60, 315–17, 364–66
  foolish, 360–61
  good, 338
  in the Lord, 317, 337–38
  true, 325
  worldly, 359–60
body of Christ, 38, 87, 146, 166, 195

Christ, 46–50, 79–82, 130–40, 147–52, 154–58, 182–86, 188–91, 204–12. *See also* Jesus
  apostles of, 335, 346
  crucified, 353–54
  death of, 82, 211–12
  exalted, 367
  face of, 160
  fools for, 60
  the glory of, 163
  gospel of, 307, 310, 323, 327, 329, 389
  judgment seat of, 189
  knowledge of, 111, 113, 118–19, 122, 124
  living, 149, 221
  love of, 198, 204, 213
  power of, 314, 357, 363
  resurrected, 140, 185, 189

  returning, 184
  salvation of, 187
  servants of, 11, 346, 356, 362–63, 373
  sufferings of, 80–81
Christian believers, 135, 145, 168–69, 231–34, 236, 352
Christian community, 38, 87–88, 117, 123, 218
Christian ministry, 109–10, 118, 124, 150–51, 161–62, 164, 214–15, 218–19
church discipline, 100, 105–6
Corinth, 26–29, 34–40, 45–51, 53–60, 62–68, 77–80, 249–53, 379–86
  believers in, 91, 93, 97, 226, 231
  the church in, 24, 91, 226, 275, 277
  the church of, 19, 54
  first-century, 188
  people in, 29, 76, 296, 379, 382
Corinthian believers, 28–29, 34, 116–17, 126, 182, 233–34
Corinthian church, 54, 58–60, 78, 83, 113–14, 269
Corinthian letters, 24, 28–30, 51–52, 58, 62
Corinthian readers, 20, 23, 189, 215, 326

darkness, 152, 155–57, 234–35, 242, 348
·death, 146–48, 167, 169–71, 177–80, 185–91, 193–95, 205, 375–76

empire, 27, 29–30, 36, 38–40, 46, 78
Ephesus, 54–56, 60, 94, 96, 252–53, 347
eternal life, 113, 115, 178, 188, 276, 278

forgiveness, 98–100, 104–5, 163–64, 222, 257–59, 285, 332–34, 371–72

Gentile Christians, 43, 63–64, 102, 252, 272
Gentile churches, 47, 272, 304, 325
Gentile Corinthians, 154, 278
Gentile readers, 236, 280
Gentiles, 30–31, 33, 63–64, 130–31, 156–59, 216–17, 271–73, 363

409

Author Index